Praise for *Unnatural Ability*

"All sports face the threat of chicanery, and Thoroughbred racing has the added complication that the carriers of illicit medications are innocent victims themselves. Milt Toby's prodigious research has produced an insightful review of villainy and the persistent efforts of those who have maintained a viable sport and industry embraced by the public over many eras."—Edward L. Bowen, Eclipse Award winner and author of numerous books on Thoroughbred racing

"*Unnatural Ability* is a seminal work in our understanding of the past, present, and future of performance-enhancing drugs in horse racing. Milt Toby takes a complex subject and masterfully breaks it down for his audience, exploring topics ranging from 'dope' in the early twentieth century to the evolution of testing to Lasix and more in the twenty-first century. This is a must-read for anyone who loves the sport and wants to learn more about this important issue."—Jennifer S. Kelly, award-winning author of *Sir Barton and the Making of the Triple Crown* and *The Foxes of Belair: Gallant Fox, Omaha, and the Quest for the Triple Crown*

"In documenting the long history of doping in horse racing, Milt Toby outlines a sport in which the cheaters, time and again, have been several steps ahead of investigators. Toby's work serves as a reminder that for racing to survive in the twenty-first century, the cheaters who have corrupted the sport and endangered the lives of horses and jockeys have to be stopped."—Frank Angst, features editor, *Blood-Horse*

"Impeccably researched, Milt Toby's *Unnatural Ability* is a valuable addition to the equine industry's library. By creating a cogent narrative of performance-enhancing drug use in horse racing, Toby organizes and catalogs the persistent omnipresence of doping, and he does not hesitate to express how that persistence has precipitated the loss of interest in and/or disapproval of the Sport of Kings. Vital. Impactful."—Becky Ryder, director, Keeneland Library

Unnatural Ability

THE HISTORY OF PERFORMANCE-ENHANCING DRUGS IN THOROUGHBRED RACING

UNNATURAL ABILITY

MILTON C. TOBY

UNIVERSITY PRESS OF KENTUCKY

A note to the reader: Several of the quotations printed in this volume contain racially insensitive language. The author has chosen to document the original terminology and descriptions to provide full historical context for the events under discussion. Discretion is advised.

Copyright © 2023 by Milton C. Toby

Published by The University Press of Kentucky,
scholarly publisher for the Commonwealth,
serving Bellarmine University, Berea College,
Centre College of Kentucky, Eastern Kentucky University,
The Filson Historical Society, Georgetown College,
Kentucky Historical Society, Kentucky State University,
Morehead State University, Murray State University,
Northern Kentucky University, Spalding University,
Transylvania University, University of Kentucky,
University of Louisville, University of Pikeville, and
Western Kentucky University.
All rights reserved.

Editorial and Sales Offices: The University Press of Kentucky
663 South Limestone Street, Lexington, Kentucky 40508-4008
www.kentuckypress.com

Library of Congress Cataloging-in-Publication Data

Names: Toby, Milton C., author.
Title: Unnatural ability : the history of performance-enhancing drugs in
    thoroughbred racing / Milton C. Toby.
Description: Lexington, Kentucky : University Press of Kentucky, [2023] |
    Series: Horses in history | Includes bibliographical references and index.
Identifiers: LCCN 2023002405 | ISBN 9780813197432 (hardcover) |
    ISBN 9780813197456 (pdf) | ISBN 9780813197449 (epub)
Subjects: LCSH: Doping in horse racing—United States. | Horse
    racing—United States—History.
Classification: LCC SF956.3 .T63 2023 | DDC
    362.290887984—dc23/eng/20230306
LC record available at https://lccn.loc.gov/2023002405

This book is printed on acid-free paper meeting
the requirements of the American National Standard
for Permanence in Paper for Printed Library Materials.

Manufactured in the United States of America.

Member of the Association
of University Presses

To my wife, Roberta, for her unwavering support
through decades of writing, ten books,
and a very challenging year.

And to the archivists and librarians who are the
front line of defense in protecting our history.
This book would have been impossible
without them.

Since the turf attained the dignity of a language of its own, there has never been coined a term which has attained the popularity that the one "dope" has achieved.

"'Dope' an American Term," *New York Times,*
April 7, 1901

Age and treachery will overcome youth and skill.

Attributed to professional cyclist and two-time
Tour de France winner Fausto Coppi

Contents

Introduction

Déjà Vu All Over Again

The genesis of horse racing was most likely a boast and a challenge—"my horse is faster than your horse"—probably with a neighborly wager to keep things interesting. The organized sport came later, and the horses had little in common with today's Thoroughbreds. Over time, the impromptu matches evolved into race meetings, and jockey clubs emerged to oversee those meetings. What started as a sport would be transformed into a multibillion-dollar business, with legal and illegal betting driving the game.

The question of who has the fastest horse remains the quintessence of racing, while the meaning of "my horse" has expanded, becoming a more abstract concept with many moving parts. Today, the success or failure of a Thoroughbred depends on the trainer, his or her assistants, the jockey, the farrier, a veterinarian or two, a nutritionist, the exercise riders and backstretch workers, the breeder, and the horse's pedigree. Wild cards in the mix—and there are many—include an unknown number of performance-enhancing drugs (PEDs).

Increasingly, it seems, sports are defined by their doping scandals.[1] This does not necessarily mean that the use of PEDs is on the rise, although that is probably true in some sports. In horse racing, it is impossible to know with certainty the extent of PED use. Extremely small numbers of positive test results are announced on a regular basis, but extrapolating a few test results to an entire sport is

1

risky, and testing every horse in every race is far too expensive and time-consuming to be practical. These numbers do not take into account the widespread use of the medication Lasix. Questions remain whether Lasix is actually a performance enhancer, but far more horses are given Lasix than need it, suggesting that trainers think the drug provides some sort of an edge.[2]

Moreover, new PEDs are always being developed, which existing tests cannot detect. In the race between the developers, distributors, and users of new PEDs on the one side and the regulators on the other side, the latter are a step or two behind and always playing catch-up because that is the nature of the doping game.

The good news is that testing for prohibited medications is getting more accurate and sensitive, and the time gap between the development of a new PED and the ability to detect it is shrinking. It also matters that drug scandals in sports attract far more attention today than in the past, especially from casual fans, through television exposure, social media, and a voracious twenty-four-hour news cycle. This increased visibility also fuels the perception that many sports have a drug problem, even if that is not the reality.

Doping incidents have plagued horse racing for more than a century. The sport has been under scrutiny for PEDs since the late 1800s, even before there were reliable chemical tests for the drugs. The modern era of systematic doping began at outlaw tracks in New Jersey. Whether legal or not, gambling has always been the lifeblood of the sport, and regulators have a long history of trying—and failing—to create a so-called level playing field to keep bettors and other participants active in the game. Even without adding PEDs to the mix, the search for a level playing field is a misguided pursuit.

Before the early 1930s, there were no reliable tests for prohibited substances in the United States. The introduction of doping on a systematic scale in the 1890s is attributed to the mysterious "Doc" Ring and his imitators. The widely publicized death of a Thoroughbred named Dr. Riddle of an apparent drug overdose in 1903 was based largely on speculation. Backstretch raids and arrests by the Federal

Bureau of Narcotics in the 1930s were reported in newspapers, and the federal criminal court records are contained in the National Archives in Chicago.

The license of prominent trainer "Silent" Tom Smith, of Seabiscuit fame, was revoked for using the stimulant ephedrine in the 1940s. The massive appellate court record is archived in Albany, New York. The Smith litigation established that penalties could be levied without a positive drug test. Proof of a violation based on nonanalytical evidence, rather than laboratory evidence, was later used by the US Anti-Doping Agency in its successful case against bicyclist Lance Armstrong. Increased reliance on nonanalytical evidence, investigation, and whistleblowers will be necessary when the delayed medication portion of the Horseracing Integrity and Safety Act of 2020 (HISA) becomes operational.

Kentucky Derby winner Dancer's Image was disqualified after a controversial positive test for a prohibited medication in 1968, followed by years of litigation.[3] Congressional hearings were held in the 1970s that attempted to link the sport to organized crime and fixed races, and amazingly, after half a century of debate about whether Lasix is a PED that should be prohibited on race day, the question remains unresolved.

More recently, there was a Derby winner on steroids in 2008. Growing threats are posed by designer drugs, blood doping, and gene doping. There was a string of federal indictments of trainers, veterinarians, and drug suppliers in 2020. To cap things off, when 2021 Kentucky Derby winner Medina Spirit tested positive for a prohibited medication, it set off a media frenzy and ultimately resulted in disqualification of the Derby winner.

It's "déjà vu all over again," as Yogi Berra might say.[4] Followers of racing could add "and again and again and again" to Berra's observation.

Distressing as these events appear when taken individually, there is a more important dilemma facing Thoroughbred racing today. Are the bad actors simply outliers in an otherwise clean sport, as many regulatory authorities and die-hard racing fans argue? Or are they players in a long-running pattern of doping culture? Are they the tip of a doping iceberg that no one wants to recognize?

It is a critical question as racing faces new challenges and competition from legal sports betting outside Nevada. The US Supreme Court decision that overturned the Professional and Amateur Sports Protection Act cleared the way for individual states to authorize sports betting.[5] A number of states moved quickly to do so, and sports betting legislation is pending in other jurisdictions.[6] Horse racing is no longer the only legal bet in town. Even with state support propping up racing in some places, integrity is vital if the sport is going to survive. Integrity is also elusive.

During the 1940s, racing vied with professional baseball for the top spot among spectator sports in America. Baseball attendance totaled approximately 10 million fans in 1940; less than 9 million midway through World War II, when many star athletes served in the military; and 11 million in 1945. In contrast, attendance at the country's racetracks increased throughout the war years, from 8.5 million in 1940 to 18 million in 1944.[7] Today, racing seldom makes the top ten on attendance lists, and sometimes not even the top twenty.[8]

Bennett Liebman is head of the Government Law Center at Albany Law School, a former New York State Racing and Wagering Board member, and a prolific writer about legal issues in Thoroughbred racing. He identified more than a dozen reasons for horse racing's precipitous decline in popularity for the *New York Times*. The integrity-related issues relevant to doping included the following:

- Corruption and the inability to prevent it: "The perception that the sport is not being conducted on a fair level has harmed racing greatly and almost destroyed the sport of harness racing. When there were no other forms of legal gambling, the sport could get by with the odor of corruption. But with faster and more honest gambling venues now at hand [before the spread of sports betting] the sport cannot tolerate corruption."

- Drugs: "The sport has not been able to prevent the use of drugs and the belief that many of the sport's leading trainers have regularly chemically enhanced the performance of their horses. We have never been able to explain or explain away the Oscar Barrera phenomenon, where one trainer in New York in the late 1970s and early 1980s seemed to be able to improve a horse's performance magically overnight."

- Public perception: "[Corruption and drugs] plus the use of whips on horses and the catastrophic injuries we have seen in major races have contributed to the perception that horse racing is a cruel sport which has little concern for the health or safety of the horse."[9]

Liebman made these observations more than a decade ago, but he could have written them yesterday.

The dilemma facing horse racing today is clear: how can we identify a nebulous "culture" of doping? A related question: are PEDs a genuine problem to be addressed by regulators, or simply a public relations concern to be managed? Regulators argue that it is the former, but a fractured web of governance by state racing commissions and inaction by legislators has hampered efforts to control PEDs, sometimes leaving bettors and fans with the impression that managing expectations about doping may be the best that racing can manage.

Finally, though, there is light at the end of the tunnel with the passage of HISA in 2020. The law's objectives include uniform national rules for medication and safety, correcting a hit-or-miss, state-by-state regulatory scheme that has always made it difficult to control the use of PEDs. The legislation received staunch support from the Jockey Club and most stakeholders but was challenged in court by a few prominent national and regional industry groups, creating a divisive split over medication control.

A decade ago, journalist Claudio Gatti asked Jörg Jaksche, a retired professional bicycle racer from Germany, about doping culture in sports. "Each new doping scandal follows the same pattern," Jaksche told Gatti. "When someone is caught, the system acts shocked and upset, declares its absolute rejection of doping and depicts the athlete as a black sheep that deserves to be slaughtered. After that, everything continues like before. But the fact is that they slaughter a scapegoat, not a black sheep, and no one ever looks at the shepherd's responsibility. I'm talking about those in the higher levels, those who govern the sports and, most importantly, those who provide the money that fuels everything."[10]

In a subsequent recorded interview, Jaksche expanded on his thoughts about how a doping culture can take over a sport, in his case, professional cycling: "It's a vicious circle," Jaksche said. "It's like a domino effect. I think in economics, it's called 'prisoner dilemma.' This is a situation where you actually don't know what the other party does and by prior experience about what happened in the past you assume that the other party is cheating. So you have to cheat as well. . . . At the end, there is an equilibrium where everyone is cheating. That's what's happening in cycling, at least in my time."[11]

Jaksche's analysis of doping culture works well for professional bicycle racing, which has been addicted to PEDs since the 1890s, when riders competing in grueling six-day races needed a chemical boost not to win but just to survive the ordeal.[12] It is not a perfect fit for Thoroughbred racing, particularly when it comes to direct involvement—or at least a blind eye—at the highest levels. There is no indication that racing is facing a government-sponsored doping conspiracy as occurred in Russia during the 1990s and East Germany in the 1970s.[13] Nor is there evidence of doping at the sport's institutional level, although comparison of a trainer's stable with Lance Armstrong's professional cycling team might be a better fit. Sadly, however, Jaksche's pattern of doping scandals at the individual level in racing is familiar enough to raise anxiety in anyone who follows the sport.

History creates a context for the present and informs the future. Much has been written about the development of PEDs and the philosophy and ethics of doping in human athletics.[14] The subject of doping in horse racing has received far less attention.[15] My goal here is to provide the first comprehensive history of PEDs in racing told from multiple perspectives—historian, journalist, and, more often than not, detective.

It is a distressing narrative for anyone who loves Thoroughbred racing but a necessary story to tell. To better understand where racing's war on drugs is going, and to answer the nagging question of whether there is a doping culture in the sport, it is essential to know where we've been and how we got here.

Part I

The Man Who Made Them Run

1

The Death of Dr. Riddle

The horse lay dead in his stall, the apparent victim of a massive dose of cocaine, heroin, arsenic, strychnine, or some combination of drugs and patent medicines intended to make a horse run faster. Instead, on an afternoon in May 1903 at Morris Park in the Bronx, dope killed a horse named Dr. Riddle.

There was nothing special about Dr. Riddle. He was a six-year-old son of Iroquois, the first American-bred to win the Epsom Derby in 1881, racing for Pierre Lorillard IV. But Dr. Riddle had inherited little of his sire's ability.[1] Instead, by 1903, he was racing mainly in "selling races" for small purses.

The winner of a selling race (a forerunner of the modern claiming race) would be put up for auction, with the listed selling price as the opening bid. The weight a horse carried in the race depended on the owner's selling price: the lower the selling price, the lower the weight. The owner could bid on his own horse but ran the risk of paying more than the horse was worth to keep. Like today's claiming races, the idea behind selling races was to create an incentive for owners to run horses in races where they would face similar competition.[2] With all the horses in the field presumed to be of more or less equal ability, selling races presented more exciting—and presumably more honest—contests and betting. That was the theory, at least. In reality, an owner could easily manipulate the outcomes of a series of races to create more lucrative wagering opportunities. One way was to instruct a rider not to ride to win in certain races but to try harder in others. Another tactic was to run a horse either doped or clean, depending on the desired outcome. Juggling drugs was the genesis of the phrase "running hot or running cold," depending on whether a horse was doped for a particular race.

"Some unscrupulous owners and trainers would hop the horses in some races and in other races would not administer the drug," W. C. Vreeland, longtime turf writer for the *Brooklyn Daily Eagle*, explained. "Hence the beginning of the phrase 'hot and cold.' The horse when stimulated with the drug showed its effects by sweating profusely. He was all steamed up. When not touched up with the drug his coat was dry and he walked and raced in listless fashion. He was cold; he had become an addict."[3]

The practice of using performance-enhancing drugs to produce convenient improvements in a horse's racing ability sometimes had unexpected consequences. Reporting on the races in New Orleans in late 1892, a writer for the *New York Times* recalled an incident involving a track official who ordered that a horse named India Rubber be injected before a race, yet the horse was beaten. The apparent intent of the order was for India Rubber to run "hot" with his usual dose of drugs—"cocaine, morphine, or whatever the stuff that is used"—instead of "cold" so that bettors would get a payoff. The plan backfired, though, when it was learned that the horse had been injected with only water.[4]

"It is the easiest thing to run a plater cold for four or five races until the price on him is around twenty or thirty to one and load him up with go-powders and turn him loose," sportswriter-turned-novelist Paul Gallico explained. "Another cheerful variation is to run a horse hot five or six times, tip him to win, turn him out cold and hold the bets off on him."[5]

There is no way to know whether Dr. Riddle was one of those horses typically running hot or cold at his owner's and trainer's discretion. The horse's performance in the month preceding the second race at Morris Park on the day he died raised the question, however.

On April 1, 1903, competing in a six-furlong selling race at the New Memphis Jockey Club track in Tennessee, Dr. Riddle was an

Grandstand at Morris Park. (Keeneland Library, John C. Hemment Collection)

also-ran. Scorpio won the race at odds of 60–1. Nine days later, in a one-mile selling race in Memphis, Dr. Riddle took the lead midway through the race and won by two lengths. The betting on Dr. Riddle that day opened at 4–1, but he started as the 8–5 favorite, an unlikely drop in odds for a horse that had been unplaced a few days earlier.

On May 3 in Jamaica, New York, Dr. Riddle started as the favorite in a one-mile, seventy-yard race but did not place. Odds on the winner, Past, opened at 10–1 but closed at 6–1 after heavy betting. On May 15 at Morris Park, the winner in Dr. Riddle's final race was Miss Buttermilk, a 40–1 long shot.

There are legitimate reasons for Dr. Riddle's uneven races leading up to Morris Park, but speculation hinted at a horse running hotter than planned and a betting scheme gone terribly wrong. Although race fixing was never proved and specific drugs were not identified, the press took the suppositions of betting chicanery and doping as fact, with sensational headlines sometimes laced with grim irony:

"Did Dope Kill Racehorse? Big Killing Planned on Dr. Riddle at Morris Park Went Wrong"[6]
"Doped for a Killing!"[7]

"Doping of Dr. Riddle Was Apparent to All"[8]
"Looked Like Case of Hops"[9]
"'Doped' Race Horse Dies"[10]
"A Scandal of the Turf: Dr. Riddle 'Doped,' Resulting in His Death"[11]

Headlines aside, there was no real proof that Dr. Riddle was doped with a particular drug before the race. Nor was there any conclusive evidence that the horse had been doped at all. A reliable chemical test to detect drugs in a horse's system was still decades away in the United States, so the lack of hard-and-fast evidence was no surprise. The conventional wisdom at the time was that the only way to identify a doped horse before a race was through close observation. The experts said that a veterinarian—and presumably an experienced layperson—could almost always pick out a drugged horse by examining the animal's eyes. Excessive sweating and erratic behavior were other indicators of a doped horse. "As soon as the drug begins to act," according to one account, "the horse breaks into a sweat. The least walking exercise will cause the animal to 'lather' as if he had been raced two miles at top speed on a hot day. His eyes begin to look unnaturally brilliant and he becomes nervous and sometimes savage. He is anxious to run every where and any where and can scarcely be restrained from running away while going to the post. Such cases are dangerous to the life of the jockey, for the horse is just as likely to run into the fence as he is to run straight."[12]

There were no published reports of any examination of Dr. Riddle's eyes that might have indicated doping. Before the race, he was already out of control in the paddock; the horse went into convulsions shortly after returning to the barn and was dying when the stewards sent a veterinarian to check on him. Dr. Riddle's decidedly abnormal behavior certainly fit the physical criteria for an artificially stimulated horse, however, and left little doubt in anyone's mind that he had been doped.

It was "one of the most flagrant cases of doping that ever came to the notice of racing men," according to one newspaper account.

"Dr. Riddle was so thoroughly saturated with some kind of 'juice' in the second race yesterday that it was apparent to the verist novice. So high in spirits was the old son of Iroquois that his head fairly touched the clouds." Dr. Riddle was only one of several horses in the race suspected of "having artificial stimulant under their hides," but he stood out from the others in the paddock because he acted like a "crazy horse."[13]

His grooms could barely control Dr. Riddle while he was being saddled, and it was obvious that the horse presented a risk to the other horses, riders, and just about everyone around him. According to another report:

> The most exciting and dangerous event of the day was the crazy actions of the horse Dr. Riddle while in the paddock previous to going to the post for the second race. The man in charge of him had a hard time of it trying to hold him. At times as he walked around the paddock with his eyeballs distended and the perspiration running off him, he would rear, carrying the man off his feet and swinging him around as if he had no more strength than a child. At one time so unmanageable did the animal become that it was almost impossible to hold him, and he knocked down a well-known Brooklynite and came very near injuring other people, who were doing their utmost to keep out of his way.

The unidentified writer concluded that "the general belief was that Dr. Riddle had been overdosed" with a stimulating drug.[14] Intentional or not, the implication of that statement was that a "normal" dose of drugs would not have been out of the ordinary on a typical day of racing.

The paddock judge, who isn't named in the newspaper accounts, should have called the bizarre situation to the Morris Park stewards' attention but chose not to do so.[15] It was a questionable decision with no apparent explanation. His nonaction lends some credence to the rumors of an insider's betting coup that would have required Dr. Riddle to race and win for the anticipated big payoff.

Dr. Riddle staggered through the post parade like an "inebriate on the Bowery," sweating and bumping into the rail.[16] The starter, a gentleman named Fitzgerald, was more conscientious about his job than his colleague in the paddock; he alerted the stewards and asked for instructions. Under these peculiar circumstances, he wanted to know, should Dr. Riddle be allowed to start the race?

This was a more complicated question than it might seem, as the answer involved the economics of operating a racetrack, rather than merely concern for horse and rider safety. If Dr. Riddle had been scratched from the race, disgruntled bettors almost certainly would have demanded refunds for their worthless bets. Those refunds would have been due from the New York Jockey Club, which operated pari-mutuel machines at the track, and from bookmakers, whose presence at Morris Park was tolerated by management.[17] But if Dr. Riddle were allowed to start the race, it could be argued that bettors at least got a run for their money, albeit a dubious one, since the horse had no real chance of winning. No refunds were required if a horse started a race but finished unplaced.

Defining a "starter" for betting purposes was the source of some confusion at the time. Under the rules in effect during the early 1890s, Dr. Riddle would not have been considered a starter until he was under the control of the official charged with actually raising the barrier—Fitzgerald, in this case. The Board of Control, which ran racing in New York for a few years, adopted a more permissive rule in 1893 that favored bookmakers at the expense of bettors. Under the new guidance, a horse became a starter for betting purposes as soon as the names of the horse and jockey were posted publicly on the official "telegraph board" at the track, even if the horse never made it to the starting gate. The purpose was to eliminate the need for bookmakers to create a so-called new book after a change in the field for a race. Bettors who wagered on a starter that didn't make it to the post had no recourse.[18] Technically,

Dr. Riddle would have been an official starter in his final race under either rule.

The stewards advised Fitzgerald to let Dr. Riddle break from the barrier with the rest of the field. However, they also instructed Fitzgerald to tell the jockey, Oscar Salling, that he had permission to pull up and not risk injury. Salling did as he was instructed, probably relieved that he didn't have to try to win. Salling "very pluckily broke away from the post, but at once pulled up the horse, which was reeling under him, and walked to the stretch long after Miss Buttermilk, a 40–1 longshot which raced out in front with Kickshaw all the way, had won the race by a head." Dr. Riddle had become so uncontrollable by then that Salling could not maneuver him back to the paddock. The rider gave up, dismounted in front of the grandstand, and turned the horse over to two grooms. Finally, and with much effort, the grooms managed to get Dr. Riddle back to the barn. The horse was so fractious, though, that he could not be cooled down as usual, so the grooms put him back in his stall. Dr. Riddle suffered convulsions and died about two hours after the race.[19] The *Daily Racing Form* simply noted that "Dr. Riddle got off poorly."[20]

The track stewards originally wanted to have a veterinarian examine Dr. Riddle in the paddock immediately following the race. But after watching the rider try and fail to get the horse to the paddock, the plan changed. The veterinarian was dispatched to the stable area to examine the horse sometime later. After reviewing the veterinarian's report, which was not made public, the stewards issued this ruling: "The stewards of the meeting order that the entries of J. Gardner and the horse Dr. Riddle be refused, and the license of Trainer William Howell be suspended." The reference to Dr. Riddle racing again became moot, of course, with the horse's death. Any further sanctions imposed on owner John Gardner and trainer Howell would be at the discretion of the Jockey Club.[21]

There was some disagreement in published reports the next day about whether Gardner and Howell went to the barn to check on

Dr. Riddle after the race, but they probably did not. There was little incentive to do so, considering their connection to the public debacle that had played out just a few minutes earlier. There were subsequent allegations that an unnamed groom employed by Howell had injected Dr. Riddle with twelve grains of cocaine before the race. The groom disappeared, however, and the report was never confirmed. Sometime later, Howell reportedly exonerated Gardner and took full responsibility for Dr. Riddle's condition and his subsequent death.[22]

A more plausible explanation was provided a few years later by John Boden, a former secretary of the New York State Racing Association. According to Boden's "strange, but almost certainly true" account, two different groups of bettors were planning to back Dr. Riddle in the Morris Park race. Each group had a groom working in trainer Howell's barn, and the two grooms, unbeknownst to each other, both doped the horse.[23]

A week later, on May 22, trainer William Howell was "ruled off the turf," presumably for life, by the stewards of the Jockey Club: August Belmont, James R. Keene, J. H. Bradford, F. R. Hitchcock, H. K. Knapp, and Andrew Miller. The stewards relied on Rule 162, which stated in part: "Any person who shall be proved to have affected the speed of a horse by the use of drugs internally, whether administered by hypodermic or any other method . . . shall be ruled off."[24] The Jockey Club stewards employed a broad definition of "proved" in reaching their decision, as there was no chemical test and only circumstantial evidence to establish that Dr. Riddle had been doped.

No action was taken against John Gardner, Dr. Riddle's owner.[25] This was surprising, given his alleged involvement in a similar doping incident in Canada. The Canadian charge against Gardner was reported, but with few details, in at least one newspaper the day after Dr. Riddle's fateful race. Although it was relevant to Dr. Riddle's death, the information was apparently not provided to the Jockey Club.[26]

Dr. Riddle's well-publicized death attracted the attention of the American Society for the Prevention of Cruelty to Animals (ASPCA), which sent a badge-wielding and probably armed investigator to Morris Park with statutory authority to arrest animal abusers. One reporter suggested that there were better ways to deal with the doping problem: "It looks, however, as though the society could better serve the purpose by assigning the task to a trained veterinary surgeon, instead of to one who has merely done patrol duty."[27] The idea of assigning a veterinarian to the paddock for every race at every track would resurface three decades later as one of several recommendations resulting from the short-lived war on illegal drugs at East Coast and Midwest racetracks waged by Federal Bureau of Narcotics commissioner Harry J. Anslinger.

Henry Bergh, a playwright and animal lover who fortunately had a large inheritance to fall back on when his writing efforts failed, formed the ASPCA during the mid-1860s. He successfully lobbied the New York legislature to approve the country's first major anti-cruelty statute. The law also granted arrest powers to the ASPCA's agents, an unusual accommodation for a nongovernmental entity.[28] More than 150 years later, animal welfare and animal rights groups play a prominent (and sometimes controversial) but unofficial role in horse racing oversight.

There is no record of anything substantive coming out of the ASPCA's investigation into Dr. Riddle's death. The mere presence of an investigator on the grounds of a racetrack was significant, however, because it demonstrated a new and expanding role for the animal welfare movement in the United States. It also illustrated a significant conflict for Bergh and his agents when it came to horse racing. One of the ASPCA's primary goals was (and still is) to reduce, if not eliminate, cruelty to animals. The conflict arose because many of the wealthy owners racing their horses at New York tracks were Bergh's friends. They were also financial and political supporters of much of the ASPCA's work, but only so long as Bergh did not interfere with horse racing, fox hunting, pigeon shooting, or their other favorite sporting pastimes.

Bergh acknowledged the ASPCA's problems related to horse racing shortly after the organization was formed. Biographer Zulma

Steele quotes him: "It is not my present purpose to protest against horse racing," he said, "for it is an 'illegal' sport sanctioned by all classes of society."[29] Although Bergh himself was welcome among the upper echelons of society and was reluctant to incur their displeasure at his perceived meddling, he eventually decided to investigate racing, despite his friendship with many of the owners.

Cooperation with ASPCA investigators was expected from racing officials and was usually provided—though sometimes grudgingly—but things did not always work out as planned. Before a race at Jerome Park in October 1884, the ASPCA was informed that a horse named Jim McGowan was entered, despite having a sore back. Agent Evans (no first name provided in the records) went to the track, investigated, and found no problem. He reported that the saddle was sufficiently padded to protect the horse's back. Before Evans could leave the grounds, however, he was approached by two prominent members of the American Jockey Club, which operated Jerome Park. Depending on which version of the story one believes, Judge A. C. Monson and David Withers either peacefully escorted Evans off the grounds (their telling) or assaulted him (Bergh's allegations).

There was conflicting testimony at the subsequent trial. Some witnesses supported the account of the American Jockey Club members, while others told a different story. There was a large crowd surrounding Evans, police inspector George W. Ditka recalled, and they were shouting "hang him," "shoot him," "put him out." According to the inspector, "As Judge Monson and Matthew Sharp [who was apparently not charged] pushed him [Evans] under the rail, I caught him in my arms and told the crowd to stop. Evans said to me that he had paid his way in and remarked that they had treated him pretty roughly. I saw that his clothes were badly torn."[30] There was also some question about whether Evans had properly flashed his badge. The charges against Withers were dismissed because there was no evidence that he had laid a hand on Evans. Charges against

Monson were also dismissed on the basis of his testimony that he had used no violence when escorting Evans off the grounds.

Press coverage of Dr. Riddle's death was extensive, even beyond New York. That lasted a few days, but interest quickly faded. After all, Dr. Riddle was an outlier in a sport where doping was presumed to be commonplace but doped horses seldom died. Reporters covering horse racing generally paid more attention to gambling's supposed evils, ongoing reform efforts, and the political machinations of racing's friends and foes than to rumors of doping.[31]

It is impossible to know the true scope of performance-enhancing drugs in Thoroughbred racing from the Gay Nineties through the first decades of the twentieth century. One way to estimate the prevalence of such drugs would be to talk to someone who used them, and that's what reporter Bob McGarry did in 1932. He asked an expert.

Peter Christian Barrie—"Paddy" to his friends, acquaintances, clients, and the authorities who chased him for decades on both sides of the Atlantic—was best known as a "painter" of horses. In other words, he had an uncommon talent for making one horse look like another—a skill essential for passing good horses off as bad ones (ringers) to win a bet at long odds. From November 21 to December 3, 1932, the *New York Daily News* published a twelve-part series based on McGarry's meetings with Barrie. The reporter and the scoundrel mostly talked about Barrie's successes and failures with ringers, but Barrie also discussed dope. "I would say without hesitation," Barrie claimed, "that fully 60% of the horses racing on the American turf are stimulated. On many racecourses the stewards, if they see any inconsistencies in a horse's racing, will call you before them and advise you that you will not be permitted to run your horse hot one day (doped) and cold (au natural) the next. You must either run him always cold or always hot, or be warned off. Hopping of horses is condoned."[32]

It's fair to be skeptical of Barrie. He was a cheater and a liar who had a habit of peddling his life story to the press whenever he ran out of money, which was often.[33] And a sensational story always sells better than a dull one. Barrie was broke and on the run from the authorities when he talked with McGarry, but his comments have a ring of truth.

A fundamental change in the use of performance-enhancing drugs was occurring as the Gilded Age was winding down. A practice once marked by occasional transgressions from a few bad actors at obscure racetracks was becoming a widespread pattern of cheating that would threaten the integrity—and ultimately the future—of horse racing. This paradigm shift, and the first equine fatality in the modern era of doping, was a legacy that began with an outlaw track in New Jersey and a shadowy figure named "Doc" Ring.

2

"Doc" Ring and the Modern Era of Doping

The loneliest man in horse racing, and maybe in the entire world, during the winter of 1892 was the "snow man" at the Guttenberg racetrack. Night after night he scanned the sky over the New Jersey Palisades, watching for the blizzard that might be coming and sounding the alarm at the first sign of snow. A contemporaneous account of a typical night for the snow man at the "Gut" appeared in the *Lewiston (ME) Evening Journal:*

> Well muffled up against the biting winter winds, with an old fur hat pulled down over his ears and a quid of tobacco in his mouth, there marches back and forth in front of a great deserted building throughout the long hours of the night an individual whose vigil is perhaps the most curious ever imposed upon any watchman on land or sea. He carries neither lantern nor club, and his frequent observations of the heavens, together with his total indifference to his immediate surroundings, show conclusively that he appre-hends danger only from above. He is engaged in a sleepless and careful watch of nothing under the heavens, but of the heavens themselves.
>
> If the night passes by with nothing more threatening than a few dark clouds and a little drizzle he continues his quiet pacing to and fro. Let those clouds, however, drop the

first few flakes of an approaching snowstorm and on the instant this watchman, like a sentinel alarmed, is all activity. At his prompt summons there issue from unexpected quarters detachments of men armed with shovels, who, as the snow thickens on the ground, industriously shovel it away. It is no uncommon thing for half a hundred men aroused from their beds at midnight by this watchman of the weather, to fight the falling snow incessantly until long after daylight or until it ceases.[1]

The snow man and his shovel brigade, identified in one report as a "small army of Italians," were necessary because racing at Guttenberg continued unabated throughout the dreary winter, regardless of how foul the weather might be. Writing under the byline Audax Minor, G. F. T. Ryall covered Thoroughbred racing for the *New Yorker* for more than half a century. When a sudden blizzard closed Pimlico Race Course late in 1957, Ryall wrote about the cold-weather experiment at Guttenberg:

> [The Pimlico snowstorm] gave the old stagers who are always grumbling that the younger generation is a bunch of softies, [an opportunity to] recall their days in the 90's at Guttenberg, a New Jersey track just across the river from 72nd street, that used to run all winter. (It was a sort of open-air horse room, where you could also bet on New Orleans & California tracks.) No matter how hard it snowed at Guttenberg—and there were blizzards in those days—a crew merely shoveled a wide path round the track for the horses, and the races went off as scheduled.[2]

Winter racing at Guttenberg was unique, at least in the northern states, where the season brought snow and freezing temperatures. Regular winter racing outside of warm-weather venues would not become popular for decades.[3]

Even on the rare occasion when racing was canceled at Gutten-berg, supposedly because of bad weather, there was usually another reason. According to management, on January 20, 1892, races were called off because the track "was unfit to race over." While it might have been true that the racing surface was worse than usual that day, bad tracks were a familiar occurrence at Guttenberg in the winter, and treacherous conditions typically did not lead to the cancellation of racing. "The excuse fooled none of the mob that patronizes the track," the *New York Times* reported, "for they know that no track is too bad to prevent the Hudson County Jockey Club from racing over it. The track was in a horrible condition, but the real reason was said to be an order received from McLaughlin not to race until his return from Trenton, for fear of interference from the Law and Order League and the Society for the Prevention of Cruelty to Animals."[4] Dennis McLaughlin was one of the "Big Four," along with Gottfried Wal-baum, Nicholas Ceusius, and John C. Carr, who operated the Gut-tenberg track. "Boss" McLaughlin was in Trenton seeking Governor Leon Abbott's help with the worrisome—and growing—number of arrests on the Guttenberg grounds.

Arrests were a persistent inconvenience at the racetrack, but the interruptions were tolerated as window dressing to assuage the Law and Order League and other antigambling reformers that wanted to close it down. In reality, the powerful Democratic political machine in Hudson County provided legal protection for the track operators, bookmakers, and patrons—extending from the local authorities up the chain of command to the state police chief.[5] To get the book-makers back to work as quickly as possible after the inevitable arrests, a local justice of the peace set up a makeshift court in a vacant stall on the backstretch, where he granted speedy releases on bail.[6]

With little competition from across the Hudson River in New York, Guttenberg's winter racing experiment proved immensely prof-itable for track owners, bookmakers, and betting shop operators. It was less popular with the Board of Control, a consortium of local jockey clubs that promoted the business interests of the elite racetracks in New York.[7] The board also hoped to standardize the rules of racing in New York and later across the country but failed to achieve this ambitious goal.

Despite its brutal winter schedule, races for underdeveloped two-year-olds started on January 1 (the official birthday for all Thoroughbreds, no matter when they were born), and a general disregard for the norms established across the river in New York, Guttenberg was the antithesis of an elite racetrack. Late in 1891 the Board of Control took action against the operators of Guttenberg with a resolution that banned owners, trainers, and horses competing during the winter in New Jersey from racing in New York when the weather improved.

The *New York Times* approved: "The *Times* has repeatedly advocated the passage of such an edict as has been formulated, because, the racing of horses in this climate in winter, and particularly the racing of youngsters as soon as they are for racing classification purposes, two years old is nothing more nor less than absolute cruelty. There is not a thing to be said in favor of racing in midwinter except that it gives people who want to gamble a chance to do so."[8] The Big Four were not bothered by the Board of Control's ban, and winter racing and gambling continued as scheduled at Guttenberg.

Legislation fully legitimizing horse racing in New Jersey (the Parker Acts) had strong support from the Democratic majority and was pushed through the state assembly and house without hearings in early 1893. Still, the safe harbor for Guttenberg was short-lived. The first blow was a ban on winter racing passed in March 1893 as a concession to reformers. Republicans won majorities in both houses of the legislature later that year; a state court ruled the Parker Acts unconstitutional in January 1894, and a few days later, the legislature repealed the pro-racing statutes. There was no racing in New Jersey for almost half a century.[9]

The Big Four were arrested a few days after the Parker Acts were repealed, based on the results of a police raid conducted two years earlier. They eventually pleaded guilty to "keeping a disorderly house in operating the Guttenberg race track."[10]

Disorderly, indeed. When a crooked jockey named McDermott was ruled off (prohibited from riding at Guttenberg) in 1892, it surprised just about everyone, but for different reasons. A few people were shocked because the decision to ban McDermott had taken so long. The majority, though, were surprised that the Big Four allowed the ban to happen at all. McDermott's reputation as a cheat was well known. He had been involved in fixing races for McLaughlin and his friends, and most people assumed that he would be protected from any disciplinary action. Apparently, though, the jockey had held his mount back in a race he was supposed to win. This cost McLaughlin and his cronies a significant amount of money, and McDermott's protection vanished.[11]

Guttenberg was not the only "disorderly house" among the "outlaw" tracks operating in New Jersey.[12] Between the fifth and sixth races on December 22, 1890, at Clifton, a fight broke out between a bookmaker named Carroll and an African American horse owner named White. A special dispatch to the *St. Louis Globe-Democrat* reported that Carroll refused to take White's bet on his horse, Cora Tanner, "using insulting language and accompanying his words with a kick which rattled against White's ribs. White then grabbed Carroll and endeavored to pull him down from his perch on the betting box. Then one of Carroll's clerks struck White on the head with a bottle of whiskey, spilling blood and an appetizing aroma for the crowd that pressed toward the belligerents and threatened to make a free fight. Special policemen forced their way to the box and stopped the disturbance." The police escorted Carroll from the grounds *after* the races were over, presumably allowing the bookmaker to take wagers on the last races of the day.[13]

Guttenberg, though, stood out among the outlaws. It was a godforsaken place by most accounts, a den of bookmakers, criminals, crooked politicians, broken-down horses, thieving jockeys, and fixed races. For all these reasons, Guttenberg was also an ideal proving ground for a visitor from the western frontier—a vanishing part of America's heritage. He brought a revolutionary new way to make horses run faster: an injection that was legal, cheap, and not against the rules of racing.

When tabulations from the 1890 US census were finally complete, superintendent of the census Robert P. Porter made a startling announcement: "Up to and including 1880, the country had a frontier of settlement, but at present the unsettled area has been so broken into by isolated bodies of settlement that there can hardly be said to be a frontier line. In the discussion of its extent, its westward movement, etc., it cannot, therefore, any longer have a place in the census reports."[14]

For decades, the census had used the limits of western migration as a significant measure of America's growth. Now, after more than a century of expansion, America's western frontier was "closed." Superintendent Porter's pronouncement did not suggest that a wall or some other physical barrier be erected on the Mississippi River's western bank; nor were there new government restrictions on travel. The closing of the frontier merely meant that an imaginary line beyond which there was still ample unexplored and unsettled land had reached the Pacific Ocean, making further westward advancement impossible. Without a moving line to monitor, the US Census Bureau lost interest in defining the frontier.

For much of the population, especially in the eastern United States, the second industrial revolution driving the country inexorably toward the twentieth century was far more relevant than any romance offered by the frontier. The future, marked by unimagined advances in communication, transportation, medicine, and science, was calling. Even Colonel William Cody—"Buffalo Bill"—recognized as much.

When Buffalo Bill offered his famous Wild West Show to the organizers of the World's Columbian Exposition in Chicago in 1893, he was turned down because of "incongruity."[15] The exposition would showcase things that were new and exciting for the world to experience; to the fair's organizers, cowboys and Indians no longer fit the image of America. Shunned by the World's Fair, Buffalo Bill found a piece of property next door, set up shop there, and had the last laugh on the exposition's selection committee. Buffalo Bill's Wild West and Congress of Rough Riders of the World ran longer than the fair and was a rousing success. "Progress" was becoming the watchword for the country, though. And Buffalo Bill's interpretation of the West was beginning to resemble a romanticized anachronism.[16]

Census numbers and perceptions of a vanishing frontier aside, the West was still mostly wild during the late 1880s, a vast expanse with plenty of opportunity and risk for the taking. It was a time of settlers and prospectors, farmers and ranchers, lawmen and outlaws, the Oklahoma land rush, the Earps, Bat Masterson, and the OK Corral. Powering the expansion were horses, and where there were horses, there was racing. By one estimate, more than three hundred racetracks were operating in the United States in 1897, many of them in the West.[17]

"Horse racing and boxing were two of the most popular sports, primarily because of the propensity of men's desire to wager a bet on just about anything," explained Marshall Trimble, Arizona's official historian and vice president of the Wild West History Association. "Wyatt Earp owned a racehorse named Dick Naylor during his time in Tombstone and he owned several during the next 20 years or so." According to Trimble, "There were some race tracks between Los Angeles and San Diego. They would have had horse racing in towns that held rodeos such as Prescott, Tucson, Phoenix, Payson in Arizona; Cheyenne, Wyoming; Denver, Colorado. Tracks were usually located at the county fairgrounds. The first in Phoenix was in 1884. The current fair site opened in 1905. Ranches competed against each other on makeshift tracks. Where you have horses, there's going to be some wagering on who had the fastest horse."[18]

And where there is racing, there will be cheaters, swindlers, and con men. Early attempts at boosting racehorses' performance were crude and usually involved "drenches," oral doses of whiskey, sherry, coffee, or some other home-mixed concoction administered before a race. Whiskey and the other ingredients of a drench were easy to come by, and the image of a frontier saloon will forever be etched in memory as one of the most iconic symbols of the Old West. Opium dens, in contrast, were rare and often linked to Chinese immigrants. Drug use is not consistent with the cowboy mystique in popular culture. In reality, however, therapeutic and recreational drug use on the frontier was fairly common. Narcotics and stimulants were cheap and could be purchased easily and legally. Opium was smoked and often dispensed by "chuck wagon cooks on the open range, railroad station managers, and train porters." Laudanum, a tincture of opium with flavoring, was prescribed as a cure-all by frontier doctors.[19] John Henry "Doc" Holliday survived the OK Corral shoot-out with the Clantons but was addicted to laudanum when he died of tuberculosis in 1887.[20]

Cocaine toothache drops, an instantaneous cure that sold for fifteen cents, were readily available. Morphine, a derivative of opium, was an essential painkiller for wounded soldiers on both sides of the Civil War. The drug later found its way into a wide variety of medicines and potions, from a supposed cure for opium addiction to Mrs. Winslow's Soothing Syrup, one of the most notorious patent medicines sold in the United States and Great Britain during the late 1800s and early 1900s. Touted as a tonic for calming restless children, relieving teething pain, and curing dysentery, Mrs. Winslow's Syrup was packed with morphine (65 mg/fluid ounce) and alcohol. The concentration of morphine was high enough to be fatal to toddlers, earning Mrs. Winslow the grim nickname "the baby killer." To be fair to caregivers, however, the dangers of morphine use were not well known at the time, and the syrup's ingredients were a mystery. Only after passage of the Pure Food and Drug Act in 1906 were manufacturers required to list the active ingredients in patent medicines.[21]

By the early 1900s, the use of opium, morphine, and cocaine was so widespread that Hamilton Wright, US opium commissioner and American delegate to the 1900 International Opium Commission in Shanghai, declared that Americans had become "the greatest drug fiends in the world. . . . We are literally the world's opium eaters. . . . The opium and morphine habits have become a national curse."

Wright had this to say about cocaine, a popular stimulant used, ironically, to treat morphine addiction, as an anesthetic, and later as a
pep pill to fight fatigue: "It is a generally known fact that during the
last twenty years, cocaine has been diverted from its original use by
the surgeon as a local anesthetic to pander to the supposed needs of
large numbers of our population. It is estimated . . . that 15,000 or
20,000 ounces of this drug are considered sufficient to satisfy the
demands of surgery in the United States. Today there are manufactured in the United States at least 150,000 ounces of the drug, the
larger part is put to improper uses."[22]

   Wright attributed the growing use of cocaine to African Americans: "In the South, the use of cocaine among the lower order of working negroes is quite common. It is current knowledge throughout the
South that on many public works, levee and railroad construction,
and in other working camps where large numbers of negroes congre-
gate, cocaine is peddled pretty openly."[23] Similar politically oriented
attempts to link the use of heroin to African Americans and marijuana to hippies and Vietnam War protesters would be put forward by
Federal Bureau of Narcotics commissioner Harry J. Anslinger.[24] This
was also a cornerstone of President Richard Nixon's war on drugs.
"You want to know what this [Nixon's war on drugs] was really all
about?" Watergate coconspirator John Ehrlichman asked Dan Baum,
writing for *Harper's* magazine:

> The Nixon campaign in 1968, and the Nixon White House
> after that, had two enemies: the antiwar left and black peo-
> ple. You understand what I'm saying? We knew we couldn't
> make it illegal to be either against the war or black, but by
> getting the public to associate the hippies with marijuana
> and blacks with heroin, and then criminalizing both heav-
> ily, we could disrupt those communities. We could arrest
> their leaders, raid their homes, break up their meetings, and
> vilify them night after night on the evening news. Did we
> know we were lying about the drugs? Of course we did.[25]

The practice of boosting racehorses was going through a dramatic change during the post–Civil War years as powerful narcotics and stimulants—legal at the time and easily purchased without a prescription—became widely available for medical and recreational use. In that landscape of familiarity with drugs and growing acceptance of their use, it was just a matter of time until someone substituted these new drugs for the old, ineffective whiskey drenches in an attempt to make horses run faster.

It is impossible to identify that person with absolute certainty. The record is scant and based mostly on secondhand reporting, very little of it contemporaneous. Conclusive proof is simply not available. Still, circumstantial evidence strongly suggests that a shadowy figure from the frontier, "Doc" Ring, ushered in the modern era of performance-enhancing drugs during the winter of 1889–1890 at Guttenberg and the other outlaw tracks in New Jersey.

What is certain is that Doc Ring did not invent the idea of doping. Trainers had been trying to boost their horses with homemade and generally ineffective potions for centuries. Instead, Doc Ring was an innovator who took much of the guesswork out of the doping equation with powerful new drugs and a new way to deliver them. He did not invent doping; he standardized it, modernized it, and pushed the practice into the twentieth century. Ironically, he may not have had any intent to cheat.

3

The Injection

Walt Whitman wrote of a man with "multitudes."[1] "Doc" Ring was a man of "maybes." Maybe he was German. Maybe his family was wealthy and his father was a successful "pork packer." Maybe he hailed from St. Louis or, as one writer speculated, "that indefinite and unbounded territory which passed by the name of the West." It is impossible to know for certain.[2]

Maybe he was a licensed veterinarian, although that is unlikely. The first college of veterinary medicine operating west of the Mississippi River was not established until 1891 in Kansas City, around the same time Ring showed up at Guttenberg and the other New Jersey tracks. Most of the individuals practicing veterinary medicine at the time—around 95 percent of them, according to one estimate—were unqualified and probably did more harm than good. They were "charlatans, harpies, mountebanks, a preponderant group whose practices were unthinkably barbarious [*sic*]."[3] Instead, the appellation "Doc" was probably acquired on the backstretch in recognition of Ring's skill at doping horses with a handful of powerful new drugs and an innovative device for their administration: the hypodermic needle.

A few facts can be verified. His name was P. B. Ring, and his background in horse racing involved trotters and pacers in the Midwest and later Thoroughbreds. Ring's name was associated with a horse named Magoozler, one of the fastest pacers racing during the mid-1860s.[4] It appears that Ring acquired Magoozler late in the horse's career, during the last months of 1867, when the horse would have been nine years old and his best days were probably behind him.[5]

Ring's subsequent ventures with Thoroughbreds were unsuccessful. He attracted some attention with a colt that was nominated to both the 1887 Kentucky Derby and the Two Thousand Guineas in England, but the horse did not run in either race and apparently did not race successfully anywhere. "Some years ago, there appeared on the turf as the nominator to a lot of stakes both in this country and Europe, P. B. Ring, a Missourian and a young man who had a little money and a colt by Volturno," according to one report. "The horse was an utter failure in stakes races, and subsequently ran at Clifton and Guttenberg [both proprietary New Jersey tracks] and other small tracks as Free Lance, but the writer does not remember of his ever having won a race of any kind. He was so bad a horse that Ring 'went broke' before he got through with him."[6]

Free Lance was apparently the last horse to race in Ring's colors. Discouraged and penniless, Doc reportedly provided some veterinary care for horses at New Jersey tracks before discovering that his real talent was skill with a hypodermic needle and a secret mixture of drugs that he called the "injection." By 1890, after successfully boosting a few horses at New York tracks the previous year, Ring was hawking his injection in the stables at Guttenberg and Clifton. He was judicious in picking his clients, favoring horses that were not racing up to their full potential because they sulked, had other temperament problems, or were just uninterested in running. He apparently thought he could help.

Oddly, Ring did not demand a fee for the injection. Instead, he asked the owner or trainer to place a bet on the horse to win, usually around $25, at the best odds offered by the bookmakers. A significant return was possible, but only if the horse won at long odds. Otherwise, Ring got nothing for his efforts. There was no indication in the sparse reporting that Ring was trying to engineer a betting coup. He just wanted horses to run as fast as they could.

Oakwood Stable's Connemara was a perfect candidate for the injection. Because of her temperament, the mare was not winning as many races as she could. When she was scratched from a race on

Suburban Handicap Day at Sheepshead Bay, the race report noted that "the fact was not deplored by those who like to see a good start, not marred by fractious animals."[7] Race notes for an event at the Elizabeth track in New Jersey reported that "Connemara spoiled several starts by refusing to break."[8] "Connemara broke in front, then refused to move," according to the summary of another race.[9] She was clearly a "notorious sulker."[10]

Ring injected Connemara before a marathon staged at a mile and five furlongs on August 27, 1889, at Morris Park on Long Island. She had run dead last at Monmouth Park in New Jersey three weeks earlier: "That wicked jade Connemara has been a most expensive mare for her backers this year," a postrace report lamented.[11] She was dismissed at odds of 10–1 for the Morris Park event. It was a promising prospect for Ring's treatment, with a potential payout of $250.

The start was delayed, but not by Connemara this time. Larchmont, with "a seventy-pound midget in the saddle," according to a report of the day, broke away and ran twice around the course in the wrong direction.[12] He was scratched, but there were no refunds for bettors because the horse had been under the starter's control when he bolted.[13]

Connemara broke well and led for most of the race before being outrun in the final furlong. Hindoocraft, carrying seventy-five pounds to Connemara's eighty, won the race and set a track record of 2:48. Connemara finished last, so there was no winning bet for Ring to collect as his fee. The race was not a total loss, though. Connemara's uncharacteristically strong performance—early pace-setting and no sulking that day—did not go unnoticed by owners and trainers, who began to ask for Ring's help.

"The mare on that day led the party for nearly a mile and a half at such a stout pace that the merits of the treatment (Ring's injection) were manifest although she did not win."[14] By the time Ring shifted his operation to the winter tracks in New Jersey later that year, demand for the injection was strong and growing. As Ring's reputation on the backstretch grew, trainers began to seek him out. No one would "admit that there was any virtue in the secret process of Ring," former racing official John Boden recalled, "but nevertheless they were neglecting no opportunity and soon the services of Ring were in as much demand as those of the crack jockeys."[15]

Despite a captive clientele clamoring for his help, Ring was careful about offering the injection to trainers. He would treat only a few horses each month, and never more than one horse in any particular race. Because most horses receiving the injection had dismal past performances and long odds, Ring made a decent living collecting on bets placed for him by the trainers of the treated horses.

The recipe for the injection was a carefully guarded secret. Speculation centered on cocaine and morphine as the active ingredients, either individually or in combination, but no one was sure.[16] Another theory was that the injection was a mixture of cocaine, nitroglycerine, carbolic acid, and rose water. In a later formulation, supposedly revised because of concerns about the side effects of the nitroglycerine, strychnine, capsicum, ginger, and "other things" were added.[17] In any case, Ring was not talking.

Not a single owner or trainer was confident enough of the rumors about Ring's recipe to experiment on their own horses—at least not at first. That would come later. Instead, they trusted Doc and his injection. Trainers readily acknowledged the existence of doping, as the practice came to be known by the mid-1890s, but they generally claimed that only the other trainers were using Ring's services.

Jim Dyer trained 1888 Suburban Handicap winner Elkwood, a horse known as much for his savage temper and his hate for jockeys as for his racing prowess. A Henry Stull painting showing Elkwood with his ears pinned back was "most faithful to life," according to author and racing historian W. S. Vosburgh.[18] In an interview with an unnamed reporter in 1900, Dyer put himself in an embarrassing position when asked to recall Doc Ring's time at Guttenberg. "I can remember very well when they began to dope horses," Dyer said:

A Prof. P. B. Ring showed up in the East several years ago, and advertised to give speed to slow horses. He charged the owners 25 for a single operation and made big money doping. Then there was no rule against the practice, and it was done openly. Several good things had been brought off in consequence of Ring's operation.

In those days, I had an old sulker by the name of Tom Sawyer, who would run like a deer if he got off in front, but would dog it anywhere else. One day I stuck him in a race, and on the morning of the race I heard that one of Prof. Ring's pupils was to start against me and everybody was going to play it. I had no jockey, so I put up a little boy no bigger than Jack Martin. For fear that something might happen to the boy, I went over to the post, and I remember the first words Jim Caldwell, who was starting, said.

Glaring at the little fellow, Jim yelled: "Where did you come from?" The little chap was too scared to make a reply. Then I went up to Jim and told him that my horse, Tom Sawyer, was a sulker, but I didn't think he would give him trouble if he would put him in front of the bunch, which he did.

At the first break the old man let them go, Tom Sawyer ran like a wild horse. The dope fiend gave him a merry chase for half a mile, and then faded. After I got back to the ring I was told that my horse was 50–1, but I was satisfied to win the purse.[19]

Maybe Tom Sawyer raced clean that unspecified day, as Dyer remembered, but that was not always the case. Perhaps Dyer conveniently forgot the other occasions when he called Ring to administer the injection.

"One of the first horses to be experimented on was old Tom Sawyer—a selling plater of roguish temperament but a usually hard campaigner," Boden wrote. "Under the treatment he won many races and 'Doc' Ring began to be talked about."[20] One of those wins came in a selling race over one mile at Guttenberg on April 3, 1890. According to the race summary, "It was a fine start, with Tom Sawyer slightly in front and attended by Thad Rowe. The pair were in close company to the lower turn, where Thad Rowe was leading slightly. In the stretch there was a great closing, and Tom Sawyer came again in a fine burst of speed and won by a neck from Re-echo, who beat Thad Rowe [by] three lengths."[21] The time for the race was 1:43¾. It was the "best race he [Tom Sawyer] has ever run."[22] In the estimation of this reporter, the injection worked exactly as advertised.

A curious situation was developing as Ring's reputation as a speed merchant and faith in his injection increased. Neither Ring nor his clients were doing anything illegal. Passage of the Harrison Narcotics Tax Act, one of the first federal attempts to control the distribution of cocaine, opium, and their derivatives, would not come until 1914. The injection was not even against the rules of racing at the time. Still, information about which horses were receiving the injection was valuable, and if this became common knowledge, it would defeat the purpose of doping. Purses were small, and a stable's profits often depended on cashing bets at long odds. Improving a long shot's chances of winning, without the bookmakers catching on to the injection scheme, gave owners and trainers a significant edge. Secrecy, though, was becoming more difficult to maintain.

Ring certainly was not popular with bookmakers, who found themselves paying off for wagers on long-shot winners with uncommon frequency, or with owners and trainers, who feared racing against a doped horse. With no legal protections against doping, bookmakers and touts began to spy on Ring, and skulkers followed him as he made his rounds. "Bookmakers and owners who had entries in a race had such a constant 'shadow' on him that frequently he had to resort to all sorts of tricks to administer his 'dope' to a horse without disclosing the fact, thereby lessening the odds against the horse," Boden wrote:

He was not satisfied as to the efficiency of the preparation if it were administered more than 45 minutes before the actual running of the race, and on more than one occasion he spent the night at some stable, smuggled into the stall, where no one who might betray the secret was at hand.

At this time the "dope" was injected hypodermically. Its principal ingredient was cocaine and it was injected in the shoulder. There was no special hour for reporting in the paddock in those days and no regularly constituted parade to the post, so it [was] possible to keep the public and the pencilers [bookmakers] from knowledge until it was practically too late either to cover or to wager on the horse.[23]

The injection almost always left a telltale swelling at the site where it was administered, which quickly identified the horse as one that had been treated by Ring. But discovery that a horse had received the injection would not affect the order of finish for the race just run; because the injection was neither illegal nor against racing rules, there were no grounds for an administrative prerace scratch or postrace disqualification. A horse with a history of injections would be marked as one that might be doped in a subsequent start. Or it might not be doped, depending on whether the owner or trainer wanted to run the horse hot or cold the next time out. To avoid detection, Ring began to inject horses either beneath the mane or under the jaw, where a lump would be less obvious to a bystander.

By 1897, when the Jockey Club instituted the country's first rule prohibiting doping, Doc Ring's monopoly on the injection was slipping away. Trainers and pharmacists had devised their own variations on Ring's formula. More important, dopers were abandoning the hypodermic needle and adopting more discreet methods of administration.

Gentian root, an herbal medicine used to reduce inflammation, was one of the new doping ingredients.[24] Heroin, digitalis, strychnine,

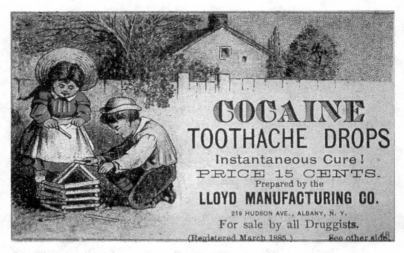

Advertisement for cocaine toothache drops. Patent medicines containing cocaine and narcotics were readily available during the late 1800s. (National Library of Medicine)

and cocaine were some of the other common drugs added to compounds that could be formed into a bolus and administered orally. With no chemical test for stimulants in an animal's system and no physical indication of an injection, a horse doped with a "ball" could be identified only indirectly by observing physical symptoms. Profuse sweating, dilation of the pupils, and agitation—all symptoms exhibited by Dr. Riddle before his final and fatal race at Morris Park—were common markers. But absent a confession from the person who administered the drugs, there was no way to establish conclusively that a horse had been doped.

Later, powdered heroin was administered alone, sprinkled on a horse's tongue as a prerace stimulant. The advantage of heroin was that it had a legitimate purpose. Heroin in liquid form—glycolheroin, a product manufactured by the Martin A. Smith Company in New York—was used therapeutically to treat colds and sore throats in both people and horses. (Glycol-heroin contained ½ grain of heroin,

24 grains of anon hypophos, 8 grains of hyoscyamus, 30 grains of white pine bark, and 2 grains of balsam tolu, mixed with enough glycerine to make an ounce of solution.)[25] Thus, by itself, possession of heroin was not proof of wrongdoing. Heroin "may be detected principally by the smell," Boden wrote, "but there almost invariably is an alibi at hand. This alibi consists in the presence in a stable of a bottle of glycol-heroin . . . so that if a horse is under scrutiny, there may be the excuse that some of it had been given to him as a remedy for a cold. Not all stables, of course, that have glycol-heroin are 'dope' stables, but in every modern 'dope' stable there is always a bottle of glycol-heroin."[26]

Other commercial products were advertised as performance-enhancing substances, both before and after the Jockey Club attempted to ban their use in 1897. One of the most popular was Speed Sustaining Elixir, which was touted as the "most valuable compound ever offered the racing public" in an 1898 advertisement. The elixir "resists exhaustion, prevents and cures thumps and heart failure, and enables an animal to endure extreme and prolonged exhaustion with least fatigue. EIGHT world's records have been made by horses that had the Elixir when the records were made."[27] The company that produced Speed Sustaining Elixir was based in New York but had sales agents in half a dozen states, and the elixir was marketed across the country. It was popular with trainers of both Standardbreds and Thoroughbreds for several years but eventually fell out of favor around the turn of the century, perhaps because of the Jockey Club's campaign against stimulants. The company was dissolved in 1900 for failure to pay taxes.[28]

Sorting out an equitable way to deal with a drug that has multiple uses, some of them allowed and some not, is still a vexing issue for racing authorities. A single medication might have a legitimate therapeutic use when administered during training to treat a horse's physical problem, but it becomes a performance-enhancing drug when given close to race time. This quandary has led to some of the sport's most famous legal battles.

In the mid-1940s trainer Tom Smith, of Seabiscuit fame, became embroiled in a dispute over the prerace use of ephedrine in some of the horses he trained for Elizabeth Arden Graham's Maine Chance Farm (see chapters 9 and 10). An herbal medicine akin to amphetamines, ephedrine is a bronchodilator that can alleviate breathing problems in humans and horses. It is also a stimulant and a prohibited performance-enhancing drug in horse racing.[29] Smith used nasal sprays containing ephedrine to treat himself, and he thought the sprays could also help his horses breathe better during training. At the time, there was no reliable chemical test to detect ephedrine in a horse's system. Instead, the evidence against Smith consisted of testimony from several people who had seen either Smith or one of his employees spray the nostrils of Maine Chance horses with a solution that, according to subsequent testing, contained ephedrine. The Jockey Club suspended Smith's trainer's license, a decision that he fought unsuccessfully in court for more than a year.

A quarter century later, Dancer's Image was the first to cross the finish line in the 1968 Kentucky Derby but was disqualified when a questionable postrace test for phenylbutazone, a nonsteroidal anti-inflammatory drug, was positive.[30] Phenylbutazone was permitted during training but not when racing in Kentucky in 1968, and the state followed a zero-tolerance policy for prohibited medications. Any trace of a prohibited drug was sufficient grounds for disqualification. Dancer's Image had been given phenylbutazone the weekend before the Derby to treat sore ankles, but the drug should have cleared his system by race day.

Peter Fuller, who owned Dancer's Image, challenged the integrity of the testing procedures and the competence of the racing commission's chemist through a series of administrative hearings and court proceedings that lasted for five years. The challenges were unsuccessful, and Calumet Farm's Forward Pass, which finished second in the race, was ultimately declared the winner. Ironically, Forward Pass had not been tested for prohibited medications after the race. At the time,

Kentucky rules required postrace tests for only two horses—the winner and a second horse selected randomly.

Fuller's legal challenges were unsuccessful, but the Dancer's Image controversy led to major improvements in track security, testing procedures, enforcement, and overall transparency. And although the positive drug test, administrative hearings, litigation, and eventual disqualification of Dancer's Image led to a redistribution of the purse and delivery of the Derby trophy to Calumet Farm, the panoply of rules, regulations, and procedures did not protect the bettors. Once the stewards declared the race "official" a few minutes after the horses crossed the finish line on the afternoon of May 4, 1968, winning tickets on Dancer's Image were cashed. Bettors who had wagered on Forward Pass to win had no recourse, although their tickets probably gained some value as collector's items.

For decades, Dancer's Image remained the only winner of the Kentucky Derby to be disqualified because of a medication violation. Then, in early 2022, following two positive tests for the prohibited corticosteroid betamethasone, 2021 Derby winner Medina Spirit was disqualified. As of this writing, litigation is still pending.

Maximum Security, which finished first in the 2019 Kentucky Derby, was disqualified for interference with another horse during the race.[31] Ten months later, Maximum Security's trainer, Jason Servis, was one of more than two dozen people indicted on federal charges related to the "systematic and covert administration of performance-enhancing drugs to racehorses competing across the United States and abroad."[32] A number of these individuals have entered guilty pleas, including Servis and prominent trainer Jorge Navarro, who was sentenced to five years in federal prison Servis was scheduled for sentencing in May 2023.

The most controversial drug at the time of this writing, and for the past forty-plus years, is furosemide, a popular medication marketed under the trade names Lasix and Salix and used to treat exercise-induced pulmonary hemorrhage in horses (more commonly called "bleeding"). Although it is useful during training, there is

conflicting research on whether furosemide enhances racing performance and confusion over whether or how to regulate race-day
administration of the drug. There are strong opinions on both sides of
the issue. Although nearly all Thoroughbreds currently race on furosemide, the Horseracing Integrity and Safety Act of 2020 will phase
out the drug's prerace use (see chapter 18).

In 1904, a year after Dr. Riddle died from an apparent drug overdose, one of the greatest Thoroughbreds of the twentieth century fell
victim to a different kind of drugging scheme. Writing in 1970, the
late Kent Hollingsworth, editor of *Blood-Horse* magazine for many
years, named Sysonby, Colin, Man o' War, and Citation as the four
best racehorses of the century.[33] Thirty years later, in one of several
retrospective volumes published by *Blood-Horse,* Sysonby ranked
thirtieth among the century's greats, between Exterminator (#29)
and Sunday Silence (#31).[34]

Sysonby's only loss came as a two-year-old in the Futurity at
Sheepshead Bay in New York. In his four previous races, Sysonby
had been perfect, winning easily by margins of six, four, six, and six
lengths. But in the Futurity, he finished a lackluster third, five
lengths behind the filly Artful and a nose behind Tradition.[35] Sysonby closed out his juvenile campaign with a three-length win in the
Junior Champion Stakes. There was no official voting for annual
championships when Sysonby was racing, but there was little doubt
that he was the best two-year-old of the season.

In his memoir published more than thirty years later, Foxhall
Keene, son of Sysonby's owner James R. Keene, explained what had
happened in the Futurity: "As the Futurity field swept up the stretch,
both my father and I could see that Sysonby was not running right.
Something was wrong. . . . Two days after the Futurity, Rowe
[Jimmy Rowe, Sysonby's trainer] caught Sysonby's negro groom, a
boy who was supposed to love Syse, sporting a roll of bills as big as
your arm, and Father succeeded in making the negro confess that he
had given the colt a dose of bromidian before the race."[36]

After finishing in a dead heat for first place in the Metropolitan Handicap in his first start as a three-year-old in 1905, Sysonby finished first in his next nine starts. Through two seasons, he won fourteen of fifteen races and earned $184,438. Sysonby fell ill early in 1906 and died of liver disease and a blood condition identified as variola. A crowd estimated at four thousand attended the colt's burial in front of the Keene barn on the backstretch at Sheepshead Bay. Sysonby's body was later exhumed, and his skeleton was prepared by S. H. Chubb for display at the Museum of Natural History in New York.[37]

Several years after the drugging incident with Sysonby, a filly named Ladana, from Harry F. Sinclair's Rancocas Stable, was apparently jabbed with a hypodermic needle containing the sedative chloral hydrate as she was being walked from the barn to the paddock for a race at Saratoga in upstate New York. By post time, she was in no condition to run, and Ladana was scratched. She had been one of the favorites in the race, which suggested a betting coup in the works.[38] Ladana's trainer, Frank M. Taylor, immediately reported the drugging, which the Saratoga stewards called "scandalous and calculated to impair confidence in racing." The stewards then censured Taylor for "not having taken measures to prevent" the drugging and ordered that no overnight entries of Rancocas horses would be accepted for the duration of the meeting.[39] A few days later, Harry Sinclair sold twenty-five horses (including Ladana for $9,500) and retired from racing.[40] Sinclair's hiatus from the sport did not last long, however. He remained a force on the turf for years after the Ladana debacle.

Fixing races by stopping the favorites—whether by bribing or otherwise inducing jockeys to pull a horse, threatening or inflicting physical injury on horse or rider, or administering drugs to a horse—has been a repugnant aspect of racing throughout the sport's history. The incidents tend to be unorganized, one-off events, but that is not always the case. During hearings conducted by the House of Representatives Select Committee on Crime in 1972, admitted race fixer Bobby Byrne (the alias he used during his race-tampering days) testified about drugging horses at tracks along the East Coast and in the Midwest. Byrne told the committee that he had tranquilized hundreds of horses from 1968 through 1970. In theory, the scheme was a simple one: target exotic wagers that offered huge payouts if a few of the favored horses in a race were guaranteed to finish out of the money. If several horses were slowed with drugs and one or two others were eliminated from contention by bribing or extorting their riders to cooperate in the fix, bettors could concentrate their wagers on the few "live" horses left.[41] Spencer Drayton, head of the Thoroughbred Racing and Protective Bureau, dismissed Byrne's testimony and similar testimony from mob enforcer Joe "The Baron" Barboza as "headline-making material provided by cheap hoodlums."[42]

Foxhall Keene's reference to Sysonby receiving "a dose of bromidian" probably meant either potassium bromide or sodium bromide, both sedatives. Or he might have been using a generic term for any sedative. Either way, using drugs to slow down or stop a horse during a race is far removed from the purposes of Doc Ring's performance-enhancing injections. There is no evidence that Ring ever attempted to manipulate a race's outcome by using drugs to prevent a favorite from winning. Instead, he simply helped underperforming horses reach their full potential. In so doing, were Ring and the owners and trainers he worked for cheating? John R. Keene, one of the founders of the Jockey Club in the 1890s, did not think so—at least not initially.

Did Doc Ring's injections, the copycat formulations that followed, and the commercially available elixirs really work? Were the American and British attempts at regulation justified, or were they solutions to a problem that did not yet exist? These are fair questions, considering that the last horse Ring owned, Free Lance, was an abject failure. If Ring had used the injection on Free Lance and it had worked as advertised, it is unlikely that Ring would have shared his knowledge with other owners and trainers. Considering Free

Lance's poor performance, that clearly was not the case. And if the injection did not help his own horses, how was Ring able to sell the procedure to others with no proof of past success?

It is likely that Ring did not start experimenting with performance-enhancing drugs until his own stable went bankrupt in the late 1880s. A contemporaneous article in the *New York Times* reported that Ring conceived the injection idea while traveling in the southern United States after giving up as a Thoroughbred owner. He was supposedly inspired by a story—maybe too good to be true—about a physician who injected a balky mule with morphine to get the animal moving: "Going alongside the obstinate mule, he jabbed the needlelike instrument into the hide of the animal. The brute reared on his hind legs, gave a bray that woke the echoes for miles around, and started down the road on a gallop such as he had never shown before."[43] With that incident in mind, Ring returned to the outlaw tracks and got to work devising his own formula for a stimulant. His injections were soon in great demand.

The problematic aspects of evaluating Ring's injections and the incidence of doping in general are twofold: the complete lack of objective proof of the drugs' efficacy, and the reliance on anecdotal evidence of doping as reported in the press. Newspapers regularly reported results from tracks in metropolitan New York with varying levels of detail, occasionally printing complete charts of the races. Bettors in the 1890s who scrutinized the best race charts of the day in the *Morning Telegraph* (a broadsheet that specialized in entertainment and horse racing news) and the *New York World* would feel at home with today's *Daily Racing Form*.[44] Those publications were the exceptions, however. Most newspaper reports were just bare-bones summaries of the conditions for each race, the order of finish, and the winning time. Eventually, postrace summaries, charts, and chronological lists of past performances became horse racing's "official" record books. These reports identified the winners, but aside from terse descriptions of how a race was run, they provided no information about why a particular horse won. For insights into gambling odds; training practices; owners' plans for their stables; racetrack gossip about owners, trainers, and jockeys; and rumors about doping, bettors relied on newspaper reports and handicapping tout sheets. They still do.

Paul Dimeo, a professor at Stirling University in Scotland, is a prolific writer about doping in human athletics and policy issues in sports regulation. He recognized the inherent danger of relying too heavily on textual sources while assembling a historical record in his award-winning monograph *A History of Drug Use in Sport*. "In essence, a story has to be told," Dimeo wrote, "but myths and ideologies have to be unpicked. . . . The documents used in this study are taken where appropriate as truthful representations, either in the truth of their production or of the straightforward facts they assert. That offers the chance to question the supposed truths that are being presented, while also recognizing the influence that texts can have, even if they are factually incorrect."[45]

Evaluating Doc Ring's injections 125 years after the fact is even more difficult because secrecy was such an essential element of doping. For the scheme to work, bookmakers and the betting public had to be kept in the dark. The few articles about Ring that made it into print identified at least a dozen horses helped by his injections: Tom Sawyer and Blackthorn in one report,[46] and Connemara, Adonis, Specialty, Lancaster, Bonanza, Barrister, Gendarme, Lottery, Cupid, and Ravelier in another.[47] Performances by Connemara at Morris Park during the summer of 1889 and Gendarme at Brighton Beach the following summer were singled out as early success stories that popularized Ring's injections.

Conventional wisdom was that the injections could enhance the performance of a sulky horse that had some talent, whereas horses that had no speed would not be helped by the injections.[48] Gendarme was an example of the former. He raced at least seventeen times in 1890, winning three races and placing twice at Guttenberg and Clifton early in the year; winning three times and finishing third in one race at Brighton Beach during the summer; and win-

ning once in three starts at Clifton in December.[49] Gendarme raced
mostly in selling races, and his record in 1890 was decent—perhaps
better than average—for a Guttenberg-class horse. He was inconsistent, winning some races and losing others, but inconsistency is
not irrefutable evidence of doping. Without reliable testing, the conclusion that any of Gendarme's wins were helped along by Ring's
injections is speculation at best. Considering the quality of racing
at Brighton Beach, though—a *New York Times* editorial called the
track a "pesthole of race-track gambling"[50]—Doc Ring and his
injections would have fit right in, just as they did at the outlaw New
Jersey tracks.

Ultimately, people's belief that the injections boosted horses
may have been more important to the jockey clubs in America and
England than whether the concoctions actually improved a horse's
performance and could alter a race's outcome. Organized horse racing has always been dependent on gambling for financial support,
and anything that threatened gambling was an existential threat to
horse racing itself.

4

Rule 162

Thoroughbred racing in the United States at the turn of the twentieth century looked a lot like racing at the turn of the twenty-first. There are differences in scale, of course, but racing today would look familiar to an owner or trainer from a hundred years ago.

There was horse racing in a dozen states in 1905, compared to thirty-eight states (plus Canada) a century later. According to *Goodwin's Official Turf Guide,* a total of thirty-four jockey clubs and racing associations (including Fort Erie and Ontario in Canada) conducted 7,763 races and distributed purses totaling $5,477,952 in 1905. In 2005 the Jockey Club reported 52,257 races in the United States, with purses totaling more than $1 billion ($1,085,005,415, to be exact). The average purse per race in 1905 was $705.64; in 2005, it was $20,763. Adjusted for inflation, total purses in 1905 were equivalent to $121,555,755 and the average purse per race was $15,650, both in 2005 dollars. Metropolitan New York was the center of racing in 1905, with the Coney Island Jockey Club (first), Westchester Racing Association (third), Brooklyn Jockey Club (fourth), and Brighton Beach Racing Association (fifth) representing four of the top five places based on purse distribution. Saratoga in upstate New York ranked eighth.[1]

Then, as now, the purse structure was inadequate to support a large number of racing stables. Gambling was an obvious way to supplement a horse's winnings, which encouraged the use of performance-enhancing drugs (PEDs) to gain an edge over the competition. Given the secrecy necessary for betting coups to work,

Bookmakers at Morris Park. Gambling, legal or otherwise, has always been the lifeblood of Thoroughbred racing. (Keeneland Library, John C. Hemment Collection)

PEDs gave owners an advantage over bookmakers as well. And a winning record, no matter how it was obtained, made a horse more marketable for both racing and breeding. The motivation for the use of PEDs, first and foremost, has always been economic gain.

A fundamental problem facing horse racing in 1905, aside from the perennial financial issues that plagued most stables and the reformers who wanted to do away with gambling altogether, was a fragmented organizational structure. The Coney Island Jockey Club operated Sheepshead Bay, the Brooklyn Jockey Club operated Gravesend, the New York Jockey Club ran racing at Morris Park, and so on. There was grudging cooperation among the clubs when it suited their individual interests, but with no central governing body at either the state or national level, there was little regard for the best interests of racing. Instead, each racetrack was operated by a different group that established its own rules and organized race meetings to serve its own interests.

"Before the Gay Nineties, every race track in America operated under its own individual rules," turf historian William H. P. Robertson wrote. "Although there was a certain amount of reciprocity among tracks concerning serious rule violators who were completely banished from the sport, not many bothered to keep tabs on minor offenders, and a person suspended by one association could merely transfer to another track, sometimes within the same city, and duck the punishment. Moreover, each track could decide its own racing dates, and simultaneous meetings in the same area, destructive to all parties concerned, were fairly common."[2]

More than a century later, the authority to regulate racing remains divided, with state racing commissions exercising local control. There is still no central governing body. Exclusive jurisdiction over racing at the state level may change, however, at least in some important areas. After several failed attempts to get legislation passed in Congress, the Horseracing Integrity and Safety Act (HISA) was finally approved by the House of Representatives and the Senate and signed into law by the president in late 2020. Initially scheduled to take effect no later than July 1, 2022, the start date for the medication regulations was pushed back to January 1, 2023. Implementation of the medication regulations was delayed again due to challenges in several federal courts. HISA is the first federal attempt to establish nationwide rules and standards for medication use and safety in horse racing. The legislation does not eliminate state racing commissions, which remain responsible for other administrative and regulatory tasks.

By the mid-1880s, some newspapers were calling for the leading New York jockey clubs to band together and enact "positive and sweeping reforms" against the "abuses and disgraces of the turf." An article in the *New York Tribune* cited the English Jockey Club as a model for regulation in the United States:

In England, the one great Jockey Club exercises a supervisory authority over all respectable race-courses. Jockeys and trainers are not allowed to ply their trades without licenses and thus a check is put upon the dishonest. Owners and jockeys who take part in races for prizes less than a hundred pounds in value are not permitted to compete on the honestly-conducted tracks. This discourages the opening of little thieving race-courses like those with which the neighborhood is infested. The American turf has none of these safeguards or restraints, and any owner or jockey, reeking with fraud, can go directly from Brighton Beach, Guttenburg [sic], Parkville, or Clifton, and take part in races at Jerome Park, Monmouth or Sheepshead Bay.

It is time to set apart the sheep from the goats. If the American and Coney Island Jockey Clubs and the Monmouth Park Racing Association will adopt a resolution excluding from their grounds all owners, trainers, jockeys and horses that take part in races at tracks not recognized by them, they will purify and elevate the turf. If they take no measures for reform, the day of their calamity is not far off.[3]

Change was necessary, but it was slow in coming.[4]

The Board of Control, a consortium of New York racetrack operators and horsemen, was formed in 1891 to supervise racing in the metropolitan area. The board's seven members were track operators D. D. Withers (Monmouth Park), J. G. K. Lawrence (Sheepshead Bay), P. J. Dwyer (Gravesend), and John A. Morris (Morris Park) and stable owners A. J. Cassatt, John Hunter, and James Galway.[5] Although horsemen were represented on the board, track operators had the majority, and there was little doubt that they were in charge.

Patterned after the English Jockey Club, the Board of Control had lofty goals, only a few of which were realized. One of its first major actions was an attempt to curb racing at Guttenberg by banning owners and horses that raced there from competing at the New York tracks. The effort was well received by the press, but ultimately, it had little effect on racing at the outlaw track (see chapter 2).

The Board of Control also promoted the use of pari-mutuel betting machines, sought to regulate the practices of owners who entered their higher-class runners in cheap selling races to win large bets, and clarified the definition of "starter." The strategy of entering good horses against bad ones persisted until selling races were replaced by claiming races, in which the winner could be purchased by anyone for the stated price.[6] The new "starter" rule—for betting purposes, a horse became a starter as soon as the names of the horse and jockey were posted on the official telegraph board—proved to be more confusing and problematic than helpful. The *New York Times* predicted that changing the definition of "starter" would encourage fraud and noted that "the rule is one that meets with the approval of a lot of horse owners whose standing is not the best, and that very fact should be its condemnation."[7]

Although the Board of Control may have been a necessary first step toward unifying New York's jockey clubs, its usefulness was short-lived. The board was mired in inefficiency, and there were ongoing complaints about conflicts of interest among the track operators who controlled it. In addition, the onset of a nationwide depression was cutting into purses. The board's demise in January 1894 had been predicted, but not mourned, by the *New York Times* a few weeks earlier:

> The energies of the men at the head of the Racing Trust, which is more commonly known as the Board of Control, were all directed to making money for the race tracks, their owners, and the chums of these owners. . . . There is absolute need for such a body [to replace the Board of Control] in the opinion of every man who loves the sport, before racing can again resume a place among the sports of gentlemen and be taken out of the list of gambling games in which

faro, roulette, rouge et noir, and baccarat are a quartet to which certain horse owners have tried to marry them.[8]

James R. Keene, a fearless Wall Street speculator and owner of one of the most successful racing stables of the day, was the driving force behind the formation of the Jockey Club to replace the defunct Board of Control. The idea of a new organization that would consolidate the activities of the leading New York tracks, and possibly govern racing on a national scale in the future, was endorsed during a meeting of horse owners at the Hoffman House in New York on December 29, 1893. The Jockey Club was incorporated a few weeks later, on February 9, 1894, with management in the hands of seven stewards: Keene, John Hunter, August Belmont II, J. O. Donner, Dr. G. L. Knapp, Colonel W. P. Thompson, and F. K. Sturgis. Hunter served as the club's first chair, with Belmont moving into that position the following year.[9]

Funding for the Jockey Club initially came from its membership —a $200 initiation fee and annual dues of $100—plus licensing fees collected from trainers and jockeys, fines collected for rule infractions, and, after 1896, administration of the breed registry and publication of the *American Stud Book*.[10]

The purposes of the Jockey Club, as set out in its certificate of incorporation, included "the investigating, ascertaining and keeping of a record of the pedigree of horses, and of instituting, maintaining, controlling and publishing a Stud Book or Book of Registry of horses in the United States of America and Canada; and of promoting and holding exhibitions of such horses and generally for the purpose of improving the breed thereof."[11] The club's "general" purposes proved expansive. Its proposed jurisdiction, made public for the first time in January 1894, included the licensing of trainers and jockeys, the forfeit list, the registration of owners and partnerships, all racing and racing matters, the rules of racing and their amendments, and the appointment of all officials associated with the sport. In other words, the Jockey Club would be in charge of everything related to racing.[12]

"The original Jockey Club ran the whole show," Robertson wrote, "frequently with an iron hand. Combining legislative, executive, and judicial functions, it wrote the rules of racing, enforced them and interpreted them as a court of last appeal. . . . The men who founded the Jockey Club were giants of their day—in industry, finance, politics, and sport—and they moved in keeping with their roles."[13]

The Jockey Club lost much of its power, but not its influence in racing matters, during the first decades of the twentieth century as state racing commissions assumed many of the responsibilities for drafting rules, licensing, allocating racing dates, and adjudicating appeals of stewards' rulings. New York, where the Jockey Club was incorporated, became the last state to assume authority for the licensing of participants. In 1951 the New York Court of Appeals ruled that the state legislature's original delegation of licensing power to the Jockey Club was unconstitutional. The power to issue licenses, the court ruled, should be vested in the state racing commission rather than a private organization like the Jockey Club.[14] Jule Fink, the winning plaintiff whose license application had been denied by the Jockey Club, reapplied with the New York State Racing Commission. That application was also denied.

Doping was among the myriad "racing matters" falling under the purview of the Jockey Club. The rules of racing, drafted after the organization was incorporated in 1894, were amended on February 11, 1897, to address performance-enhancing drugs with an addition to Rule 162, section VI. The amendment banned "any person who shall be proved to have affected the speed of a horse by the use of drugs, internally, whether administered by hypodermic or any other method, or who shall have used appliances, electrical or mechanical, other [than] the ordinary whip and spur. Every person so offending shall be ruled off."[15] A later version of Rule 162 added a specific reference to a "drug or stimulant" and replaced the requirement of proof that the speed of a horse had been affected with a broader

prohibition against simply administering the drug.[16] Identification
of specific prohibited substances would come later.

Early on, there was some dissension about the Jockey Club's
position on doping. Later, after the organization took up the fight
against performance-enhancing drugs, W. C. Vreeland, veteran turf
writer for the *Brooklyn Daily Eagle,* asked James R. Keene for his
thoughts on the subject. Surprisingly, the man who had championed
the formation of the Jockey Club and been one of its original stewards seemed to consider doping a potentially useful training method.
The problems with doping, Keene said, were harmful side effects
and public relations. "It is not the use of stimulants that we object
to," Keene told Vreeland. "Anything that is helpful to improve the
speed of horses is all right. But it is harmful to the horse itself and
makes him a dope fiend. Then too, its use at times and its failure to
do so at other periods smacks of trickery. That is why it has been
banned."[17] It seems that Keene was more concerned about running
horses hot or cold and the negative impact on gambling, rather than
the effects of doping itself.

There was a problem with Rule 162, however, and it was a serious
one. The attempt to prohibit doping was years ahead of its time. With
reliable chemical tests to detect stimulants in a horse's system decades
away, there was no way to prove that a horse had been doped. Proof
of an infraction required more than circumstantial evidence; it
required either a confession or observation of a drug being administered. For obvious reasons, both were highly unlikely. The new rule,
which was supposed to prevent doping, was actually an affront to
fairness by punishing an owner or trainer for an offense that could
not be established with certainty. Apparently, this shortcoming was
not a problem for the Jockey Club's stewards. They meted out penalties for doping based solely on observation of a horse's erratic behavior
and other circumstantial evidence.

Despite its flaws, Rule 162 was noteworthy because it marked
the first significant antidoping regulation enacted by any sport's governing body. A similar effort to curb performance-enhancing drugs

in human athletics would not come for more than a quarter century, during a meeting of the International Amateur Athletic Federation (IAAF) held during the 1928 Olympic Games in Amsterdam. The proposal was straightforward: the federation would ban anyone involved in the doping of competitors with "drugs or stimulants internally by hypodermic or other methods." A mechanism for enforcing the rule was not addressed.[18] The antidoping proposal received scant notice because the meetings were focused on more pressing issues, including whether women should be allowed to compete in future Olympics and the accuracy of timing watches that measured to one-tenth of a second. About the antidoping proposal, the *New York Times* reported, "Under America's leadership, however, the administering of drugs to athletes was recognized by the I.A.A.F. for the first time as an existing evil, and provision was made for the exclusion of any person knowingly administering drugs or assisting in the act anywhere that I.A.A.F. rules prevail."[19]

Another sign of the times was the decision that women could compete in future Olympic Games. There were misgivings about that decision, but they were eased by a German identified only as Dr. Bergmann, who was the "examining physician of the women athletes of Berlin." According to the *Times,* Dr. Bergmann told the IAAF that, based on ten years' experience, he was convinced that participation in sports was not injurious to female competitors. Women athletes, the doctor said, "got married and had children just as did non-athletes."[20]

The first significant action by the Jockey Club in response to an alleged doping infraction came a few days after the death of Dr. Riddle in May 1903 after a race at Morris Park (see chapter 1). William Howell, who trained Dr. Riddle, was ruled off the turf, the most severe penalty available to Jockey Club stewards. No action was taken against owner John Gardner, despite rumors of a previous doping incident in Canada.[21]

The tragic and very public death of a horse following an alleged drug overdose, and the press outrage that followed, demanded action

August Belmont II, one of the most influential early chairmen of the Jockey Club. (Keeneland Library, Charles Christian Cook Collection)

by the Jockey Club, even without conclusive proof of doping. Subsequent rulings were sometimes based on far less "evidence" of doping than in the case of Dr. Riddle. For example, following a race at Brighton Beach on July 15, 1903, successful trainer Lee Brown was ruled off after his horse, If You Dare, "was sent to the post manifestly in a drugged condition." The only evidence was the horse's unusual behavior that day and an investigation into If You Dare's physical condition. The horse was also ruled off for life, and tracks were ordered to refuse future entries from the owner. After announcing the stewards' ruling, August Belmont II said the Jockey Club was prepared to resort to extreme measures to stop doping. Brown applied for reinstatement later that year, but the stewards denied his request.[22]

In 1906, in a surprise decision called a "bolt from a clear sky," the Jockey Club ruled off owner Robert L. Rogers, assistant trainer

John Wilson, and the horse Garnish for violations of Rule 162. No specific instances of doping were mentioned, but Garnish's erratic record was seemingly a factor. The horse had won handily at decent odds in late October, following poor efforts in his two previous races. Although not uncommon, Garnish's inconsistency was deemed sufficient circumstantial evidence of doping to satisfy the stewards. The ruling as it applied to Garnish was nonsensical: the horse had obviously not been a willing participant in his own doping, if in fact he had been doped. And there was no conclusive evidence of that, beyond Garnish's spotty race record. "The inference then," according to a report about the Jockey Club's ruling, "is that Garnish is accused of 'doping,' that Garnish is a 'dope horse' and that his whimsical running hereabouts has been due to the fact that the 'dope' has not been steadily used on him."[23] The basis of the ruling was apparently a growing concern about horses running hot and cold. Inconsistent performance was becoming an indicator of doping and a threat to the supposed level playing field for bookmakers and gamblers.

There was some recognition that ruling off owners, trainers, and occasionally horses without hard evidence—scientific tests for doping did not yet exist—could create unfair hardships, but protecting the betting public was deemed more important. Reporting on the opening of the fall 1902 meeting at Hawthorne near Chicago, the *Tribune* praised the efforts of local officials for "ferreting out some of the flagrant form reversals and 'doping' practices which have caused the pessimistic to call the present year the worst in the recent history of the local sport." The report acknowledged the difficulty of securing incriminating evidence and recognized that "barring a horse inflicts financial punishment on owners." Nevertheless, the *Tribune* urged protection for bettors, despite the possibility of errors in judging the intentions of owners: "Allowing markedly inconsistent horses to run is an injustice to the public which supports the game."[24]

Occasionally, suspicions of doping were based on more than just observation and speculation. In March 1903 stewards at the Crescent City Jockey Club in New Orleans ruled off W. H. Fizer, a successful trainer who had been suspected of doping horses in his stable for several years. There had been some troubling incidents, including the sudden improvement of a horse named Swordsman while under Fizer's care. After being claimed, Swordsman could not replicate his prior form, and the horse was later sold to one of Fizer's friends. Swordsman was an easy winner his next time out, and it was assumed that Fizer had shared the winning dope recipe with his friend. The Crescent City stewards took no action against Fizer, however, until investigators located prescriptions for stimulants that he had filled at a local pharmacy. The trainer was ruled off after he could offer no reasonable explanation for purchasing the drugs.[25] Perhaps it was a coincidence, but Fizer also reportedly trained If You Dare, the horse ruled off by the Jockey Club in New York a few months later.[26]

What began as a seemingly simple prohibition against doping eventually grew into the Jockey Club's "Reformed Racing Medication Rules," released on August 12, 2012. Guided by the overriding principle that horses should be allowed to compete "only when free from the influences of medication," sixteen pages of rules addressed definitions, trainer responsibility, general regulations and duties for veterinarians, prohibited substances and the use of therapeutic medications, and how violations and penalties should be determined and assessed. The document also noted that all racing jurisdictions in the United States allowed the use of furosemide on the day of a race, and it encouraged "alignment with other racing nations that prohibit the use of furosemide on race day."[27] However, the reformed rules recognized that addressing the furosemide problem would not happen quickly.

On the other side of the Atlantic, the British were facing a doping problem of their own, one that they tended to blame on the Americans. "One north country vet boasted that he had been injecting cocaine-based 'speedy balls' for years," award-winning journalist and racing historian Chris McGrath explained, "but it was the

Americans who began producing 'horses who were notorious rogues running and winning as if they were possessed of the devil, with eyes starting out of their heads and the sweat pouring off them.'"[28]

George Lambton, a legend among turn-of-the-century British trainers, sent out thirteen classic winners, including Epsom Derby and St. Leger Stakes winner Hyperion. In his memoir *Men and Horses I Have Known,* he credited American trainers with introducing doping to Great Britain:

> There is no doubt that the Americans started the practice of doping, though it must not be supposed that they all doped their horses. Both [John] Huggins and [A. J.] Joyner detested it. They had seen too much of the mischief it caused in their own country, but, when they came over [to the UK], there was no law against doping and those people who, like Wishard, made a study of it were perfectly within their rights. . . . After the Americans brought the dope over here, many Englishmen took it up, but they were not very successful, as they did not really understand enough about it.[29]

Lambton was referring to Enoch Wishard, a successful trainer in the United States before moving to England. He had a reputation for transforming nondescript horses into winners, often at long odds, and he was one of the most prominent targets of early doping accusations. Among his best horses was Royal Flush, a long-shot winner of the 1900 Royal Hunt Cup at Ascot. Royal Flush worked well at home but seldom carried that form to the racecourse. A history of the Hunt Cup noted that Wishard had "perfected the technique of doping and was able to induce the necessary improvement" in Royal Flush to win the race. The unexpected victory "netted a fortune for his unscrupulous American owners."[30]

Wishard was a "very shrewd man, who won a great deal of money," Lambton said of the American:

He went in for a different class of race, and trained for a different class of owner, but I personally liked him very much.
He was a remarkably clever man with horses. There is no
doubt that he supplemented his great skill as a trainer by
making use of the dope. In those days, there was no law
against this pernicious practice. . . . I always thought it was
a real pity that Wishard ever took to doping, for he was
somewhat of a genius with horses, and would, I am sure,
have made a great name for himself without it.[31]

Although Lambton never discussed doping with Wishard, he argued
that the trainer's success with Royal Flush proved that the American
was a "great trainer as well as a good doper." Lambton did not know
whether Royal Flush had actually been boosted for the Hunt Cup or
any other race, but if he had been, the treatment "cannot have been
a very injurious one, or he would not have kept his form throughout
the season as he did, with the appearance of a perfectly trained
horse."[32]

Lambton was initially skeptical of rumors about the use of
performance-enhancing drugs in England but changed his mind
when three veterinarians told him that doping would be the "ruin
of horse-breeding and should be stopped." After a steward of the
English Jockey Club dismissed Lambton's concerns, the trainer
announced that he was going to dope rogue horses in his own stable
to evaluate the effects of stimulants. "I obtained six dopes from a
well-known veterinary surgeon," Lambton wrote. The horses "were
not injected with a needle, just given [the drugs] from a bottle. Their
effect on a horse was astonishing. I used five of them, and had four
winners and a second." Lambton gave the last dope to a friend to use
on Cheers, a horse that had raced without success all season. After
being doped, Cheers won against a large field that, ironically,
included one of Lambton's horses.[33] A year later, in 1903, following
the Jockey Club's lead in America six years earlier, the English Jockey
Club banned doping.

Suspicions of doping lingered, but it was not until 1930 that any English trainer was punished under the 1903 rule. That year, Charles Chapman and David Taylor were ruled off the turf when saliva tests of horses they trained showed the presence of caffeine, a prohibited stimulant.[34] *Blood-Horse* magazine reported on the penalties in an October 11, 1930, editorial by Thomas B. Cromwell, who noted that doping in America "is considered to be a part of the routine of racing horses." The American Jockey Club's rule against performance-enhancing drugs had become a laughing matter, Cromwell added. "The iniquity of drugging has become a part of the American system to such an extent that it is no longer considered to be a matter worthy of the attention of our racing officials. This condition is the shame of American racing."[35] Both Chapman and Taylor claimed they were innocent of doping. Chapman took it a step further and filed a lawsuit against the Jockey Club for libel, arguing that being accused of doping the horse Don Pat for a race at Kempton Park had ruined his career. It took a while, but the court eventually agreed and awarded the trainer £16,000 in damages from the Jockey Club and others.[36]

Early attempts to regulate doping in the United States and England were important first steps, but they shared two similarities that pitted principle against practicality. The rules of racing in both countries banned the use of performance-enhancing drugs, a goal that few people questioned, but the inability to detect the presence of such drugs made the bans unworkable.

Part II

Anslinger's War

5

The Drug Czar Goes Racing

Prohibition, a largely unpopular and generally unsuccessful attempt at social engineering put in place by the Eighteenth Amendment to the US Constitution, lasted for fourteen turbulent years. It came to a welcome end in 1933, in the most unlikely place imaginable.[1]

On December 5 of that year, in Salt Lake City, Utah, a group of elected delegates met to consider whether to ratify the Twenty-First Amendment that would repeal Prohibition. Thirty-three states had already approved the proposed amendment—thirty-six states were required for ratification at the time—and the delegates in Utah were intent on having their state cast the deciding vote. "We are determined no other State shall take this glory away from Utah," delegate Franklin Ritter explained. The Utah delegates waited for several hours until similar constitutional conventions in Pennsylvania and Ohio had approved the proposed amendment; then they hustled to vote ahead of a similar referendum later that day in Maine.[2]

The vote in Utah, when it finally came at 5:32 p.m. eastern standard time, was unanimous.[3] Reactions were immediate. President Franklin Roosevelt said he trusted "the good sense of the American people" to avoid drinking to excess and implored citizens to work toward a goal of national manliness, whatever that was. The speakeasy and bootleg prices for alcoholic drinks suddenly dropped by half in New York, and the Atlas Tack Corporation received an order for 4.5 million gross of bottle caps, for delivery no later than January 1, 1934.[4]

"Within minutes of Utah's ratification, liquor legally began to flow in some American cities as patrons purchased their first authorized drinks since 1920," journalist Christopher Klein wrote in a summary of the first post-Prohibition evening. "Delivery truck engines purred as they left liquor warehouses. Thousands of champagne corks popped, and hundreds of thousands of glasses clinked to toast drinkers' regained freedom. Licensed hotels, restaurants and nightclubs dusted off their dormant glassware, and waiters relied on muscle memory to mix drinks from the 'cocktail wagons' that they wheeled to customers' tables. By late night, licensed establishments were packed as jazz bands played and drinkers rightfully sang 'Happy Days Are Here Again.'"[5]

Ironically, although no one seemed to notice at the time, the Utah vote ending Prohibition appeared to contradict a long-standing tenet of Mormonism. A century earlier, during a meeting of the faithful in Kirtland, Ohio, Mormon leader Joseph Smith received a revelation—a "Word of Wisdom" codified as section 89 of *The Doctrine and Covenants*—limiting alcohol use to "wine for the Sacrament and hard liquor for washing the body."[6] In practice, though, neither Prohibition nor Utah's restrictive state law nor a Mormon majority in the population and legislature had been able to curb the production and consumption of alcohol. Historian Allen Kent Powell noted that from 1923 through 1932, the height of the Prohibition era, "Utah law enforcement officials uncovered 448 distilleries, 702 stills, thousands of pieces of distilling apparatus, 47,000 gallons of spirits, malt liquor, wine and cider, and 332,000 gallons of mash."[7]

The repeal of Prohibition was hardly a surprise. It was failed public policy that was unpopular and rife with corruption, did little to reduce alcohol consumption, and cost the United States hundreds of millions of dollars in tax revenue. Most important, Prohibition arguably led to the rapid expansion of organized crime in the United States, as gangsters built lucrative networks to smuggle and distribute illegal liquor.[8]

One of those gangsters was Arnold Rothstein, a bootlegger, horse owner, racetrack operator, and gambler who, despite his denials, is credited with fixing the 1919 World Series.[9] Racing historian

Brien Bouyea suggests that, two years later, Rothstein fixed the 1921 Travers Stakes at Saratoga.[10] Rumors also circulated that Rothstein helped engineer a betting coup for his biggest score, $300,000, when Belmont Stakes winner Hourless defeated Kentucky Derby winner Omar Khayam in a rich 1917 match race.[11]

Rothstein made more money than he could spend smuggling alcohol during the early years of Prohibition, but he soon traded liquor for illegal drugs—mainly opium, heroin, and cocaine—and quickly made even more money. Author and historian David Pietrusza called Rothstein, who was murdered in a Manhattan hotel room in 1928, the "founder and mastermind of the modern American drug trade."[12]

The "Black Sox" gambling scandal in the 1919 World Series raised serious questions about the integrity of America's most popular sport. In response, baseball executives replaced a national commission that had governed the sport ineffectively for years and appointed respected federal judge Kenesaw Mountain Landis as the first commissioner of baseball. Soon after taking over as commissioner, Landis imposed a lifetime ban on the eight White Sox players involved in fixing the series, even though all eight had been acquitted at trial.[13] Landis's tenure as commissioner was characterized by action, not idle talk.

Similar demands for a strong-willed national commissioner to bolster Thoroughbred racing's integrity and public image would come up from time to time over the next hundred years or so. Still, nothing of substance happened until passage of the Horseracing Integrity and Safety Act of 2020, which would resolve some, but not all, of the problems arising from racing's splintered governance structure.[14] A commissioner of racing was not part of the proposed fix.

When the Jockey Club was incorporated in 1894, the organizers' intent was to vest complete operational control over Thoroughbred racing in the United States in one governing body. It was a bold plan that never materialized. The reasons included travel and communications limitations that made organizing the sport on a national scale impractical, fiercely independent owners and trainers who bristled at "outside" interference in their sport, and the growth of state racing commissions that ultimately usurped much of the Jockey Club's authority over the day-to-day activities at racetracks.

The concept of a national commissioner for horse racing—or any sort of central governance structure at the expense of state-level control—languished until the early 1930s, when Harry J. Anslinger Jr., commissioner of the new Federal Bureau of Narcotics, revived the idea. Noted turf columnist G. F. T. Ryall, who wrote "The Race Track" column in the *New Yorker* for more than half a century, visited Anslinger in his Washington, DC, office in late 1933. The solution to racing's doping problem, Anslinger told Ryall, was a central governing body charged with the enforcement of drug rules. He envisioned a clandestine team of investigators, veterinarians, and chemists that would travel from track to track. "This squad might be at Belmont Park, or Churchill Downs, or Pimlico—no one would know where it would be except one member of the governing board, to whom it would report and turn in its evidence," Ryall wrote in *Polo* magazine. "Such a squad would not only do much to stamp out the narcotic evil, but also the spongers and the other undesirables. It's a swell idea—but the only trouble is all the governing bodies of racing wouldn't cooperate."[15]

During a meeting in Washington in mid-September 1934, Anslinger convinced representatives from eighteen states where racing was conducted that centralized control was necessary. Anslinger's support for a federal role in the regulation of racing was disingenuous at best, however. The original purpose of the meeting was more modest. A saliva test for a few alkaloids (primarily heroin, morphine, and cocaine) was being imported from Europe for use in the United States, and Anslinger wanted states to standardize the methods for collecting and testing samples from horses to detect the prohibited drugs. Instead, the racing representatives approved a

Harry J. Anslinger, commissioner of the Federal Bureau of Narcotics for more than thirty years, led a brief war on illegal narcotics at racetracks during the 1930s. (Library of Congress)

much broader resolution approving federal oversight of some aspects of horse racing—or so it appeared:

> RESOLVED: That we the veterinarians and chemists represent- ing the State Racing Commissions of the respective states gathered at this meeting request the Racing Commissions separately and collectively, and the U.S. Treasury Depart- ment through the Federal Bureau of Narcotics, to unite and assist in the formation of a Central Bureau in the Treasury Department in Washington to direct and preform [sic] such research studies that may be necessary to unify the proce- dure to be followed by the Racing Commissions in each state, and that all information so gained by these studies be distributed to the various Commissions and be it further
>
> RESOLVED: That the veterinarians and chemists assembled form the necessary sub-committee to carry out the neces- sary technical work in a cooperative manner to develop standardization, through the Bureau of Narcotics, pending the establishment of the Central Bureau.[16]

It is unlikely that the commissioners, veterinarians, and chemists assembled in Washington that day had the authority to commit their racing commissions to any sort of collaborative agreement, especially with the federal government as a player. There was some concurrent support for a unified national racing commission, but without federal involvement.

A few days after attending the meeting with Anslinger, Walter H. Donovan, secretary of the Florida State Racing Commission, wrote to treasury secretary Henry Morgenthau proposing a national racing commission. He was not suggesting direct federal oversight of horse racing, but he acknowledged the need for a single governing body because state commissions were "not adequate" to police the sport. The commissions, he claimed, were prone to a "predominating indifference, or the occasional extreme of zealous unsympathetic interference" when it came to regulation. "If racing is not regulated from within," Donovan wrote in closing, "it will be from without; and, the alternative is not shall it be done, but who shall do it. . . . A 'Landis' of racing would be smart and profitable, created voluntarily before it is forced on the industry."[17] Regulation within the industry was a long shot at best; direct federal involvement in regulating racing was a nonstarter.

Nine months before the Washington meeting, on December 18, 1933, Anslinger presented a budget proposal for the Federal Bureau of Narcotics to a House of Representatives subcommittee responsible for the Treasury Department appropriations bill for 1935. "We ran into a serious situation last year on racetracks," Anslinger told the committee, "where we found, in making just a cursory investigation—I mean we did not go into the matter deeply—one man observing 1,200 horses found that as many as 300 had been doctored just before a race. We have made over 50 arrests, and have a number under indictment. We are trying to get the help of the racing commissions of the several States and also of the racing associations to cooperate in stamping out the abuse of narcotic drugs. We are committed by legislation and by treaty to suppress the abuse of narcotic drugs in any form."[18]

Pressed later by committee member Louis Ludlow about possible federal legislation to regulate the doping of racehorses, Anslinger acknowledged that doping was not a federal offense and was not likely to become one. "I take the position that the Federal Government is not trying to regulate this matter," he said. "Congress has passed legislation on the subject of narcotic drugs, which does not permit the stimulation of horses by racetrack racketeers." The Harrison Narcotics Tax Act, passed in 1914, regulated opioids and cocaine by imposing a tax on the importation, production, and distribution of the drugs.[19] Although Anslinger seemed to be saying that the Harrison Act also prohibited doping simply because it regulated some of the drugs used by dopers, the legislation did not mention horse racing.

"I am afraid that the constitutional restrictions are so great that we could not put a veterinarian on a race track to examine horses," Anslinger added. Two months earlier, in a request to Congressman John J. Cochran, Judge Joseph A. Murphy had floated that suggestion.[20] "We are looking into that phase of the matter," Anslinger continued. "Up to this point, I have not been able to figure out any sort of legislation that would touch it (doping) except in the way we are going about it now." Regulation of doping was best left to individual state racing commissions, Anslinger explained to the committee. "They have greater police powers to protect the health, morals, and general welfare of the people," Anslinger said. "We only have the revenue measure [the Harrison Act]."[21]

A possible federal role in the war on doping resurfaced in October 1935, when Narragansett Park owner Walter O'Hara proposed that Anslinger create a "flying squad" of federal investigators traveling from track to track. O'Hara acknowledged that the government had no money to pay for the program and offered to contribute $10,000 to a fund administered by Anslinger. Andrew J. Cummings, president of the Maryland State Fair, called the proposal "rubbish" and "utterly impractical" in a *Baltimore Evening Sun* article. "Why should the race tracks spend money to help the Bureau of Narcotics do their work," Cummings was quoted as saying. "We in Maryland have no trouble with horse dopers."[22] O'Hara's flying squad, like similar proposals, was never enacted.

Anslinger's public warnings of federal intervention in the absence of state action were idle threats. For the commissioner's purposes, enforcement of the Harrison Act was sufficient justification for more than a year of undercover investigations, raids, and arrests at American racetracks. Indictments were based on violations of the Harrison Act, not doping. But headlines, encouraged by Anslinger, told a more popular story: "Waging War on the Cruel Horse Dopers."[23]

Anslinger was a competent and effective bureaucrat who quickly rose through the ranks in Washington. After working as a railroad detective and then carrying out diplomatic assignments overseas for the State Department as World War I wound down, he became chief of the Division of Foreign Control in the government's Prohibition Unit in the mid-1920s. In 1929 he was promoted to assistant commissioner of Prohibition in the Division of Foreign Control. His responsibilities there expanded beyond Prohibition enforcement to include a review of the growing problem of international drug trafficking.

The Federal Bureau of Narcotics was created the following year to deal exclusively with enforcement of the Harrison Act, and on July 1, 1930, Anslinger was named acting commissioner of the bureau. Three months later, President Herbert Hoover made Anslinger's appointment permanent, pending approval by Congress. There is no conclusive evidence that the appointment hinged on personal relationships. However, the new Federal Bureau of Narcotics operated out of the Treasury Department, and Anslinger's wife was a close relative of treasury secretary Andrew Mellon.

There was some congressional opposition to Anslinger's appointment. By coincidence (or perhaps not), the confirmation vote came one day after Anslinger made national headlines for seizing half a ton of illegal narcotics, worth $1 million, from the *Alesia,* a ship arriving in New York from Turkey. The seizure was a cooperative effort between agents of the Federal Bureau of Narcotics and the Customs Bureau, but Anslinger was the primary beneficiary of the timely news.[24] His appointment became official in December. It would not be the last time Anslinger would capitalize on favorable treatment in the press.

Anslinger and the Federal Bureau of Narcotics were a good fit. Although the public was growing weary of Prohibition and restrictions on alcohol, the use of illegal drugs was seen as a much more serious societal problem. The new bureau chief was smart, energetic, and ambitious, and his stand against illegal drugs was generally popular. He was also a bigot and a racist who used almost any means available, questionable or not, to expand the bureau's power beyond its original mandate and intimidate those who opposed his policies.

Anslinger campaigned against organized crime throughout his tenure as commissioner, starting years before the Federal Bureau of Investigation even acknowledged that the Mafia existed. At the same time, he exploited questionable data about addiction and smuggling to suit his objectives. Anslinger circulated exaggerated claims associating heroin, marijuana, and violence with racial and ethnic minorities that still plague the justice system today. He also manipulated the press and engaged in harassment campaigns designed to destroy the reputations, and sometimes the lives, of perceived enemies such as African American singer Billie Holiday, who epitomized Anslinger's misunderstanding of the nation's race and drug problems.[25] Holiday was known best for "Strange Fruit," a powerful anthem against lynchings in the South.[26] Named Song of the Century by *Time* magazine in 1999, "Strange Fruit" remains relevant today.[27]

For more than thirty years, until he retired in 1962, Anslinger wielded enormous influence in how federal narcotics legislation was written and enforced. He served during five administrations, and his hard-line approach to drug policy and enforcement survived his tenure as director of the Federal Bureau of Narcotics.[28]

Anslinger died in November 1975. He had suffered from several serious health problems, including angina, a painful heart condition for which he took morphine to ease the discomfort.[29] His obituary in the *New York Times* included a quotation that summarized his philosophy: "You can't give up the fight," Anslinger said. "We intend to get the killer-pushers and their willing customers out of selling and buying dangerous drugs. The answer to the problem is simple— get rid of drugs, pushers, and, users. Period."[30] When Richard Nixon announced his "war on drugs" on June 18, 1971, nearly a decade after Anslinger's retirement, the president officially endorsed many of the former drug czar's draconian policies.[31] The impact of those policies is still being felt.

A short entry on Anslinger's resumé, seldom remembered today and generally ignored or glossed over by his biographers, was a short-lived campaign aggressively targeting the possession and distribution of illegal drugs at East Coast and midwestern racetracks during the early 1930s. The Federal Bureau of Narcotics had no jurisdiction to actually clean up racing, despite the press crediting Anslinger's efforts to do so, because doping horses was not a federal offense. Nevertheless, Anslinger garnered a tremendous amount of favorable publicity by associating his racetrack investigation with the humane treatment of horses.

The investigation spanned more than two years, starting early in 1932 and still active during the first months of 1934. During that period, agents from the Federal Bureau of Narcotics followed the Thoroughbred racing circuit, looping from Louisiana to Florida to Maryland in the winter and spring; heading up to Illinois and Ohio in the summer; then making stops in Michigan, Maryland, Kentucky, and New York before returning to Louisiana in the fall. The agents conducted hundreds of undercover investigations on the backstretches of at least fifteen racetracks in eight states (see appendix 2). This was a significant commitment of men and resources for the bureau, which in the early 1930s averaged between 200 and 220 field agents and an annual budget of less than $1.5 million.[32]

Although the racetrack sweep generated favorable publicity for Anslinger and the bureau, the investigations had minimal effect on doping. Anslinger admitted as much in 1936 when he told state racing commissioners that they had one more chance to clean up the sport. If not, Anslinger said, he was prepared to introduce legislation drafted by the Treasury Department that would ban the interstate shipment of horses with undefined "bad records for the use of narcotics."[33] It was not the first time he had criticized state racing commissions for their inaction on doping, and it would not be the last. But federal intervention never happened, and doping continued.

The scope of the Federal Bureau of Narcotics investigation is summarized in documents among Anslinger's papers archived at the Pennsylvania State University Library. Though not comprehensive, the summaries provide substantial overviews of the doping problem from 1932 through 1934 in several related areas: horses, owners, race-tracks, and dates associated with reported incidents of doping; violators implicated in doping incidents; and individuals indicted for drug offenses. Anslinger's papers also include a lengthy formulary of doping prescriptions in use at the time (see appendix 3). The prescriptions were collected by federal agents during the investigation, and they indicate that dopers were still using many of the drugs first introduced to the sport by Doc Ring and his contemporaries in the 1890s. Change was coming in human athletics and horse racing, but cocaine, heroin, and morphine continued to be the main performance-enhancing drugs in use at the nation's racetracks during the 1930s.[34]

Aslinger told the House Appropriations Subcommittee that his agents had observed twelve hundred horses and found that three hundred—25 percent—had been "doctored" before a race.[35] The summary in Anslinger's papers identifies 348 separate incidents of suspected doping during the relevant period (29 percent of the horses reportedly observed) involving 254 individual horses (21 percent). Four of those horses were named in five separate doping incidents; four others were named in four separate incidents each. Of the 254 identified horses, 56 were implicated in more than one doping incident.

Nearly one-third of alleged doping incidents reported by the Federal Bureau of Narcotics from late 1932 through early 1934—104 of 348 reports—occurred at Jefferson Park in New Orleans. Ironically, in December 1931 Jefferson Park stewards T. C. Bradley and John T. Ireland had issued a stern warning to owners and trainers that anyone caught with illegal narcotics or liquor (Prohibition would not be repealed for another two years) would be prosecuted. Bradley and Ireland also gave notice that horsemen would be responsible for drug and liquor violations by their employees.[36] The warning had little effect, and two years later, it was repeated. A statement from the stewards warned owners and trainers that the track veterinarian, Dr. Hamlet Moore, would "exercise the closest possible scrutiny in detecting any mispractice and to report any such findings to the stewards, as well as the government officials." The goal, the stewards added, was "to give the government all the aid possible toward stamping out the practice of doping horses."[37]

After Jefferson Park, the racetracks with the most suspicious incidents of possible doping were Arlington Park (64), Hialeah (32), Detroit Fair Grounds (29), and Lincoln Fields in Illinois (22).[38] The statistics showed a lack of either ability or interest (maybe both) on the part of track owners and racing officials to control doping and added credence to Anslinger's worries that racing could not police itself. One doped horse out of every four does not necessarily indicate a general acceptance of performance-enhancing drugs in horse racing, as Anslinger, Thomas Cromwell, and others claimed. Still, it was an astonishing number.

The horses on the list were a generally nondescript lot. One name stood out, however: W. S. Kilmer's Herowin, a homophone for the potent drug often found in doping prescriptions. Whether the name was intentionally ironic or an accidental coincidence that slipped past the Jockey Club is lost to history. Anslinger's summaries named several prominent owners, including Audley Farm, E. R. Bradley, Hal Price Headley, Greentree, Coldstream Stud, Jack Howard, C. V. Whitney, and Brookmeade Stable.

A separate summary identified seventy-four individuals by case number, name, track, dates of arrest and indictment, and disposition of the case where available. Of the seventy-four named individuals, fifty-nine were indicted on narcotics charges. Of those indicted, forty-four were convicted and received sentences ranging from thirty days to fifteen years; five were fugitives when the list was compiled; and three cases were dismissed (including one because a motion to exclude the prosecution's evidence was granted). A third summary named 105 "violators," including three pharmacies. There are handwritten notations listing fifty-three convictions (with jail and prison sentences totaling "110 years, 7 months"), twelve cases pending, three cases closed, five dismissed, and seven fugitives. There is substantial duplication of names on the three lists, but each summary also contains information not included on the others.[39]

There are significant caveats about taking these numbers, names, and allegations at face value. The most important ones involve the sample size (small and possibly statistically insignificant) and the way the lists were compiled. Anslinger's undercover agents made the rounds of the Thoroughbred racing circuit for two years, posing as owners, touts, gamblers, and often just interested hangers-on. They generally had complete discretion when it came to deciding which horses to watch and which ones to ignore. Also, the dispositions of the reported doping incidents—whether there were arrests, indictments, trials, verdicts, dismissals, and so on—are often unknown.

Another problem with the investigation was the narrow geographic scope of the undercover operation. Anslinger's agents visited more than a dozen racetracks over fourteen months, but none of them were west of the Mississippi River. Any sweeping conclusions from the investigation must be tempered by the failure to recognize or address the fact that Thoroughbred racing, and possible doping, was taking place throughout the United States.

A saliva test to detect a few prohibited medications in a horse's system was not introduced in the United States until 1934 at Hialeah. Although Anslinger would claim much of the credit for bringing the saliva test to America, it did not figure into his investigation. As a result, allegations, indictments, and prosecutions were based primarily on the reports of agents who observed substances being administered to horses before races. Subsequent chemical testing of the substances themselves, testing of bottles or other containers confiscated from individuals or barns (often without search warrants), and the possession of hypodermic needles and other drug paraphernalia bolstered the agents' field reports. Even when couched in the clinical language typical of police files, the investigative reports of Federal Bureau of Narcotics agents tell a sordid story of a sport in serious trouble.

6

Reports from the Field

Anslinger's list of narcotics law "violators" includes two arrests at Hawthorne in October 1929, which makes no sense because the Federal Bureau of Narcotics had not yet been created. However, federal agents were on the backstretch at Hialeah in January 1932 when jockey Charles Underwood, trainer I. G. Underwood, and owner Charles Burton were arrested after a lengthy investigation into a "narcotic ring of racketeers." The arrests were based on the agents' purchase of narcotics, not on reported doping incidents, and it is unclear whether these arrests were part of Anslinger's subsequent racetrack crusade.[1]

The undercover investigations initiated by Anslinger and cited during his testimony before the House Appropriations Subcommittee on December 18, 1933, began in December 1932, continued in earnest through 1933, and then tapered off in early 1934. The written field reports cited in this chapter are from Anslinger's personal papers, archived at Pennsylvania State University, and are quoted verbatim.[2] Agents' names were redacted in several of the reports retrieved from the Penn State files.

It is not clear from Anslinger's records whether prosecutions resulted from any of these field reports. Most likely, they did not. The reports are, however, representative of conduct by trainers and grooms observed and reported by narcotics agents during the undercover investigation.

Of the seven horses that are the subjects of these reports, three won their races, one finished second, one ran third, one was unplaced, and one collapsed and died during the race.

Report 1. Confidential, Jefferson Park
New Orleans, Louisiana
December 19, 1932
Sir:

At 2:40 this afternoon, while making observations in the vicinity of the Receiving Barn at Jefferson Park, my attention was called to a stall occupied by a horse under the name of CONFIDENTIAL, a brown mare of six years, owned by J. Somersby and trained by the owner.

One man in a gray overcoat was working about the stall. On the ground outside was a bucket containing bandages, bottles and a syringe. Taking a white enameled cup the man poured a quantity of liquid from one of the bottles and drew it up into the syringe. He then injected it down the throat of the horse CONFIDENTIAL. The man then closed the lower half of the stall door and stood outside, waiting.

After almost an hour had elapsed and the horse had not been removed, I strolled over to the stall and stood conversing with a man I knew and after a time included the gray overcoated man in the conversation.

At 3:40, this man took out his watch and said, "They told me to get the mare ready at 3:30 [to] race." The man with me said, "No, you're going in the 7th." The gray overcoated man then said, "I guess I'll have to hit her again," and taking the syringe went into the stall. I strolled on with my companion so as not to create suspicion and he told me that the name of the horse was CONFIDENTIAL.

I went to the paddock and watched the horse led into paddock stall No. 1. The animal was very nervous and apparently difficult to control.

The horses went to the post at 4:49½ and were at the post 5½ minutes. CONFIDENTIAL well in hand the first 5/8, worked her way to the lead entering the stretch but faltered in the final 1/8 and finished 3rd in the race.

Respectfully submitted,

Report 2. La Salle, Jefferson Park
New Orleans, Louisiana
January 10, 1933
Sir:

At 3:30 P.M. today, while making observations in the receiving barn at Jefferson Park, my attention was attracted to a stall in that barn occupied by a horse under the name of LA SALLE, a chestnut gelding of 5 yrs. owned by Shandon Farm and trained by J. J. Greely, Sr. The horse was entered in the 6th race, a claiming affair for 4 year olds and upwards. The horse was ridden in the race by M. Lewis.

Two men were working about the stall and as one of them walked over to where I was standing, the other called out and asked him what time it was. The man near me answered, "They'll be coming out in a minute, you'd better get busy. I'm going over to watch the filly run." The other man took a white piece of paper from his pocket and, securing a rub rag, pulled the horse's tongue out and wiped it dry. He then poured the powder on the tongue of the horse LA SALLE and rubbed it well in. Then he made a second rubbing and wiped out the mouth of the animal. The horse was then allowed to stand and began to get nervous and to kick the stall. After a time he was led out by a white man wearing a green sweater, the horse had a large S on the blanket so I felt that I could not miss him on the way to the paddock.

LA SALLE got away 9th and did nothing in the race, it was not his race to win but there was so much gratification over the winning of the 5th race by At Top of same stables, that the men did not seem to care that LA SALLE did nothing in the 6th.

Respectfully submitted,

Report 3. My Joanne, Jefferson Park
New Orleans, Louisiana
January 12, 1933
Sir:

At 1:30 P.M. today while making observations in the vicinity of the receiving barn at Jefferson Park, I was advised by one of the men who sells apples to place a bet on MY JOANNE in the second race because the horse had been given a big "shot" and would get another before long. I asked where the stall was and later strolled over there and saw two men working about the stall.

One man had a long horse syringe and was drawing some liquid up into it from a cup and squirting it back again as if mixing it. He then sprinkled in the contents of a paper he took from his pocket and stirred the mixture. He then drew it up into the syringe and injected it down the throat of the horse MY JOANNE. The horse looked badly and her eyes were blood shot. She was allowed to rest a while and later was led to the paddock for the second race.

The horses went to the post at 2:33 P.M. and were at the post 1½ minutes.

MY JOANNE got away 9th in this furlong race but was pulled up about the ½ and dropped dead after three furlongs.

The general talk about the receiving barn was that the horse had been given too much to make her run. I asked one of the trainers of another animal and he said that the combination of nitro glycerine and heroin makes the heart pump too strong and sudden strain will stop the heart beating. It was generally conceded that this combination was what MY JOANNE had received.

Respectfully submitted,

The chart caller for the *Daily Racing Form* was terse: "MY JOANNE, internally distressed before going a quarter, was pulled up in the stretch and died shortly after approaching the finish."[3]

Report 4. Field Goal, Coney Island
August 22, 1933
Mr. Ralph H. Oyler
District No. 9
Chicago, Illinois
Sir:—

At 4:45 P.M. today at Coney Island, the horse named FIELD GOAL was given the liquid contents of a brass colored metal syringe in the following described manner:

At the above mentioned time, the man who is addressed as "Jim" and whom had previously been observed administering to the horse named SKY HAVEN at Lincoln Fields, Chicago, came to Stall No. 3 in Barn No. 29. Here, he removed a small bottle of liquid from the hip-pocket of his trousers and after he had unscrewed the nozzle from a metal syringe, he poured the contents from the bottle into the barrel of the syringe and then replaced the nozzle on the end of it. With the filled syringe in his hand he approached FIELD GOAL, which occupied Stall No. 3, and inserting the nozzle of the syringe into the mouth of this horse he released the contents therein. After he had done this, he placed the empty syringe in the right hand corner of the stall and came outside.

FIELD GOAL is a brown gelding three years old, owned and trained by S. Haughton and entered the Seventh Race in Post Position No. 5 ridden by Jockey G. South. The horses went to Post at 5:35½ P.M. Cincinnati time. Were off at 5:36½ P.M. FIELD GOAL moved into contention after three-eighths, gave a mild bid entering the stretch, but hung slightly in drive to finish second in a field of six.

Respectfully,
Walter S. North,
Narcotic Agent
Edward P. Bertin,
Narcotic Inspector

Report 5. Okapi, Bowie Race Course
Washington
December 1, 1933
Confidential Report
Mr. H. J. Anslinger,
Commissioner of Narcotics
Washington, D.C.
Sir:

On or about 1:45 P.M. Nov. 30, 1933, while making investigations at the Bowie race track, the following happened.

A horse named "Okapi" from the Brookmeade stable, stabled in "M" barn, was entered in the fourth race. Agt. Burton and myself went to the vicinity of this stable where we could watch the stall in which this horse was being made ready for the race. A man in a blue suit and light felt hat walked toward the tap room and Agt. Burton told me that if he entered the tack room that I was to rush into the stall and get the syringe and man. The man left the tack room with his left hand in his pocket and entered the stall with the horse closing the doors behind him. Another man stood in front of the stall, I caught him and threw him away from the door and entered the stall, the man was holding the horse's mouth open with his left hand and giving the horse the contents of the syringe, I grasped the syringe with my left hand, pulling it out of the horse's mouth and caught the man's right hand, telling him that I was an officer. I jammed the nozzle of the syringe against the wall, bending it back along the barrel of the syringe to retain any liquid which it might still contain. By this time the man outside the door of the stall had come into the stall and had threw both arms around me while the man in the blue suit tried to get the syringe, at the same time crying don't let him get away, get that syringe. He snatched off my glasses and threw them in the bedding, we struggled around the stall and I finally got out of the stall. When we reached the outside the man in blue called to the men around the stable to help him and not let me get away. Several men had hold of me by this time and a negro jammed a pitchfork against my stomach, holding my back against the side of the stall. Agt. Burton came to my assistance and pulled the man with the fork away. Two men had my right arm and the man in blue and another had my left arm and was twisting my fingers and arm trying to get the syringe. They finally bent my finger back and twisted the syringe out of my hand and the man in blue threw it to another stable boy telling him to get rid of it. He ran around the other side of the stable and that was the last I saw of the syringe. Agt. Burton, seeing the number of men who had hold of me had gone for the police after pulling the negro with the pitchfork away from me. When he returned with two policemen it was too late as they had gotten the evidence away from me.

The man in blue told the policemen that he was giving the horse some cough medicine as he had a cold and that if he had had a gun he would have shot me as he thought that I was trying to sponge his horse.

I felt that we had a very good case, could I have retained the evidence. I did all in my power to get away with it but never had a chance, due to the number who piled onto me.

"Okapi" ran the race and won. He was picked to run fifth but some of the track tipsters had picked him for second money.

Respectfully,
F. E. Walker,
Narcotic Agent

Report 6. Come Seven, Jefferson Park
New Orleans, La.
December 26, 1933
Mr. Ralph H. Oyler,
District Supervisor
Detroit, Michigan
Sir:

At about 1:10 P.M. the following occurred at barn 15, Jefferson Park Race Track:

On this date, at the above mentioned time A. Gaignard entered the tack room, at the end of the barn, and emerged in about a minute carrying a metal horse syringe concealed in a cotton leg bandage. He walked to the stall occupied by the horse named COME SEVEN. Here he handed the syringe to a stable hand, who had preceded him into the stall. As the stable hand entered the stall he swung the horse's head to the left hand side of the stall. In about a minute the stable hand handed Gaignard the syringe still wrapped in the cotton leg bandage, who took the syringe to the tack room where he rinsed it in a bucket of water. Some time later Gaignard led the horse to the ¾ chute, where he boosted an exercise boy on COME SEVEN's back. This boy galloped the horse around the track to the paddock. While Gaignard walked around the track to the paddock.

COME SEVEN, is a bay colored filly, 2 years old, owned by A. Gaignard Jr. and trained by A. Gaignard. This horse entered the 1st race in No. 12 post position, ridden by Jockey L. Pichon. The horses went to post 2:01 P.M. were off in 5 minutes. COME SEVEN, slow to begin, moved up fast in the turn and, continuing gamely, took the lead and won easing up.

Respectfully,
Robert Jacobs,
Narcotic Inspector

Report 7. Idle Along, Jefferson Park
New Orleans, La.
December 28, 1933
Mr. Ralph H. Oyler,
District Supervisor
Detroit, Michigan
Sir:

At about 1:10 P.M. this date the following occurred at Barn 10, Jefferson Park Race Track:

At the above mentioned time and date, Gaignard entered the tackroom at the far end of the barn and in a moment came out with a syringe hidden under a blanket. He handed this to a white stable employee who entered the stall and used the syringe on the horse, IDLE ALONG. In about 2 minutes he came out of this stall and walked to the tack room where he rinsed the syringe in a bucket of water, in front of Gaignard, who had stood there all the while. Some time later the same stable hand that had used the syringe on this horse led her to the paddock for the 1st race.

IDLE ALONG is a chestnut colored filly, 2 years old, owned by A. Gaignard and trained by A. Gaignard. This horse entered the 1st race in No. 1 post position, ridden by Jockey L. Pichon. IDLE ALONG broke fast, cut out a stiff pace and, opening a commanding lead, won easing up, in a field of 12 horses.

Respectfully,
Robert Jacobs,
Narcotic Inspector

As noted in Report 5, these undercover investigations sometimes involved risk. Narcotics agent F. E. Walker reported that he was roughed up by a couple of grooms from Brookmeade Stable, one armed with a pitchfork, after he tried to snatch a suspicious-looking syringe from one of the men. Walker lost the syringe in the struggle but escaped uninjured when his partner showed up with two policemen in tow for backup. The report in Anslinger's file at Penn State University, dated December 1, 1933, has a handwritten notation on the first of two typed pages, probably made by Anslinger himself, pointing out that Brookmeade is the "Best stable in U.S." Brookmeade, owned by Mrs. Isabel Dodge Sloane, may have been among the best stables in the United States in 1933, but it did not top the list of winning owners until 1934. That was the year Cavalcade won the Kentucky Derby, High Quest won the Preakness, and the stable earned $251,138.[4]

Okapi, the subject of the report, is the only Brookmeade horse appearing on Anslinger's master list of "Horses Involved in Racetrack Investigation." The horse had apparently been under scrutiny for a while; five days earlier, another possible doping incident had been reported. There is no indication that charges were ever filed against Robert A. Smith, the Brookmeade trainer.

7

The United States v.
Ivan H. Parke

Harry Anslinger managed to keep his undercover backstretch investigations out of the papers for the first half of 1933. There were arrests and indictments, but mainly at smaller tracks such as Jefferson Downs in Louisiana, and mainly involving obscure trainers and grooms unlikely to attract national press attention. A Newspapers.com search for the keywords "Anslinger" and "horse" for the period January 1 through mid-July 1933 turned up only nineteen references, none of which involved drugs at the country's racetracks. When Anslinger was mentioned at all, the articles addressed topics one would expect to see about the nation's first drug czar: a push for uniform state drug laws; taking credit for higher street prices for narcotics as a result of the bureau's antismuggling efforts; the development of a new pain reliever (Dilaudid) six times more potent than heroin; and, most notably for Anslinger, his retention as commissioner of the Federal Bureau of Narcotics.[1]

The press blackout was almost certainly part of Anslinger's strategy. He hardly ever shied away from favorable publicity and always took credit, deserved or not, for good outcomes. But he was looking for a strong case that would garner national attention, and too much early publicity from arrests at the smaller tracks would expose the undercover investigation and drive the dopers into hiding.

By midsummer, though, the political landscape in Washington had changed. Anslinger was a staunch Republican appointed in 1930 by Republican president Herbert Hoover, but his job security was in question after a Democratic landslide victory in the 1932 elections. Despite their party differences, new president Franklin D. Roosevelt reappointed Anslinger in March 1933. Still, by July, rumors were circulating that Anslinger would be replaced by Dr. L. S. Booker, a Democrat from North Carolina.[2]

Anslinger needed a big score, similar to the timely and possibly coincidental million-dollar seizure of illegal drugs shortly before his congressional confirmation as the first narcotics commissioner in 1930. He found what he was looking for at one of the country's premier racetracks: Arlington Park on the northwest side of Chicago. Late in the day on July 28, 1933, just as a successful meeting at Arlington Park was wrapping up, Anslinger and federal narcotics agents raided the backstretch. They arrested several trainers and grooms; searched tack rooms and living quarters; and seized equipment trunks, medicine cabinets, and various narcotics, stimulants, and doping paraphernalia. According to Ralph Oyler, head of the bureau's Chicago division, between 400 and 500 grains of narcotics were seized, as well as syringes, hypodermic needles, and bottles of a patent medicine containing a mixture of drugs.[3] When the cases were presented to a grand jury, however, Oyler's estimate proved to be inflated.

The raid at Arlington Park brought Anslinger and the Federal Bureau of Narcotics the national publicity he sought, but it was uncertain whether the initial flurry of high-profile arrests, indictments, and convictions and those that followed could hold the long-term attention of the public. Trade publications had been regular critics of horse racing's drug culture for several years. *Blood-Horse* magazine had run more than thirty editorials condemning the failure to address doping, and that coverage continued. To guarantee consistent reporting in national newspapers and general circulation magazines, Anslinger tied the backstretch raids to a pair of newsworthy causes likely to be popular among both racing fans and the general public: a crackdown on the doping of racehorses and the prevention of cruelty to animals. The strategy worked. A Newspapers.

com search for the keywords "Anslinger" and "horse" found 519 references for the second half of 1933. It was a remarkable turnaround from the first half of the year. The strategy was also a blatant manipulation of the press, a skill that Anslinger would put to good use throughout his three-decades-long career as drug czar. Reporters latched onto Anslinger's misdirection immediately after the Arlington Park raids without recognizing, or admitting, that there were problems with the story he was telling them.

Unlike J. Edgar Hoover, Anslinger's counterpart at the Federal Bureau of Investigation, there is no indication that the head of the Federal Bureau of Narcotics had any particular interest in horse racing or betting. Also, even if Anslinger had intended to clean up racing, he lacked the authority to do anything about it. The mandate of the Federal Bureau of Narcotics was enforcement of the Harrison Act, which had nothing to do with horse racing. Also, while most state racing commissions had rules against the use of performance-enhancing drugs, there was no federal statute and few state laws that prohibited doping a Thoroughbred prior to a race. When pressed by reporters, Anslinger admitted he was interested only in the possession of illegal narcotics, not doping itself. The investigation's impact on doping, if any, was indirect and not the bureau's intent.

Even more disingenuous was linking the investigations to animal welfare, which was little more than an appeal to the public's emotional attachment to horses. This is clear in an internal memo to Anslinger from someone identified only as "H.T.H.," dated October 18, 1933. Although the memo is tagged "purely personal" and carries a handwritten instruction stating, "P.S.—This is 'personal'—do not file," it was archived with Anslinger's papers at Pennsylvania State University. The writer referred to a January 1933 field report about the alleged doping of a two-year-old named Race Street at Jefferson Park. He urged Anslinger to "have Menke play up the atrocious practice of ruining young horses—mere babies." Reporter Frank G. Menke was one of Anslinger's staunchest supporters. He wrote a fourteen-part series on Anslinger's investigations for the *San*

Francisco Examiner that ran daily in October 1933, as well as a laudatory article in *Esquire*.[4] The memo continued:

> Visualize the poor innocent RACE STREET getting its first shot of dope. It comes out on the track bewildered. It does not know what it is all about. It is fractious at the post and the assistant starter adds to the torture by putting a twitch on it in order to get it in the starting stall. The race starts. The horse dashes off like wild. It is crazy with fright—of what it does not know. It never experienced such inward sensation before. The brain is on fire. It wants to run on and on—to get *away from* something—*not to* the finish line. The jockey does not get it pulled up until the half-mile post is reach [*sic*] and the other horses have turned and started back to the judges' stand.
>
> A couple of paragraphs about the "Slaughter of the innocents" will cause the sob-sisters and uplifters to shed tears aplenty. Great human interest stuff (I should say animal interest stuff). His [Menke's] animal-batting-its-brains-out-in-the-stall story was a corker, but the poor little two year old can be played up just as well. Anyway, tell him to give the story both barrels.[5]

Anslinger apparently did not forward the suggestion to Menke, or perhaps the reporter did not take the hint. The latter is unlikely, though, because Menke's articles tended to be very favorable toward Anslinger and usually included inside information and lengthy quotes directly from the narcotics bureau chief. Menke's articles appeared regularly in William Randolph Hearst's chain of newspapers and reached a nationwide audience. In a letter written on November 23, 1933, Anslinger thanked Hearst for his support and added that he had no intention of involving the federal government in the regulation of Thoroughbred racing.[6]

Around the same time, *Blood-Horse* magazine was critical of Menke's coverage: "A series of dope articles, more or less rehash, written in sensational vein by Frank G. Menke and played up under large headlines, has appeared in recent numbers of the William Randolph Hearst newspapers. They have not done racing any good unless it shall work out that they have served recalcitrant racing officials to action."[7] *Blood-Horse* was also opposed to federal involvement in racing and was of the opinion that racing could police itself. A few months after the Arlington Park raid, editor Thomas B. Cromwell explained that racing's "house cleaning" should be left to the "Turf's own forces," not outsiders. "The Blood-Horse, a believer in state's rights and not in further centralization of power at Washington, is in favor of racing's control by the people of the states in which the tracks are located, just as we have it, in the greater number of such states, by State Racing Commissions," Cromwell wrote. "If those in the various states who are fond of racing are unwilling, or are not sufficiently powerful, to keep it clean without Government control or supervision, then they should not be entitled to have it at all."[8] In a few months, Anslinger would come to agree with Cromwell.

John C. McWilliams, one of Anslinger's biographers, argued that the narcotics bureau's backstretch campaign against illegal drugs was little more than a clever political ploy to garner attention and convince President Roosevelt to keep Anslinger on as commissioner.[9] If so, it worked. He headed the Federal Bureau of Narcotics for more than thirty years and through five administrations, both Republican and Democrat. The "sob-sisters and uplifters" in the 1930s probably never realized they were being manipulated.

The first sweep through the Arlington Park backstretch by narcotics agents resulted in seven arrests, including two men prominent enough to capture the national attention that Anslinger sought.[10] One was Hall of Fame jockey Ivan Parke; the second was prominent Kentucky owner and breeder Hal Price Headley, who in 2018 was recognized as a "Pillar of the Turf" by the National Museum of Racing. Other arrests and prosecutions followed. Anslinger tallied the results of the undercover investigations in undated spreadsheets archived with his

papers at Penn State: 102 "violators"; 53 convictions; sentences totaling 110 years, 7 months, 15 days; fines totaling $2,560. A dozen other
cases were listed as "pending"; three as "closed," without further explanation; five as "dismissed." Seven people were listed as "fugitives."

Racetrack officials expressed surprise, and sometimes indigna-
tion, in the wake of the raid at Arlington. Judge Joseph A. Murphy,
acting president of the Chicago Businessmen's Racing Association,
offered to pay the expenses for a government veterinarian to be stationed in the paddock of every track under his jurisdiction: Chicago,
Detroit, New Orleans, Arlington Downs, and Tanforan. He promised cooperation but complained that the federal agents "were snoopers who made a play for the galleries and publicity."[11]

Anslinger's investigations targeted several individuals prominent
in the Thoroughbred community. Among casual racing fans and the
general public, Ivan H. Parke was probably the best known. He was
North America's leading apprentice rider in 1923 (winning 173 races)
and leading rider the next year in both races won (205) and money
won ($290,395).[12] Parke would later train a Kentucky Derby winner
and be inducted into the National Museum of Racing Hall of Fame.
He was indicted, along with backstretch employee Benjamin Creech
and groom and exercise boy William Payne, in Federal District Court
for the Northern District of Illinois (case number 27518).[13] The trio
was charged with five counts of violating the Harrison Act (unlaw-
fully purchasing narcotics, including 120 grains of heroin hydrochloride, 16 grains of cocaine hydrochloride, and unknown amounts of
heroin, morphine, and cocaine), the Narcotic Drugs Import and
Export Act (concealing narcotics after unlawful importation), and
conspiracy. The conspiracy count was based on eleven alleged "overt
acts," presumably witnessed by Anslinger's agents at Arlington Park
from June 27 through July 28, 1933. These overt acts included the
administration of heroin to the horses Portcodine (once), Dr. Parrish
(twice), Threat (five times), Street Singer (once), and Timorous (once),
plus possession of heroin hydrochloride, cocaine hydrochloride, heroin, and morphine in Barn S.[14]

According to Anslinger, Parke admitted to possession of "enough heroin to dope 150 horses" when a narcotics agent came across a lady's handbag during the search of a tack trunk. "Them's the cakes," Parke reportedly said when questioned about the contents of the purse.

The charges were serious ones. Violation of the Harrison Act carried maximum penalties of five years in federal prison and a fine of up to $2,000. For a violation of the Narcotic Drugs Import and Export Act, the maximum penalties were five years in prison and a fine of $5,000. Conviction of conspiracy could result in two years in prison and a fine of $10,000.

Anslinger considered the evidence presented against Parke, Creech, and Payne to be "one of the clearest cases of 'horse doping' we have so far developed." He must have been frustrated when the prosecution dragged on for more than two years in federal district court without a trial. Finally, on November 1, 1935, he received word from the US attorney in Chicago that the trial was set to begin on January 6, 1936. Anslinger was anxious to get started because the Sixth Circuit Court of Appeals had affirmed the convictions of Audley Farm trainer Joseph Patterson, trainer Robert Wingfield, and groom Horace Moore on November 1. But things did not work out as he had hoped. Anslinger wrote:

> Our officers were ready to proceed to Chicago to present the evidence at the trial, when I learned, to my consternation, that on November 26, 1935, in spite of the [Patterson] decision, without notice to any representative of this Bureau, without knowledge on the part of the Assistant United States Attorney assigned to handle narcotics cases, whom our Chicago office was contacting almost daily, and despite the fact that the Attorney General had previously ordered that no indictment should be dismissed without the consent of his office, Parke and Payne had been permitted to withdraw their pleas of not guilty and enter pleas of guilty, followed by the imposition of fines of $500 and $200, respectively; and

the cause as to the defendant Creech had been dismissed on motion of the United States Attorney's office.

Because of the action taken in this case, the receipt of reliable information that considerable political pressure had been brought therein, and a report that a large sum of money had been collected for the purpose of securing a disposition [of] these charges in a manner favorable to the defendants, the Attorney General is being requested to make an immediate investigation, to remove from the supervision of the United States Attorney's office in Chicago cases pending in that city involving the doping of race horses, and to designate a special assistant to the Attorney General to handle the remaining cases.[15]

There is no record of Anslinger's requests being granted.

Anslinger had expected to use the Sixth Circuit's decision in the Patterson case to bolster the case against Parke, Creech, and Payne.[16] Ironically, that appellate decision may have contributed to the unexpected pretrial disposition. Despite the seriousness of the alleged offenses and the potential penalties, the district court had imposed minor sentences of six months each for Patterson, Wingfield, and Moore and relatively small fines of $1,000, $250, and $500, respectively.[17] When the Sixth Circuit affirmed the three men's convictions, this may have encouraged the federal district court to accept guilty pleas and minor fines for Parke, Creech, and Payne.

Although Anslinger's interest in illegal drugs at the country's racetracks soon waned, he continued to track Parke's growing fame as a trainer. When Parke saddled Fred Hooper's Hoop Jr. to win the 1945 Kentucky Derby, the drug czar questioned why the Kentucky commission had granted Parke a trainer's license in the first place. Before Hoop Jr. ran in the Preakness Stakes two weeks later, Anslinger asked George Mahoney, a racing commissioner in Maryland, to obtain a saliva sample from the horse, even if "he came in last." Hoop Jr. ran third, but Mahoney apparently delivered the requested saliva sample. When it was tested, the chemist found crystals from a "drug that could not be identified." Anslinger suspected the crystals were from a previous doping that had not cleared the horse's system, but he was grasping at straws by then. "We were all set for his [Hoop Jr.'s] appearance at Belmont for the big stake race but the horse was not entered because of an alleged injury." Anslinger was convinced that Mahoney was fired because he helped obtain the saliva sample from Hoop Jr. after the Preakness.[18]

To Anslinger's consternation, Ivan Parke would always be the one that got away.

Dr. Nelson Edward Southard, prominent racetrack veterinarian from Louisville, Kentucky, was indicted in Federal District Court for the Northern District of Illinois (case number 27523). Dr. Southard denied doping a horse named Louis Dear that was trained by Jack Howard. He told Leslie E. Salter, assistant attorney general in charge of the investigation, that he had been treating Louis Dear for a year with a non-narcotic medication for a painful left foreleg.[19]

The charges against Dr. Southard were based on a search and seizure of his medical bag, which contained "various medicines, medical instruments, and supplies." Also in the bag was a sealed envelope containing 9 grains of heroin hydrochloride, a drug with legitimate therapeutic uses in addition to being a doping agent. Dr. Southard petitioned to suppress the seized evidence, arguing that he was the lawful owner of the bag and its contents and that the search and seizure were unconstitutional. The case went to trial in late July 1934. Dr. Southard waived a jury trial, and after a bench trial he was found not guilty and released by the court.[20]

The vexing question of a medication with legitimate therapeutic uses that can also be administered as a performance-enhancing drug remains an issue in both horse racing and human athletics today.

Joseph F. Patterson, Robert Wingfield, Thomas Murray, Morton Smith, and Horace Moore were charged with violating the Harrison

Hall of Fame jockey Ivan H. Parke. He was dogged by the Federal
Bureau of Narcotics for years following a raid on Arlington Park in 1933.
(Courtesy of National Museum of Racing and Hall of Fame)

Act, the narcotic import statute, and conspiracy. The trial court acquitted Patterson on the Harrison Act charge, but he was found guilty of violating the import statute and of conspiracy. Wingfield and Moore were convicted on all three charges. Smith and Murray were acquitted on all charges. Reviewing the lower court decision, the Sixth Circuit Court of Appeals stated the facts as follows:

> Appellants Patterson, Wingfield, and Moore were sentenced upon the third count alone. They challenge the denial of a directed verdict. Inasmuch as they were sentenced upon the one count only, the question is whether the evidence was sufficient to sustain the verdict thereon. There are certain undisputed facts.
>
> On October 7, 1933, the Audley Farms, of which appellants were employees, had three race horses, Knights Gal, Royal Blunder, and Cloudet, at the state fair grounds race track near Detroit. Patterson was a trainer and manager. Wingfield was in charge of the horses at Detroit, and took his orders from Patterson. Appellant Moore, and Smith, were employed as grooms. Murray was trainer for another stable. Wingfield, Moore, and Murray were at the track on the above date, but Patterson was with other horses at Lincoln Fields, near Chicago.
>
> It was the duty of Oyler and Bell, agents of the Bureau of Narcotics, to investigate the use of narcotics at race tracks, and they were at the Detroit track on October 7. Knights Gal was entered to run at about 4:30 p.m. on that day, and about 3:30 p.m. these two narcotics agents saw Murray and appellant Moore together in a stall occupied by Knights Gal. Moore was in the act of inserting a syringe in the horse's mouth, and both agents testified that Murray was holding the horse by a halter. They arrested both Moore and Murray, and took from Moore the syringe and a small bottle, Exhibit 3, and seized another small bottle, Exhibit 4,

which Moore had taken from his pocket, and had dropped on the floor of the stall, after removing the cork. A small packet, containing a powder, Exhibit 4-B, was attached by a rubber band to Exhibit 4. The two small bottles had labels, Exhibits 3-A and 4-A attached. Upon Exhibit 3-A appeared the following notation in pencil: "325–340 Royal Blunder. First dose. Give this dose which"— then an erasure and the following conclusion: "one hour before post time." The notation in pencil upon Exhibit 4-A was as follows: "335 kg. First dose. Give this dose which"— then an erasure, and, "one hour before post time." The syringe and bottles, Exhibits 2 and 3, were found to contain, or to have contained, heroin, a derivative of opium. None of the containers bore internal revenue stamps. The unstamped paper packet, Exhibit 4-B, contained four grains of heroin.

Moore admitted that he received the two bottles (Exhibits 3 and 4) from Wingfield at about 1:30 p.m. with instructions to give the contents to the horses about one hour before running time, but disclaimed any knowledge that the bottles contained narcotics. Wingfield did not testify, but admitted to the agents that he had given the bottles to Moore, and that they contained heroin which he had directed Moore to give to the horses. He admitted further that he had asked Murray to assist Moore. He explained that he had purchased the heroin as well as 47 grains of cocaine, found in his possession, some four years before in Cuba. The agents found in a cigar box in Wingfield's room still another unstamped bottle, Exhibit 11, containing heroin, which bore a label, Exhibit 11-A, reading as follows: "Knights Gal. Give this dose * * * one hour before post time," and also a letter, Exhibit 8, dated September 20, 1933, addressed to Wingfield and signed by Patterson and bearing instructions relative to the three horses, Knights Gal, Royal Blunder, and Cloudet. In it appeared this sentence: "Am sending some bottles along with Morton Smith with full instructions on each." Patterson did send the horses by Smith to Detroit about September 22.

On October 11 the agents interviewed Patterson in Chicago, and he then, as well as later in his testimony, admitted that he wrote the letter to Wingfield dated September 20. He also wrote, for the agents, Exhibit 9, which contains some of the words appearing on the labels of the small bottles, Exhibits 3 and 4. He admitted to the agents that he had sent bottles of medicine to Wingfield at Detroit by Smith, but he denied that he had sent the small bottles, Exhibits 3 and 4, and also denied that he had written the labels thereon. However, Patterson admitted in his testimony not only that he had written Exhibit 8, but also that he had written the instructions on the labels of the small bottles, Exhibits 3 and 4, and that he had sent these bottles to Wingfield by a boy named Stevens, but denied that they contained heroin when they left Chicago. He testified that they contained bromides to be given to the horses for nervousness, and that the instructions on the labels to give a dose to Knights Gal one hour before post time was to settle her nerves. An expert in handwriting testified that the "request" handwriting of Patterson on Exhibit 9 showed a distinct effort to get away from habit.[21]

The Sixth Circuit affirmed the convictions of Patterson, Wingfield, and Moore. The US Supreme Court was asked to review the Sixth Circuit decision but declined.[22]

Wingfield, trainer and manager for Audley Farm, had his training license suspended after his arrest. He and Murray, trainer for W. F. Knebelkamp Murray, were subsequently ruled off the turf while their cases continued in court.[23]

Hal Price Headley, prominent Kentucky owner and breeder, was indicted along with Marvin Hardin, a groom at Headley's stable, in Federal District Court for the Northern District of Illinois (case number 27514). They were charged with three counts of violating the Harrison Act and the Narcotic Drug Import and Export Act.

On June 27, 1934, almost a year after the Arlington Park raid, Headley and Hardin petitioned the court to suppress the evidence seized by narcotics agents, claiming the agents had failed to obtain a search warrant and the seizure was therefore unlawful. Federal prosecutor Michael L. Igoe disagreed. He claimed that Headley's employee and codefendant Hardin gave permission for the search when he responded to an agent's question about where he kept the narcotics by saying, "You help yourselves—go around and try to find them."

The trial began in November 1936, with Headley and Hardin and owner A. A. Baroni as defendants. The disposition of this case is not known.[24] The only mention of the trial in Chicago newspapers was that a motion to suppress evidence was being argued. The outcome of that motion and of the trial itself received no press coverage. Apparently, the charges were dismissed, although a dismissal is not recorded in the court record.

Baroni was initially named in a separate federal indictment, along with his groom James Hexham (case number 27511). Baroni and Hexham filed separate petitions to suppress evidence. They argued that the search of a medicine cabinet that yielded "one syringe, one graduate glass, and two bottles of proprietary medicine" was done without a search warrant and was therefore unconstitutional. US attorney Michael L. Igoe claimed that on two occasions narcotics agents saw the defendants using a syringe to "drench" a horse with "certain fluids 45 minutes to one hour just before post time." Igoe also argued that the search was legal because Hexham had given permission by telling the agents, "You can help yourselves. You go and look around." This alleged statement sounds remarkably similar to the permission supposedly given by Hardin that led to Headley's indictment ("You help yourselves—go around and try to find them"). It is probably no coincidence that Igoe was the prosecutor in both cases.

Trainer Jack Howard was indicted along with his employee Charles Porter Mitchell in Federal District Court for the Northern District of Illinois (case number 27515). Howard was quoted by the Associated Press as saying that he "had never doped a horse in his life" and had never instructed one of his employees to do so. Howard added that any medications given to his horses were prescribed by a licensed veterinarian for an ailment the horse was suffering.[25]

After their motion to suppress evidence seized by narcotics agents was denied by the court, Howard and Mitchell were found guilty on two of the five counts in the indictment: violating the Harrison Act and conspiracy to violate the Harrison Act and the Narcotic Drug Import and Export Act. They were sentenced to ten days in jail on each count, to run concurrently, and fined $300. The conviction and sentences were affirmed by the Sixth Circuit Court of Appeals on May 7, 1935.[26]

Three grooms were also charged:

- Chauncey Berger pleaded guilty and was sentenced to three years in the federal prison at Leavenworth, Kansas.
- William (Bottoms Up) Cooney pleaded guilty and was sentenced to two years in the federal prison at Leavenworth.
- John (Tip East or Tip Easy) Pride pleaded guilty and was sentenced to two years in the federal prison at Leavenworth.[27]

The lesson here is that grooms without the resources to hire decent lawyers, many of them African Americans, fared much worse in the justice system than owners and trainers. Little has changed in that regard.

In an article published in the Hearst newspapers, Frank G. Menke pitched Anslinger's promise that "wholesale drugging of race horses will be a thing of the past on major race tracks in 1934. . . . The big drive to banish narcotics from racetracks really gets underway early next year, and this is a fight that will be won."[28] Strangely, it was not clear who was going to do the fighting.

Arrests by federal agents continued on a haphazard basis after the Arlington Park raid,[29] but Anslinger terminated his undercover investigations in early 1934 and shifted primary responsibility to the state racing commissions. He did so partly because the Federal Bureau of Narcotics had "too many other more important things which demand our attention and prevent our going into the racing situation as comprehensively as we'd like." And the investigations had served their political purpose by helping to secure Anslinger's position as head of the Federal Bureau of Narcotics. "Anslinger's supporters . . . included a strange alliance of conservative law and order politicians (who equated any drug use with anti-Americanism), pharmaceutical executives who wanted to protect their monopoly in the importation of opium, and race track owners embarrassed by horse-doping scandals. Having quickly established influential allies, Anslinger effectively neutralized an early threat to his status as narcotics commissioner."[30]

Instead, he wanted the state racing commissions to be the bureau's boots on the ground, with federal agents available if necessary. There is no record that this attempt at cooperation bore fruit. Three years later, in 1936, Anslinger was still waiting for substantive action at the state level. He said the federal government was willing to give the state commissions one final chance to rein in doping. Otherwise, the federal government was prepared to implement legislation banning the interstate shipment of horses with "bad records for the use of narcotics."[31] That did not happen, although several states did approve regulations intended to curb doping.[32]

Many state racing commissions had little inclination to take meaningful action, however, which led to Anslinger's idle threats of federal intervention. Money was also an issue. In New York, for example, the racing commission wanted to contract with Cornell Medical Center to conduct research on the use of saliva tests to detect performance-enhancing drugs in horses. The contract would cost $500, but because there was no specific statutory allowance for drug research, the commission asked for an opinion from the state attorney general.

"I regret that my answer must be in the negative," John J. Bennett Jr. wrote on October 9, 1934:

> The State Finance Law, section 36, requires that money appropriated for a specific purpose cannot be used for any other purpose; and the Comptroller shall not draw a warrant for the payment of any sum appropriated, unless it appears from the detailed statement presented to him by the person demanding the same, as required by this chapter, that the purpose for which money is demanded are those for which it was appropriated.
>
> I have carefully examined the State Racing Act (chapter 440 law 1926, as amended), but cannot find therein any authority for the expenditure of money by the Racing Commission for research and experimentation work.
>
> The matter, of course, can be taken care of at the next session of the Legislature.[33]

For the most part, aside from his preoccupation with tracking the training career of Ivan Parke, Anslinger's campaign against drugs on the backstretch was quickly forgotten. Instead, he tackled his genuine interest: the fight against the international production, trafficking, possession, and use of illegal narcotics, cocaine, and marijuana. He was remarkably successful in shepherding repressive drug laws through Congress, including the Uniform State Narcotic Drug Act; the Boggs Act, which imposed mandatory minimum prison sentences for simple drug possession; and the Narcotic Control Act.[34]

Anslinger never revisited the doping of racehorses. Federal involvement aimed at regulating the use of performance-enhancing drugs in horse racing would not happen again for another eighty-seven years.

8

The Spit Box, Trainer Responsibility, and the Modern Era of Drug Testing

Ernest Hemingway called them "boosted" horses, the ones that ran with the aid of performance-enhancing drugs (PEDs) at the Hippodrome d'Enghien-Soisy north of Paris or at the Hippodrome d'Auteil to the west of the city during the early 1920s. He was introduced to the sport during the summer of 1918 at the San Siro racecourse in Milan, Italy, where he was recuperating from wounds suffered while driving an ambulance for the Red Cross during World War I.[1] He continued going to the races with his new wife, Hadley, after they moved to Paris in December 1921.

Hemingway enjoyed Thoroughbred racing—the spectacle, the danger, and most certainly the gambling. The last was a problem. Money was usually scarce for Hemingway, who was trying to make a living as a journalist. He and Hadley went to the races whenever they could afford it, in hopes of adding to their meager resources with well-placed bets.[2] Hemingway believed a dedicated bettor could make money through what he called "intelligent handicapping," but making a profitable study of horses' form was a full-time job that interfered with his writing. Sporting newspapers that published past performances and race predictions were one shortcut for handicappers; another was to look for horses that had been stimulated with performance-enhancing drugs, or what Hemingway referred to as "boosted beasts."[3]

"It was before the days of saliva tests and other methods of detecting artificially encouraged horses," Hemingway wrote, "and doping was very extensively practiced. But handicapping beasts that are receiving stimulants, and detecting the symptoms in the paddock and acting on your perceptions, which sometimes bordered on the extrasensory, then backing them with money that you cannot afford to lose, is not the way for a young man supporting a wife and child to get ahead in the full-time job of learning to write prose."[4]

Hemingway chronicled his time at the Paris racetracks in a memoir, *A Moveable Feast*. An enduring question about the still-popular book is whether it is fact, fiction, or something of both. In a preface that Hemingway wrote in 1960, while living in Cuba, he had this to say: "For reasons sufficient to the writer, many places, people, observations and impressions have been left out of this book. Some were secrets and some were well-known by everyone and everyone has written about them and will doubtless write more. . . . If the reader prefers, this book may be regarded as fiction. But there is always the chance that such a book of fiction may throw some light on what has been written as fact."[5]

Hemingway recognized that performance-enhancing drugs presented an obvious advantage to unscrupulous owners and trainers, but also to bettors (at least on those rare occasions when bettors knew the fix was in). He also understood that drug tests could take away that potentially valuable edge. What Hemingway could not have known was that horse racing was on the cusp of a campaign to rid the sport of PEDs, a war waged on the backstretches, in Congress and state legislatures, and in laboratories and courtrooms. It is a war that continues to this day.[6]

Hemingway's handicapping involved close observation of horses in the paddock and, if he was lucky, an occasional bit of inside information about which horses were boosted. It was the same imperfect strategy used by Harry Anslinger's federal narcotics agents during their undercover backstretch raids a decade later. Wide application of a newly developed saliva test probably would have reduced doping in Paris and, in the process, made Hemingway's betting strategy less profitable. In the United States, it would have made Anslinger's campaign against illegal narcotics at racetracks much easier to pursue by providing substantive proof that a horse had been doped.

Chemical analysis to identify some of the common doping agents used at the time, such as morphine, heroin, and cocaine, was not difficult. A first-year college student majoring in organic chemistry could probably do it in a lab. A bigger problem was identifying those same drugs in the system of a horse. The difficulty for regulators, then and now, is that the development of new performance-enhancing drugs, or the adoption of old ones, always outpaces the development of reliable chemical tests to detect them. This lag time creates a "grace period" for dopers that can last many months. For racing in the United States, this grace period would last more than thirty years.

In 1803 Frederick Sertürner, a self-taught chemist who never even attended college, was the first experimenter to isolate the potent painkiller morphine from the sap of the opium poppy. Called "God's own medicine" by some physicians, morphine was used extensively during the American Civil War. The drug's efficacy as a painkiller was eventually overshadowed by its addictive qualities.[7]

Experimenting with Sertürner's new alkaloid several decades later, English chemist C. R. Alder Wright, working at St. Mary's Hospital in London, came up with a new derivative drug with a difficult-to-pronounce chemical name: diacetylmorphine. Wright's interest was strictly academic; he wanted to learn more about the chemical structure of morphine and other naturally occurring alkaloids. Perhaps he didn't recognize the new drug's potential market value as a substitute for morphine, or perhaps he was simply uninterested in the economic benefits of his discovery.[8] The German pharmaceutical giant Bayer did care about the economics, however. By the end of the 1800s, Bayer was aggressively marketing diacetylmorphine under a more familiar name: heroin. The initial reaction of the medical community was positive. Ironically, one of the hoped-for benefits was that heroin would be less addictive than morphine.[9]

Cocaine, a powerful stimulant derived from the coca plant grown in the Andes mountains of South America, was isolated in pure form during the mid-1800s. Psychiatrist Dr. Sigmund Freud endorsed the medical use of cocaine, as did US Army surgeon-general Dr. William Alexander Hammond. In 1886 Atlanta pharmacist John Pemberton began selling a carbonated, fruit-flavored elixir named Coca-Cola that included extracts from coca leaves and kola nuts. (Cocaine was dropped from the recipe a few years later.)[10] Even Sherlock Holmes, the world's most famous fictional detective, had a habit of injecting cocaine on those slow days when there were no exciting cases afoot.[11]

This is not to suggest that heroin and cocaine were developed with even a casual thought about doping racehorses. There is no denying the unintended connection, however. Heroin, morphine, and cocaine, along with the hypodermic syringe—a relatively new device that made it easier to inject drugs and made dosing more accurate—were the tools that fostered a culture of systematic doping begun by Doc Ring in around 1890.

By the mid-1920s, with a reliable chemical test still a decade away in America, doping had become so prevalent that Peter Burnaugh, one of the best-known turf writers of his day, wrote in the *Atlantic:* "And where is the noble sport of racing when the race itself becomes, not an issue between the blood of St. Simon and the blood of Lexington, nor even a test of riding skill between a Sande and a Maiben, but a Drug Store Derby between Heroin and Cocaine?"[12]

The spread of PEDs did not go unnoticed. Rules prohibiting their use were quickly enacted by the Jockey Club in the United States, by several state-level racing authorities, and by governing bodies in England, France, and half a dozen other European countries. It was a worthy mission, but there was an inherent problem. Although a relatively simple chemical assay could positively identify a substance like heroin, cocaine, or some other stimulant in a laboratory, there was no way to detect the presence of those same drugs in a horse's system. For example, it has been suggested that trainer H. G. Bedwell doped Sir Barton with strychnine, but there was no hard evidence to either exonerate or condemn him.[13] Detection of doping at the time was based on prerace observations made *after* a horse was injected or fed a drug that turned out to be a PED, or it was confirmed through a confession. The former was difficult to orchestrate; the latter was unlikely, although Bedwell admitted giving strychnine to Sir Barton.

The effective detection and prosecution of doping depend on a reliable and repeatable testing procedure that can detect drugs in a horse's system at the time of a race. By 1910, Polish pharmacist Alfons Bukowski had one—an analytical method of finding alkaloids such as heroin and cocaine in a horse's saliva. On the hundredth anniversary of his discovery, an article in the journal *Drug Testing Analysis* explained the development of the first reliable test for PEDs.[14] According to the authors, doping associated with American jockeys had become a serious problem in European racing around the turn of the twentieth century. Chemical analysis of horses' urine and feces to detect PEDs was possible but difficult and time-consuming, and it caused unreasonable delays in awarding purse money to owners. In 1910 the Warsaw Jockey Club hired Bukowski to develop a faster but still reliable test. Based on his observations of "profuse salivation of horses following a race," Bukowski hit on the idea of testing saliva for prohibited medications, and he developed a saliva test for alkaloids, including heroin, morphine, cocaine, and caffeine. Bukowski also developed a protocol to ensure consistent sampling procedures, some of which are still in use today. His saliva test was particularly valuable because it detected only drugs given to a horse on the day of a race, not earlier. This weakened the excuse that a drug had been given during training but not on race day. The test was adopted in several European countries soon after Bukowski's breakthrough, but acceptance in the United States came much more slowly.

The new test was a significant step in the right direction, and Bukowski's reputation as a "pioneer of anti-doping research" is well deserved.[15] Nevertheless, any hope that Bukowski's new procedure would be a panacea for horse racing's growing doping ills was sadly misplaced. There were shortcomings with the procedure that continue to hamper effective drug testing today. First, the test's specificity was limited to some—but not all—of the alkaloids used for doping. Second, and more important, the test could not detect new drugs, so chemists had to play catch-up whenever a new PED showed up at racetracks.

Joseph E. Widener finally adopted the saliva test at Hialeah for the Florida racetrack's winter meeting in 1934, twenty-four years after the test was introduced in Europe.[16] But Harry Anslinger took credit—this time, with some justification. A few days after the raid at Arlington Park, Anslinger proposed that every racetrack implement "dope boxes," special stalls in the paddock where horses suspected of being doped would be sent for the collection of samples for drug testing. The drug czar hoped that state racing commissions would impose lifetime bans on owners and trainers whose horses tested positive.[17] Widener had a different recollection and claimed that "he and his associates had prompted the government to investigate the use of stimulants in American racing in the first place."[18]

Widener was optimistic about implementing the saliva test at Hialeah. At a meeting of the National Association of Racing Commissioners at Churchill Downs in May 1934, he announced that the doping of horses was being eliminated. He claimed that the use of narcotics had been completely deterred by reliance on the saliva test in France, and he was sending veterinarian James Cattlett and chemist Charles Morgan there to study the test's use. Widener was wrong, of course. All pronouncements about the elimination—or even the control—of doping have been premature.[19]

Racing commissions were reluctant to rule owners off the turf, especially forever, and penalties for trainers were far less severe than

Anslinger would have liked. Still, the Hialeah experiment was a positive response. In an undated narrative, Anslinger overstated the influence of the Federal Bureau of Narcotics and, like Widener, promised a positive impact on racing. "Our investigations, raids and convictions led to the establishment of a saliva test at every race track in the country with competent chemists and veterinarians checking on stimulants administered to horses," Anslinger wrote. He should have stopped there, but instead he continued with a heavy dose of wishful thinking: "With few exceptions, the practice of drugging horses with narcotic drugs such as heroin and cocaine has virtually disappeared from American race tracks, as well as from foreign tracks. We had a veritable procession of foreign race track officials come to our door for advice and suggestions."[20]

During an early race meeting at Tropical Park, three veterinarians (representing the federal government, the state of Florida, and the racetrack) managed the dope box. Racing writer W. C. Vreeland saw evidence that the saliva test was working as intended. "No longer do the Thoroughbreds come out of the paddock with heads held high, pupils of their eyes distended, prancing as though stepping on air, and with rivulets of sweat dropping off their bodies," Vreeland wrote. "There's a reason, and a good one—no hop-along-juice, commonly called dope. And that's another good thing that President Roosevelt is responsible for—driving away dope dealers from race tracks."[21] Vreeland was probably was giving Roosevelt credit for keeping Anslinger on as director of the Federal Bureau of Narcotics, which, considering his lasting impact on drug policy in the United States, might not have been such a good idea.

Unlike at Tropical Park, where there were no reports of doping, drug testing got off to a rocky start at Hialeah. More than one hundred horsemen threatened to strike on the final day of racing, March 17, when the $10,000 Florida Derby was scheduled to be run.[22] Hialeah's adoption of the new and controversial saliva test was the impetus behind the threatened strike, but trainers had been grumbling

Hialeah walking ring. The first saliva test for prohibited drugs was introduced at Hialeah Park in 1934. (Keeneland Library, Charles Christian Clark Collection)

throughout the race meeting. Five trainers had been ruled off all Florida tracks based on their horses' positive saliva tests, mostly for traces of caffeine. Although Anslinger supported the saliva test, its use sometimes created a conflict between the narcotics bureau's enforcement of the Harrison Act and state regulations. Caffeine, a stimulant, was not an illegal drug subject to federal control. However, caffeine was prohibited under Florida rules, and stewards were required to suspend trainers whose horses tested positive for the substance.

The state racing commission could reverse the stewards' decision on appeal. This happened on at least one occasion when trainer John Partridge, who suspected his horse had been doped, scratched the horse *before* the race and *requested* a drug test. Although the test was positive, Partridge was exonerated. In another case, H. C. Trotter also thought a horse he trained had been doped and requested a saliva test, but not until *after* the race. Trotter was suspended for the remainder of the Florida racing season but avoided a lifetime ban, apparently because he had requested the test. There were still no penalties for owners.[23]

Another trainer, Nat Ray, was suspended by Hialeah stewards without a hearing after a horse tested positive for PEDs. Ray finally got a hearing, after a protest, and he was exonerated when veterinarian Major Schofield testified that strychnine was not a stimulant, was nothing more than a tonic, and could not be considered "dope," even when given in large doses. After the Ray decision, the racing commission changed its rules to ban the administration of "drugs, chemicals, patented medicines, narcotics, tonics, cough syrup or any other medication whatever . . . within 49 [*sic*] hours of a race in which the horse is to participate."[24]

Hialeah stewards held trainers liable for positive drug tests, but trainers demanded that the racing commission take complete charge of the horses entered in each day's races and accept responsibility for positive drug tests. The trainers argued that some of their colleagues who had been ruled off were innocent, that a horse could be doped without a trainer's knowledge, and that there was no right to appeal the commission's decision. The commission had already assumed responsibility for a horse's condition an hour before each race and offered to extend that oversight to two hours. The commissioners refused to assume complete responsibility for positive drug tests, however, and imposed an early version of the "absolute insurer rule" that remains in effect today.[25] This rule assigns liability for a positive drug test to the trainer, even without direct involvement in the doping, and it remains one of racing's most potent rules to combat the use of prohibited PEDs. With some amendments, including giving accused trainers the right to produce mitigating evidence in many states, the rule has stood the test of time.[26]

Dissatisfied with the commission's offer, 125 horsemen threatened to strike and not enter their horses on closing day at Hialeah. The Florida Derby and an important race for juveniles already had full fields, but there were few entries for the other five races on the card. There was also concern that the strike would extend to the twelve-day Tropical Park meeting scheduled to start the following week. In the end, the strike was averted. Four so-called agitators were expelled from the track grounds.[27] Widener declared, "We will race tomorrow even if there is only one horse in each field." The next day, the five races on the undercard had between three and nine entries by post time.[28] Opening day at Tropical Park drew sixty-nine entries for seven races.

Harry Anslinger's backstretch raids garnered a significant amount of favorable publicity for him and the Federal Bureau of Narcotics, but his optimistic promises about the imminent end to doping never came to fruition. There were positive results, however. Although Anslinger was not solely responsible for introducing saliva tests, as he would claim, support from the drug czar and his excellent working relationship with Hialeah president Joseph Widener certainly helped.

The federal agents also collected dozens of doping recipes during their raids (see appendix 3). These showed that the same PEDs introduced by Doc Ring and his colleagues in the 1890s—morphine, heroin, and cocaine—were still in wide use more than thirty years later. However, most of the positive drug tests at Hialeah in 1934 involved caffeine, suggesting a shift away from the use of illegal drugs that came with time in federal prison.

During the 1937–1938 season in Florida, 443 saliva tests were conducted, with one sample positive and one sample suspicious. J. J. Bauer, trainer of the horse that tested positive for an unidentified drug, was suspended for sixty days.[29]

With other states adopting the saliva test, the modern era of drug testing in the United States had finally arrived, albeit with a quarter-century head start ceded to the dopers. Ironically, the first drug scandal involving a high-profile Thoroughbred trainer would come a decade later and was not the result of a positive saliva test.

Part III

Silent Tom's Atomizers

9

"Those Bastards"

An unusual thing happened at Churchill Downs on the afternoon of May 3, 1947: Tom Smith smiled. Not the broad, face-cracking smile one might expect from someone who had just saddled a Kentucky Derby winner, but a tight-lipped half grin that might have gone unnoticed except for famed sportswriter Walter Wellesley "Red" Smith. It happened again minutes later in the winner's circle with Jet Pilot, the Maine Chance Farm colt that had just won the Derby for Tom Smith and Maine Chance owner and cosmetics queen Elizabeth Arden Graham. Jet Pilot "was standing on the track with Eric Guerin still on his back and his trainer, Tom Smith, holding his bridle," Red Smith wrote. "Tom Smith almost grinned—with him that amounts to laughing like a loon—as he fondled the horse's head. They went into the floral horseshoe followed by Mrs. Graham, who shook hands with Smith, shook hands with Guerin, then stood on tiptoe to pat Jet Pilot's neck. She is not a tall lady." Winning the Kentucky Derby is reason enough to celebrate in any year, but Jet Pilot's victory must have been doubly satisfying for both owner and trainer. A "large dose of poetic justice," Red Smith called it when the winner edged out Phalanx and Faultless in a three-horse photo finish.[1] He was right.

The year before, with the 1946 Kentucky Derby just two days away, a fire at Arlington Park near Chicago destroyed a barn and killed twenty-three horses belonging to Mrs. Graham. The horses, most of them two-year-olds, were valued at $500,000; insurance on the horses totaled $300,000.[2] As fate would have it, Jet Pilot was not among the juveniles lost in the fire. The colt had been shipped to Churchill Downs, where he broke his maiden in a race run on Derby Day. Maine Chance's three entries in the 1946 Derby—Bluegrass Stakes winner Lord Boswell, with Eddie Arcaro in the saddle; Santa Anita Derby winner Knockdown; and Perfect Bahram—were odds-on, but they all finished out of the money. King Ranch's Assault won the Kentucky Derby and went on to become a Triple Crown winner and Horse of the Year in 1946.[3]

Tom Smith had his own problems and was lucky to be training horses for Maine Chance Farm—or anyone else—on the first Saturday in May 1947. Eighteen months earlier, stewards of the Jockey Club and representatives of the New York State Racing Commission had revoked Smith's trainer's license for allegedly doping a Maine Chance horse, Magnific Duel, with ephedrine before a race at the old Jamaica track in Queens, New York. Smith had achieved national prominence as the trainer of champion Seabiscuit, and it was the first time a trainer with his reputation had been charged with a medication violation. The incident triggered a flurry of administrative hearings and litigation that lasted through most of 1946 before Smith finally gave up the fight. His license was restored by the Jockey Club a few weeks before Jet Pilot's Derby, and Smith returned to Mrs. Graham's employ as the trainer of record.

Mrs. Graham never gave up on Smith, and he never really stopped training for Maine Chance, although the license revocation required him to ply his trade on the sly. This was against the rules, but that didn't seem to bother anyone. When a reporter asked Mrs. Graham if, despite the license revocation, Smith had seen the Maine Chance horses Knockdown and Star Pilot (trained on paper by Smith's son Jimmy) run one-two in the 1946 Santa Anita Derby, she had a quick answer. "Of course," she said, "the old fellow wouldn't break a rule for the world, but he has powerful glasses and probably was up in a tree."[4]

Losing his trainer's license was a bitter blow to Tom Smith, who had been having a banner year with the Maine Chance horses, maybe his best year ever. And that's saying a lot for the man who trained 1938 Horse of the Year Seabiscuit.

Warren Wright's Calumet Farm was the face of Thoroughbred racing in the 1940s:

- Two Triple Crown winners: Whirlaway in 1941 and Citation in 1948
- Five Horses of the Year: Whirlaway in 1941 and 1942, Twilight Tear in 1944, Armed in 1947, and Citation in 1948
- A total of nine champions that earned an impressive nineteen titles among them[5]

Calumet was the leading owner in money won seven times (1941, 1943, 1944, 1946, 1947, 1948, and 1949) and the leading owner in races won during the same years—a formidable showing of quality and quantity.

One of the few chinks in the Calumet armor came in 1945, when Maine Chance Farm topped the owner's list with earnings of $589,170. Tom Smith was the leading trainer in money won that year, with $510,655. The difference between the stable's earnings and the trainer's earnings ($78,515) was due to Smith's license revocation, which put him on the sidelines—officially, at least—through most of November and all of December. That year marked the second title for Smith, who had also led all trainers in 1940, when he was on the payroll of Seabiscuit's owner Charles Howard.[6]

To make matters worse for Smith, if that was possible, Maine Chance horses captured championship honors in both two-year-old divisions in 1945: Star Pilot as juvenile male and Beaugay as juvenile filly. Although he developed both horses, Smith received "official" credit for only one. For the information of bettors, past performances for both horses included the line "previously trained by T. Smith."

Thanks to the license revocation, Roy Waldron had taken over training the Maine Chance horses on a temporary basis before Star

Pilot won the Pimlico Futurity on November 24, 1945. By 1946, Waldron was out and Smith's son, J. W. "Jimmy" Smith, was the trainer of record for Maine Chance, making it easier for the elder Smith to orchestrate the stable's campaign.[7]

Thursday, November 1, 1945, began like many other days for Tom Smith. Three horses were being shipped from Maine Chance's base of operations at Belmont Park on Long Island to Jamaica, a few miles north, for the afternoon card. All three were maidens—two-year-old Gay Garland in the second race, three-year-old gelding Magnific Duel in the third, and two-year-old filly Easton Queen in the fourth—and all three started as favorites at very short odds, owing to the reputations of Smith and Maine Chance, which had had a very successful year. Gay Garland won by a head, Magnific Duel won by 1¼ lengths, and Easton Queen finished third. Two dollars to win on each of the three would have netted a bettor $1.20.

It was another successful afternoon in a season full of them for Maine Chance horses, and Smith went into the weekend thinking everything was all right. He was wrong. Early on Monday morning, Smith got a puzzling telephone call. The caller, who refused to identify himself, told Smith that he would be called before the stewards later in the day "for Magnific Duel." The caller also told Smith to "bring the groom for Magnific Duel," but he did not explain why.[8] Left to guess what the stewards wanted with him, Smith would not receive official notice of the charges against him for more than a month, in a December 13 letter sent to John T. Cahill, one of his attorneys. According to that letter, Smith was accused of purchasing a "quantity of three per cent ephedrine, an improper medication or drug which affects the racing condition of a horse in a race"; keeping the ephedrine in one atomizer (the so-called white atomizer) and a mixture of vinegar, salt, and water in a second atomizer (the brown atomizer), and not keeping the two atomizers separate; and "us[ing] it, direct[ing] it to be used, or negligently allow[ing] it to be used in atomizing with ephedrine the nostrils of horses of the Maine Chance

Farm in the receiving barn at Jamaica Race Track immediately before the races in which such horses ran."[9]

Of those allegations, only the last was a violation of Rule 216(f) that would justify a penalty. The rule in effect at the time read:

> If the Stewards of the Meeting shall find that any improper medication or drug has been administered, internally or externally, which affects the racing condition of a horse in a race, such Stewards shall impose such penalty and take such other action as they may deem proper under any of the Rules of Racing against every person found by them to have administered or to have caused to be administered, or to have conspired with another person to administer such medication or drug and shall immediately refer the same to the Stewards of The Jockey Club; and such person or persons shall have his or their licenses, if any, suspended or revoked and/or otherwise punished in the discretion of said Stewards of The Jockey Club.
>
> Although the trainer or groom of such horse, or any other person having charge of or access to such horse, may not be shown to have known of or participated in such act or administration, he may be punished as if he had known or participated therein.[10]

Although the administrative hearings and subsequent litigation focused on Magnific Duel, the notice of charges referred to other incidents of doping with ephedrine on a "number of occasions." It was a small number: October 20, when Lord Boswell and Star Pilot were reportedly dosed with an ephedrine atomizer, and October 25, when "several horses of names unknown" got the same treatment.[11]

The Stewards' Hearing

The stewards' hearing was held at Belmont Park on November 5–6, 1945. Present were stewards Marshall Cassidy, Francis P. Dunne,

Harold O. Vosburgh, and F. S. von Stade. Appearing at the hearing were Tom Smith, Ernest Pevler (foreman, Barn 28), Allen Choate (groom), James Shelley (foreman, Barn 3), Francis Turner (groom), and Lacey Smith (groom).[12]

Smith's hearing before the stewards was an affront to due process. The officials were prepared with the rules and the facts as they understood them, along with witness statements implicating Smith and a report from the racing commission's chief chemist, C. E. Morgan. Based on a sample from an atomizer recovered from one of the stalls in the receiving barn occupied by the Maine Chance horses on November 1, the "almost colorless liquid with a faintly aromatic odor" contained "ephedrine in quantity equivalent to 2.6 grams per 100 milliliters."[13]

Smith, in contrast, was ill prepared for the interrogation. He was not represented by counsel, he was excused from the room when other witnesses testified, he was not permitted to cross-examine those witnesses, and he had no opportunity to dispute their statements. The only explanation of the charges was an opening question from Cassidy: "Mr. Smith, we have a report that you have administered or caused to be administered by atomizer spray a medication for horses prior to a race. Have you?"

"Only vinegar and water and salt," Smith answered. "That's all I have ever administered before or maybe Vick's." Smith acknowledged that he occasionally used an ephedrine spray on horses that were bleeders, but only during morning workouts and never before a race. He said he had purchased a 3 percent solution of ephedrine at the Elmont Pharmacy without a prescription and that the druggist had assured him the medication was not a narcotic or a stimulant. Smith added that he sometimes used ephedrine himself to clear up nasal congestion. Later in the hearing, Cassidy commented that he did the same thing.

Smith denied spraying the nostrils of any of the Maine Chance horses that raced on November 1. He claimed that none of his employees would have used the ephedrine unless he instructed them to do so, and he testified that he had not given such instructions to anyone that day.

A complication was that Smith had two similar atomizers: one with a white (or clear) glass bowl that contained the ephedrine, and one with a brown glass bowl that contained the vinegar, salt, and water solution. Neither was labeled. Smith knew which was which, but it was unclear whether any of his employees could make that distinction. A mix-up of the two atomizers was a mistake waiting to happen, and Smith argued that one did.

Ernest Pevler, Smith's foreman in Barn 28, acknowledged that Magnific Duel had been sprayed with an atomizer he found in a bucket of equipment brought to the receiving barn by James Shelley, Smith's Barn 3 foreman.

"Who told you to spray Magnific Duel?" Cassidy asked.

"Well, Jimmy [Shelley] brought this thing over and he said before we run him, we'd better spray his nose with salt and vinegar and water and I said all right *so Jimmy said Mr. Smith* said to spray his nose the day we run him."

"Mr. Smith said that?" Cassidy asked.

"Yes, he said it that morning," Pevler answered.[14]

Given Smith's lack of counsel and inability to cross-examine witnesses, the question of whether the trainer had told Pevler directly to spray Magnific Duel or whether the foreman relied on Shelley's recollection of Smith's instructions went unanswered until later in the hearing. At the close of Pevler's testimony, Francis Dunne resolved that question.

"Well, as I understand it," Dunne said, "the groom brought the spray over and as far as you know, the spray consisted of vinegar, salt, and water. This horse was not in your stable. Is that right?"

"Yes, he is in the other foreman's stable," Pevler said.

"No one told you to spray his nose out?"

"That's right."[15]

That answer supported Smith's testimony, but the trainer should not have been forced to rely on the help of one of the stewards to resolve the confusion.

The other witnesses had little to add. Allen Choate was a groom for Smith in Barn 3. He testified that he did not take the atomizer to the receiving barn. He said that Pevler had an atomizer, but Choate did not see him use it and did not know where the atomizer had come from.

James Shelley, the Barn 3 foreman, said that all three horses racing on November 1 were his responsibility and that he was at the receiving barn in the afternoon. He acknowledged that two atomizers were usually kept on the desk in Smith's office, "one that the boss usually uses and one with vinegar, salt and water." He said one atomizer (the one Smith used) went to the receiving barn with the horses and Pevler later took the other atomizer.

"Then both atomizers were at the Receiving Barn?" Dunne asked.

"Yes, sir," Shelley responded. He added that he did not see Smith at the receiving barn on November 1 and then recounted a later conversation he had with the trainer.

"Did Mr. Smith say anything to you about this investigation?" Dunne asked.

"No, he didn't say anything," Shelley responded. "He said that they got the wrong spray."

"When did he tell you that?"

"The other day when they took the spray away."

"You were told they took the wrong spray."

"He said we took the wrong one. Should have taken the one for salt and water."

"How did he happen to say that?"

"They came and took the spray away. He seen the end of it. He said this spray is my spray. Where is the other spray?" Shelley seemed to be saying that someone from the stable picked up the ephedrine atomizer by mistake, and later in the day it was confiscated by officials.

Groom Francis Turner took care of Lord Boswell, Gay Garland, and Harvey's Pal. He testified that he did not see an atomizer, that

Smith was not at the receiving barn until later, and that he did not see an atomizer used on any of the Maine Chance horses. He added that he had worked for Smith for only a couple of weeks.

Easton Queen's groom, Lacey Smith, anticipated the "Sergeant Schultz" defense from the television comedy *Hogan's Heroes:* "I know nothing." After a series of less than useful answers, among them "Can't say," "I don't know," "I didn't," and "I don't remember," Dunne made one final attempt: "As far as you know, you know nothing about it."

"No sir, nothing at all."

Tom Smith suspected that he was being watched before November 1, and that was confirmed by Cassidy during the stewards' hearing. "You have had a great deal of success," Cassidy said. "We have had to have a man stationed at your stable every time you ran a horse. We did that in preference to suspending the stable."[16]

"Well, whatever you do is all right," Smith replied, "because I sure didn't want to do anything that's against racing rules. If I were to run horses back a couple of times and then if I gambled on the races, it would be a different thing, but I don't. I just run them for the pleasure of it and for the public and it hurts me to run a favorite and have him beat."

Finally, as an afterthought, the stewards added a parenthetical note to the transcript after Smith's testimony: "In the opinion of the stewards, Mr. Smith was extremely nervous which is entirely different from his usual bearing." Apparently, the stewards regarded Smith's demeanor to be an indicator of his guilt in the doping incident.

The case was immediately referred to the Jockey Club for further hearings.

The Jockey Club Hearing

The Jockey Club hearing was held on November 8, 1945, at the club's office at 230 Park Avenue in New York City. Present were William Woodward (chairman), A. H. Morris, Joseph E. Davis, Robert

A. Fairbairn, Walter N. Jefferts (probably Walter M. Jeffords), F. S. von Stade, Marshall Cassidy (executive secretary), Ashley T. Cole (representing the state racing commission), and attorney H. C. McCollom. Exhibits included a transcript of the stewards' hearing; notarized affidavits from Dr. James G. Cattlett, Dr. M. H. Gilman, Dr. Thomas E. Corwin Jr., Townsend MacAllister, Dr. M. J. Dair, and Frank La Boyne; and excerpts from *New and Non-Official Remedies of 1943, Milks Veterinary Materia Medica,* and the report of chief commission chemist C. E. Morgan.[17]

The first witness was Dr. James G. Cattlett, a veterinarian called to explain the effects of ephedrine spray on a Thoroughbred. He was the first witness to clarify the track stewards' presumption that ephedrine was, in fact, a stimulant. Ephedrine is currently a class 2 drug in the racing commissioners' Uniform Classification Guidelines, defined as a medication that has "a high potential for affecting the outcome of a race."[18] The drug was a "heart stimulant" and a "respiratory stimulant," Dr. Cattlett explained, and "a very powerful drug." He added that ephedrine would be a heart stimulant only in small doses; in large doses, it would be a heart depressant. "It is not a narcotic, but it is definitely a stimulant."

Whether the drug could be detected by the saliva test in use at the time was an open question, and an important one. The postrace tests on all three Maine Chance horses that ran on November 1, including Magnific Duel, were reportedly negative. A negative test for ephedrine would favor Smith, but only if the drug could actually be detected in a horse's saliva.

"Wouldn't ephedrine show in a saliva test?" A. H. Morris asked.

"I can't answer that," Dr. Cattlett responded. "I haven't heard of it being found."

"You have never found it as yet?"

"No, sir. I don't think so. Now, I will not make that statement for sure, because I don't know. I do not think so. I have been away for several years, and I do not know that it has been found since I have been gone."

"They have never made any experiments of giving it and then found out if it would show?"

"I believe not. Not to my knowledge."

"My point would be that if ephedrine does not show, it would be a very clever thing to use it to avoid detection." The stewards' thinking was becoming clear: doping with ephedrine would be a "clever" way for Smith to cheat.

"It is quite evident from the testimony that ephedrine is a stimulant," Chairman Woodward said. "The question is, then, to determine whether it was used or not; that is the only question before us, really. That is, whether it was used in this case."

"It looks like a foolproof thing to you," Jefferts said to Woodward.

"I think it is," the chairman replied.

By the end of Dr. Cattlett's testimony, there was little doubt about the outcome of the hearing.

There were only two witnesses after Dr. Cattlett: Tom Smith and Ernest Pevler. Neither man had much to offer beyond their testimony at the stewards' hearing, but the questioning produced some interesting details.

Before transporting Magnific Duel to Jamaica, Smith said the gelding went out for a gallop and a short breeze, "just an eighth of a mile." Aside from checking on Magnific Duel in his stall at the Belmont barn after that workout, Smith said he did not see the horse again until he was brought from the receiving barn at Jamaica to the paddock for saddling. Smith testified that he went to the receiving barn after arriving at the track but left before the van with Magnific Duel and Gay Garland arrived. Smith acknowledged that he sometimes sprayed horses with a vinegar, salt, and water mixture before a race, but never with ephedrine. Smith later corrected his testimony about when he was at the receiving barn and revealed a superstition. "I was there—just a minute," he said. "I will tell you the truth. Always, when I can, I go in the stalls and urinate [in] the stalls for luck. I do that always, if I can. I went back [to the receiving barn]

Trainer Tom Smith and champion Seabiscuit. During the Jockey Club hearing on Magnific Duel, chairman William Woodward changed tactics and asked whether Smith had doped Seabiscuit with ephedrine. (Keeneland Library, Morgan Collection)

when 'Gay Garland' was in the stall, and urinated, and went back [to the track]. I did not see the other horses at all."

Woodward asked about Smith's contract with Mrs. Graham, and Smith explained that he was paid a flat salary and a percentage of the horses' winnings. Woodward also asked about Smith's time with Charles S. Howard. Neither the contract nor his employment history was relevant to the issue before the Jockey Club stewards, but the questions about Howard were leading to what Woodward really wanted to know. "Did you ever use this ephedrine on 'Seabiscuit' in the morning or other times?" the Jockey Club chairman asked.

Whether Smith was surprised by this unexpected inquiry about Seabiscuit is not apparent from the written transcript, but he must have wondered about the purpose of the question. One possibility is that Woodward was hoping to learn that Smith had used performance-enhancing drugs to develop Seabiscuit into a champion. Woodward had employed trainer James "Sunny Jim" Fitzsimmons for years, but that legendary horseman had failed badly with Seabiscuit before Howard purchased the future Horse of the Year. Perhaps Woodward was looking to bolster his own trainer's reputation with evidence that excused Sunny Jim's lack of success with Seabiscuit.

"No, I did not, because I did not find anything—well, he never had a head cold, or anything," Smith explained. "He had leg troubles. That was all."

Smith reiterated that he had not sent the ephedrine spray to the receiving barn and did not know why any of his employees would have taken it there. He also tried to clear up an apparent misunderstanding on Marshall Cassidy's part about whether Smith had ever sprayed horses before a race. He had sprayed them with the vinegar, salt, and water solution, Smith said, but never with ephedrine.

Woodward next questioned Smith about his success in 1945, again implying that the trainer's horses needed chemical help to win races.

"You have had great success this year," Woodward said.

"And that is why I hate to have this thing come up," Smith said, "because the lady [Mrs. Graham] spent a lot of money, and I am telling you, those are running horses. There is nothing making those horses run but good hay and oats."

"Do you feel the treatment in the mornings, I don't mean before a race, but in the mornings, of this ephedrine, and occasionally with vinegar, do you feel it helps their running?" Woodward continued.

"No, no, because the horses are just good horses," Smith said:

> That is all there is to it, and there is nothing making those horses run except just hay and oats; good, strong, fat horses, and good horses. There isn't a thing. They have got a report around the track that I have a hundred thousand dollar radar and I braid their tails up and put a wire in it and stand in the center. They have been watching me do that. I don't like to go up in Miss Arden's [Mrs. Graham's] box, because it makes me nervous to go up around a bunch of people that way, and I go around and stay on that little platform at the odds board, where they put up the Daily Double. There is a bench over there.
>
> That is the report that they have all over now, that I use radar. I don't do a thing on them.
>
> I get up at four o'clock in the morning, and try to keep them strong and ready to run.

Smith probably brought up the "radar" accusation to illustrate the many wild theories accounting for his success that year. He might have hoped the stewards would consider the ephedrine charges just another one of those outlandish claims.

Smith's testimony wrapped up with questions about an altercation he had with a groom and whether that man might have a grudge against the trainer. "Mr. Smith," Cassidy said, "some time early in the summer, you had some trouble with one of your men. He hit you with a hammer, and you fired him."

"Yes," Smith replied.

"Would you have any reason to believe that man had any animosity towards you and would attempt to get you in trouble because of that?"

"Yes, I do."

"Do you think in any way he could be responsible for anything that happened recently?"

"I don't know that he was, because I haven't seen him. I haven't heard of him. He was working at the other barn, Barn 28, when I had the trouble."

The groom received a six-month jail sentence for the assault on Smith and was probably still incarcerated when the alleged doping occurred.[19]

Ernest Pevler acknowledged once again that he sprayed Magnific Duel with the white atomizer before his race and that he also sprayed Easton Queen with the same atomizer before she raced. He again claimed that he dosed Magnific Duel because he understood that's what Smith wanted. Pevler testified that he thought the atomizer contained the vinegar, salt, and water solution and said he still did not know what the atomizer actually contained. The confusion about when, or whether, Smith had instructed the other barn foreman, James Shelley, to spray Magnific Duel and which atomizer to use was not resolved at the hearing. Before Pevler was excused, the questioning returned to Seabiscuit's owner.

"Did you use it [an atomizer, with or without ephedrine] in your work for Mr. Smith when he was with Howard before?" Cassidy asked.

"No, sir," Pevler said.

"You never used a spray?"

"No, sir."

Following a discussion of the suspicions that had prompted the investigation into Smith's activities with an atomizer during the weeks before November 1, the inevitable ruling was made:

The trainer's license of Tom Smith has been revoked and he is denied all privileges on tracks under the authority of The Jockey Club for the period of one year, terminating on November 1, 1946. Ernest Pevler and James Shelley, foremen in the stable of Maine Chance Farm, for which Tom Smith was training, are denied all privileges of any track operating under the jurisdiction of The Jockey Club for a period of 30 days, starting November 8.

The reason for this action is violation of Rule 216(f) of the rules of racing, which prohibits the administration of any medicine or drug to any horse, internally or externally, which affects the racing condition of the horse in a race.

The report of the State chemist identified the medication as ephedrine.

Smith received official notification of the ruling in a letter dated November 10, 1945.

The language of the ruling was critical. Although contemporaneous reports often used the terms "suspension" and "revocation" interchangeably, a revocation allowed an appeal. At the time, the suspension of a license apparently did not.[20]

After the ruling was announced, Smith told the *Daily Racing Form* that he was innocent of any wrongdoing. In a subsequent statement, Smith continued to claim his innocence:

The saliva tests of every Maine Chance entry were negative. During my 28 years as a trainer I have never done anything which to my knowledge was in violation of the rules. I am sure the officials will vindicate me when the full story is told.

The so-called drug used on Magnific Duel is infinitesimal and could not have affected his racing condition. He was examined after his winning effort and the tests were negative. I knew I was being watched, and I wouldn't deliberately put myself in this position had I thought I was doing anything wrong.[21]

On November 21, 1945, through attorney Arthur F. Driscoll, Smith appealed the Jockey Club's ruling. A hearing before the Joint Board, composed of three New York State Racing Commission members and two stewards of the Jockey Club, began on December 14, 1945. This time, the emphasis would be on the chemical nature of ephedrine and, most important, Smith finally would be represented by legal counsel.

10

The Joint Board and the Courts

Facing criticism about Tom Smith's lack of legal counsel at the stewards' hearing, Marshall Cassidy, executive secretary of the Jockey Club, issued an explanation that explained nothing:

> Tom Smith appeared before us for a full hour last Monday after the close of the Belmont Park meeting. And he was present at a hearing on Wednesday that lasted from 10 in the morning until well after noon. He not only had a chance to explain himself at this hearing, but he did explain himself fully.
>
> It has also been said that Smith was not notified of his year's suspension until he read about it in the papers. Naturally Smith was not represented after the stewards had heard all the testimony relative to the case and while they were making their decision. He was perfectly aware, however, that he would be penalized.[1]

It was disingenuous for Cassidy to excuse Smith's lack of legal representation during the stewards' deliberations when it was during the hearings that he would have benefited greatly from the advice of counsel. The damage done to Smith's case by a lack of representation would become painfully obvious at the upcoming Joint Board hearing.

Officials also had to defend their ruling against Smith for the use of a medication—ephedrine—that was often prescribed for people with head colds. Francis P. Dunne, the track steward appointed by the Jockey Club, issued a statement of his own. "It is easy to say that ephedrine is a common medicine for humans, that it requires no prescription at a drug store," Dunne said:

> But that reasoning can easily lead to a misrepresentation of the stewards' point of view. In speaking of this case, where Magnific Duel was involved, or any case of this sort, two things should be emphasized: First, that the dosage of any medicine may completely alter the effect it may have. Second, that some medicines—such as quinine, benzedrine, ephedrine—may conceivably mask the presence of a stronger drug.
>
> The reason the stewards must take an absolutely firm attitude in these cases is because any letting down of barriers might lead to flagrant abuse. We have to be inflexible on the subject of stimulants and every horseman understands the very explicit ruling that applies to these cases. It is Rule 216(f) of the Rules of Racing.[2]

Maine Chance Farm owner Elizabeth Graham got into the game, making a statement that managed to be a weak assertion of her confidence in both the Jockey Club and Smith. "I shall start an investigation immediately," she said:

> This is a terrible thing to have happen just at a time when we were so proud of our victories. My horses don't need stimulants to win races. But I have sufficient confidence in Mr. Woodward and the other members of The Jockey Club to know that they would not take this action without giving the entire matter full consideration. We are going to ask The Jockey Club to cooperate with us in investigating every race

we have won. And if our right to any purses is questioned, I will return the money.

Whether or not Mr. Smith appeals his decision, I shall reserve judgment on him until I complete my own investigation. I just cannot understand it. His record has been spotless and I made sure that he was not a betting man before I employed him. I do not bet and as for ephedrine, I have been using it for years.[3]

The *New York Herald Tribune* got the facts painfully wrong but managed to inject a bit of humor into an otherwise serious situation. The now-defunct and, on this occasion, poorly proofread newspaper noted that the state chemist "reported traces of ephedrine in the saliva test taken from Mrs. Elizabeth [Arden] Graham."[4]

The Joint Board Hearing

The hearing conducted by the Joint Board was held at the office of the New York State Racing Commission, 745 Fifth Avenue, New York City, on December 14–15, 1945, and January 9, 11, and 14, 1946. Present for the racing commission were Ashley T. Cole, chairman; members William C. Langley and David Dows; John P. Powers, assistant attorney general; and Howard D. Danihy, assistant attorney general. Present for the Jockey Club were stewards William Woodward and George D. Widener. Appearing at the hearing and representing the Jockey Club were attorneys Martin A. Schenk and Harold C. McCollom of the law firm Davies, Auerbach, Cornell & Hardy. Representing Tom Smith were attorneys from the law firm Cahill, Zachry, Gordon & Reindel: John T. Cahill; Jerome Doyle and Turner McBaine, of counsel; and Neil S. McCarthy.[5]

The two previous hearings involving Tom Smith, conducted by the Jamaica track stewards and stewards from the Jockey Club, focused on who did what and when. By the end of the second hearing, the consensus was that Barn 28 foreman Ernest Pevler had sprayed the nostrils of Magnific Duel with an atomizer containing a solution of ephedrine before the third race at Jamaica on November 1. Magnific Duel won that race, and postrace tests were negative for prohibited substances. Confusion lingered about whether Smith told Pevler to spray the gelding, whether Smith told someone else to use the spray and that person told Pevler to do it, or whether Smith did not tell anyone to use the atomizer. That detail did not really matter; the absolute insurer rule made Smith liable for the condition of any horses he trained.[6]

Although both Smith and Pevler testified at the Joint Board hearing, the question of whether ephedrine is a stimulant was the real issue. Neither the trainer nor the foreman could speak to that question, and a procession of veterinarians, researchers, and medical doctors were the main event. Schenk and McCollom presented the Jockey Club's case against Smith, with Schenk doing most of the talking; Cahill was the main spokesman for Smith.

Alex Bower, executive editor of *Blood-Horse* magazine, attended the first days of the hearing and described the attorneys: "Cahill and Schenk made an interesting contrast as they squared off when Chairman Cole tapped his gavel at the start of the hearing," Bower wrote. "Cahill, dressed meticulously, and full of nervous energy, italicized his points by bouncing from his chair and moving close to the board or to the witness under examination. Schenk, tall and a bit shabby, remained seated during the entire hearing and metered his words as if he were assembling them a letter at a time, or as though he had already exceeded his quota for 1945."[7] Bower did not mention how the attorneys' participation impacted the proceedings. While the November hearings had moved along smoothly and fairly quickly, this one was riddled with substantive and procedural objections from both sides as the testimony dragged on.

According to Bower, during one of the breaks in the hearing Smith commented, "I have the same opinion now as I had before. I don't see why they didn't give me a break in the first place. I wasn't trying to break the rules." Smith also noted that Roy Waldron, the temporary trainer who had taken over for him, was doing a good job. That was not a surprise, given that Smith was still running the show and talking to Waldron a couple of times a day. "I think this was perfectly all right," he said. "[Waldron] and the horses would have been at a disadvantage otherwise. He did exactly as I told him."[8]

The first witnesses were Drs. Corwin and Gilman, both examining veterinarians for the state racing commission. They testified about alleged spraying incidents that occurred *before* November 1, which were relevant only because they appeared to show a pattern of misconduct on Smith's part. Dr. Corwin testified that he saw Smith spray horses on October 20 at Jamaica, using an atomizer with a brown glass bowl. Testimony at the previous hearings, however, had established that the brown atomizer contained a vinegar, salt, and water solution that was not prohibited.

Dr. Gilman testified that he saw Smith using an atomizer at Jamaica on October 25 and that he was "pretty sure that it was the white atomizer [previously established as the one containing an ephedrine solution]." Smith's attorney objected to the testimony about the atomizer if the witness was only "pretty sure"—an objection he would raise frequently during the hearing—and Chairman Cole struck the testimony. Dr. Gilman had taken samples from a bottle and an atomizer found in a stall on October 25. Those samples were then analyzed by C. E. Morgan, the racing commission's chief chemist, who reported "epinephrine absent. Sample inadequate for further tests."[9] Neither Dr. Corwin nor Dr. Gilman questioned Smith about the atomizers or reported their suspicions to anyone.

Frank Lorentzen and James La Boyne, both employees in the horse identification department, were present at the receiving barn on November 1 and were responsible for confiscating the white atomizer from Smith's employees. Interestingly, neither of them could positively identify Smith as the "white man" at the receiving barn with the atomizer and the Maine Chance horses. Morgan confirmed that he tested the liquid in the white atomizer confiscated by Lorentzen and La Boyne and that the sample contained "ephedrine in quantity equivalent to 2.6 grams per 100 milliliters, calculated as anhydrous ephedrine."[10] Morgan testified that the liquid had a faintly aromatic odor, ruling out the possibility that it was Smith's vinegar, salt, and water treatment for congestion. The concentration of ephedrine in the atomizer, and whether that amount would "affect the racing condition of a horse in a race" pursuant to Rule 216(f), would become the main point of contention throughout the rest of the hearing.[11]

The next witness for the commission was Dr. James Cattlett, the veterinarian who supervised the examination and identification of horses at all New York tracks and at Hialeah Park in Florida. Dr. Cattlett also supervised saliva and urine tests for prohibited substances. Ephedrine, he said, is "an alkaloid of this Chinese drug, mahuang, and it is used as a stimulant, both a heart stimulant and respiratory stimulant."[12] When Dr. Cattlett was asked about the effect of ephedrine on a horse in a race, Smith's attorney objected. "We are not here concerned with ephedrine," Cahill said. "We are concerned with the 2.6 percent solution of ephedrine, so that what the effect of 100 percent ephedrine may be is immaterial and irrelevant." Cahill raised the same objection nearly every time "ephedrine" was mentioned without the 2.6 percent solution qualifier.

The next issue was how much of the 2.6 percent solution would be required to affect the racing condition of a horse and how much of the drug would be lost if the horse sneezed after being sprayed. Dr. Cattlett said the amount of ephedrine necessary to have a "systemic" effect (enter the bloodstream) depended on the size of the horse. He also testified that he did not know how much of the drug would be lost if the horse sneezed after being sprayed.

At the conclusion of Dr. Cattlett's testimony, the commission rested its case. Cahill moved that the charges against Smith be dismissed on the grounds that the evidence "does not prove any offense under Rule 216(f)." Racing commission chairman Cole, who was running the Joint Board hearing, reserved his decision until all the evidence had been heard.

There followed a procession of expert witnesses in support of Tom Smith.

Dr. Harry Gold, a physician who specialized in cardiology and pharmacology, stated that he had done a great deal of original research on the effect of ephedrine on animals. He testified that ephedrine is not a narcotic and is not habit-forming, that there is a direct relationship between the weight of an animal and the dosage necessary to have an effect, and that the principal use of ephedrine is to clear nasal congestion. Dr. Gold had conducted experiments using an atomizer identical to Smith's white one and found that it took about five hundred squeezes of the bulb to get a dose equivalent to two-thirds of an ounce, the amount Dr. Cattlett testified would be necessary to affect a horse's racing condition. Pevler testified that he had sprayed Magnific Duel four times in each nostril and then the horse had sneezed, losing some of the spray.

"Assume that the proof will show that the weight of Magnific Duel is 600 kilograms," Cahill stated, "and assume that the proof in this case will further show that he was sprayed four times in each nostril from Exhibit 5, what would be the systemic dose per kilogram of body weight of this particular horse without regard to any loss by sneezing?"

"The systemic dose which that horse would have received," Dr. Gold answered, "by that I mean the amount of the drug that would have entered his system to produce effects on the body, under those conditions, would be 0.003, 3/1000ths of a milligram. Approximately 1/300th of a milligram, per kilogram."

"Now, I ask you whether any such amount of ephedrine solution would have any effect on a horse," Cahill continued.

"I doubt if it would have an effect on a flea," Dr. Gold replied. "That is like so much water."

"I want to ask you specifically whether such amount would have any effect whatsoever on the ability of a horse to run faster or slower," Cahill persisted.

"None whatsoever," Dr. Gold concluded.

Dr. Gold had also conducted experiments with ephedrine on Magnific Duel before the horse was shipped to California earlier in December.

"As a result of this experiment," Cahill asked, "is it your conclusion that the amount of ephedrine solution received by the horse [Magnific Duel] in the experiment that you described could not affect the racing condition of a horse?"

"Not at all," Dr. Gold replied.

"And it would follow," Cahill continued, "that an amount— what was the amount, Doctor?"

"1/100th as much."

"Given by eight compresses of the spray, by Exhibit 5, could not have had the slightest effect on the horse, is that true?"

"None whatsoever."

Dr. Gold's testimony regarding ephedrine was supported by a cadre of experts: Dr. Robert S. MacKellar, a New York veterinarian with fifty years' experience, said that use of an ephedrine spray on a horse that bled or that was congested was proper treatment. Dr. David E. Buckingham, a practicing veterinarian and university professor from Washington, DC, testified that ephedrine could be useful for a horse that was a bleeder and that, in his opinion, only an "enormous" amount of ephedrine could affect the racing condition of a horse. He added that he was not even "sure of that."

Ernest Pevler and Tom Smith were the next witnesses to testify. Pevler said he knew about the white and brown atomizers kept on Smith's desk in the stable office and that he thought they both contained the vinegar, salt, and water solution. He acknowledged spraying Magnific Duel and recalled that there was no reaction from the horse other than a sneeze. He said that no one, including Smith, had told him that one of the atomizers contained ephedrine, and he had no doubt the white atomizer contained only the vinegar, salt, and water solution.

On cross-examination by Schenk, Pevler either denied making some of the statements attributed to him in transcripts of the track stewards' and Jockey Club hearings or said he did not remember making them. This included the statement that "Jimmy said Mr. Smith said to spray his [Magnific Duel's] nose the day he run." He also denied trying to hide the white atomizer in the straw and said it had fallen there by accident. There was nothing in Pevler's testimony that directly, or even indirectly, implicated Smith.

Tom Smith was up next. Cahill led him through his history as a trainer: working for C. B. Erwin, George Adams, John Spreckles, Mrs. Erwin, Neil McCarthy (one of Smith's attorneys, who had recommended him to Elizabeth Graham), Charles Howard, and finally Maine Chance Farm starting on March 7, 1944. Smith said his first experience with ephedrine was using the drug for his own nasal congestion, the result of a broken nose. He started using ephedrine on the Maine Chance horses in spring 1945, when an epidemic of coughs hit the barns at Belmont Park.

Smith repeated prior testimony that he had not instructed any of his employees to spray horses on November 1. Asked by Cahill whether he had ever "administered or caused to be administered any drugs or stimulants for the purpose of affecting the speed of horses in races in which they were about to participate," Smith said he had not.

There were also questions about the "tonics" Smith gave his horses. Those tonics, he said, were prepared by Dr. Southard, a racetrack veterinarian who had an office on the Belmont Park backstretch "right next to the superintendent's office." This was most likely Dr. Nelson Edward Southard, a racetrack veterinarian indicted on federal drug charges during the Federal Bureau of Narcotics raid at Arlington Park in 1933. After a bench trial in Chicago, he was found not guilty (see chapter 7).

At the close of his case, Cahill renewed his motion to dismiss the charges against Smith. Cole again preferred to wait until the hearing was over to rule on the motion.

Schenk called one rebuttal witness: Dr. Hubert S. Howe. He testified that ephedrine in a 2.6 percent solution would be a stimulant in a horse, but he also stated that he had no notes and had not published anything about the effect of ephedrine on horses in any academic journal. On cross-examination by Cahill, Dr. Howe admitted that he had no personal experience regarding ephedrine and horses.

"Did you ask the attorneys for The Jockey Club to supply you with a horse so that you could make an experiment with the 3 per cent solution of ephedrine on a horse?" Cahill asked.

"No," Dr. Howe replied.

"Did you make any attempt to get a horse in order that you could make an experiment of the effect of this solution on a horse?" Cahill pressed.

"No."

At this point, Cahill asked to have Dr. Howe disqualified as an expert witness because of his lack of experience with horses. The request was denied on the basis of substantial testimony already taken from witnesses for both sides about the effect of ephedrine on humans. Chairman Cole allowed Dr. Howe to testify, with the qualifier that his lack of experience with horses would be considered in deliberations.

At the close of testimony, Neil McCarthy, one of Smith's attorneys, suggested that further tests be conducted on Magnific Duel. After a recess, Chairman Cole announced that neither the racing commission nor the Jockey Club would conduct such tests for fear of creating a precedent for future cases. Cole added that the record would be kept open if Smith's attorneys wanted to commission further tests. A few days later, Smith's attorneys announced that no additional testing would be conducted: "Upon consulting with and on the advice of our scientific experts, it is our opinion that no practical method of conducting tests on Magnific Duel other than that presented by our expert testimony, could more conclusively establish the absence of a systemic effect of ephedrine in the dosage with which this case is concerned."[13] The decision not to proceed was based on a December 21 letter from Dr. Harry Gold, who had testified for Smith, and Bernard L. Oser, PhD, who had assisted in the prehearing tests on Magnific Duel but did not testify. The letter went into detail about the validity of the tests conducted on the horse and the lack of any relevant testing by the other side. "We, therefore, do not believe that tests on Magnific Duel conducted in any other manner [different from the tests Gold and Oser had already conducted] would be likely to throw further light on the question at issue," the authors concluded.

The letter appeared to clear the way for briefs to be filed and a decision to be rendered. Instead, it generated several hundred pages of generally repetitive testimony and three more days of hearings in early January. The only new information was testimony from Dr. Manual Gilman, who had conducted tests on eleven horses, including several Thoroughbreds. Those tests, Dr. Gilman said, showed that ephedrine administered by nasal spray produced a uniform increase in blood pressure and a change in respiration.

Before the hearing began, attorney McCarthy had been confident that his client's license revocation would be reversed. "I have known Smith for a great many years," McCarthy told famed sportswriter Grantland Rice:

> He is a quiet, simple fellow with a brief vocabulary who has no cunning nor guile in his system, but one who happens to be one of the best trainers racing has. Smith is a fine trainer because he is a hard worker who knows conditioning. And this season, he happened to have the best stable in the country with which to work.
>
> Now, it has been proved and admitted that Smith was not even near the place where the Maine Chance groom applied the touch of ephedrine in the horse's nostrils. He knew nothing about it. The groom says he thought the application was another mixture, known to be completely legal and harmless.

Also, the groom made no effort to hide or cover up his action and certainly made no effort to hide any atomizer. Also, I made a complete test with Magnific Duel with the same application of ephedrine and found that it had no effect whatever as a stimulant. Again, Smith was given no chance in the closed meeting to examine any witnesses. I don't believe he received a fair deal and the facts back me up.

As trainer of the most successful stable of the year, Smith was bound to be the object of envy on the part of others not so successful. Smith knew he was being watched for months, but as he had nothing to hide he was never worried about it. I know he is completely innocent of any wrong or attempted wrong.[14]

McCarthy was correct that much of the evidence tilted in Smith's favor. Nevertheless, the absolute insurer rule allowed a penalty to be imposed on a trainer who neither knew of nor participated in a doping incident. On February 14, 1946, the Joint Board upheld Smith's license revocation: "After hearing the evidence and examining the briefs and memoranda of counsel, the Joint Session of the State Racing Commission and two Stewards of The Jockey Club, acting as a Board, has unanimously determined that the Stewards of The Jockey Club for the purpose of maintaining a proper control over race meetings and to punish persons concerned in fraudulent turf practices properly exercised their discretion in revoking the trainer's license for the year 1945 of R. Tom Smith."[15]

The decision, which should have surprised no one, meant that Smith had exhausted his administrative remedies. An appeal to the judicial system was his only option. His attorneys asked the state supreme court for a stay of the original revocation, which was denied, but on appeal, Smith was granted a stay of sorts. On April 5, 1946, the court denied Smith's motion to order the Jockey Club to give him a trainer's license, but it stayed execution of the order barring Smith from training in New York until November 2, 1946. The court ruled that the Jockey Club had the discretion to decide whether to give Smith a trainer's license if he applied for one, but his application could not be refused based on the original revocation order.[16]

A month later, the First Department of the Appellate Division of the Supreme Court of New York reached the substantive question of setting aside the Jockey Club's revocation of Smith's license. The only question before the appellate court was whether there was substantial evidence to support the Joint Board's decision.[17] The court determined that there was:

> There was substantial evidence before the administrative body [the Joint Board] that ephedrine had certain qualities as a stimulant, and that it also might affect the racing condition of a horse by increasing its respiratory capacity. Expert opinion evidence, contradictory in view, was received from both sides to the controversy concerning the possibility of the dosage administered in this case acting as a stimulant, particularly in view of the method of its application. Under the controlling authorities we may not consider the weight of the evidence relating to this question. Nor may we choose to believe one set of experts rather than the other. If we could, it might well be that we should arrive at a different conclusion from that arrived at by the board as to whether the evidence established any actual stimulation of the horse in question.
>
> We find that a fair hearing was afforded the petitioner and that there was substantial evidence to support the finding made. Accordingly, the determination cannot be said to be arbitrary or capricious, and we may not set it aside.[18]

Smith initially appealed the decision but withdrew the appeal in early September.[19] His license was reinstated in April 1947, a month before he saddled Jet Pilot to win the Kentucky Derby for Maine Chance Farm.[20]

11

The Not-so-Absolute
Insurer Rule?

Proving that a horse had been boosted with performance-enhancing drugs was an aspirational goal at best for regulators until a saliva test was introduced to American racing at Hialeah in 1934. The principle of trainer responsibility for doping, however, was familiar much earlier. Following the death of Dr. Riddle from an apparent drug overdose after a race at Morris Park in May 1903, for example, there were rumors, but no facts, about what led to the horse's demise (see chapter 1). William Howell, the trainer of Dr. Riddle, made no defense to the allegations of doping and acknowledged that he alone was responsible for the horse's condition. He was ruled off, apparently for life, by stewards of the Jockey Club. Implicit in that action was an early application of New York's version of the absolute insurer rule.[1] There is no record of an appeal.

The Tom Smith affair was one of the first serious challenges to the absolute insurer rule by a Thoroughbred trainer whose license had been revoked (see chapters 9 and 10). Smith's case reached the appellate court, and even though he lost his appeal (see appendix 4), things turned out all right for "Silent Tom." He saddled Jet Pilot, winner of the 1947 Kentucky Derby for Maine Chance Farm, a few weeks after the one-year revocation had run its course and his license had been reinstated. He made it into the Hall of Fame at the National Museum of Racing in Saratoga—after a ridiculously long delay—in 2001.[2]

In concept, the absolute insurer rule was a stroke of genius, and the new saliva test made it workable. Assigning liability without fault to the trainer of record for a horse's positive drug test was a shrewd piece of rule making and a racing commissioner's dream. Based solely on an analytical test result, without the need to prove what really happened or who was responsible, racing commissions now had someone to blame in every doping incident, along with the authority to impose a severe penalty.

The absolute insurer rule also made good common sense. Who other than the trainer was in the best position to monitor the horses and be responsible for their condition? Whether the trainer was involved in the doping, either directly or indirectly, was irrelevant. Ironically, the charges against Tom Smith were not based on a positive postrace test result for a prohibited medication. In fact, Magnific Duel tested negative for any prohibited substances after winning the race in question. Instead, the liquid in a confiscated atomizer used to spray the nostrils of Magnific Duel was found to contain ephedrine.

In practice, and especially when courts got involved, the rule was on shaky constitutional ground. This was particularly true—and remains so—in those jurisdictions where racing commissions interpreted "absolute" liability without fault on the trainer's part to mean no provision of adequate notice to the accused trainer, no meaningful hearings, no legal representation, and no right of appeal. The US Constitution and many state constitutions impose more exacting requirements to satisfy the basics of due process.[3] A question that has dogged litigation over the absolute insurer rule for three-quarters of a century, however, is how much "process" is "due" to protect a trainer's rights.

Setting the legal wrangling aside, the absolute insurer rule remains "undeniably the most important in racing," according to attorney Robert L. Heleringer. It "go[es] to the heart of maintaining the integrity of the sport. Strict enforcement of the prohibition against the use of banned or controlled substances is paramount in the sport of horse racing."⁴ More importantly, the Smith case set the stage for decades of litigation over the constitutionality of the rule's most basic and controversial concept: trainers are guilty until proved innocent of doping, sometimes without any meaningful opportunity to defend themselves.

The debate revolves around a fundamental issue: what is the proper balance between a trainer's rights under the due process clause of the Fourteenth Amendment to the US Constitution and a state's right and obligation to protect the integrity of Thoroughbred racing? Constitutionality was raised by Tom Smith's attorneys but never seriously argued. This was likely because Smith received three administrative hearings (albeit two without legal counsel), notice of the charges against him (though arriving very late in the game), and the right to judicial appeal, which he exercised without success.⁵

Two hundred miles to the south, the balancing act became a fundamental question in a series of doping cases in Maryland. The situation was called a developing "crisis in racing."⁶

One of the first signs of the doping crisis was a feud brewing between the Maryland Racing Commission and the New York State Racing Commission over the competence of the latter's testing laboratory and its chief chemist C. E. Morgan. The New York lab had been testing saliva and urine samples for the Maryland commission for a decade with no problems or complaints. In mid-November 1945, however, Morgan began to see strange results from the Maryland samples. The Maryland specimens contained so much water that obtaining a reaction of any kind was impossible. "We have noticed that your saliva samples recently appear to be mostly water, containing very little saliva," Morgan wrote to the Maryland commission. "It is suggested that you investigate." As it turned out, no investigation was necessary. It was an inside job: the last batch of saliva samples from Maryland was bogus, taken from farm horses instead of Thoroughbreds.

The deception was orchestrated by Maryland Racing Commission chairman Charles E. Mahoney, an ally and sometimes accomplice of Harry Anslinger, director of the Federal Bureau of Narcotics, who complained that the New York lab had detected only four cases of performance-enhancing drugs during several years of testing. Convinced that the New York lab was lax, Mahoney secretly sent legitimate samples to Professor J. C. Munch at Temple University. According to Mahoney, Munch had already found five positive samples from horses racing at Pimlico on November 17 and 19, and the five trainers involved had been suspended pending a hearing.

Officials in New York refuted Maryland's claims. "We found two cases of stimulation of Maryland horses last month alone, before this mystifying change," a puzzled Morgan said. "Those were on October 16 and October 18, and we notified the Maryland commission of these. We found caffeine in one specimen and benzedrine in the other. The Maryland commission imposed penalties on the trainers concerned in both cases." Ashley T. Cole, chair of the New York Racing Commission, was more direct. In a letter, Cole instructed his counterpart in Maryland not to send any more samples to the New York lab because they would be returned untested. "Specimens which have been received at our laboratory since about the middle of November have not originated at Pimlico and do not seem to be intended to be accepted seriously," Cole explained.[7]

Regardless of whether the deception was warranted, Maryland was clearly in the throes of a doping crisis. Three trainers were accused of stimulating their horses early in the fall meeting at Pimlico, and two of those cases had already been adjudicated. James McGee, trainer for the Morris Wexler Stable, was suspended for a year after one of his horses tested positive for caffeine; J. J. Bauer, trainer for the Norwalk Stable, was ruled off for life after one of his horses tested positive for benzedrine. No action had yet been taken against J. Daliet "Dolly" Byers, who was charged with doping a steeplechaser named Cosey with benzedrine prior to a race on November 14.

Byers's hearing was scheduled for November 28, but his attorneys requested additional time to gather exculpatory evidence. Apparently, they found nothing to support the trainer's claim of innocence. On

December 10 he was suspended for a year. The difference between Byers's one-year suspension and Bauer's lifetime ban for similar violations was likely related to the prominence of Cosey's owner, Mrs. F. Ambrose Clark.[8] The stable had been one of the most successful in steeplechasing for several years, and the Clarks hardly seemed the type to dope their horses. "Mrs. Clark and her husband, a colorful, English squire type of character who wears gaiters and square, pearl-gray derby hats, have long been pillars of steeple chase racing," reporter Dan Parker wrote. "They represent the highest type associated with racing, being in the game only because of their love of horses and of the sport itself."[9]

When the Maryland Racing Commission started another round of hearings on December 10, L. Harold Sothoron, a state senator and counsel for the Maryland Horsemen's Protective Association, introduced a statement from the group. It suggested that the racing commission was taking unfair advantage of controversial statutory language and predicted that the commission's vigorous campaign against doping would "destroy" the state's horse racing industry. The issue was a single word in the regulation: "conclusive," when considering the impact of a positive drug test. The rule stated, "The fact that the analysis shows the presence of a drug shall be *conclusive* evidence either that there was knowledge of the fact on the part of the trainer or that he was guilty of carelessness in permitting it to be administered." The trainers' organization suggested that the rule be changed to read: "the presence of the drug shall be *prima facie* evidence."[10]

The difference might seem like minor legal semantics, but the consequences of the change would be significant. Whereas the former wording essentially guaranteed a suspension after a positive drug test, with no meaningful opportunity for accused trainers to present their case, the latter created only a presumption of liability that accused trainers could rebut with evidence of their innocence. The outcome of commission hearings based on the then-current rule was predetermined. *Before* a series of December hearings, Mahoney stated that the trainers would be suspended for a year and that the best outcome they could hope for would be to avoid longer terms.[11]

As the hearings continued and suspensions mounted, Byers and a few other trainers went to court. The first decision came in a combined lawsuit filed by owners W. L. Brann and Sylvester E. Labrot, their trainers E. A. Christmas and Clay Sutphin, trainer Robert W. Curran, and the American Trainers Association. Circuit judge Emory H. Niles found that the "conclusive evidence" provision of Rule 146(d) was invalid and denied accused trainers "due process of law" guaranteed by the US Constitution:

> No case has been found or cited to the court in which either a statutory or administrative rule establishing a conclusive presumption of guilt has been upheld, and in the face of the cases cited, the court has no hesitation in concluding that Rule 146(d), insofar as it established a conclusive presumption of the guilt of the trainer, is unconstitutional as violating both the Fourteenth Amendment to the Constitution of the United States and Article 23 of the Maryland Declaration of Rights.
>
> Namely, that where a presumption is made conclusive, it deprives the defendant of all opportunity to make a defense. The right to make a defense under reasonable conditions is a basic element of due process, and where a conclusive presumption of guilt is laid down, that right is taken away.[12]

The Maryland Racing Commission took a second legal hit a few days later when superior court judge Edwin T. Dickerson granted a petition from Dolly Byers and ordered the commission to "restore [Byers] to good standing as a trainer of race horses in the State of Maryland."[13] The commission appealed the Byers ruling and lost again in Maryland's highest court. The court of appeals wrote:

> From the fact that benzedrine was found in the saliva taken from the horse after the race, this irrebuttable presumption

[Rule 146(d)] is substituted for facts necessary to find the appellee [Byers] guilty under paragraph (d) of the rule. No facts or circumstances surrounding the stabling, care and attention given the horse after it arrived at Pimlico is to be considered.

The appellee's reputation as a clean, straight, decent jockey and trainer, which he has borne among the racing world for years, and which was attested to by many witnesses of high standing, is not to be considered in determining his guilt or innocence. In fact, the Commission attested to [Byers's] fine record as will appear from the remarks made by its Chairman, contained in the record. All of this, like so much chaff, is to be blown away as waste in the operation of the machinery set up under this paragraph [Rule 146(d)]. This irrebuttable presumption destroyed the right of [Byers] to offer evidence to establish his innocence. If this is "just," then the term "unjust" is without meaning.[14]

The day after the appellate court's decision was announced, a steeplechaser entered under the name All Flo was scheduled to compete in the first race at Bel Air. The stewards became suspicious about the horse's true identity, however, and after some investigation, it was discovered that All Flo was actually a ringer named Don't Delay. The horse was scratched and drug-tested, and the test was positive for an unidentified stimulant. Paul E. Middleton and William F. Mink, owners of Don't Delay, were charged with "conspiracy to defraud the Harford County Fair Association," which operated the Bel Air track.

Meanwhile, Mahoney was livid. He hit back at the courts, claiming that the two rulings left the racing commission powerless to take *any* action against doping. The saliva and urine tests had become virtually useless, he said. "Their only value now," Mahoney told reporters, "is to let us know what is going on. We can't do anything about it."[15] That was not true, of course. The decisions did not strip the racing commission of any power to enforce its regulations; however, it could no longer rely on automatic suspensions and would be bound by due process requirements. It would have to offer timely notice and meaningful hearings to trainers accused of doping. When Middleton and Mink entered guilty pleas and paid fines of $1,000 each, Mahoney took the opportunity to repeat his claim that the racing commission could do nothing about doping. But apparently, trying to run a ringer was within the commission's jurisdiction. The two owners were ruled off a few days later.[16]

Based on the lower court decisions, the licenses of Byers, Christmas, and Sutphin had been provisionally restored months earlier, pending the outcome of the appeal in the Byers case.[17]

While the appeal was pending, Mahoney announced a plan to provide immediate postrace saliva testing through a mobile laboratory. Federal Bureau of Narcotics commissioner Anslinger, who had led the drug raid at Arlington Park more than a decade earlier, endorsed the plan. "I have carefully reviewed the procedure recommended in your paper . . . and extend my congratulations for this skillful and ingenious proposal," Anslinger said. "I am in complete agreement with the enforcement angle and particularly with the safeguards which you have set up for those who will be held responsible. Your recommendation for a mobile laboratory is reasonable and practical. It eliminates many loopholes in connection with the handling of samples. It serves better to protect the chain of custody so necessary in this type of evidence."[18]

Anslinger's support for the program was not a surprise. Two years earlier, Anslinger had still been trying to catch jockey-turned-trainer Ivan Parke in a medication violation. He asked Mahoney to procure samples from Jet Pilot, a Maine Chance Farm horse running in the Preakness, even if the horse did not win the race (Jet Pilot finished third). Mahoney was happy to help, but the samples produced nothing that could be identified; they contained only crystals that Anslinger claimed resembled heroin, and he speculated that

the unidentified drug (if it was a drug) were remnants from an earlier stimulation. Anslinger later called Mahoney "the finest racing
official I knew. He stood for clean, honest sport of kings and he was
determined to clean out the rackets. His ideas were of the best and
were honest."[19] Mahoney also ran the racing commission with a
heavy hand, which Anslinger surely would have appreciated.

The full details of Mahoney's plan were not revealed until the fall
meeting at Laurel, and the new regulations almost caused a strike
among trainers. The original plan called for a mandatory receiving
barn where horses would be taken two hours before their scheduled
races. Members of the Horsemen's Benevolent and Protective Association (HBPA) voted unanimously to boycott the Laurel meeting if
the receiving barn was mandatory. After a six-hour meeting with
HBPA leaders, Mahoney announced some changes to the rules. The
receiving barn would remain mandatory, and after arriving at the
barn, all horses would be subject to a prerace drug test. If the test
was positive, the horse would be scratched, but the result would not
be "officially" announced, and the prerace samples would not be
retained. Upon arrival at the receiving barn, each horse would also be
assigned a "watchman" who would remain with the horse until it was
saddled and left the paddock. The watchman would not touch either
the horse or the tack. Perhaps the most important change was this
one: even if a horse tested positive for a prohibited substance after a
race, "the owner or trainer shall not be held responsible for such stimulation or drugging, no sample shall be preserved for the owner or
trainer, and no charges will be preferred." Trainers agreed with the
new conditions, and there was no strike.[20]

Baltimore Sun staff correspondent J. E. Wild reported on the
first appearance of the watchmen on opening day at Laurel:

> For the first time, the Governor's Horse Guards paraded
> here today, as the Laurel fall race meeting began.
> The first troop of His Excellency's only squadron of
> Horse Guards, nattily attired in horizon blue uniforms,

wearing gold and black brassards, swung down in front of the grandstand.

But they walked with their horses instead of riding as a National Guard troop might do. They walked because they are the men assigned to guard the horses from the time they reach the receiving barn until they go to the post in an effort to stamp out doping.[21]

The idea of shifting responsibility for a horse's condition from the trainer to the racing commission after the horse came under the commission's control in the receiving barn was a good one in theory, but the prerace test used was questionable. Detection of the presence of a prohibited medication was based on the Straub reaction in mice, a biological rather than a chemical test. Dr. Thomas Tobin, a veterinarian and professor at the University of Kentucky's Gluck Equine Research Center, is one of the leading researchers on performance-enhancing drugs in horse racing. He described the Straub reaction as a "vertical S-shaped curve in which a mouse injected with morphine carries its tail." The test is nonspecific, however; in addition to morphine, the reaction occurs in the presence of other similar substances.[22]

There were conflicting reports at the time regarding the utility of the mouse test. In an editor's note to the first annual report of the Thoroughbred Racing Protective Bureau (TRPB), two studies were mentioned. The first, authored by Drs. J. C. Munch (who tested Mahoney's secret samples during the feud with the New York testing lab) and A. B. Sloan, was presented at the annual meeting of the Pharmaceutical Society of the United States. The second was based on research conducted by Dr. Alfred Gellhorn and C. E. Morgan (chief chemist of the New York lab). "The Munch-Sloan report recommends the use of the test in racing work," the editor's note stated, "and the Gellhorn-Morgan study discredits it even as a preliminary screening process in racing work."[23]

In addition to uncertainty about the accuracy of the Straub test, prerace testing using mice was expensive. According to the *Balti-*

more Sun, each mouse cost $0.27, and three mice were required to confirm positive or negative test results for each horse tested. Figuring approximately 300 mice per day for Maryland's 150 racing days in 1947, the racing commission's proposed budget was around $12,000 for 45,000 mice. "Saliva from each horse is shot into the mice," the *Sun* reported. "They are kept in glass cages, and the pharmacologist [at an annual salary of $6,000] watches to see what reaction each mouse has. Mr. Mahoney said that the reaction takes place within five minutes after a mouse has been given a sample of the saliva. The mice are destroyed after one test."[24]

Appellate courts in the Tom Smith and Dolly Byers cases had differing opinions about whether New York's and Maryland's absolute insurer rules were valid exercises of a racing commission's authority or unconstitutional violations of due process. Over the next decades and into the present, the jurisprudence surrounding absolute insurer rules split along similar lines.[25]

A recent dispute in Kentucky showed such a split between the trial court and the appellate court in the same case. A filly named Kitten's Joy, owned by George Strawbridge Jr. and trained by H. Graham Motion, finished first in the 2015 Bewitch Stakes at Keeneland Race Course but was disqualified after a postrace test showed methocarbamol at a concentration of 2.9 nanograms per milliliter. The threshold for the drug in Kentucky at the time was 1.0 nanogram per milliliter. (A "threshold" can be a safe-harbor level for a drug approved for therapeutic use but not for racing. No action is taken when a horse tests positive for certain drugs at the threshold concentration or lower.)

The case went to an administrative hearing officer, who affirmed two violations and recommended that the Kentucky Horse Racing Commission (KHRC) suspend Motion's license for five days, fine him $500, and disqualify Kitten's Joy from the Bewitch. As a result of the disqualification, Strawbridge would forfeit a $90,000 purse. The KHRC adopted the hearing officer's recommendations regarding the fine and disqualification of Kitten's Joy but not the five-day suspension for Motion.

Strawbridge and Motion appealed the decision to Franklin (County) Circuit Court, a state trial court with jurisdiction over actions taken by state administrative agencies in Kentucky. In August 2017, two years after the Bewitch Stakes, Judge Thomas Wingate determined that the KHRC had ruled in an arbitrary fashion because there was no scientific evidence that such a small amount of methocarbamol (either the actual test result for Kitten's Joy or the threshold amount) could affect the outcome of a race or harm a horse. The decision was apparently based on testimony from Dr. Richard Sams, a KHRC witness, that the effects of such a small dose of the drug had not been established due to a lack of testing. Almost as an afterthought, though potentially far more significant, Judge Wingate then ruled that Kentucky's absolute insurer rule was unconstitutional because it was, in fact, absolute. The rule, he said, did not provide an opportunity for accused trainers to present evidence rebutting their liability.

There was some question at the time whether the KHRC would appeal Judge Wingate's decision and risk an appellate ruling in Motion's favor or simply let the trial court's ruling stand. Unlike a trial court decision, an appellate court ruling affirming the trial court would have value as legal precedent. Despite the risk, the KHRC appealed. On December 21, 2018, the Kentucky Court of Appeals affirmed the circuit court's jurisdiction to hear Strawbridge's and Motion's appeal but reversed the lower court on the substantive issues. "The Commission's expert witness, Dr. Richard Sams, testified that the pharmacological effects of methocarbamol were not fully understood," the court said. "Dr. Sams and other witnesses testified that when given large doses of methocarbamol, a horse's impairment can be seen with the naked eye. Dr. Sams also testified that it is unknown what subtle effects smaller doses have on the cellular level because there has been no scientific testing to determine such and it cannot be readily observable. Limiting the amount of a

drug in a horse's system that is not fully understood is a rational reason for a low threshold. This is especially true in light of the broad
powers given to the Commission."

As to the trial court's ruling on the constitutionality of the state's
absolute insurer rule, the court of appeals said that Strawbridge and
Motion "were provided with sufficient due process in this case." The
court agreed with the KHRC that the state's absolute insurer rule
"does not violate due process because [the KHRC] must still prove a
violation occurred before the trainer is penalized." Also, "the Commission must consider any mitigating circumstances presented by
the trainer. . . . Mitigating factors were in fact considered and discussed by the hearing officer in this case. These facts also underscore
the reason for our finding that the absolute insurer rule does not violate due process."[26] Based on a similar argument about administrative hearings, the appeals court in the Byers case in Maryland found
a due process violation, despite the fact that the state commission
had held hearings.

In February 2020 the Kentucky Supreme Court denied a discre-
tionary review of the appeals court's decision. A month later, on
March 25, the KHRC imposed a $500 fine on Motion and con-
firmed Strawbridge's loss of the Bewitch Stakes purse. "Obviously I
am disappointed that the Supreme Court of Kentucky did not agree
to hear the case as it did involve important issues related to drug
testing and rules," said attorney W. Craig Robertson, who represented Strawbridge and Motion. "In my opinion, nothing could be
more important than what we raised in this case. That being said,
there is nothing more we can do at this point."[27]

Although the constitutionality of the KHRC rule was eventually upheld, the commission had already taken corrective action
between the circuit court and appellate court rulings. Major changes
in the rules included the addition of language specifying that accused
trainers can present evidence in their own defense and that trainers
are responsible for the condition of their horses after a positive drug
test in the "absence of substantial evidence to the contrary."[28]

As of this writing, Robertson is one of the attorneys representing trainer Bob Baffert, whose 2021 Kentucky Derby winner Medina Spirit tested positive for trace amounts (above the threshold) of the corticosteroid betamethasone. Among the proposed mitigating factors is the argument that the positive tests from two samples resulted from the topical application of an ointment containing the drug for Medina Spirit's skin rash rather than a joint injection. (Only a joint injection with a "stand down" period of fourteen days is specifically addressed in the regulations.[29]) Baffert initially denied using betamethasone on Medina Spirit but later admitted that, until the day before the Derby, the horse had been treated with an ointment called Otomax that contains the drug.[30] On February 1, 2022, the KHRC formally disqualified Medina Spirit. Two months earlier, the horse suffered fatal injuries during a workout at Santa Anita.[31]

With the status of a true absolute insurer rule still subject to debate in the courts, attorney and scholar Bennet Liebman published a comprehensive law review article on the subject. After reviewing the history of the rule and the applicability of strict liability in other nonracing situations, Liebman offered a compelling argument for state racing commissions to abandon the absolute insurer standard and adopt a rebuttable presumption of trainer liability. "Eliminating the absolute insurer rule and utilizing the rebuttable presumption of trainer responsibility will inject a measure of fairness into the system by helping to protect the innocent trainer from punishment," Liebman wrote. "At the same time, in the majority of cases, the rebuttable presumption will assure that there is adequate responsibility for drug positives. There will be certainty of punishment, and by reintroducing the factor of trainer intent into the penalty equation, the elimination of the absolute insurer rule can help establish a system that adequately deters racetrack licensees from intentional misconduct with penalties that fit the crime."[32]

12

The Thoroughbred Racing
Protective Bureau and the
Defection of Dr. Kater

J. Edgar Hoover, director of the Federal Bureau of Investigation (FBI), loved Thoroughbred races; he loved the sport and the gambling to the point that one of his biographers suggested that his passion reached the level of addiction. That addiction played out at Hialeah, Del Mar, Bowie, Pimlico, Charles Town, Belmont Park, and other tracks, where for forty years Hoover and his companion Clyde Tolson routinely enjoyed private tables and complimentary box seats.

"An in-house joke," Anthony Summers wrote, "had it that the FBI agent whose hair grayed fastest was the man who had to get the Director to the track through rush-hour traffic. Headquarters staff were dispatched to the Library of Congress to dig out racing information. . . . Racing got Edgar overexcited. After a run of bad luck one afternoon, former Speaker Tip O'Neill recalled, he took another man's car and drove it all the way back to Washington."[1]

A fair question is why Harry Anslinger, who knew next to nothing about horse racing, took on the job of ridding the backstretches of narcotics and cocaine in the 1930s, instead of Hoover. There are several reasons for what seems like a gross oversight. Most important was the mandate of the Federal Bureau of Narcotics (FBN) to enforce the Harrison Act, while the FBI dealt with other crimes.

Also, Anslinger had already linked organized crime to drug trafficking and racetrack corruption early in his tenure at the FBN.

Hoover, in contrast, had questioned the Mafia's existence for years. Then, on November 17, 1957, he read in his Sunday newspaper about a mob conclave in Apalachin, a village in Tioga County, New York. The meeting attracted dozens of mafiosi from major crime families across the country. The purpose was to emphasize the "organized" part of organized crime and work out a number of intramural conflicts. A state trooper got suspicious about the number of limousines heading to the home of Joseph Barbara Sr., a soft drink distributor with a long rap sheet, and Barbara's order for an unusually large number of prime steaks from a local butcher. New York State Police sergeant Edgar Croswell, another officer, and two FBN agents set up a roadblock on the only road leading to Barbara's property. Word about the roadblock spread quickly, and Barbara's guests "panicked and spilled out of the house by the dozens." With the driveway obstructed, many of them tried to flee on foot, struggling through trees and brush until they reached the road—only to be seized by reinforcements called in by Croswell. As Croswell later recalled, "These middle-aged men looked pretty silly as they stumbled through the foliage: 'Some of them lost their hats and they were full of cockleburs.'"[2]

Hoover was utterly blindsided by the Apalachin fiasco. One biographer wrote: "According to a headquarters official at the time, the FBI not only had no idea that the hoodlums were going to meet but didn't even know who they were." A total of sixty-three people were "rounded up, identified, and released." Another forty or so stayed in Barbara's house and avoided interrogation. Most of the people detained claimed they had heard that Barbara was not feeling well and had decided to visit. Showing up on the same day was just a coincidence.[3]

Hoover and the FBI somehow weathered the public relations crisis, and the bureau began its war on the Mafia in earnest, a quarter century after Anslinger's covert racetrack investigations. Either Hoover was ignorant of the Mafia for all that time, which is difficult to believe, or he chose to turn a blind eye to the possible criminal involvement of some of the people he socialized with at the races and elsewhere.

It was no surprise, then, that Hoover was having lunch in the club-house at Pimlico on Wednesday, November 29, 1945. Perhaps it was a slow day at the FBI. After the first race, America's top cop wandered over to an adjacent table and sat down with Harry Parr III, president of Pimlico, and Alfred G. Vanderbilt. Their conversation involved a job offer and a question: was Hoover interested in leaving the FBI to head a new organization to police Thoroughbred racing?

After the FBN's backstretch raids in 1933, many racing officials argued that they could clean up the sport on their own and did not need federal oversight. Anslinger threatened federal intervention if the self-policing failed, which it did, but government action never materialized. By the mid-1940s, despite racing's popularity with fans, it was evident that the sport was facing other major threats. The most pressing was a growing belief among bettors that horse racing was not operating on the up-and-up, and it was becoming obvious that state racing commissions lacked the ability and the resources to deal with the problem on an individual basis. Some of the reasons for a skeptical view of racing were doping, ringers (good horses entered under different names to hide their talent), and no way to reliably identify undesirable individuals applying for licenses and frequenting racetracks.

"Racing was in danger of losing its patronage," Parr later explained in an annual Thoroughbred Racing Protective Bureau (TRPB) report in the mid-1960s:

> All sports were being held suspect because of prevalent scandals of bribery and game-fixing. Racing had its ringer cases, stimulation cases, jockeys who were trying to fix races, unscrupulous trainers and shady owners. The TRPB was to reveal that the backstretch was rife with loose characters

having police records ranging from petty larceny to arson. Touts and bookmakers roamed the grandstands of the country's tracks victimizing the racegoers, cheating the tracks and the States of revenue. There was only one way to rid racing of all these ills, if possible, and that was to do it ourselves.

Why racing itself? Because independent track security and supervision at that time was, for one reason or another, insufficient and inadequate.

Security was insufficient, perhaps, because during the War, manpower was extremely short. Inadequate for the simple reason that independent track security at that time was able only to cope with hirelings, bookmakers' runners and small operators among the touts. Many of these were arrested daily and chased off tracks, but the next day somebody else would be operating in their place.[4]

Parr was also president of a new trade organization formed after World War II, the Thoroughbred Racing Associations (TRA), and he set out to identify someone to lead a national private security agency. J. Edgar Hoover was the obvious choice, given his parallel interests in law enforcement and racing, but he turned down the offer. Instead, Hoover recommended Spencer Drayton Sr., a former FBI agent who had recently left the bureau to work at an advertising agency. Drayton accepted the offer and signed on to head the newly created Thoroughbred Racing Protective Bureau in January 1946.[5] "I was a $2 bettor before I ever became associated with the TRA," Drayton told *Daily Racing Form* reporter Oscar Otis in 1971. "I saw my first race at Timonium just after I had joined the FBI. The boss, J. Edgar Hoover, was a race fan even then, finding it ideal relaxation. Anyway, I figured if the boss liked it, racing must have something special in the way of appeal."[6]

Drayton had worked primarily in administration and accounting during his tenure with the FBI; now he would have a free hand at the TRPB to organize Thoroughbred racing's first national police force. For more than three decades, Drayton would be a powerful figure in the racing community. "Drayton will have absolute and complete authority to engage the necessary personnel and direct their operations to deal with any dishonest practices affecting racing and to prosecute all offenders," Parr said when he announced Drayton's appointment. The TRPB would "supersede any police agency at any of the tracks which are members of the TRA," Parr explained. "The squad will work on and off the tracks. Whatever evidence they find of evil-doing they will turn over to the respective tracks, or to the affected states, for punitive action."[7]

Drayton's initial hires were FBI agents—some retired, others looking for a change of scenery—and he modeled the TRPB along the lines of the FBI, with regional departments in New York, Boston, Baltimore, Miami, Chicago, and Los Angeles.[8] He recognized doping as one of several immediate concerns, and a few months later, TRPB agents Joseph Sullivan and Francis Gleason made the agency's first significant collar at the old Jamaica track on Long Island.

A horse named Old Westbury had a positive drug test after winning a race on March 9, 1946, at Tropical Park in Florida. Trainer Clarence Reynolds and James Newton, Old Westbury's groom, were arrested in Florida. Both entered guilty pleas there on October 17 and received suspended sentences. The TRPB's investigation of the race also connected veterinarian Harold O. Sheetz to the doping, and he was taken into custody at Jamaica a few days later. Dr. Sheetz was held as a fugitive until he could be returned to Florida to stand trial.[9] The detention of Dr. Sheetz was a successful exercise of the TRPB's national reach, which was why the agency had been formed in the first place. Two days later, James Scaffidi, owner of Old Westbury, was arrested in Philadelphia. In 1935 he had received a two- to five-year sentence and a $1,000 fine in New Jersey on "lottery charges."[10]

By 1955, Drayton was confident enough to assert that "racing today is the most cleanly run sport in the world."[11] The next year, the TRA published a booklet extolling Drayton and the agency and highlighting the "fine record of the TRPB in protecting the interests of Thoroughbred Racing at our member tracks through the country." The TRPB's success stories included wins against doping, a forger who doctored pari-mutuel tickets, an attempt to fix a race by using a homemade air gun to shoot a pelleted depressant into the flank of the favorite (Horse of the Year Assault), the bogus registration of foals supposedly sired by a stallion that was dead, and a Pennsylvania man's illegal betting shop.[12] The doping case was typical of the success stories:

> Stimulating a horse, to give it greater speed, by administering a drug to an animal before a race is one of the most serious crimes in racing. Therefore, when the TRPB agents at Rockingham Park in New Hampshire heard, through confidential sources, that Apprentice Jockey Nicholas Restivo was going to attempt to stimulate a horse named King Eric they quickly moved in to prevent it and to capture Restivo.
>
> An agent was "planted," disguised as a groom, in a tack room opposite King Eric's stall. He rigged a shaving mirror on the tack room wall so that it showed the entire area of King Eric's stall. With this device, he could keep his back to the stall and appear to be working and not paying any attention to the comings and goings outside the tack room.
>
> Nothing happened for some time, then shortly after noon, just when the TRPB agent was beginning to think the stimulation story was just a baseless rumor, Jockey Restivo appeared in the mirror, heading for King Eric's stall.
>
> The agent kept his back to the shed row down which Restivo strode, observing him in the glass.
>
> He approached the wire netting of the stall and called out to the horse, then pushed his hand through the wires and held it toward the horse. The agent moved swiftly and silently from the tack room, between the shed rows and up behind Restivo. Before the jockey could move, the agent

had seized his arm, pulled it back from inside the stall and grabbed the piece of sugar Restivo held in his hand.

Laboratory analysis of the sugar showed that it had been saturated in a solution of strychnine and brucine, central nervous stimulants.

Restivo confessed that he was hard up for money and hoped to win some by stimulating King Eric and betting on him.

He received an 18-month suspension from the New Hampshire Racing Commission and was successfully prosecuted in the Salem, New Hampshire courts on a charge of "attempting maliciously to interfere with or tamper with a horse used for racing purposes."[13]

There were, of course, rough spots during the TRPB's early years. One of the people who attracted Drayton's attention during the mid-1950s was Dr. Alex Harthill, a young Louisville veterinarian suspected of participating in a doping incident at the Fair Grounds in New Orleans. Drayton supposedly became interested in Harthill after the veterinarian was suspended in Illinois over the doping of a horse named Mr. Black. The horse had won the Grassland Handicap at Washington Park three days after being given a medication containing a stimulant. At a stewards' hearing, Harthill said he had given the horse a stimulant because it had "tightened up" and could not urinate. He admitted the mistake and was suspended for sixty days, not because he administered the stimulant but because he failed to notify anyone about the medication, including the trainer and the racing commission. Dr. Harthill then took the racing commission to court, and a judge granted a stay of the suspension to "a man of Harthill's stature pending a full hearing later."[14] There is no record of a subsequent hearing, and when Dr. Harthill applied for a license in Illinois three years later, it was granted.

In the *Louisville Courier-Journal* on March 6, 1955, a photograph of Dr. Harthill appeared with the cutline "Louisville Vet in

Trouble Again." The accompanying article reported his arrest in New Orleans for doping horses and public bribery. The charges arose from the alleged doping of four horses in January and February 1955. Harthill was arrested along with Cassius Clay, director of the Food and Drug Division of the Louisiana State Board of Health, and trainer Harvey H. Vanier. "I figured we had enough evidence without letting the public be duped again," Major Aaron Edgecombe of the Louisiana State Police explained. Of the four horses, Mrs. L. E. Vanier's Smasher was the only winner. A fifth horse suspected of being doped was scratched.

Harthill and trainer Vanier were charged with "unnatural stimulation" of racehorses, allegedly with caffeine; Harthill and Clay were charged with attempting to bribe a public official—in this case, a testing laboratory employee. Drayton told reporters he had been watching Harthill for several months, ever since the alleged doping of a horse named Tonight at Keeneland Race Course in Kentucky and the veterinarian's short-lived suspension in Illinois. Drayton claimed he had set a trap that produced "adequate evidence" against the veterinarian, including recorded conversations between Harthill and Vanier.[15]

The evidence was not as adequate as Drayton thought. The case against Harthill and Clay went to trial a year later, but it ended in a mistrial when the prosecution asked to amend the charges. The second trial a month later included testimony from Cecil M. Shilstone, a partner in Shilstone Laboratories, which performed drug testing for the state. Shilstone claimed he and Clay had discussed a plan to destroy samples from certain horses to prevent officials from discovering the horses had been doped. He testified that Clay would bet $100 on the doped horses and give Shilstone one-third of the winnings.

H. O. Couvillon, a former employee at Shilstone Laboratories, testified that Clay told him "it would be worthwhile" to destroy selected urine and saliva samples. He testified that Clay gave him the numbers of the horses whose samples were to be destroyed.

Dr. Robert Copeland, a prominent central Kentucky veterinarian, testified for the defense. He said that caffeine, the drug reportedly given to Smasher, would not make the horse run faster than usual and would not give a horse increased stamina.

Other evidence included a statement given to the police and apparently signed by Clay that Dr. Harthill "wanted to give some race horses a caffeine stimulant and they did not want to get caught," as well as wire recordings of conversations between Harthill, Clay, and Shilstone. Nevertheless, a five-person jury acquitted both men.[16] Dr. Harthill would later figure prominently in the debate over the drug Lasix and the disqualification of 1968 Kentucky Derby winner Dancer's Image.[17]

Around the same time as the trial in New Orleans, the TRPB faced an existential threat from an unlikely source: *Life* magazine, one of the country's most popular periodicals. Dr. John McA. Kater, formerly the TRPB's chief scientist, wrote a scathing article for *Life* suggesting that the agency had done little to reduce doping during the first decade of its existence.[18]

Intrigued by a wave of swamp fever (also known as equine infectious anemia) at northeastern tracks in 1947, Dr. Kater studied the outbreak, focusing on how the disease spread among Thoroughbreds in New England. The usual mode of transmission from horse to horse, with mosquitoes and horseflies as the vectors, was not efficient enough to account for the large number of sick and dying horses, so he looked for a human vector. What he found was an odd distribution of the disease between geldings ("nearly one gelding out of every three came down with the disease") and ungelded colts and horses ("the proportion was only one out of eight"). Gelding made horses more tractable, Kater noted, but it also "weakens their spirit." The real problem, he decided, was a shift in performance-enhancing drugs from narcotics and cocaine to the hormone testosterone. He wrote:

A much publicized drug called testosterone, the male hormone, was available to trainers looking for a way to put more spirit into geldings and thus make them win. As a physiologist, I doubt that it would actually help a horse run a better race, but the swamp fever epidemic indicates, I am convinced, that a lot of racing people felt otherwise. They must have figured that a shot of testosterone administered with a hypodermic needle would impart to their geldings the fire of the stallion—and a man furtively doping a horse would probably not bother to sterilize his needle.[19]

Dr. Kater did not identify any particular trainers he suspected of going through the shed row spreading swamp fever with a dirty hypodermic needle and a syringe filled with testosterone, but one name stands out: H. G. Bedwell, trainer of Sir Barton, the first Triple Crown winner. Plagued throughout his career by suspicions of doping, Bedwell lost a total of fourteen horses during the outbreak, more than any other trainer.[20]

Ironically, around the time Dr. Kater was investigating the doping of geldings with testosterone, two Horses of the Year, Calumet Farm's Armed (1947) and King Ranch's Assault (1946), met in a $100,000 match race at Belmont Park. Armed, a gelding, led for the entire 1¼ miles and won by eight lengths. There is no suggestion that Armed was doped with testosterone or anything else, showing that some geldings need no chemical help.

Dr. Kater left the TRPB in 1953 "in disgust," he wrote in *Life*:

The swamp fever epidemic opened my eyes to the doping menace and I spent most of my time studying it for the next seven years. I can flatly state that it is still easy to dope a horse and get away with it—the saliva-urine test and the TRPB notwithstanding. . . .

Since the late '30s at a few tracks and since the '40s at most of them, both tests have been used. A few tests have showed up positive and the trainers promptly suspended. But mostly, the tests have been used by racing to advertise how free it now is from the doping evil.

The facts are quite otherwise. Any smart operator can get around the saliva and urine tests—and the TRPB knows it because I kept saying so inside the TRPB for years. The tests never were a real safeguard against doping and they still are not as of this day. . . .

Who is to blame for the whole sham of dope-prevention in racing? It is certainly not the fault of the breeders of horses, who detest the very thought of filling a horse's blood with some foul dope that will help him make money for a crooked owner at the peril of his future or even his life. (All dopes are dangerous and are probably never or only very rarely used on really top horses.) It is not the fault of the many fine sportsmen who own and train horses and would themselves never descend to doping, which amounts to unfair competition against them in the struggle for purse money. It is not the fault of the track owners, who must naturally frown on crookedness in racing as a threat to their investments. Indeed, I am sure that the disclosures I have made here will be as great a shock to many track officials as to the public.

The people I blame are the men who know but cover up: the front men of racing who have managed to make a fine living by persuading their employers that everything is sweetness and light.[21]

Dr. Kater's comments may have been in retaliation for the TRPB's failure to fund his request for a comprehensive drug research program. Still, the article in *Life* from a recognized expert and TRPB insider had the ring of truth.

Racing's supporters responded as one might expect. Spencer Drayton said: "Many of Kater's statements are inaccurate, obsolete, or grossly exaggerated. . . . There is no evidence . . . to substantiate his conclusion that doping is widespread and undetected. . . . Metrazol is now routinely detected. . . . If Kater or anyone else thinks he can dope along the lines suggested in this article and get away with it, he had better not try it." Dr. Roger W. Truesdail, chairman of the executive board of the Association of Official Racing Chemists, noted that the Kater article "contains many half-truths, innuendoes, and completely erroneous statements." Ashley T. Cole, chairman of the New York State Racing Commission, observed: "The general scheme of Kater's paper is one which he has presented to several people here, including myself, that chemists are unable to invariably detect drugs in saliva and urine of horses, and that that only can be done by pharmacologists, of which he is one. . . . Kater's paper is simply the reaction of a man who has failed to sell his services." These comments appeared in an editorial in *Blood-Horse* magazine, which stated:

> However much the article is calculated to exaggerate the extent of malpractice, it should not be dismissed with nothing but refutation and resentment. . . . The best refutation of the Kater article is not in any attack on the man himself, but in a detailed statement of the procedures used in protecting the sport against doping, and of the research through which new procedures are developed as they become necessary. Improvement of those procedures should be, and is, a primary concern for racing authorities. Kater's blast appears an unduly emotional attack, but it should be answered with fact, not fury.[22]

Two months later, at the annual convention of the National Association of State Racing Commissioners, Drayton explained that the TRPB has always dealt in facts. "No other sport has devoted as much attention or has invested as much money as Thoroughbred racing in its determined efforts to keep their sport clean and to merit the confidence of millions of fans. No other sport goes to such extremes to see that wrongdoers are prosecuted and expelled."[23]

Although it was a long time coming, the TRPB was racing's first and best response to Anslinger's challenge for racing to police itself. Of

Drayton's three original mandates for the TRPB—rein in doping, eliminate ringers, and identify bad actors—the agency's success in curbing doping is debatable. Doping scandals, some of them increasingly sophisticated, continue today. Success in achieving the other two goals is unquestionable. In 1947 the TRPB instituted a lip-tattoo system to positively identify horses. That system worked well for decades until it was replaced by microchip identification in 2020.[24] Over the years, the TRPB has conducted many thousands of interviews and investigations and compiled a vast repository of information that can be used by racing commissions to identify wrongdoers and determine whether to grant licenses.

More recently, except for major events like the Triple Crown races and the Breeders' Cup, day-to-day racing has morphed from a popular in-person activity for fans and bettors into an online wagering platform that requires a major shift in security and integrity procedures. The TRPB has changed along with racing to emphasize wagering networks and business interests. It is worth noting that while "race-fixing" receives at least a general mention in the TRPB's mission statement, specific antidoping efforts do not:

1. To provide and/or manage integrity analysis and security services for TRA racetrack wagering networks and those wagering networks for all other clients under contract.
2. To manage, administer, and safeguard the horse identification tattoo program.
3. To address integrity matters that have a negative impact on the business interests of TRA tracks and upon request to conduct a due diligence background examination whenever a TRA member track is evaluating new business associates and enterprises or hiring key employees.
4. To concentrate attention on those areas which significantly affect the integrity of racing, including race-fixing, horse substitution, hidden ownership, and organized crime influences/association with licensees.

5.   To create and operate a modernized, effective system for the collection and evaluation of information on matters affecting the integrity of horse racing.
6.   To utilize the investigative, analytic, and information resources of the TRPB in the development of new business opportunities within the equine and racing industry at large.[25]

In an interview with *Paulick Report* editor-in-chief Natalie Voss, one of the best investigative reporters covering horse racing today, past TRPB president Paul Berube attributed the change in strategy to smaller crowds at the tracks that require smaller security forces, a shift from on-track betting to offtrack and online wagering, and changes in track ownership. "When I started and through a good bit of my career you had some real leaders and giants who were in the TRA," Berube said, "the big names in racing and the good names in racing. And mostly, the tracks were privately owned. And today, obviously, the landscape of ownership has changed. It started even when I was president, the diminishment and erosion of the commitment to have a viable TRPB. Since 2005, it's just faded away."[26]

In the background, always near the action, was Dr. Alex Harthill, Thoroughbred racing's controversial version of Dr. Jekyll and Mr. Hyde.

Part IV

NSAIDs, Lasix, and Steroids

13

The Derby and the Doctor

Exploring the history of performance-enhancing drugs and their place in Thoroughbred racing from the 1890s into the twenty-first century is complicated by constant shifts in the game and the players. Medications used to boost horses, testing protocols, rules and regulations, and public attitudes toward doping change; most important, the owners, trainers, bettors, and fans change. Yet it seems that the dopers are always one step ahead of the regulators. The racing commissions and the chemists are forced to play catch-up, developing tests to detect whatever new drugs start to show up at racetracks. Coming up with a reliable test for a new drug can take months, which means that, for a while at least, the dopers are free to cheat.

Jumping from decade to decade and from one doping scandal to another without a unifying presence can be a dizzying ride. No single individual has been around long enough to connect all the parts of this 130-plus-year narrative, but one name keeps popping up from the late 1940s until his death in 2005. Central Kentucky veterinarian Alexander Harthill was unquestionably brilliant, one of the best of his time. He was also a rogue and a scoundrel, if the rumors and stories, some of them coming from Harthill himself, are to be believed. Perhaps he was both or neither. Whatever the truth, the legend—most of it, at least—lives on.[1]

If anyone was born to be a veterinarian, it was Alex Harthill. His great-grandfather had been a veterinarian in Scotland during the nineteenth century, and his grandfather and father maintained veterinary practices in Louisville, Kentucky. Alex started college the day after he finished prep school, and he found work almost immediately after graduating from Ohio State University in March 1948 with a degree in veterinary medicine.

Finding clients can be a struggle, especially for a new vet school graduate, but Dr. Harthill had connections in the stratosphere of Thoroughbred racing. Hall of Fame trainers Ben Jones and Jimmy Jones, a father-and-son team that sent out a succession of champions and Triple Crown winners for Calumet Farm, were friends of Dr. Harthill's father, and the new graduate made a quick transition from the halls of academia directly to Calumet's shed row. One of the first horses he treated was Citation, winner of the Triple Crown just a few weeks after Harthill graduated from Ohio State.

That same spring, Dr. Harthill saved the life of Ponder, a Calumet two-year-old colt that had been stabbed in the chest by a groom carrying a pitchfork. A serious infection set in, and for days it was unclear whether Ponder would even survive, let alone race. He did both, winning the Kentucky Derby the next year. One of many Calumet legends, Ponder was the son of Derby winner Pensive, and he sired a Derby winner himself (Needles). Dr. Harthill later explained how the injury happened:

> A groom started in to clean [Ponder's] stall and had a pitchfork in his hand. As grooms do, he ducked underneath the half door. When he went to straighten up, he saw Ponder rear and start to come down on him. In a reflex action, he hit him in the chest with the business end of that pitchfork.
>
> The colt's chest was punctured, he swelled up and got something like blood-poisoning. That was before antibiotics were as efficient as they are today, and he was in desperate shape. We worked with poultices and everything else we could find and it took several days before we knew he was safe.[2]

Dr. Harthill also worked miracles for Warner L. Jones, owner of Hermitage Farm. In the spring of 1949 Harthill was called to treat a pregnant mare named Isolde. She was in serious trouble: her foal was dead and positioned in such a way that it could not be delivered normally. Isolde was a very well-bred broodmare that Jones did not want to lose, but two other veterinarians had already given up, and her prospects for survival were grim. Harthill performed a fetotomy using a thin, flexible wire with sharp teeth to methodically dismember the dead foal in utero. The gruesome procedure took hours to complete, and it was exhausting for the young veterinarian, but his heroic efforts saved the mare's life. Isolde recovered quickly, and later in the year she was healthy enough to be bred to the stallion Royal Gem. That breeding produced Dark Star, winner of the 1953 Kentucky Derby and the only horse to defeat Native Dancer.

Word of the young veterinarian with extraordinary skills spread quickly, and soon Harthill's name was linked with one good horse after another. His ascension from just another racetrack veterinarian to the "Derby Doc" had begun. He was the attending veterinarian for more than two dozen Kentucky Derby winners, including Triple Crown winners Citation and Affirmed, as well as Hill Gail, Dark Star, Swaps, Iron Liege, Tim Tam, Carry Back, Decidedly, Northern Dancer, Lucky Debonair, Proud Clarion, Spectacular Bid, Lil E. Tee, and Grindstone. At the same time, Harthill was developing a reputation for chicanery, including allegations of doping, race fixing, hidden ownership, and practicing veterinary medicine in states without the proper temporary license.

In 1954 Texas oilman Sam E. Wilson Jr. complained to the FBI after one of his horses won a race at Hawthorne in Chicago. According to Wilson, Harthill had fixed the race and wanted to be paid $1,500. Wilson later recanted, claiming the $1,500 had been a commission on the sale of some horses. The FBI investigation was dropped.

Dr. Harthill came under scrutiny again later that year when the winner of a race at Keeneland Race Course in Kentucky tested positive for a prohibited stimulant. A groom testified that Harthill had injected the horse with something prior to the race, but the veterinarian denied any wrongdoing. He claimed the shots were koagamin and vitamin K, permitted medications often used in horses that bled during a race. The trainer and groom were handed sixty-day suspensions by the Kentucky State Racing Commission, but Harthill was not disciplined.

Still later in 1954, Dr. Harthill was suspended for sixty days by the Illinois Racing Board after a horse named Mr. Black tested positive for a prohibited stimulant. A court later overturned that suspension. Then authorities in Louisiana claimed that Harthill was involved in a multihorse drugging and bribery scheme at the Fair Grounds in 1955, but he was acquitted on all charges by a five-person jury (see chapter 12).

In October 1980 thieves supposedly stole Dr. Harthill's Cadillac from a service garage. A few days later, an anonymous caller reported to the sheriff's office in Hartford County, Maryland, that a satchel had been found in a parking lot. The bag contained a set of clippers, several small glass vials, and Dr. Harthill's racing license. Chemical analysis determined that the vials contained Voltaren, a product manufactured in Germany that had supposedly been found in postrace drug tests.[3] Voltaren, the trade name for the drug diclofenac, is a powerful nonsteroidal anti-inflammatory drug (NSAID) that treats pain and inflammation. The drug was later approved for over-the-counter use by human arthritis sufferers.[4]

Noted trainer and racing official John Veitch recounted a slightly different version of the stolen Cadillac story. According to Veitch, the police had been tipped off that Dr. Harthill had illegal drugs in his car (Voltaren was legal in Canada but not in the United States). Harthill claimed the car had been stolen, he had never seen the drugs, and he was being framed. Harthill "was a brilliant veterinarian," said Veitch. "He loved the edge. I don't care where the medication was made, whether it was in Europe or Canada or Mexico, Alex was right on it—and often before it was legal in the United States. Day or night, if you called Alex, and if he liked you, he was there for you."[5]

For better or (possibly) worse, Dr. Harthill started his practice at a time when there was a paradigm shift in the use of performance-enhancing drugs in Thoroughbred racing. Plant-based narcotics (opium, heroin, and morphine) and stimulants (cocaine and ephedrine) had been in vogue during the 1890s, and based on Harry Anslinger's investigations and the hearings related to Tom Smith's license revocation, they were still being used in the 1930s and 1940s. By then, however, these "natural" drugs were being replaced by more sophisticated and effective drugs developed in laboratories.

Amphetamine was one of the first drugs to be synthesized in a laboratory during the 1920s. It was used extensively during World War II to combat fatigue in ground and air forces, and by the 1950s, athletes were experimenting with the drug. Anabolic steroids were introduced around the same time, and testosterone was already being used in horse racing by the late 1940s (see chapter 12).

In 1990 Dr. Harthill reportedly told another veterinarian that he had treated Northern Dancer with Lasix before the horse won the 1964 Kentucky Derby. Lasix was prohibited in Kentucky at the time.[6] Harthill may have been one of the first racetrack veterinarians, if not *the* first, to use the drug. Repercussions from the introduction of Lasix to horse racing are still being felt. Writing in 2009, blogger Jim Squires called it "the most incendiary and controversial of the remaining drug issues that plague horse racing." He noted, "Lasix is a testament to both the nefarious genius of Harthill and the likely unstoppable quest for whatever undetectable and not yet prohibited magic that can be worked to gain an edge in the Derby."[7]

The investigations of Dr. Harthill continued at Churchill Downs, Oaklawn Park, and other tracks over the years, but suspicion and innuendo never led to any hard evidence of wrongdoing. Harthill shrugged off the rumors of his misdeeds as ingenious tall tales fueled by professional jealousy and hostile reporters. His supporters—and there were many—probably agreed. Asked about those rumors by one reporter, Harthill said they were figments of the imagination:

I was at Monmouth Park one time working on a horse and the groom says to me, "have you ever heard of Doc Harthill?" I said, "yeah, I've heard of him," and the groom goes on to tell me a story about Doc Harthill having shown up at some track in New England the night before a certain horse was . . . run, having gone into the stall, and how the horse went out the next day and not only won but set a track record. When he was finished the groom said to me, "that Harthill, he must be something else, huh?"

What else could I say? I just laughed and agreed with him. But truthfully, most of these tales are just that, racetrack tales. I guess I should be flattered but I've got family and friends like anybody else and I wouldn't want to have them hurt or shamed because of things said about me that have no foundation.[8]

There were some allegations, however, that Dr. Harthill could not shrug off as "racetrack tales."

Early in 1995 the Drug Enforcement Administration (DEA) visited Dr. Harthill's office at Churchill Veterinary Supply Company, 3737 South Fourth Street, Louisville, as part of a routine investigation into his record-keeping practices for controlled medications. Both the DEA and the individual states have comprehensive requirements for tracking controlled substances in veterinary practices, and the penalties for failure to follow the regulations can be severe. "Simply put, DEA controlled substance logbooks must contain sufficient information to maintain accurate records of your controlled substances," explained Jack Teitelman, a retired DEA supervisory special agent and CEO of Titan Group, DEA Compliance Experts. "If the DEA knocks on your door and you can tell them with the utmost confidence the whereabouts of every drug that enters your doors, goes into your safe, is administered to an animal, or is sent to the reverse distributor, you will never have a problem."[9]

When the DEA agents knocked on Dr. Harthill's door, they discovered serious discrepancies in his records and evidence of unusual drug purchasing activities. On May 8, 1995, a criminal case was initiated against Harthill in the US District Court for the Western District of Kentucky, but it was terminated three days later. Proceedings for the case are listed in a federal database as "not available." Seven months later, a civil complaint was filed in the same court. The defendants were Dr. Harthill and his wife, Mary Alice Harthill (referred to only as "et al." in the case name), who was the co-owner of Churchill Veterinary Supply.

The complaint alleged that Dr. Harthill was ordering unusually large quantities of controlled drugs typically not used in horses, including thousands of sleeping pills, narcotic painkillers, and amphetamines. Between August 1991 and September 1994, Harthill ordered approximately four thousand Halcion pills and another two hundred in 1995. He reportedly told DEA agents that the sleeping pills were for his and his wife's personal use. Veterinarians are licensed to prescribe drugs for animals but not for humans. Harthill also reportedly ordered quantities of methadone and oxycodone, tightly controlled painkillers. The complaint charged that the Harthills kept no records of the drugs, that some drugs were missing, and that falsified records had been submitted to the DEA.

"It's all over bookkeeping," the *Louisville Courier-Journal* quoted Dr. Harthill as explaining:

I'm a busy vet, but I'm not a very good bookkeeper.

I prescribe various drugs after surgery to keep horses quiet. Some of them are quite innocuous but nevertheless are controlled substances. It's just hard for me to remember if I gave them one or two pills.

This has been going on for over a year. And I've tried to be as cooperative as possible. I didn't do anything wrong and I won't do anything wrong.[10]

The lawsuit sought $2.5 million in civil penalties and a court order requiring Dr. Harthill to keep accurate records of controlled substances. Two years and three months later, after seventy-eight court filings, extensions for discovery and depositions, and various court orders, the lawsuit against the Harthills was dismissed. The motion for dismissal was filed by the US attorney, which typically means there was a settlement.

Dr. Harthill died in 2005 from complications of pneumonia and a stroke. He was eighty years old and had been practicing cutting-edge veterinary medicine for more than half a century. For many, his death was the end of an era. Journalist and Thoroughbred owner Barry Irwin may have put it best: "What I will remember most about Doc was the twinkle in those blue eyes," Irwin wrote in an obituary in *Blood-Horse* magazine. "It would have been nicer if they didn't seem to dance most when he recounted an old larceny. But I was able to separate the admirable part from the dark side. I hope that when he is remembered, others might be able to do the same."[11]

More likely, though, even as Dr. Harthill's well-earned reputation as a skilled veterinarian fades from generation to generation, his legacy may be his rumored but unproven role in the first disqualification of a Kentucky Derby winner.

14

Permissive Medication and the "E" in PED

The Kentucky Derby is arguably the most famous and most important horse race in the world. In 1968 the Derby was also a perfect storm of controversy and complications: disqualification of the winner because of a positive drug test; elevation of the second-place horse to first place, despite the lack of a drug test; a drug that many people still think is dope but is not; conspiracy theories and claims of chicanery; weeks of agency hearings; and years of litigation. And at the center of things was Dr. Alex Harthill.

Boston automobile dealer Peter Fuller had a very nice three-year-old colt named Dancer's Image entered in the Kentucky Derby that year. He spent a lot of time on the phone during the weeks leading up to the race. When it became clear that Dancer's Image was headed for Churchill Downs after a win in the Wood Memorial in New York, there were airplane reservations to make, hotel rooms to secure, and Derby tickets to negotiate. Fuller was extremely confident about Dancer's Image, and his excitement was contagious. He wanted to share the experience with as many people as possible. Counting family, friends, and business associates, Fuller needed at least sixty tickets for race day, maybe more. This was well above the usual allotment set aside for owners of Derby horses and many more tickets than Churchill Downs president Walthen Knebelkamp was inclined to dole out. It would have been like driving up to Fort Knox and requesting a few bars of gold, except that talking the soldiers out of the gold might have been easier.

Fuller made at least two telephone calls to Hermitage Farm owner Warner L. Jones Jr., a prominent Thoroughbred breeder who also happened to be chairman of the board of Churchill Downs. Fuller needed some advice about a couple of important matters. One was security for Dancer's Image after the horse arrived in Louisville. Considered a damn Yankee by many Kentuckians who were still fighting the Civil War, Fuller had been receiving hateful letters since it became public knowledge that he donated the purse from a rich race in Maryland to Coretta Scott King, widow of civil rights leader Dr. Martin Luther King, who had been assassinated on April 3 (just a month before the Derby). The letters were probably written by crackpots, but Fuller thought it would be foolish to totally ignore the threats. He told Jones he was thinking about bringing some people down from the "homeland" for added protection, but Jones assured Fuller that there was great security at Churchill Downs, and Fuller finally acquiesced.

Dancer's Image had a history of ankle problems, so Fuller also asked Jones to recommend a good veterinarian to attend to the colt in Kentucky. Perhaps recalling the Isolde incident two decades earlier, Jones suggested Dr. Harthill. Fuller did not know the Derby Doc, but he was willing to rely on Jones's recommendation. Harthill agreed to treat Dancer's Image because Odie Clellan, a longtime friend who had trained some horses for Fuller in New England, asked him to help. Just what that help might have entailed remains a mystery more than half a century later.[1]

On Derby Day, Dancer's Image crossed the finish line first, 1½ lengths in front of the favorite, Calumet Farm's Forward Pass. The winner's postrace urine test was positive for the prohibited drug phenylbutazone, a nonsteroidal anti-inflammatory drug (NSAID) marketed under the trade name Butazolidin but universally called "Bute" by trainers and veterinarians. Dr. Harthill acknowledged treating Dancer's Image with Bute on the Sunday before the Derby but steadfastly denied giving the colt the drug on any other occasion.

Dr. Harthill's veterinary bill to Peter Fuller for the period from April 26 through May 6, 1968, included ten separate entries. There were several sets of x-rays, doses of vitamins, Azium (an NSAID with analgesic properties similar to Bute but allowed in Kentucky), and, on April 28, a single dose of Bute. The bill totaled $325, including a charge of $7.50 for Bute. Fuller paid the bill with check number 352, drawn on a special account from Shawmut Bank in Boston.[2]

One of the first NSAIDs developed—aspirin was the first—Bute is a powerful anti-inflammatory.[3] It was synthesized for human use in 1946 but soon attracted the attention of Thoroughbred trainers. Bute is neither a stimulant nor a depressant, the drugs most often associated with cheating, but it still has an image problem. In the public's eye, Bute is dope.

State racing commissions began testing for Bute in the early 1950s, and by 1962, the drug was strictly controlled everywhere. Kentucky, which has one of the most permissive drug policies, was the last jurisdiction to regulate Bute, and it did so reluctantly, primarily to adhere to a uniform medication rule. Although Kentucky was testing for Bute throughout much of the 1960s, no horse was disqualified for the drug until Dancer's Image.[4] That fact seems to belie anecdotal evidence of the widespread use of Bute during the 1960s. It suggests that these reports of Bute use came from disgruntled trainers looking for excuses when their own horses did not run well. Just as likely, however, is that state racing officials had little interest in regulating the drug.

Most states allowed Bute for training but adopted a zero-tolerance policy for racing, with even the smallest trace counting as a positive test. Zero tolerance presented a serious dilemma for trainers and veterinarians because the drug could often be detected in a horse's system long after any analgesic effect had ended. For Bute, the typical clearance time from a horse's system is seventy-two hours, so the dose given to Dancer's Image six days before the Derby should have left no trace. Under the circumstances, the colt's positive test made no sense, unless he had received a second dose of Bute.

Unlike trainer Tom Smith's hearings in the mid-1940s, where the main point of contention was whether ephedrine was a stimulant that could affect the outcome of a race,[5] the Dancer's Image case challenged the reliability of drug tests and the competence of the state's chemist. Today, an owner or trainer can request a second test of a positive sample at an independent laboratory, but that option was not available in 1968. At the time, there was no requirement for a split sample, and the state's chemist used all the urine collected for his own testing. Today, a contested positive test is considered evidence of a violation only if both tests are positive for the prohibited medication.

In the court of public opinion, where many of horse racing's drug controversies are won or lost, reporters found it necessary to remind people that phenylbutazone is not "dope" but a painkiller. "Phenylbutazone is not a stimulant and not a narcotic," David Condon wrote in the *Chicago Tribune* a few days after the 1968 Derby. "Phenylbutazone is not a bad word. It is not pushed by the junkies or favored by the hippies. If you're a horse player, it's likely that you've wagered on several thoroughbreds that have been treated by phenylbutazone. Not many years ago the Illinois tracks daily informed patrons what entries were going postward with phenylbutazone still in their systems. Many knowledgeable horsemen still favor removing restrictions disciplining its use prior to a race."[6]

In the same vein, Thomas Rivera called the belief that Bute is dope "one of racing's greatest public misconceptions. In the public mind, the use of the word drug, which so often is turned into 'doping,' means simply that the horse involved has been given something to pep him up or hypo him to perform better than he normally could."[7]

Almost half a century after the disqualification of Dancer's Image, an article appeared in the *International Journal of the History of Sport* that took a different tack and examined what the authors called "the relationship between humans and domesticated animals." Reviewing the historical records from the 1968 Derby, the authors found a dichotomy in the treatment of Dancer's Image. On the one hand, the colt was anthropomorphized and treated as the "possessor of a human-like moral code centered on the noble pursuit of athletic victory. When stripped of his victory, Dancer's Image is shown in these representations as suffering a tremendous emotional blow." On the other hand, "alongside such instances of anthropomorphism . . . one can find numerous cases in which the horse's disqualification is discussed in purely monetary terms."[8]

No one represented both views better than the late Peter Fuller, who bred and raced Dancer's Image. During his testimony before the Kentucky State Racing Commission in November 1968, Fuller talked about Dancer's Image being "libeled," the personal distress he felt because Dancer's Image was no longer the Derby champion, and his concern that people would not know whether Dancer's Image was "a real horse, or just a horse that had to be helped. . . . I have to clear the horse's name." He also mentioned the potential syndication money that would be lost because of the disqualification.[9]

The Dancer's Image case came on the cusp of a decade of "permissive medication," during which the strict rules of the 1960s were liberalized. The zero-tolerance standard that cost Dancer's Image the Kentucky Derby soon was dropped in favor of testing for allowable threshold levels of certain drugs. The rationale for relaxing the testing standard was largely based on the growing sophistication of tests that can detect minuscule traces of drugs long after any therapeutic effects have dissipated.[10]

Caught up in the liberalization of medication policies was another popular therapeutic medication and possible performance-enhancing drug (PED): Lasix (trade name for the diuretic furosemide, which is used to treat exercise-induced pulmonary hemorrhage in horses). Lasix, like Bute, has wreaked havoc among racing officials, bettors, fans, and trainers. Research has been inconclusive as to whether Lasix actually enhances performance. One of the first studies of the efficacy of Lasix as a PED, commissioned by the Jockey Club in 1988 and performed at the University of Pennsylvania, found that Lasix did improve horses' performance: at a mile, horses administered Lasix ran faster, by an average of 0.48 second, whether or not they were bleeders; for older geldings, the improvement was greater, as much as nine lengths. More often than not, bleeders treated with the drug continued to bleed.[11]

Subsequent research contradicted the Pennsylvania study, leaving regulators with a quandary: how to regulate Lasix when an estimated 95 percent of horses raced on the drug, even those that were not bleeders. One solution was to ban it on race day, an unpopular option for trainers and some veterinarians; another was to not regulate the drug at all, an unpopular option for just about everyone else. The middle ground, which took years to reach, was a phaseout of Lasix, starting with stakes races. By the end of 2020, more than half a dozen states had imposed restrictions on Lasix, with more to come.

Dr. Dionne Benson, chief veterinarian of the Stronach Group, which operates racetracks in Maryland, Florida, and California, discussed the eventual banning of race-day Lasix with journalist Victor Ryan. "First, obviously there is a perception issue," Dr. Benson explained:

Whether you believe Lasix is an issue when it comes to integrity . . . the public sees something that is concerning—that we allow horses to be medicated on race day. While some people might see it that, if a horse has an issue, let's give it some medication and let [it] race, others may see it that if a horse has an issue, why race? So there is an issue of public perception that's out there.

Secondly, there is a concern that horses who would not necessarily need the medication were receiving it for the performance-enhancing effects. We know it exists. It's just not being used for EIPH [exercise-induced pulmonary hemorrhage], and I'm not sure how you draw the line for those that need it for EIPH and those that are using it to keep up with the other horses.[12]

The Horsemen's Benevolent and Protective Association (HBPA), the largest organization of Thoroughbred trainers in the country, had a different view. "We always point to the fact that if there was research or a better medication that is legal and non-performance enhancing, we would be the first to sign up," said Eric Hamelback, CEO of the HBPA. "But right now, all the science, all the research, points to furosemide—using Lasix—on race day four hours out as being in the best interest of equine health and welfare."[13]

Opponents of the HBPA position argue that since racing gets along fine without race-day medication everywhere else in the world—which is generally true—why should the United States be any different? It's a compelling argument, but it misses two important points. The first is that racing in the United States has become a year-round sport. In most other countries, race meetings are shorter, and there is an off-season during which horses can rest and recover. Second, and possibly more important, is the economic disparity between wealthy horse owners and everyone else in the horse racing business. Well-to-do owners can afford to take a horse out of training when it needs a rest. But owners of small stables may need to keep their horses racing, ailing or not, to pay the mortgage and put food on the table.

The Horseracing Integrity and Safety Act (HISA) was signed into law on December 27, 2020, implementing nationwide rules and enforcement. The portion of the law dealing with safety took effect on July 1, 2022; the effective date of the medication-related portion was pushed back until January 1, 2023. As of this writing, the proposed medication regulations had not been submitted to the Federal Trade Commission for approval; they include a phaseout plan for Lasix and a three-year research study of the drug. Legal issues involving the HISA medication rules would further delay implementation.

Funding to implement the rules and regulations promulgated under HISA, including the Lasix study, was another issue. There were also questions about whether the US Anti-Doping Agency (USADA) would manage the medication portion of HISA. The agency's participation was a major selling point for HISA in the Thoroughbred community, but in late 2021, after months of contract talks between the HISA Authority and USADA, negotiations broke down (see chapter 18). The HISA Authority eventually settled on another agency, Drug Free Sport International, as a substitute to handle medication control.[14]

As the medication debate dragged on, it was becoming clear that there should be two definitions of PED: performance-*enhancing* drug, or those medications with no legitimate use beyond allowing a horse to perform beyond its natural ability, and performance-*enabling* drug, or those therapeutic medications with legitimate uses to allow a horse to reach its full potential and that might or might not be allowed on race day. It can be a subtle difference because a drug that enables might also enhance, an important distinction for regulators.

The 2021 Kentucky Derby, for example, was embroiled in controversy when the winner, Medina Spirit, tested positive for traces of betamethasone, a corticosteroid often injected into horses' joints. Kentucky rules allow the use of betamethasone during training, but there is a withdrawal period to allow the drug to clear a horse's system before race day. Testing of Medina Spirit's second sample confirmed the initial test, and further testing apparently showed that the drug had not been injected; instead, it had been applied topically to treat a skin rash. The rules made no mention of betamethasone in any context other than as an injectable drug, leaving the racing commission with a dilemma that was resolved in 2022 with the disqualification of Medina Spirit and the suspension of trainer Bob Baffert.

A positive development occurred at the 2021 Breeders' Cup, where for the first time all race-day medications were prohibited. The previous year, race-day medications had been prohibited only for two-year-olds. "This is extremely important for Breeders' Cup because we're on the global stage of racing and we want to have uniform rules and regulations across the world," CEO Drew Fleming said. "The world as a whole has been running Lasix-free for quite a while, and it's important that the Breeders' Cup now joins them." The two-day Lasix-free event was a rousing success.[15]

15

The Steroid Derby

It is difficult to know what to make of the 2008 Kentucky Derby. It was a tour de force for the winner, Big Brown, but the race was marred by the tragic breakdown of the filly Eight Belles after crossing the finish line in second place. Eight Belles suffered serious fractures in both front legs, and she was euthanized on the track in front of a crowd of more than 150,000 and a television audience of millions. It was a devastating blow to the filly's owner, trainer, jockey, and grooms. On a larger scale, the catastrophe was another punch in the gut for Thoroughbred racing's already sagging public image.

Then, just when it seemed things could not get any worse, amazingly, they did. A few days after the Derby, Big Brown's trainer, Richard Dutrow, casually mentioned that the horse had been receiving monthly injections of the anabolic steroid Winstrol (brand name of the drug stanozolol).[1] This is the same steroid that showed up in the drug test of Canadian sprinter Ben Johnson after he set a world record in the 100-meter dash at the Seoul Olympics in 1988. Johnson was stripped of his gold medal and world record in what one writer called the "Dirtiest Race in History" because a majority of the runners were, had been, or would be involved in doping scandals.[2] Coming in the midst of Major League Baseball's "steroid era," the timing of Dutrow's announcement could not have been worse.

Big Brown won the Preakness Stakes two weeks later, finishing 5¼ lengths ahead of Macho Again. With a Triple Crown on the line, a confident Dutrow said he had not injected Big Brown with Winstrol since April 15, a couple of weeks before the Kentucky Derby, and he assured the public that the colt would run without the drug in the upcoming Belmont Stakes. At the time, all three states where the Triple Crown races are run (Kentucky, Maryland, and New York) allowed steroids.

There was one major question leading up to the 2008 Belmont Stakes. If Big Brown had last been injected with Winstrol in mid-April—taking Dutrow's statement at face value—would the drug still be in the horse's system when he tried to win the last leg of the Triple Crown? And if so, would it matter? Joe Drape, who covers racing for the *New York Times,* asked several experts. Two told Drape that Winstrol was unlikely to have any effect on the outcome of a race six or seven weeks after the last injection; a third called Winstrol a "training drug" and added that "it's really immaterial that he is not doing it now."[3]

Thoroughbreds obviously cannot report whether anabolic steroids improve their performance, but a world-class power lifter who has extensive personal experience with Winstrol and other anabolic steroids had this to say: "Steroids allow me to train harder and to train more in preparation for an event, and that training allows me to lift more weight," he explained, suggesting at least an indirect enhancement of athletic performance. "They also help with attitude, and to keep the aggression and fire that you need for hard training. It also means that I can get away with a mistake in training at times." But does taking steroids immediately before an event improve performance, as an amphetamine would? "Taking steroids just before an event won't do jack shit," he said.[4]

Big Brown started as the odds-on favorite in the Belmont Stakes but finished a disappointing last in the ten-horse field.[5] The colt raced twice more, winning the Haskell Invitational and the Monmouth Stakes before suffering a career-ending injury during a workout. He won seven of eight races and earned $3,614,500.[6]

A lingering question about performance-enhancing drugs since the 1930s is whether they can affect a horse's breeding success as a stallion. Big Brown was a sought-after stallion for breeding, and the stud fee for his initial season at Robert N. Clay's Three Chimneys Farm in Lexington, Kentucky, was set at $65,000.[7] Classic winner or not, that was pricey for a first-year stallion in an economy heading toward a major depression, and the horse's association with Dutrow and Winstrol did not help matters. After some success as a sire, Big Brown wound up in New York standing for a fee of $6,000.[8]

It is important to remember that despite mounting criticism, Dutrow probably did nothing wrong except talk out of turn. Assuming that Big Brown's Winstrol injections were prescribed by a veterinarian—and there is nothing in the record to indicate otherwise —use of the drug was not prohibited. There was no rule against the use of steroids in Kentucky or most other racing jurisdictions. That was about to change.

The response of state racing commissions to the sudden steroid crisis was rapid. At a June 19, 2008, hearing before the House Subcommittee on Commerce, Trade, and Consumer Protection, Alexander Waldrop, CEO of the National Thoroughbred Racing Association, commented on interstate cooperation and the steroid epidemic:

> One of the foremost examples of cooperative uniform solutions to industrywide challenges is the Racing Medication and Testing Consortium (RMTC). The RMTC is governed by a board of directors consisting of 23 industry stakeholders, including regulators, veterinarians, chemists, as well as owners, trainers, breeders, and racetracks from all breeds. Working with the guidance from the RMTC, the RCI (Racing Commissioners International) has developed a comprehensive set of model rules which govern the use of drugs and therapeutic medications in racing. These model rules have now been adopted in 32 of 38 racing jurisdictions, including all major racing States.
>
> The RMTC has also helped the RCI develop tough but standardized penalties for drug violations, and these tough penalties are now in place in almost half of all States that

conduct horseracing, with more States expected to adopt these penalties soon.

More recently we worked closely on a policy regarding anabolic steroids. With the full support of the industry, the RCI has called for all racing States to adopt a standardized rule removing anabolic steroids from racing and race training by the end of 2008. Some 28 states are now in the process of removing anabolic steroids from competition, with the remaining 10 expected to follow suit shortly. Importantly, in the case of anabolic steroids, we have made progress in a matter of months, not years, proving that we can act quickly, collectively, and constructively. This industry is no longer a rudderless ship.[9]

One of the individuals invited to testify before the committee was Rick Dutrow. He did not appear, reportedly due to illness. "I know they wanted me to go down to Washington to ask me a bunch of questions," Dutrow explained, but "I wasn't feeling on top of my game. If I had a gun to my head, I would have went. But no one put a gun to my head."[10] Dutrow was apparently referring to the fact that he had not been subpoenaed by the committee, making his appearance voluntary. Voluntary or not, the empty seat behind the "Mr. Dutrow" nameplate at the witness table did not sit well with Representative Cliff Stearns. "The fact that he didn't show says volumes about him," Stearns commented after the hearing.[11]

A few days after he failed to attend the committee hearing, Dutrow was suspended for fifteen days in Kentucky for a positive drug test in another horse. Salute the Count finished second in the Aegon Turf Sprint at Churchill Downs the day before Big Brown's win in the Kentucky Derby. The horse tested positive for an excessive amount (called an "overage") of the drug clenbuterol, a bronchodilator that helps horses breathe but also has steroidal qualities.[12] Clenbuterol is a legal medication for training, but there is a cutoff time that varies from state to state, as well as a limit on how much of the drug can be present in a postrace test.[13] The test on Salute the Count showed a concentration of 41 picograms of clenbuterol, more than twice the legal limit in Kentucky.[14]

Imposing a suspension for a positive drug test and having a trainer actually serve it in a timely fashion is a problem for racing. Dutrow's first delay came when he requested a second drug test on the split sample, as was his right. That due process requirement had become an industry standard after the disqualification of Dancer's Image in the 1968 Kentucky Derby. The second lab reported a similar result for the clenbuterol overage, at which point Dutrow exercised his right to appeal the stewards' ruling, earning a second delay. He was allowed to continue training while the appeal was pending.

Appeals and delays come with risk, however. On July 8, 2009, more than a year after the appeal began, the Kentucky State Racing Commission upped Dutrow's penalty from fifteen days to thirty days. The commission approved the longer suspension by a vote of six to five. Commission executive director Lisa Underwood said the higher penalty (which was still within the rules) was imposed because the commission thought Dutrow was intentionally delaying the process. And of course, he was, legally. "He flagrantly worked the system," Underwood was quoted as saying. "I think a lot of what was going through the commissioners' minds was to protect the integrity of racing. Frankly, it's offensive for the betting public to see trainers still out there who have a violation, who have admitted they have a violation."[15] It is disingenuous, however, to allege that Dutrow was gaming the system when everything he did—from treating Big Brown with Winstrol before the Kentucky Derby to appealing the clenbuterol overage—was within the rules in force at the time.

Offending the betting public, a constant concern for racing commissioners everywhere, should not trump due process rights, and balancing both concerns remains a major dilemma for racing.

The use of steroids in horse racing, like the use of most other PEDs, mirrored their use in human athletics. Following the synthesis of testosterone in Germany during the mid-1930s and its use to treat depression in humans, anabolic steroids made an appearance during the 1954 Olympics, when they were reportedly used by Russian weight lifters.[16] Around the same time, Dr. John McA. Kater, working for the Thoroughbred Racing Protective Bureau, began to investigate the use of testosterone in racehorses, especially in geldings (see chapter 12). *New York Times* sportswriter Bill Finley places the start of steroid use in horse racing a bit later and quotes trainer Elliott Burch, who first heard about steroids in the mid-1960s.[17]

The International Olympic Committee added anabolic steroids to its list of prohibited medications in 1976.[18] In 1990 Congress passed and the president signed the Anabolic Steroids Control Act, criminalizing the possession of steroids without a prescription. By the 2000s, steroid use was becoming widespread in many professional sports, including horse racing and baseball.

During the 2005 preseason, Major League Baseball instituted strict penalties for steroid users: a fifty-game suspension for first-time offenders, one hundred games for a second offense, and a lifetime ban for a third offense. Then, an investigation led by former senator George J. Mitchell resulted in a report released on December 13, 2007. It implicated more than eighty current and past baseball players, including potential Hall of Famers, as steroid users.[19] The next year, a report on steroid use by Thoroughbred trainers in Pennsylvania estimated that more than 60 percent of horses racing in the state had been treated with at least one steroid.[20] Still, racing officials seemed to be ignoring steroids. Finally, after Big Brown won the 2008 Kentucky Derby after receiving regular Winstrol injections, the Thoroughbred community took notice of a problem that had plagued human athletics for years.

Rick Dutrow and Big Brown took advantage of a regulatory gray area in 2008, when steroids were legal with a veterinarian's prescription and the drugs were not banned in the Triple Crown states and most other racing jurisdictions. Although he did nothing illegal or against the rules, Dutrow lost in the court of public opinion.

In October 2011 the New York State Racing and Wagering Board suspended Dutrow for ten years, citing a long history of suspensions and fines that were "unbecoming and detrimental to the best interests of racing" (see appendix 6). Although the suspension applied only to New York tracks, it was honored elsewhere as a result of reciprocity among jurisdictions. Dutrow began serving the longer-than-normal suspension in January 2013. Through 2021, efforts to reduce the penalty had been unsuccessful.

Part V

New Challenges,
New Solutions

16

Indictments and Wiretaps

Skeptics about the existence of a doping culture in American horse racing were shaken to their cores on March 9, 2020. That day the US attorney for the Southern District of New York unsealed four indictments alleging the involvement of twenty-seven people in various conspiracies and obstruction and smuggling activities linked to performance-enhancing drugs (PEDs) in racing.[1] The indictments were the result of a cooperative investigation conducted by the FBI's New York Joint Eurasian Organized Crime Task Force, the New York State Police, the Food and Drug Administration (FDA), the Drug Enforcement Administration (DEA), and private investigative services.

"Today's unsealing of four indictments for widespread doping of racehorses is the largest ever of its kind from the Department of Justice," Manhattan US attorney Geoffrey S. Berman said. "These defendants engaged in this conduct not for the love of the sport, and certainly not out of concern for the horses, but for money. And it was the racehorses that paid the price for the defendants' greed. The care and respect due to the animals competing, as well as the integrity of racing, are matters of deep concern to the people of this District and to this office."[2]

The indicted individuals included two of the country's leading trainers in recent years, Jason Servis and Jorge Navarro. In 2018 Servis ranked thirteenth among trainers, according to Equibase, with earnings of $7,577,894. Navarro was sixteenth, with earnings of $7,092,228. Among the top twenty trainers that year, only three had win percentages above 30 percent: Navarro (34 percent), Servis (32 percent), and Bob Baffert (32 percent). Only four had win-place-show percentages of 60 percent or higher: Navarro (66 percent), Servis (65 percent), and Baffert (60 percent). The figures were similar in 2019. Servis ranked eighth, with earnings of $11,089,040; Navarro ranked fourteenth, with earnings of $8,307,311. No trainer that year had a win percentage of 30 or above, and only four trainers had win-place-show percentages in the 60s: Servis (66 percent), Chad Brown (62 percent), Baffert (61 percent), and Brad Cox (60 percent).[3]

On March 8, 2020, Servis started a horse at Aqueduct in New York and Navarro started a horse at Gulfstream Park in Florida. The next day, the federal indictments were unsealed, and their training careers came to a crashing halt. Through March 8, horses trained by Servis had officially earned $1,201,827, and horses trained by Navarro had earned $657,696. At the end of the year, with no more starters, Servis ranked 129th among trainers, and Navarro was 305th.

Not included in the 2020 total for Servis was the $10 million earned by Maximum Security for winning the inaugural Saudi Cup held at King Abduaziz Racetrack in Riyadh a few days before the indictments were made public. Based on the federal charges, the Jockey Club of Saudi Arabia (JCSA) withheld the winner's purse, pending further investigation—keeping in mind that Maximum Security's drug tests were apparently negative after the race and that Servis is innocent until proved guilty. Had the $10 million been distributed in a timely fashion, Servis would have ranked seventh among trainers in 2020, with total earnings of $11,201,827. The JCSA explained its decision:

This decision has been taken in the interests of safeguarding the integrity of racing in the Kingdom of Saudi Arabia, and is based on the following considerations:
Following the running of the 2020 Saudi Cup, Servis and others were indicted in the U.S. The sealed indictment,

which covers a period of time between 2018 up to February 2020, alleges that Servis administered performance-enhancing drugs to horses in his care, including Maximum Security.

The administration of PEDs is prohibited under the JCSA rules and the horsemen's guide to the Saudi Cup, to secure the integrity of racing and the welfare of racehorses. Prior to the race the JCSA received no allegation and no indication that Maximum Security had ever been administered PEDs.

However, as a result of the indictment the JCSA received an objection to the participation of Maximum Security in the race. As a result of that objection and the indictment, the JCSA commenced its own investigation into the allegations which was notified to all connections of runners in the race, and to the wider public.

That investigation remains ongoing but has been hampered by the COVID-19 crisis and the fact that the JCSA is not a party to the ongoing legal proceeding in the U.S. Therefore, unless and until the evidence that supports the sealed indictment in the U.S. proceedings is placed in the public domain, that evidence is unavailable to the JCSA's investigation and to any JCSA inquiry.

The JCSA is bound to reach a fair and reasonable decision on the objection and circumstances of Maximum Security's running in the race and it cannot do so without the consideration of relevant evidence that has been gathered by the prosecution authorities in the U.S. proceedings in respect of the sealed indictment.

Therefore, the JCSA cannot properly conclude its investigation and any inquiry by its stewards committee cannot be commenced without consideration of all relevant evidence including that gathered by the prosecution authorities in the U.S.[4]

Servis entered a guilty plea on December 9, 2022, with sentencing in May 2023. Maximum Security's owner, Gary West, said that he supported the redistribution of the Saudi Cup purse.[5]

Following the indictments, training of Maximum Security was transferred from Servis to Baffert. After the transfer, Maximum Security won the TVG Pacific Classic Stakes and the San Diego Handicap before being retired to stand at Ashford Stud in Kentucky.[6]

Making sense of the tangled web of defendants, alleged conspiracies, and other charged offenses requires a scorecard. Luckily, the US attorney's office provided one.[7] Each of the twenty-seven defendants initially pleaded not guilty at arraignment. (Tables 1–4, later in this chapter, outline the status of the cases through August 2022. As of December 31, 2022, all the initial defendants had been tried and convicted or entered guilty pleas.) According to the US attorney's office, "The Indictments unsealed today each allege the shipment and administration of adulterated and misbranded drugs designed to secretly and dangerously enhance the racing performance of horses beyond their natural ability, a dishonest practice that places the lives of affected animals at risk."[8]

Superseding indictments were filed by the prosecution on November 5, 2020, and March 11, 2021.[9] They added more serious charges of mail and wire fraud for some of the defendants, which carry maximum sentences of twenty years' imprisonment. The new indictments also included detailed descriptions of some of the performance-enhancing drugs allegedly manufactured, distributed, and used by the defendants:

- Erythropoietin (EPO) and its analogs. EPO boosts a horse's red blood cell count to increase endurance and improve recovery time after a race. Among the code names for so-called blood builders were BB3 and Monkey. EPO was also popular with professional bicycle racers, especially during the Lance Armstrong era. When combined with strenuous physical exertion, use of EPO can lead to cardiac failure and death of the human or equine athlete.

- SGF-1000 is a "customized PED purportedly containing 'growth factors' . . . which are intended to promote tissue repair and increase a racehorse's stamina and endurance beyond its natural capability," according to the indictment.
- Customized analgesics to "mask physical injuries in a racehorse, which can cause a racehorse to overexert itself during periods of intense physical exercise, and thereby sustain a leg injury or break during a race."
- "Red acid" is a generic term for customized PEDs designed to reduce joint inflammation.

It's worth noting that one of the most successful horses trained by Jorge Navarro, XY Jet, died of an apparent heart attack in January 2020. Ten months earlier, XY Jet won the Dubai Golden Shaheen, worth $1.5 million. According to the original indictment, Navarro discussed administering "Monkey" to XY Jet on numerous occasions: "During an April 3, 2019, call between Navarro and [defendant] Marcos Zulueta," the indictment alleged, "the two discussed, among other things, Navarro's administration of PEDs to XY Jet in the weeks leading up [to], and on the day of, the race in Dubai, and Navarro explained: 'I gave it to him through 50 injections. I gave it to him through the mouth.'"[10]

Although the doping of racehorses was mentioned often in court documents and likely will continue to be the focus of conversations about these indictments, the allegations were only indirectly based on how PEDs were used. Without a federal law specifically criminalizing doping, the prosecution relied on laws targeting conspiracies for drug misbranding and adulteration, obstruction, and smuggling.[11] Harry Anslinger faced a similar problem in 1933 when he publicly condemned doping in racing but could charge owners, trainers, and backstretch workers only with illegal drug possession and trafficking under the Harrison Act (see chapter 6).

March 9, 2020, Indictments

Table 1. Navarro Indictment

Count	Charge	Defendant	Plea; Disposition	Maximum Penalty
Count 1	Misbranding conspiracy 18 U.S.C. §371	Jorge Navarro	Guilty; sentenced to 5 years	5 years' imprisonment
		Erica Garcia	Not guilty; trial scheduled for late 2022, along with Michael Tannuzzo	
		Marcos Zulueta	Guilty; sentenced to 33 months	
		Michael Tannuzzo	Not guilty; trial scheduled for late 2022, along with Erica Garcia	
		Ross Cohen	No longer under indictment; testified against Seth Fishman	
		Seth Fishman	Convicted at trial of two counts of conspiracy	
		Christopher Oakes	Guilty; sentenced to 3 years	
		Nicholas Surick	No longer under indictment	

Count	Charge	Defendant	Plea; Disposition	Maximum Penalty
Count 2	Misbranding conspiracy 18 U.S.C. §371	Seth Fishman	Convicted at trial of two counts of conspiracy	5 years' imprisonment
		Lisa Giannelli	Convicted at trial of one count of drug alteration and misbranding with intent to defraud and mislead	
		Jordan Fishman	Guilty; sentenced to 15 months	
		Rick Dane Jr.	Guilty	
Count 3	Misbranding conspiracy 18 U.S.C. §371	Jason Servis	Not guilty; trial scheduled for early 2023, along with Alexander Chan	5 years' imprisonment
		Kristian Rhein	Guilty; sentenced to 3 years	
		Michael Kegley Jr.	Guilty; sentenced to 30 months	
		Alexander Chan	Not guilty; trial postponed until 2023, along with Jason Servis	
		Henry Argueta (former assistant to Jason Servis)	No longer under indictment; likely a prosecution witness against Servis	
		Jorge Navarro	Guilty; sentenced to 5 years	

Count	Charge	Defendant	Plea; Disposition	Maximum Penalty
Count 4	Misbranding conspiracy 18 U.S.C. §371	Nicholas Surick	No longer under indictment	5 years' imprisonment
		Rebecca Linke	Prosecution deferred based on several conditions	
		Christopher Marino	Not guilty	
Count 5	Obstruction 18 U.S.C. §§1512(b)(3) and 2	Nicholas Surick	No longer under indictment	20 years' imprisonment
Count 6	Obstruction 18 U.S.C. §§1512(c) and 2	Nicholas Surick	No longer under indictment	20 years' imprisonment

Table 2. Izhaki Indictment

Count	Charge	Defendant	Plea; Disposition	Maximum Penalty
Count 1	Misbranding conspiracy 18 U.S.C. §371	Sarah Izhaki	Guilty; sentenced to time served plus 3 years supervised release	5 years' imprisonment
		Ashley Lebowitz	Entered into nonprosecution agreement with the government	
Count 2	Smuggling 18 U.S.C. §§545 and 2	Sarah Izhaki	Guilty; sentenced to time served plus 3 years supervised release	20 years' imprisonment

Table 3. Grasso Indictment

Count	Charge	Defendants	Plea	Maximum Penalty
Count 1	Misbranding conspiracy 18 U.S.C. §371	Louis Grasso	Guilty	5 years' imprisonment
		Donato Poliseno	Not guilty	
		Conor Flynn	Not guilty	
		Thomas Guido III	Not guilty	

Evidence in the Navarro and Izhaki cases was summarized as follows:

The discovery in the Navarro case is voluminous. From approximately October 2018 through approximately October 2019, the Government obtained authorization for wiretaps over the cellular telephones of, among others, the defendants Nicholas Surick, Jorge Navarro, Jason Servis, Christopher Oakes, Lisa Giannelli, Seth Fishman, and Kristian Rhein. The Government obtained search warrants for over a dozen email accounts, online storage accounts, and electronic devices (principally cellular telephones) prior to the March 9, 2020, arrests, and conducted two covert searches on barns associated with the Navarro defendants. Additionally, at the time of arrests, the Government executed multiple searches of various premises associated with the Navarro defendants, including residential and commercial premises at which large volumes of drugs and electronics were obtained.

The discovery in the Izhaki case is more limited, consisting largely of consensual recordings, draft transcripts of those recordings, surveillance photographs and reports, drugs sold by each of the defendants, and cellular telephone geolocation information.[12]

The evidence in the Grasso case included the following:

Of the 4 defendants charged in the Grasso Indictment, each was arrested on the morning of March 9, 2020. . . . Among other materials, the Government intends to produce [at trial]:

- Linesheets and audio recordings from three separate cell phones, one that involved interceptions over a cellular telephone belonging to defendant Grasso, and two that involved interceptions over cellular telephones belonging, respectively, to Seth Fishman and Lisa Giannelli, each of whom is charged in the Navarro case before Judge Vyskocil. Grasso's cellphone was intercepted from in or about September 2019 through in or about November 2019; Fishman's cellphone was intercepted from in or about February 2019 through in or about June 2019; and Giannelli's cellphone was intercepted from in or about April 2019 through in or about May 2019.

- The contents of multiple electronic devices, including devices seized on or about March 9, 2020, at the time of the arrests in this case. Those devices include one cellular telephone apiece seized from defendants Poliseno, Grasso, and Guido, and over 15 computers, hard drives, and other storage media seized from premises belonging to or associated with the activities of these defendants.

- Documents, photographs, and inventories (reflecting, among other things, PEDs), seized from premises belonging to defendants Poliseno and Grasso, respectively, and from premises at which defendants Grasso and Flynn, among other individuals, administered PEDs to racehorses under their care and control.

Table 4. Robinson Indictment

Count	Charge	Defendant	Plea; Disposition	Maximum Penalty
Count 1	Misbranding conspiracy 18 U.S.C. §371	Scott Robinson	Guilty; sentenced to 18 months	5 years' imprisonment
		Scott Mangini	Guilty; sentenced to 18 months	
Count 2	Misbranding conspiracy 18 U.S.C. §371	Scott Robinson	Guilty; sentenced to 18 months	5 years' imprisonment
Count 3	Misbranding conspiracy 18 U.S.C. §371	Scott Mangini	Guilty; sentenced to 18 months	5 years' imprisonment

- Reports, related records, photographs, and/or audio reflecting covert approaches and purchases of PEDs from Grasso, Poliseno, and Guido.
- Subpoena returns from, among others, compounding pharmacies and pharmaceutical wholesale companies and telecommunication providers.[13]

The fourth indictment charged Scott Robinson and Scott Mangini:

The Indictment in this case charges the two defendants, together, in a single conspiracy to violate the drug misbranding and adulteration laws of the United States, and charges the defendants separately in one additional count each of conspiracy to violate federal drug misbranding and adulteration laws, based on conduct subsequent to the period of their joint conspiracy charged in Count One. In each instance, the allegations in the Indictment describe the production, sale, and distribution of various performance-enhancing drugs ("PEDs") for use in doping racehorses throughout the United States and abroad. The defendants operated largely through the use of online marketplaces catering to racehorse trainers and owners, and, as alleged, the drugs sold were designed and packaged in such a way as to evade standard anti-doping drug screens and interdiction by state and federal drug and racing regulators.[14]

Since March 2020, when the US attorney's office first referred to the "voluminous" evidence supporting the indictments, there have been questions about what exactly that evidence is. It was assumed that wiretaps had produced essential evidence, but the prosecution did not release transcripts of some of those wiretaps until September 2, 2021. Those transcripts were part of a 140-plus-page omnibus brief in response to a motion from Jason Servis to suppress the wiretap evidence. At the time of this writing, the district court had not yet ruled on the suppression motion.[15] Even if the transcripts are never presented to a jury, however, they are now in the public domain, and the reputations of the defendants have suffered irreparable harm.

The following excerpts are taken verbatim from the omnibus brief opposing the motion to suppress the wiretap evidence. The explanatory text in italics is from the prosecution and is excerpted from the indictments.

Omnibus Brief Page 88

March 3, 2019—Jorge Navarro and Michael Tannuzzo
March 5, 2019—Jorge Navarro and Jason Servis
At the time of the initial Servis wiretap on April 30, 2019, the evidence made amply clear that Navarro, Servis, and others understood that

"SGF" was a performance-enhancing drug, and one that was discussed in the context of other such substances. For example, on March 3, 2019, Navarro and defendant Michael Tannuzzo engaged in the following conversation:

Navarro: What I'm going to do is tap his ankles, put him in a series every week with SGF. I'm just trying [to get] my vet to give me a good price man because I want to fucking charge to fucking tap every week.

Tannuzzo: You're going to tap him every week.

Navarro: Yeah with SGF that's what I did with XY Jet. I'm going to call my vet up north to see, my surgeon to see how he did it to XY Jet and that's it. Don't worry man you're in good hands don't worry.

Tannuzzo: You're talking about the HGF not the SGF.

Navarro: Yeah yeah yeah whatever the SGF whatever. The thing that you sent me the syringe.

Tannuzzo: Yeah.

Navarro: Yeah. Yeah and he [a horse] is getting one of those SGF 1000 whatever. He's getting one today.

As relayed in the April 30 affidavit, on March 5, 2019, Navarro and Servis discussed drugs, and made their first mention (to each other) of a drug that they, like Navarro and Tannuzzo, also referred to as "SGF":

Navarro: And if you know something new, if you know about something new don't forget about your man ok? Don't forget about your man.

Servis: I'll tell you what, Jorge I'm using that fucking uh shot what is it SGF?

Navarro: Oh yeah yeah yeah I got uh I got more than 12 horses on that so I'll let you know ok?

Servis: I've been using it on everything almost.

Navarro: Jay we'll sit down and talk about this shit. I don't want to
talk about this shit on the phone ok.
Servis: Alright you're right.

Omnibus Brief Page 95

June 5, 2019—Jason Servis and Kristian Rhein
*Shortly after [having a] conversation with Argueta . . . Servis called
Rhein to discuss an additional concern with the testing, namely the possibility that the Commission would discover Servis' use of SGF. At 1:55
p.m., Servis called to confirm that Rhein was alone and available to talk:*

Servis: You got a minute.
Rhein: Sure sure sure.
Servis: Are you by yourself?
Rhein: Yeah yeah yeah I just walked out of the barn.

One minute later, the two spoke again:

Servis: Hey. So they've been doing some out of competition testing
which I have no problem with. Um they took Maximum Secu-
rity Monday and they came back again today. But Monday he
got the "KS" I just want to make sure we are all good with that.
Rhein: Wait what did he get?
Servis: I'm sorry I said "KS" the . . . you know your shot the . . .
Rhein: Oh the SG . . .
Servis: Yeah that stuff.
Rhein: Yeah no no no the Jockey Club tested it and I met the guy
who tested it way back when. It comes back as collagen. They
don't even have a test for it.
Servis: It will probably come up with Dex probably right.
Rhein: Yeah that's it. It will be Dex. It will be Dex. It will be like
that's it. And I've had them. I had them pull some stuff and I was
like "oh shit" I wonder what will happen. Nothing. Nothing.

I mean and the guy said SGF doesn't even test close thank god. But the only thing will be the AZM and you can just say he has like hives or something but . . .

Servis: Right but they're not even going to ask me about it.

Rhein: They won't even.

Servis: Because you're allowed to have that anyways. Dex I mean.

Rhein: He's allowed. He's allowed. So [unidentified individual; hereafter U/I] I don't know. I've done it. I've had it tested. Jockey Club did it and I've had at least three different times it's been tested on horses that I gave it the day before and nothing. Not a word.

Servis: Yup.

Rhein: There's no test for it in America. There's no testing. There's nothing.

Servis: Okay that's fine.

Rhein: There's nothing you did that would test.

Servis: So Monday they took Max and they got three other horses. Actually they got two they were looking for Sunny Razor and I told them he's at Belmont. I think they got him today Henry [Argueta] said. But they took a two-year-old filly that ran the other day and finished fourth. Um and I'm thinking why the fuck would they want to take her. But maybe they are just doing random or maybe looking for Clenbuterol I don't know.

Rhein: Yeah that's what I am wondering. I'm wondering if it's Clenbuterol they are looking for.

As discussed further below, the defendants' concern with racing authorities' scrutiny of their use of clenbuterol undermines their current professed view that the substance is entirely innocuous.

Servis: Right because Parx you are not allowed to have it on the grounds. . . .

Rhein: That's really an odd thing and that horse I guarantee has never had any shit that. I mean I know because I met the guy inadvertently when the Jockey Club took a box of the SGF. They took it and I met the guy and I met the guy down at the conference and he goes "The Jockey Club" and he saw the hat that I had on was the same company and he goes "Oh man I just tested a box of that stuff" and I go "What stuff" and he goes "Medivet. You've got a hat on. SGF. Yeah Jockey Club sent it to me out in California. Yeah it came back as just a bunch of collagen. Nothing interesting [U/I]. These guys think it's got something that can be like a performance enhancing drug." He goes "There's nothing in it," and he was the actual head of the testing lab.

Servis: Yeah I think you told me.

Rhein: Yeah so you are golden. And like I said we have had it done two or three times here. Nothing.

Servis: Okay.

Rhein: Shit I just had that I gave to some horses and they just took it.

Servis: Well that's what I'm saying that horse got it Monday.

Rhein: Yeah.

Servis: And then they come in and test it [U/I].

Rhein: No but they won't. It's you know I promise. It's never been anywhere, anyway, anyhow and I got guys going through FEI testing. Which is the French International Federation that is 50 million times stricter because these guys are giving it for their horses in the Grand Prix. They give it to them. The Grand Prix jumping. So I have like three horses that are gold medal . . . well medal winning horses in the Olympics and they are all on it. And they go right through the box for FEI and it's far stricter than anything we got.

Servis: Alright Kristian. Just want to make sure.

Omnibus Brief Page 98

June 5, 2019—Jason Servis and unnamed individual
June 6, 2019—Jason Servis and Kristian Rhein
On the same day, following his conversation with Rhein, Servis placed a call to another individual regarding falsely listing "Dex" (presumably

the corticosteroid dexamethasone) in veterinary records to obscure his use of SGF-1000—the drug that Servis now claims was innocuous:

Servis: Yeah. So I just want to give you a heads up. So they pulled blood on some horses Monday one of them is Maximum Security and then they pulled it again today. Um . . . and I talked to Kristian [Rhein]. I mean the shots shouldn't be a problem because you know it may come up as Dex. I don't know if you cover your ass if they want to look at a bill and see if the horse why he got Dex or some . . .

Servis: I just wanted to give you a heads up with the Dex because that horse you gave it to him Monday I think right.

Individual-1: Yeah he got the Dex Monday.

Servis: Yeah I don't know if they might try to put why did he get Dex it's not on the bill or something.

Individual-1: Nah [U/I] put it down. [U/I] put it down. Got it.

On the following day, June 6, 2019, Servis and Rhein continued their conversation about SGF-1000, and the wiretap affidavit submitted on June 27, 2019, again disclosed the untestable nature of that drug:

Rhein: On what we were talking about the other day. There is no problem with it, but, like somebody squealed around here about it.

Servis: Okay.

Rhein: So, that is the only thing that we should be cautious of. I got a . . . I got a couple of . . .

Servis: That's the SGF?

Rhein: Uh huh.

Servis: Ok.

Rhein: So somebody squealed. Not that it is testing, or that . . . there's no . . . it's untestable. It's that they were crying about it. I don't know why. They didn't tell me who. But somebody is crying about it.

Servis: Ok.

Rhein: So it's just, just that we know. I just wanted to let you know that I, you know. . . . The guy said this is a big, higher up official. I was like, "What are they? Is it some weird test? Or is something coming back?" And he was like, "No, not at all."

Servis: Ok, I just . . . like I said they pulled blood the same day that he got it, that is what threw me off.

Rhein: Yeah, well, this was the . . . I'm not worried in the sense of anything going wrong with it because. . . . Like I said, the guy already tested it, so it's not that. It's more people crying.

Servis: Right, right.

Rhein: It's more people crying about it and I am sure, as you will hear. Believe me, more people come up to me and bitch and cry about you. They are like "Oh, he is cheating, he is cheating, he is cheating." I was like "Yep, sure." I said, "They test all of his horses over and over and over again."

Servis: I know, I hear it all the time.

Rhein: I know you do. So, but . . . between you and me because the testing, they called me from the test center here and I was like "What's up?" They go "Do you know anything?" So what they called it, they called it "growth hormone." They were like "You're using some sheep growth hormone." I go "No, it has no growth hormone what-so-ever in it." And I said "It tested as collagen, which is a protein. A fine . . . there is nothing wrong with it." I told him the name of the gentleman that did it in California. I said "His name is [redacted]." He goes "Oh, I know him." I said "The Jockey Club had it tested." They were all freaked out, they thought it was this, they thought it was that. I said "So, it has been tested up and down." And he said "Listen, somebody dropped a dime on me." And I was like "What?" They are like "Yeah." So all we need to do . . . I'm not going to say anything to anything else. I'm just going to tell Alex [Chan] and people like that. Like it is not on any of our bills, it never is.

Servis: What about, is it on your truck?

Rhein: No, nah, I don't take it on my truck. I just, when they call for it I just have it, come and get it.

Servis: Well, if you want us to back off I mean I have no problem with that.

Rhein: No, no. No, no, I mean, I'm going to find out some more. I just wanted you to know. I mean, I'm not worried. I am not worried because it has been tested, you know. And the person that just called me is the guy who tests. So I'm not worried about that. We do it further out. I mean all those things. So I am not trying to be clever, or tricky or anything. This guy said "Listen, I am letting you know." And I said . . .

Servis: Right, somebody dropped a dime on you. . . .

Rhein: Put it this way, they have no test period, but we don't get close. We never do. I mean I don't get close with it.

Servis: Yeah, we are ten, twelve days.

Rhein: Exactly, the rules of New York say anything outside of seven days is anything that is not listed. And this is truly listed as a biologic so if they really want to fight, guess what, a biologic in New York is forty-eight hours.

Servis: Right.

Rhein: Because that's all it is.

Servis: The only thing I was concerned with is, is it FDA approved?

Rhein: Well, no, no. Not that I know of.

Servis: That's the only thing I was thinking, I don't . . . does it have to be?

Rhein: Well, no, because, no. I mean, there is so many things. That is the beauty of being a veterinarian. As a veterinarian you are allowed to use any drug that you think would be . . . and this is not even considered a drug. It has no drug in it, it is literally just a purified protein from a sheep's placenta.

Servis: Right.

Rhein: So, I was like, look this isn't a drug, this isn't manufactured. So the Federal Drug Administration, they wouldn't approve it anyway, just because it is not a drug. Yeah, so, I just want to beware. I am not like "Oh my God" panicked.

Servis: Yeah, because I use it down here.

Rhein: Shit, I love the stuff. I mean, you should see like tendons. . . .

Rhein: He [an individual Servis had previously complained about] is such a little bitch. He just is a little sawed-off bitch. I worked for him. I mean I worked for him. He had me shock waving horses. He would leave me these notes. They were hidden in his drawer and then we used to use Decadurabalin. I used to use Winstrol [an anabolic steroid] and he was like "don't you dare put that on the bill."

Servis: Wow.

Rhein: I'm like . . . you know . . . so this guy, he talks out of both sides of his mouth.

Servis: Yeah he does and one day somebody is going to write a fucking book. It is going to be a groom or a vet somebody and he is going to hang them all out.

Rhein: Yeah, believe me we could. I was there. I mean, I know these hypocrites. I mean I did all these guys' work. I know who was using and who was not, who needed to, who didn't, I mean. I don't say it lightly, but shit. I was doing [several other individuals], I had all those barns. I was doing all their lameness. And these guys were the first ones that wanted you to do it, "hey what can we do?"

Servis: Yeah.

Rhein: And then they were like . . . so . . . we will be fine. Like I said, it is never on a bill. It is never on a bill. That is the problem.

Servis: I have been billing it Baycox in Florida and here.

Rhein: Oh, good. Good, no, I think we do . . . ours are totally innocuous so . . . and I bill a lot of mine as like acupuncture. I'm an acupuncturist. I'm a trained, I'm a licensed acupuncturist. So, that is for me why I do it. They can't say I am not. I have my advanced degree for equine acupuncture so.

Omnibus Brief Page 104

Date uncertain—Kristian Rhein and Michael Kegley Jr.
*Rhein and convicted codefendant Michael Kegley Jr., the sales director
for the company that compounded and sold SGF-1000 and TB-1000,
also discussed testing of SGF-1000 in the context of ongoing regulatory
scrutiny of Jason Servis. In this conversation, Rhein himself acknowledged a fear that SGF-1000, notwithstanding prior "clean" tests, might
well contain growth hormone in addition to the advertised growth
factors:*

> Make sure there is no growth hormone in there because if
> they are calling it that and it is in there then we'll—we need
> to—but I can't imagine there is. There's no—I can't—
> I don't think a fetus [the source of the purported sheep
> placenta from which SGF-1000 is derived] has growth
> hormone in it. There's just—I don't—I don't think fetal pla-
> centa membranes have growth hormones. You know, I'll do
> some research tonight but I don't believe that's correct. I
> think it could have something that stimulates it. . . . Well
> here's the thing is, I don't think it does. And just because
> they can test for it, it doesn't mean they will. Now if it has
> growth hormone, I mean, it costs them a lot of money to
> test. A lot of money. And then the second thing is, how long
> is something in there. Well if we're giving it five to seven
> days out then we're fine. It's not gonna hang around. It's—
> nothing hangs around long. EPO doesn't hang around that
> long. (Id. at 119–20, emphasis added; see also id. at 125–26:
> "Yeah, well, that's when your Dad called me. So [a Ken-
> tucky veterinarian] didn't get it [SGF-1000] [tested] for
> growth hormone. And I was like . . . So I said, "all we have
> to prove is there's no growth hormone, that's it." Cuz that's
> all they're saying. And if we, we prove that, cuz fuck, right
> now, I told your Dad, "We don't want those results going

out, cuz right now it's not saying [U/I] growth factor." . . .
And I'm like, "fuck it, I don't know why it works.")

Rhein and others besides Servis continued to discuss their efforts to hide the administration of certain drugs. With Chan, in particular, Rhein discussed the fact that their administration of SGF-1000 was not to be committed to writing in their records. (See, e.g., id. at 123: "The main thing is just that it will never—we're just not writing it down and we just need them to not say a lot about it.") With others, Rhein discussed efforts to conceal the possession of his drugs. (Id. at 103: "I keep it [a performance-enhancing paste sold by Rhein] hidden in the honey graham box"; see also id. at 103–17, reciting multiple calls between Rhein and people other than Servis regarding the administration of various drugs, including efforts to "backdate" the records reflecting the administration of certain drugs.)

Omnibus Brief Page 108

Date uncertain—Jason Servis and Jorge Navarro
Among the early interceptions of incriminating communications between Servis and Navarro was a discussion that reflected Navarro's provision of an irregular (as opposed to "regular") clenbuterol to Servis, and Servis' desire to use that drug, if and when Navarro could provide it in a covert manner. The same early conversations revealed Servis' willingness to tip off Navarro about racetrack officials and Navarro's indication that a racetrack insider was similarly willing to tip him off about anti-doping scrutiny. With respect to Navarro's use and distribution of "irregular" clenbuterol, Navarro and Servis engaged in the following conversation:

Navarro: Yeah he's going to—he's going to look at Gastroguard. Make sure they label he's going to confiscate them going to take them. He's going to make sure . . . he can could be a dickhead about thyroid oil. Okay.

Servis: Okay.

Navarro: Alright besides that the Clenbuterol is not there huh.

Servis: I left a little bit with 14 day withdrawal because . . . no not that the regular.

Navarro: Okay you left the regular one. Not the other one.

Servis: No no.

Navarro: Okay good good.

Servis: You got my message yesterday right.

Navarro: Yeah yeah I got it.

Servis: I mean . . .

Navarro: But also the head of security was looking for me, he's a good friend of mine, so I think he was going to tell me too.

Servis: Okay.

Navarro: Just just just follow everything he does cause he could be a fucking dickhead.

Servis: Ok.

Navarro: Alright the only thing—any medications, pills and stuff you have to have it under lock.

Servis: That was the only thing we didn't have cause [U/I] didn't go in today, [U/I] said [U/I] got to have everything locked up.

Navarro: Yeah yes that's the only thing and I have cases of Gastroguard—I—he confiscated all that three years ago, but he gave it right back to me, cause I had an attorney and everything that I was going to sue him and ah like generic Gastroguard so everything has to be labeled.

Servis: He gave [U/I] a bunch of shit about generic acid. I got expensive colt that went to Palm Beach equine. They want omeprazole with uh something else in it.

Navarro: Yeah yeah yeah he could be a fucking jerkoff about that. He could be a fucking jerkoff.

Servis: I mean Jorge [U/I] time to bullshit around about regular Clenbuterol. Them horses the three win the other day they are just on regular.

Navarro: Yeah well I . . .
Servis: You know how long.
Navarro: Well it came in already. I have it at home but fuck I'm
    afraid. I'm afraid to bring it over.
Servis: No I'm scared to death right now.
Navarro: Ha ha ha.
Servis: The horses are running like crazy.
Navarro: Buddy you're killing them buddy. You're killing them.
Servis: But I ain't doing it. I'm fucking just regular. . . .
Servis: Okay but when the dust settles I'd like to get some. Get Rigo
    and my guy to [U/I] or something.

Omnibus Brief Page 114

July 10, 2019—Jason Servis and Henry Argueta
*With respect to the final period of interception over the Servis and Rhein
phones, the July 30 affidavit further recounts an additional conversation
on July 10, 2019, between Servis and Argueta in which Servis directly
acknowledges the problems with his use of that substance:*

Servis: Be careful man. Henry with that. Really careful because.
Argueta: Yes.
Servis: Because we are getting really good.
Argueta: Yeah no.
Servis: All we need is a problem like that. Oh with the Derby and
    shit. Oh my god.
Argueta: Yeah. Then they glad they are looking for us in the tree.
Servis: Yeah they will.
Argueta: They are going to be in the tree looking for you with their
    binoculars. [U/I].
Servis: What.
Argueta: The mounts right after the road.
Servis: Right.
Argueta: They'll be over there. They be there looking for you.

Servis: No they'll be in a can or a car with black windows you won't
be able to see in.

Argueta: Ha ha.

Servis: You know what I am saying. But they can see out.

Argueta: Yeah but what are they going to see. Nobody going to see
nothing. What are they going to see. Nothing.

Servis: Right.

Argueta: We don't do nothing ha ha. They can look wherever they
want to look.

Servis: It means that Clen is supposed to be for Sunny Ridge.

Argueta: Yeah but what it's legal.

Servis: I know but [U/I] told me it's supposed to be for whatever you
got the prescription for. [U/I].

Argueta: Yeah it might be having a problem but it's legal. It's a
14 day rules.

Servis: Yeah but it's not. In New York it's supposed to be for a horse
you have a prescription for and you have to get permission from
the Gaming Commission to even get a prescription.

Argueta: Yeah I know. Yeah that's a little problem but the rest . . . it's
little it's not like you're doing something very illegal.

Servis: Yeah but I know but what I'm saying is they [U/I] it out.

Argueta: The only problem you get is what you don't report about it.
That's it.

Servis: Yeah it's not reported right.

Argueta: That's it. What else can they do.

Servis: Well they might do shit.

Argueta: Okay.

Servis: Got to be careful.

Argueta: Yup.

Servis: Like Navarro is doing it at midnight.

Argueta: What do you mean?

Servis: He's got . . . Quachi says he sees him 11 o'clock at night.

Argueta: Probably right. [U/I] It's like daywatch like nightwatch.

The words of Servis, Navarro, and the other defendants make it difficult to deny that racing has a serious drug problem.

The names of most of the twenty-seven individuals indicted in March 2020 are unfamiliar even to most racing insiders and fans. The principal exceptions are Jason Servis and Jorge Navarro. Navarro changed his plea to guilty on August 11, 2021. On December 17, 2021, he was sentenced to five years in federal prison on one count of a superseding indictment charging drug misbranding and adulteration. As part of Navarro's plea deal, he also agreed to pay restitution of $26,860,514 to the victims of his criminal activities. Names of the recipients of the restitution were filed under seal.[16]

"Jorge Navarro's case reflects failings, greed, and corruption at virtually every level of the world of professional horse racing," US attorney Damian Williams said in a press release:

> For money and fame, corrupt trainers went to increasing extremes to dope horses under their care. Unscrupulous owners, who stood to profit directly, encouraged and pressured trainers to win at any cost. Veterinarians sworn to the care and protection of their patients routinely violated their oaths in service of corrupt trainers and to line their own pockets. Assistants and grooms all witnessed animal abuse in the service of greed, but did little to stop such conduct, and engaged in myriad ways to support notoriously corrupt trainers. Structures designed for the protection of the horses abused in this case failed repeatedly; fixtures of the industry—owners, veterinarians, and trainers—flouted rules and disregarded their animals' health while hypocritically incanting a love for the horses under their control and ostensible protection. Standing as the keystone for this structure of abuse, corruption, and duplicity was Jorge Navarro, a trainer who treated his animals as expendable commodities

in the service of his "sport." Today's sentence appropriately condemns the danger inherent in Navarro's crime and reflects the seriousness with which this Office takes the kind of abuse that Navarro practiced. . . .

The charges in the Navarro case arise from an investigation of widespread schemes by racehorse trainers, veterinarians, PED distributors, and others to manufacture, distribute, and receive adulterated and misbranded PEDs and to secretly administer those PEDs to racehorses competing at all levels of professional horseracing. By evading PED prohibitions and deceiving regulators and horse racing officials, participants in these schemes sought to improve race performance and obtain prize money from racetracks throughout the United States and other countries, including in New York, New Jersey, Florida, Ohio, Kentucky, and the United Arab Emirates ("UAE"), all to the detriment and risk of the health and well-being of the racehorses. Trainers, like Navarro, who participated in the schemes stood to profit from the success of racehorses under their control by earning a share of their horses' winnings, and by improving their horses' racing records, thereby yielding higher trainer fees and increasing the number of racehorses under their control. Veterinarians, including those whom Navarro directed in the corrupt administration of illegal substances, profited from the sale and administration of these medically unnecessary, misbranded, and adulterated substances. . . .

Navarro operated his doping scheme covertly, importing misbranded "clenbuterol" that he both used and distributed to others, avoiding explicit discussion of PEDs during telephone calls, and working with others to coordinate the administration of PEDs at times that racing officials would not detect such cheating. Among the horses that Navarro trained and doped was XY Jet, a thoroughbred horse that won the 2019 Golden Shaheen race in Dubai. Among

Navarro's preferred PEDs were various "blood building" drugs, which, when administered before intense physical exertion, can lead to cardiac issues or death.

Navarro's crime was far from a single lapse in judgment. Rather, Navarro engaged in repeated and persistent efforts to cheat over the course of years, cycling through various sources of supply, and pursuing aggressively new means to illegally dope horses. Throughout, Navarro maintained a flippant attitude towards his dangerous and illegal conduct. Navarro, notoriously known in the horse racing world as the "Juice Man" due to his routine doping, kept a pair of customized shoes in his barn with the words "#JUICE MAN" emblazoned across the front.[17]

Navarro was scheduled to start serving his sentence on February 17, 2022. The court recommended that he be housed in a facility in Florida so that it was possible for his family to visit. Following his release from prison, Navarro will be subject to supervised release for an additional three years.[18] Having pleaded guilty to a felony, he will likely be deported to Mexico upon his release.

17

The Balkanization of Thoroughbred Racing in America

During his short-lived campaign to eliminate illegal drugs from the country's racetracks during the 1930s, Harry Anslinger insisted that racing authorities cooperate in policing their own sport and threatened federal intervention if they did not. The threats were hollow ones. There were promises of interstate cooperation from some racing commissions, but nothing of substance came of those assurances. Anslinger's threats of government action never materialized either, and he soon shifted the resources of the Federal Bureau of Narcotics back to fighting international drug trafficking.

This lack of cooperation from the states could not have been a surprise. The mandate of the Federal Bureau of Narcotics was to enforce the Harrison Act's prohibitions against illegal drugs, not to take over and manage a sport. There was also a strong states' rights argument that the feds should keep their hands off horse racing. The main reason, though, involved each individual state racing commission's efforts to protect its own political turf, a common problem with a long history in the sport.

America's first racing commission was created by the New York legislature in 1895 as part of the Percy-Gray Act. Championed by August Belmont II, chairman of the Jockey Club, Percy-Gray was comprehensive legislation that delegated regulatory authority over most aspects of Thoroughbred racing in New York to a commission composed of political appointees. Belmont was the logical choice for chairman of the new commission, and until his death in 1924 he wielded enormous power and influence through dual leadership of the Jockey Club and the New York State Racing Commission.[1]

Kentucky soon followed New York's example (borrowing a good bit of the Percy-Gray language in the process), and in 1906 it became the second state to establish its own racing commission. A constitutional challenge followed almost immediately when the commission awarded lucrative spring racing dates to Churchill Downs instead of a competing track. A federal district court issued an injunction ordering the commission to grant the contested dates to Douglas Park, but the Sixth Circuit Court of Appeals reversed the lower court, noting: "The power to assign dates for race meetings involves not only the power to limit their duration but the power to limit the number of associations within the state or in any given community that may operate during the same period of time, and even to limit to one association the right to operate its race track during any period of time."[2] The race for states to establish commissions to regulate the sport within their own borders—and to provide governors the opportunity to make attractive political appointments—was on in earnest.

In 1951 a New York court ruled that the state legislature's delegation of authority to license trainers, jockeys, and other participants to the Jockey Club—a private organization—was not permitted.[3] By then, every state with Thoroughbred racing had its own appointed commission responsible for operational aspects of the sport. This balkanization of horse racing would continue for more than eighty years, until the Horseracing Integrity and Safety Act (HISA) was passed by Congress in late 2020. On December 27 HISA became law with the signature of outgoing president Donald Trump. The legislation grants the authority to regulate safety and medications on a national basis but does not completely usurp the authority of state racing commissions. The commissions retain responsibility for other administrative matters such as licensing and the assignment of racing dates.

Tucked away near the back of a huge omnibus spending bill consisting of more than five thousand pages, HISA went unnoticed by almost everyone outside the Thoroughbred community. Among racing's stakeholders, reactions were mixed but generally supportive of HISA's dual goals of uniform rules and standards for medication control and safety. There were a few important exceptions, however. The national Horsemen's Benevolent and Protective Association (HBPA) and several state racing commissions challenged the legislation in a Texas federal district court; the states of Oklahoma and West Virginia, their racing commissions, and other plaintiffs filed a second lawsuit in Kentucky. Both lawsuits challenged the constitutionality of granting regulatory authority to a private entity; both lawsuits were dismissed, but litigation continued. Legislation giving the Federal Trade Commission more oversight of HISA may have solved the constitutionality question, but through early 2023, the issue remained unsettled.[4]

The passage of HISA is a testament to the perseverance of congressmen Andy Barr, a Republican from Kentucky, and Paul D. Tonko, a New York Democrat, a bipartisan duo who did not know when to quit. Barr and Tonko had introduced similar legislation several times before, but they persisted until then–Senate majority leader Mitch McConnell, a Republican from Kentucky, finally got on board.

The HISA backstory is more complicated, though, and its origins can be traced to a series of articles in *Sports Illustrated* that, ironically, generally supported racing's fragmented regulatory status quo.

During the summer of 1969, *Sports Illustrated* ran a three-part series on drugs in sports that publisher Garry Valk called the "first comprehensive and authoritative study of a vastly complicated problem."[5] The magazine had written about drugs before, but an earlier article focused mainly on amphetamines, cocaine, and human athletes. The only reference to horse racing in the earlier article, made in passing, was a comparison of painkillers: "Novocain has a counterpart for today's athlete in the pain-killing Butazolidin [Bute], an analgesic legally (in some states) administered to race horses to permit them to run on sore limbs."[6] Eight years later, in a state where Bute was not legal for racing, the winner of the Kentucky Derby would be disqualified (see chapter 14).

The first two parts of Bil Gilbert's series covered increased drug use—both legal and prohibited—in human athletics, with examples from the World Series, the Sugar Bowl, the National Basketball Association championships, soccer, cycling, and the Olympics. Horse racing took center stage in the third article as an exemplar of how drug regulation should work. Gilbert did not address the potential problems of having different rules in each state. Instead, he focused on the proposition that *any* rules prohibiting doping were better than no rules. "It can be claimed that horse racing is the sport with the worst reputation for doping," Gilbert wrote:

> In a technical sense the reputation is deserved, since nowhere else in U.S. sports do any drug regulations exist that can be broken. . . . Racing has admitted that drugs can affect athletic performance, defined what doping is and established an apparatus to detect the practice and punish offenders. . . . One thing that makes the racing situation particularly instructive is that since the competition is between animals, the issues are not obscured by real or phony sentimentality.[7] There is little pretense that anti-doping regulations exist for the good of the horses. The rules are for what racing potentates consider the good of the sport.

And, Gilbert might have added, for the good of the bettors whose wagers drive horse racing. The substantive issue for Gilbert in the medication debate was that "drugs can corrupt a sport." No argument there. "This is the key premise that has been accepted by racing. Without becoming embroiled in humane or metaphysical debates, racing has defined what sport is—or at least should be. Sport is a matching of two or more peers to determine who can best perform certain physical feats. For sport to be of interest, to have emotional impact, to be an artistic or a commercial success, the contestants must be as equal as possible. None should have an artificial advantage over the others and, just as important, all suspicion of such advantage should be eliminated." The appearance of impropriety, the author correctly noted, can be as destructive to the reputation of a sport as actual doping.[8]

Suggesting that coverage of horse racing's problems in *Sports Illustrated* and other news outlets had any real influence on matters taken up by Congress is speculative at best, especially considering that Gilbert's articles investigated PEDs, while Congress initially focused on race fixing, or manipulating the outcomes of races with sedatives, bribes, and intimidation. Nevertheless, the timing of the legislative hearings is instructive.

In May 1972, three years after Gilbert's series on doping, the House Select Committee on Crime opened the first congressional hearings that focused on organized crime and sports. The original intent of the hearings was to investigate a number of sports. As the hearings stretched into 1973, however, "it became apparent that the investigation into criminal activities in pari-mutuel racing alone was sufficient to keep the committee and its investigators active through the end of the year," according to a report issued by the committee. "The public hearings produced some shocking disclosures," the preface to the report stated. "These included a full revelation of the scandalous events that led to syndicate takeover of one racetrack and a near successful effort to secure a second; testimony by individuals that bribes were routinely made to racing commissioners and public officials in exchange for racing licenses or favorable racing dates; sophisticated methods employed by small groups of unscrupulous individuals to fix races for high returns on modest investments, and the exposure of racing's Achilles' heel—a small and inadequate security force in desperate need of increased manpower and authority to conduct unhampered interstate investigations."[9]

Public interest in the hearings was high because of racing's alleged ties to organized crime and a few "celebrity" witnesses. As a result, many of the sessions were televised, a rarity in the early 1970s.

The broadcasts reinforced an image of horse racing as a game where cheaters win and bettors and fans lose. For more than half a century, little has happened to erase that perception.

One of the star witnesses was admitted race fixer Bobby Byrne. Byrne had been arrested by Thoroughbred Racing Protective Bureau agents in April 1971 as he tried to enter the backstretch at Suffolk Downs in Massachusetts while carrying two syringes filled with an unnamed tranquilizer. He showed up at the hearing wearing dark sunglasses, a lime-green suit, and a yellow shirt—all unimpressive in the black-and-white newspaper photographs—and testified about drugging horses with tranquilizers hundreds of times at East Coast and Midwest tracks during 1968, 1969, and 1970. The objective, he said, was to manipulate the order of finish and engage in exotic betting to collect large payoffs for modest wagers. "The public don't stand a chance," Byrne told the committee:

> There is no way. . . . The public is getting swindled every day. . . . They are so gullible. They know it is cooked, they suspected it, and there are people that know definitely it is, and yet they come back every day looking for more. They are a glutton for punishment. Let's face it. The American people are. We are noted for being the biggest suckers in the world, and other countries take our money and here I am, I take the American people's money because there's more of it. So, it's the same way. You will never clear it up in a million years. There is no way.[10]

Responding to a question from committee member Larry Winn Jr., from Kansas, Byrne supported the idea of a federal takeover of racing. He even offered his help:

Winn: In other words, you are endorsing the idea of a federal commission; do I understand you right?

Byrne: No question in my mind.

Winn: You think it would be tougher?

Byrne: No doubt about it. And I'll tell you, I would like to be hired for the job to see if we could get to fix a race. If we can't, then you know you were successful.

Winn: I tell you, with your background and your experience, you might be the type of man we want to hire, because you could save us a lot of time.[11]

Byrne also admitted having connections to the Gambino crime family and testified about an unidentified drug that defied detection and could slow a horse by a few seconds in a race. "It is like putting a baby to sleep with a bottle or pacifier," Byrne said of the drug. "That is how good it is." Responding to a question from Joseph A. Phillips, chief counsel for the committee, Byrne explained how the drug could be used to manipulate the outcome of a race:

Phillips: It substantially affects his running speed?

Byrne: Yes, it does. He will go through the motions. See, a horse can cover his own length in one-fifth of a second. And the horse travels, let's say, the average thoroughbred travels 40 miles an hour. Let's say 38–43 miles an hour, depending on his condition. Now this horse will go through this motion, but his time is going to increase. And he is going to be travelling like probably 33 miles an hour. Seconds are a vital thing in horseracing, so he will go through the motions, but he just is not going to win. I don't care what anybody says, he is not going to win.

Phillips: In all of these situations where you actually hit the horse [with the drug], the horse ran out of the money?

Byrne: Definitely, out of the money.

The confessed race fixer also told the committee about experimenting with every drug he could get, both legal and illegal, on a Thoroughbred named Robert Kope, a durable but unfortunate son of Intentionally that raced 108 times.[12]

Witnesses also included Joseph "The Baron" Barboza, a mob enforcer implicated in at least two dozen murders.[13] The Baron had no particular interest in horse racing or in fixing the outcomes, but he testified about strong-arming jockeys to cooperate in race-fixing schemes for other gamblers. He also suggested that entertainer Frank Sinatra had ties to organized crime, a connection the singer denied.[14]

Spencer J. Drayton, president of the Thoroughbred Racing Protective Bureau (TRPB), played down the testimony about race fixing, telling reporters these sensational claims by "cheap hoodlums" gave horse racing "an undeserved black eye." This was not an altogether unexpected assessment from the man charged with eliminating race fixing. Drayton also discounted the impact of organized crime. "Our experience is that organized crime isn't an important factor in racing," he said at a press conference. "They're trying to beat the bookies. They're fighting among themselves."[15] However, a string of indictments in the Northeast and Midwest a few years later gave credence to the testimony of Byrne and other witnesses.

The mastermind of numerous race-fixing schemes during the mid-1970s was Tony Ciulla, whose grand jury testimony led to indictments and convictions in Michigan and New Jersey. Placed under government protection in exchange for his testimony, Ciulla also implicated several prominent jockeys—including Angel Cordero Jr., Jorge Velazquez, Braulio Baeza, and Jacinto Vasquez—as accessories in his race-fixing activities. The riders denied the allegations. Ciulla was reportedly Bobby Byrne's boss before Byrne changed sides and became a witness for the federal government.[16]

The committee's final report included recommendations directed at Congress, state legislatures, and state racing commissions. Those recommendations included congressional action to make race fixing a federal crime, interstate cooperation in the creation of an enhanced racetrack security force, establishment of a national database for offenders, conflict-of-interest prohibitions, and limits on exotic betting to make race fixing less profitable. Drayton's TRPB was already working on some of these recommendations, including a national database and security force; however, a congressional mandate for state racing commissions to cooperate across state borders was virtually impossible to enforce.

The committee stopped short of recommending direct federal involvement to stop race fixing, as some of the witnesses had proposed. "Several members of the committee suggested the need for a U.S. Commissioner of Racing and for a strong, Federal security force with interstate capabilities," the final report noted. "This approach was seriously considered; however, we believe that the states should have the opportunity to act individual[ly] and jointly to restore and retain public confidence in their ability to police the sport of racing. It became obvious from the hearings that the adequacy of enforcement differed widely from State to State and that vigorous investigations frequently stopped at state lines."[17]

Apparently, a regulatory framework composed of scattered racing commission fiefdoms—the status quo Gilbert praised in *Sports Illustrated* and cited as a model for doping regulation in other sports—was good enough, at least for a while. Congress also seemed satisfied with racing's fragmented regulatory framework for the next decade.

Intentionally or not—and the press had questions about the committee's real purpose—the organized crime hearings cast horse racing in a terrible light, just as Harry Anslinger's drug raids and the attendant negative publicity had done forty years earlier. Triple Crown winners Secretariat, Seattle Slew, and Affirmed, as well as a decade of exceptional racing during the 1970s, managed to shift the public's focus away from the hearings. Meanwhile, congressional attention toward racing continued, albeit with a shifting emphasis.

In 1978 Congress passed the Interstate Horseracing Act (IHA).[18] The act legalized interstate wagering and set the stage for simulcasting, remote betting, and a fundamental change in racing's business model. Horse racing, which had been the most popular *spectator* sport for decades, when bettors had to actually show up at a racetrack to place a legal bet, quickly became a nonspectator vehicle for offtrack wagering. In 2019 (the last year not affected by the COVID-19 pandemic) 91.75 percent of the betting handle was wagered somewhere other than at a racetrack.[19] Except for "event" days such as the Triple Crown and Breeders' Cup races, on most days there are few spectators present at tracks to place bets and buy hot dogs, beer, programs, and souvenirs.

Then, in 2000, in response to a Department of Justice argument that interstate remote wagering violated the federal Wire Act, despite the language of the IHA, Congress came to racing's defense with a clarifying amendment establishing the legality of remote wagering.[20] The stated government policy behind the IHA was limited to the regulation of interstate wagering on horse races.[21] However, the legislation suggested that Congress had the jurisdiction (if not necessarily the will) under the US Constitution's commerce clause to regulate other aspects of Thoroughbred racing affecting interstate commerce.[22] That nascent will to act would not manifest for another decade, when Congress took up legislation with a different focus. The target then would not be an outside influence like organized crime; it would be the sport's inability to police itself.

Why the pivot? Perhaps because Congress began to pay attention to the critics of "permissive medication," a policy shift during the early 1970s that liberalized drug rules in most racing states. "During the past four years a series of public disclosures concerning the wide-spread abuse of so-called 'permissive medication' rules in horse racing has contributed to increased public distrust in the sport," attorney Russell J. Gaspar said in a prepared statement to a House Subcommittee on Criminal Justice in 1983. "Racing writers in the *Washington Post, Philadelphia Inquirer, New York Daily News,* and in *Sports Illustrated,* have discussed in great detail how drugs can not only contribute to astonishing changes in form, but are used to fix races and to permit horses that would otherwise be unable to compete to enter the starting gate."[23]

One of those racing writers was Andrew Beyer, who covered the sport for the *Washington Post* for decades. He was one of the first individuals to rail against Lasix in the 1970s, when he noticed dramatic improvements in the form of some horses in Maryland. For a time, Beyer must have felt like a voice crying in the wilderness.[24] "The entire racing establishment was lying to us and cheating us," Beyer wrote:

> The veterinarians who were made the all-powerful men on the backstretch by the legalization of drugs which they administered; the trainers, who were given a perfect tool with which to manipulate their horses' form, and the Maryland Racing Commission which so casually ignored the interests of the betting public. . . .
>
> It all started about four years ago, when one trainer discovered the drug [Lasix] and saw that it could improve some horses by 20 lengths overnight. A few more trainers started using it, illegally, and suddenly they were accomplishing feats that the greatest horsemen in history would have envied. The Racing Form's past performances were becoming almost irrelevant. And when Lasix finally was legalized, everybody was given a license to steal.[25]

Two years later, Beyer would make a similar warning about a new drug: "Sublimaze, known generically as fentanyl, was created in the laboratory by a Belgian pharmaceutical firm a decade ago," Beyer wrote. "It was devised primarily to relieve postoperative pain in humans. But when it started showing up at the nation's race tracks three or four years ago, unscrupulous veterinarians and trainers found it was almost the perfect illegal drug."[26]

Another organization that was late getting to the table was the national Jockeys' Guild, which finally took a public stand against permissive medication in 1979. "Maybe the Jockeys' Guild has waited too long to say what it's about to say now," the guild's managing director Nick Jemas said, "but controlled and permissive medication should be banned entirely to stop the constant and increasing parade of lame, sore, worn out, and completely exhausted horses from going to the post every day. The public is not being given good racing. More and more jockeys are injured, seriously, and killed."[27]

"Permissive medication rules are a relatively new phenomenon," Gaspar's statement continued:

> Prior to 1968, it was illegal in nearly every racing jurisdiction to permit a horse to run while medicated. However, the disqualification of Dancer's Image, then 1968 Kentucky Derby winner, for running on phenylbutazone, was the impetus for change. During the late 1960s and early 1970s permissive medication rules were adopted in most states.
>
> A variety of reasons were given for liberalization of the drug rules. The foremost was that the expansion of racing seasons created year-round pressures to field horses, pressures that could only be relieved if lame or aching horses could be medicated rather than rested. Phenylbutazone ("Bute") was the drug most horsemen wanted for this purpose. Another argument was that "bleeders"—horses that bled from the nose or lungs during a race—needed medication to help control their hemorrhages. As a result, furosemide ("Lasix") was legalized. These, and a wide variety of other drugs, including corticosteroids, were permitted on the theory that they were legitimate medications that merely let a horse perform at its potential, rather than distorting of altering the animal's performance.[28]

The distinction between therapeutic medications and performance-enabling or performance-enhancing drugs is a contentious issue that continues to be debated today in both horse racing and human athletics.

During 1982 and 1983, the House Subcommittee on Criminal Justice staged a series of hearings targeting corrupt horse racing practices, performance-enhancing drugs, and legislation to establish uniform rules to control the use of drugs in racehorses and test for the presence of prohibited medications. Federal intervention was overdue, according to Representative Bruce F. Vento, author of the Corrupt Horseracing Act of 1981. In a prepared statement, Vento said this legislation was necessary because, "with control in the hands of independent state racing commissions, there is no centralized body with the facilities comparable to the federal government in USDA, DEA, FDA, to develop tests for the detection of new drugs." Vento added that doping was a "real" threat to the integrity of horse racing, that most bettors believe "horse races are fixed pretty often," and that the legal use of drugs could have "a harmful effect on the breeding industry" by masking "inherited unsoundness" in horses used for breeding.[29]

The Senate Subcommittee on Criminal Law held similar hearings in 1982. Subcommittee chair Charles Mathias Jr. acknowledged "some progress" by the states in adopting uniform medication rules but cautioned the racing community about a "small, dark cloud on the horizon, the possibility of Federal legislation to deal with the medication problem." Mathias noted that, "since 'Preakness Week' a year ago":

> I have watched the progress of the States in coming to grips with this problem on their own. Although some progress has been made by the States in accepting a uniform set of medication guidelines, I think it is clear, and I think that most fair-minded people would conclude that the States have not yet solved the problem. . . . While some medication is, of course, necessary from time to time to cure illnesses that could keep these magnificent animals healthy, it seems to me that race-day medication is hard on the horses; it is unfair to the horses and unfair to the bettors, since the records of past performances are worthless without an accompanying record of medication.

The Corrupt Horseracing Practices Act, Mathias explained, would require "prerace testing of all horses," would ban "the race-day use of all drugs, including bute and lasix," and would "prohibit the icing, numbing or freezing of all horses prior to a race." He concluded, "It is a tough bill, but it is a tough problem."[30]

Despite an ominous title that raised the specter of widespread wrongdoing that demanded action on a national level, the Corrupt Horseracing Practices Act of 1981 made little progress in either the House or the Senate. The hearings were significant for a different reason, however. They signaled a shift in congressional attention away from wise-guy witnesses, racketeering, fixed races, and organized crime and toward essential issues that still shape the debate about drugs in horse racing: the important difference between therapeutic medications and performance-enhancing drugs, race-day medication, the welfare and safety of horses and their riders, and federal intervention to create uniform rules and testing procedures versus state-directed programs.

More hearings followed in subsequent sessions of Congress and suffered the same ultimate fate—no action. A few weeks after the tragic breakdown of Eight Belles in the 2008 Kentucky Derby, the House Subcommittee on Commerce, Trade, and Consumer Protection held a hearing on "Breeding, Drugs, and Breakdowns: The State of Thoroughbred Horseracing and the Welfare of the Thoroughbred Horse." One of the issues raised by the committee was a familiar one: a central authority for medication regulation. Another was steroids.

"What is going on here?" Representative Jan Schakowsky asked in her opening statement to the committee. "What is happening to the Sport of Kings? Unlike every other professional and amateur sport, horseracing lacks a central regulatory authority or league that can promulgate uniform rules and regulations. While baseball and football now impose strict rules that severely penalize players for steroid and performance-enhancing drugs, horseracing remains a patchwork of different regulations from State to State."[31]

The witness lists at these hearings included organizations and individuals that would become familiar whenever Congress tackled medication reform: the Humane Society of the United States, the Jockey Club, the National Association of State Racing Commissioners, the Horsemen's Benevolent and Protective Association, the American Veterinary Medical Association, the American Association of Equine Practitioners, the American Horse Council, the National Thoroughbred Racing Association, the Thoroughbred Horsemen's Association, animal welfare and aftercare groups, and a succession of veterinarians, racing chemists, racing commissioners, owners, trainers, jockeys, legislators, and the occasional journalist. While the names of the organizations' representatives changed over the years, organizational policies—either for or against the legislation—seldom wavered.

Congress was beginning to do a good job of identifying the drug issues that dogged horse racing, but reaching a consensus about federal intervention seemed an impossible goal.

18

Legislating Integrity?

The public perception that horse racing is a crooked game fueled by a seemingly endless string of doping scandals can be as damaging to the sport's reputation as actual wrongdoing, although there is plenty of that as well. Both perception and reality were on the mind of Jockey Club chairman Ogden Mills Phipps Jr. at the 2007 Jockey Club Round Table in Saratoga, New York. "The stewards of The Jockey Club cannot stand the pace that we're going at," Phipps said of industry efforts to resolve doping concerns. "Integrity issues, or even the perception of integrity issues, cause grave concern to anyone overseeing a business of any kind. They are especially troublesome for businesses involved with spectator sports." He could have added that spectator sports that depend on gambling revenue to survive are particularly vulnerable when integrity is in question. Customers' trust can be easy to lose and difficult to regain, especially with the growing number of legal sports betting options. "To be quite candid," Phipps said:

> the stewards of The Jockey Club think it's a disgrace that numerous horses in our sport's most prominent and highly visible races are routinely trained by people who have repeated medication-related violations.
>
> At the present time, there are no penalties for owners of horses who test positive for a banned substance. In the past, we believed that was correct. But if owners are picking trainers who are routinely fined or suspended for medication

infractions, we should reconsider an owner-responsibility rule.

I might also add that we firmly believe anabolic steroids should be banned at racetracks and, for that matter, in horses at yearling and 2-year-old sales.

We agree with Andy Beyer: the use of illegal medication is indeed "a raging forest fire" and if we don't put it out soon, it will consume us.

There is nothing more important to The Jockey Club and the stewards of The Jockey Club than resolving the medication dilemma. We have to level the playing field for the sake of this industry.[1]

In a few sentences, Phipps foreshadowed coming disasters, including a Kentucky Derby winner racing on steroids the next year (Big Brown, 2008) and the disqualification of another Derby winner conditioned by a trainer with a long history of medication violations (Medina Spirit, 2021). Phipps did not specifically address the possibility of federal intervention in racing's fight against doping. Nevertheless, legislation was coming, albeit in fits and starts.

First up was the Interstate Horseracing Improvement Act of 2011, which garnered a surprising amount of attention. Committee hearings were held in both houses of Congress: "A Review of Efforts to Protect Jockeys and Horses in Horseracing" in the House Subcommittee on Health, and "Medication and Performance-Enhancing Drugs in Horseracing" in the Senate Committee on Commerce, Science, and Transportation. Once again, federal intervention was a prominent focus during the hearings, although the proposed law did not create a federal oversight agency.

"Today's hearing will look at the effects of drug use in horseracing, how it impacts the health and well-being of jockeys, and whether adequate rules and uniform enforcement exists to prevent doping in horseracing," Joseph R. Pitts, chair of the House Subcommittee on Health, explained in his opening statement:

> In 2008, members of the Energy and Commerce Committee held a hearing on "Breeding, Drugs, and Breakdowns: The State of Thoroughbred Horseracing and the Welfare of the Thoroughbred Racehorse." At that time, we heard testimony and promises that reform was needed and would be forthcoming. . . .
>
> We will consider the need for a national set of uniform rules to prohibit the use of performance-enhancing drugs with a set of consequential penalties for violations. We can look at whether it is possible to create a uniform set of rules for drug use—perhaps zero tolerance—so that every State, every race, is conducted on a level playing field which is fair to all competitors, similar to what we have in other professional sports.[2]

In the Senate, Tom Udall further explained the purposes of the legislation: "Number one, ban race-day medication and horses from racing under the influence of performance-enhancing drugs. Number two, kick the cheaters out of the sport after three violations of the rules. And three, require drug testing of independent labs."[3]

This legislation, which would have amended the Interstate Horseracing Act of 1978, included policy requirements for racing associations, civil penalties for individuals administering prohibited substances, and, for the first time, suspension of a doped horse. In summary:

> H.R. 1733 / S. 886: Interstate Horseracing Improvement Act of 2011—Amends the Interstate Horseracing Act of 1978 to prohibit: (1) entering a horse in a race that is subject to an interstate off-track wager if the person knows the horse

is under the influence of a performance-enhancing drug; or
(2) knowingly providing a horse with such a drug if the
horse, while under the influence of such drug, will participate in a race that is subject to an interstate off-track wager.

Prohibits a host racing association from conducting
a race that is the subject of an interstate off-track wager
unless it has in place a policy that: (1) bans providing a
performance-enhancing drug to a horse that will participate
in such race while under the influence of the drug, (2) bans
the racing of a horse that is under the influence, and
(3) requires that an accredited third party conformity assessment body test the first-place horse and one additional randomly selected horse for any such drug and report any test
results demonstrating that a horse may have participated
while under the influence to the Federal Trade Commission
(FTC) and any host racing commission that entered into an
agreement to enforce this Act's provisions.

Sets forth penalties for violations, including: (1) civil
penalties and suspension of a person providing a horse with
such drug, and (2) suspension of a horse that is provided
with such a drug or that is raced in violation of this Act.
Provides for enforcement of this Act through private civil
actions and by the FTC, including through an agreement
with a host state's racing commission.[4]

Despite interest in the legislation and the hearings, the Interstate
Horseracing Improvement Act of 2011 never advanced beyond the
House and Senate committees.

The Horseracing Integrity and Safety Act of 2013 introduced some
new elements related to proposed federal intervention. First, the
legislation required the creation of an independent antidoping organization pursuant to the Office of National Drug Control Policy
Reauthorization Act of 2006. Second, the act provided a two-year

grace period for the race-day use of Lasix. Third, consent of the anti-doping organization would be required for any offtrack wagering. In summary:

> Horseracing Integrity and Safety Act of 2013—Requires: (1) there to be an independent anti-doping organization with responsibility for ensuring the integrity and safety of horse races that are the subject of interstate off-track wagers, and (2) the independent anti-doping organization designated pursuant to the Office of National Drug Control Policy Reauthorization Act of 2006 to serve as such organization.
>
> Sets forth as the duties of such organization: (1) developing, publishing, and maintaining rules regarding substances, methods, and treatments that may and may not be administered to a horse participating in such a race; (2) implementing programing relating to anti-doping education, research, testing, and adjudication to prevent any horse participating in such a race from racing under the effect of any prohibited substance, method, or treatment; and (3) excluding from participation in any such race any person who is determined to have violated such a rule or who is subject to a suspension from horse racing activities by any state racing commission.
>
> Prescribes conditions under which such organization may: (1) suspend the period a person is excluded from participation; and (2) permit the use of furosemide by a horse participating in such a race during the two-year period following enactment of this Act.
>
> Permits a host racing association to conduct a horse race that is the subject of an interstate off-track wager, and permits an interstate off-track wager to be accepted by an off-track betting system, only if consent is obtained from such organization. Requires such organization to ensure that all costs incurred in carrying out its duties are defrayed pursuant to agreements for such consent.[5]

Although the US Anti-Doping Agency (USADA) was not specifically mentioned as the independent organization required by the law, there seemed to be a general assumption at the hearing that it would fill this role. Travis T. Tygart, the CEO of USADA, was one of the witnesses, and his responses to submitted questions anticipated a role for his agency.[6] Moving forward, the USADA's involvement in any federal antidoping program was a central element in obtaining the support of the Thoroughbred community.

Like previous attempts, the Horseracing Integrity and Safety Act of 2013 failed to make it out of committee.

More promising (and similar to legislation that would pass a few years later) was the Thoroughbred Horseracing Integrity Act of 2015, the first of a trio of bipartisan bills introduced in the House over the next five years by Andy Barr (R-KY) and Paul D. Tonko (D-NY). The Barr-Tonko bill would have established the Thoroughbred Horseracing Anti-Doping Authority, tasked with developing lists of permitted and prohibited substances, a schedule of penalties, research and testing programs, investigative procedures, and laboratory accreditation standards. The racing industry would be responsible for funding the authority. In summary:

Thoroughbred Horseracing Integrity Act of 2015— Establishes the Thoroughbred Horseracing Anti-Doping Authority as an independent organization with responsibility for developing and administering an anti-doping program for Thoroughbred horses (covered horses), the trainers, owners, veterinarians, and employees of such persons and other personnel who are engaged in the care, training, or racing of such horses (covered persons), and horseraces that involve only Thoroughbreds and that are the subject of interstate off-track wagers (covered horseraces). Grants the Authority exclusive jurisdiction for anti-doping matters over all covered horses, persons, and horseraces, effective January 1, 2017.

Imposes the jurisdiction and authority of the Authority as conditions upon the privilege to accept, receive, or transmit wagers on, and to participate in, covered horseraces. Vests the Authority with the same powers over Thoroughbred horseracing licensees as the state racing commissions have.

Directs the Authority to develop and administer the Thoroughbred horseracing anti-doping program, which shall include:

- lists of permitted and prohibited substances and methods;
- a schedule of sanctions for violations;
- programs relating to anti-doping research and education;
- testing procedures, standards, and protocols for in-competition and out-of-competition testing;
- procedures for investigating, charging, and adjudicating violations and for the enforcement of sanctions for violations; and
- laboratory standards for accreditation and testing requirements, procedures, and protocols.

Conditions eligibility to participate in covered horseraces on covered persons agreeing that they and their covered horses shall be bound by the provisions of the program.

Directs the Authority to establish: (1) a list of anti-doping rule violations applicable to either horses or covered persons; (2) standards of accreditation for laboratories involved in the testing of samples taken from Thoroughbred horses, the process for achieving and maintaining accreditation, and the standards and protocols for testing of samples; (3) rules for anti-doping results management and the disciplinary process for anti-doping rule violations; and (4) uniform rules imposing sanctions against covered persons and/or covered horses for anti-doping rule violations.

Requires funds for the establishment and administration of the anti-doping program to be paid by the Thoroughbred horseracing industry.[7]

This legislation would not have affected the Interstate Horseracing Act. It compared the congressional commitment to fairness in Thoroughbred racing to its commitment to fair competition in human athletics and cited USADA as "an independent anti-doping organization possessing high-level expertise and credibility in the development and administration of an anti-doping program." The bill died in the House Subcommittee on Commerce, Manufacturing, and Trade, but it set the stage for future efforts.

In the same session of Congress, Representative Joseph R. Pitts introduced the Horseracing Integrity and Safety Act of 2015. Similar to legislation Pitts introduced two years earlier, this version also died in committee.

The Horseracing Integrity Act of 2017, introduced by Barr and Tonko, was substantially similar to their first try two years earlier, except for a new name for the regulatory authority and a few important twists. The bill would have given the Federal Trade Commission (FTC) exclusive jurisdiction over all antidoping and medication programs in horse racing, with USADA providing oversight and playing a substantial role in program development and implementation; eliminated race-day medication, with no exception for Lasix; and imposed levies on state racing commissions to fund the antidoping authority, based on the number of starters in each state. In summary:

> Horseracing Integrity Act of 2017—This bill establishes the Horseracing Anti-Doping and Medication Control Authority as an independent non-profit corporation with responsibility for developing and administering an anti-doping and medication control program for: (1) Thoroughbred, Quarter, and Standardbred horses that participate in

horse races that have a substantial relation to interstate commerce, (2) such horse races, and (3) the personnel engaged in the care, training, or racing of such horses.

The Federal Trade Commission (FTC) shall have exclusive jurisdiction over all horse racing anti-doping and medication control matters. The Authority and such FTC jurisdiction shall terminate if an interstate compact providing for services consistent with such program is established within five years after the program takes effect.

The Authority may enter into agreements with state racing commissions to implement the program within their jurisdictions.

Program elements shall include:

- anti-doping and medication control rules,
- lists of permitted and prohibited substances and methods,
- a prohibition on the administration of any such substance within 24 hours of a horse's next racing start, and
- testing and laboratory standards.

The Authority shall:

- develop, maintain, and publish such lists;
- establish a list of anti-doping and medication control rule violations applicable to either covered horses or persons;
- establish standards and the process for laboratory accreditation and sample testing; and
- promulgate rules for anti-doping and medication control results management, for the disciplinary process for violation results management, and for imposing sanctions for violations.

The bill sets forth civil enforcement provisions.

Activities under this bill are funded by an assessment placed on state racing commissions based on the calculation of cost per racing starter.[8]

The House Subcommittee on Digital Commerce and Protection held a contentious hearing on the bill. There was opposition from major horse racing groups, and the legislation never made it beyond the subcommittee.

According to Barr, the legislation was necessary because of the fragmented regulatory framework of American racing. "Our signature racing industry labors under a patchwork of conflicting and inconsistent, state-based rules governing prohibited substances, lab accreditation, testing, and penalties for violations," said the congressman from Kentucky:

> This lack of uniformity has impeded interstate commerce, compromised the international competitiveness of the industry, and undermined public confidence in the integrity of the sport.
>
> This legislation would remedy these problems by authorizing the creation of a non-governmental anti-doping authority, the Horseracing Anti-Doping and Medication Control Authority (HADA), governed by representatives of all major constituencies of the industry and responsible for implementing a national, uniform medication program for the entire horse racing industry. These reforms would eliminate the perception of unfair competition and enhance the reputation of U.S. racing on both national and international levels.[9]

Denied twice, Barr and Tonko tried again in 2019. This legislation was nearly identical to their 2017 bill, but this time, there was growing enthusiasm among their colleagues in the House of Representatives and support from the Coalition for Horseracing Authority (representing eighteen racing organizations, racetracks, owners and breeders associations, and animal welfare groups) and the Water, Hay, Oats Alliance (a coalition of more than seventeen hundred owners, breeders, trainers, and industry leaders).

By early September 2020, the Barr-Tonko Horseracing Integrity and Safety Act had 259 sponsors. It was approved by the House Energy and Commerce Committee by a vote of forty-six to five on September 9. Concerns raised by the committee members voting against approval included the lack of a strong veterinary presence during the development phase of the legislation and the restrictions on Lasix. Tonko assured critics that there would be veterinarian input going forward, but veterinarians would be subject to the bill's conflict-of-interest provisions. He added that there had already been a compromise on the use of Lasix during the three-year research study mandated by the bill.[10] At this point, granting the FTC authority over all safety and medication control issues garnered little attention. That would quickly change.

On the same day the bill cleared the House committee, Senate majority leader Mitch McConnell introduced his version of the legislation. Approved by a voice vote in the House of Representatives in September 2020 and by the Senate three months later, the Horseracing Integrity and Safety Act of 2020 (HISA) was included in a mammoth $2.3 trillion spending bill.[11] Part of a multisubject category labeled "Other Matters," which included bankruptcy relief, western water and Indian affairs, Sudan claims resolution, and other unrelated bills, HISA became law when President Trump signed the spending bill on December 27, 2020. In summary:

Horseracing Integrity and Safety Act of 2020—This bill recognizes the Horseracing Integrity and Safety Authority for purposes of developing and implementing a horseracing anti-doping and medication control program and a racetrack safety program.

The authority shall establish an anti-doping and medication control standing committee and a racetrack safety standing committee to provide guidance to the authority on the development and maintenance of the programs.

The Federal Trade Commission (FTC) shall have oversight over the authority. The authority shall submit to the FTC any proposed rule, standard, or procedure developed by the authority to carry out the horseracing anti-doping and medication control program or the racetrack safety program. The authority shall seek to enter into an agreement with the U.S. Anti-Doping Agency or an entity equal in qualification under which the entity acts as the anti-doping and medication control enforcement agency under this bill.

Among the required elements of the horseracing safety program are sets of training and racing safety standards consistent with the humane treatment of horses, a system to maintain track surface quality, programs for injury and fatality analysis, investigation and disciplinary procedures, and an evaluation and accreditation program.

The bill sets forth other provisions regarding (1) funding, conflicts of interest, and jurisdiction; (2) registration with the authority; (3) program enforcement; (4) rule violations and civil sanctions; (5) testing laboratories; (6) review of final decisions of the authority by an administrative law judge; (7) unfair or deceptive acts or practices; and (8) agreements with state racing commissions.[12]

The new law was hailed as the "most significant safety and integrity development in the history of Thoroughbred racing," a "pivotal moment for the future of horseracing," and a "landmark moment."[13] However, there was also criticism from some major players, including the Horsemen's Benevolent and Protective Association (HBPA), the US Trotting Association (USTA), and several state racing commissions.

The first lawsuit challenging HISA was filed by the national HBPA and eleven state affiliates in US District Court for the Northern District of Texas, Lubbock Division, on March 15, 2021. The complaint for declaratory and injunctive relief argued in part that Congress's delegation of regulatory authority to the Horseracing Integrity and Safety Authority, and then by that authority to the Horseracing Integrity and Safety Authority Inc., a private, nonprofit Delaware corporation, was unconstitutional. The plaintiffs argued that the delegation of regulatory authority to a private entity was a violation of the well-established "nondelegation doctrine."[14]

A month later, the Oklahoma and West Virginia state racing commissions, the USTA, Hanover Shoe Farm, and several Oklahoma stakeholders filed a similar lawsuit in US District Court for the Eastern District of Kentucky, Lexington Division. Those plaintiffs claimed a number of constitutional violations, including violation of the nondelegation doctrine.[15]

The federal response was that the HBPA lawsuit was "premature" because the "complaint questions the validity of a law that currently subjects them to no obligation or penalty."[16] A similar response was applicable to the Oklahoma lawsuit filed in Kentucky. Both lawsuits were dismissed at the district court level in 2022, but appeals followed. Such lawsuits are commonly filed to challenge new laws, and they are anticipated by the laws' supporters. A more serious challenge to HISA, however, came as a surprise.

An essential component of HISA is USADA involvement in rule making and enforcement. In early November 2021 USADA CEO Travis T. Tygart gave the impression that the agency was fully on board: "We are honored to be involved at this stage to help draft and ultimately finalize gold-standard rules on anti-doping and medication control for the equine industry. We are excited with where this process is headed and with proposed rules being published for two additional rounds of public feedback."[17]

Although the law includes an important backup provision allowing the Horseracing Integrity and Safety Authority to enter into an agreement with USADA "or an entity equal in qualification," in reality, there are few options. As negotiations with USADA dragged on month after month, concerns were raised. During the University of Arizona's Global Symposium on Racing, Horseracing Integrity and Safety Authority chairman Charles Scheeler announced that not all parts of HISA would be ready for implementation by the statutory deadline of July 1, 2022. USADA's role in medication policy and enforcement would start with out-of-competition testing and investigation, Scheeler said, and postrace drug testing would remain the responsibility of state racing commissions until 2023. Scheeler justified the change in plans by explaining that a "mid-season handoff of race day testing was fraught with danger and fraught with risk," and the delay would permit synchronization with state racing commission schedules, allow laboratories to adopt new standards, and provide more time for feedback.[18]

The delay in implementation was certainly worrisome, but the announcement two weeks later that the Horseracing Integrity and Safety Authority and USADA were suspending contract negotiations was a surprise and a shock to HISA supporters. "We are deeply disappointed to announce that we have been unable to reach an agreement with the Horseracing Integrity and Safety Authority for USADA to become the enforcement agency for the anti-doping and medication control program for thoroughbred racing under the Horseracing Integrity and Safety Act," Tygart said in a December 23 statement:

> After months of negotiations, we have been unable to enter an agreement in line with the requirements of the Act, and one which would have given us a reasonable chance to put in place a credible and effective program. While we are obviously saddened by the outcome at this stage, we tried our absolute best to find a way forward but without success.
>
> While we desperately tried to reach an agreement to implement the program, without compromising our values, we have always said the passing of the legislation and the finalization of uniform, robust rules are huge victories for

the horses and the equine industry. We are honored to have been involved with these efforts to restore the integrity of thoroughbred horse racing. Though we are unsure what the future holds for USADA—if any—in this effort, we have offered to assist the Authority and others in the industry to ensure that the sport gets the program it needs and that the horses deserve.[19]

The Horseracing Integrity and Safety Authority released a similar statement, raising questions about what comes next.[20]

Turf writer Bill Finley spoke for much of the Thoroughbred racing community when he called for the Horseracing Integrity and Safety Authority and USADA to resolve their differences. "Thanks to the passage of the Horse Racing Integrity and Safety Act racing finally seemed ready to clean up a game where cheating trainers and the use of performance-enhancing drugs is a serious problem," Finley wrote in *Thoroughbred Daily News:*

> USADA was not only the best choice to take over the policing of the sport. It was the only choice. There is no one else.
>
> With USADA's announcement, HISA is in shambles and picking up the pieces will be a daunting, if not impossible task. USADA's involvement was the reason so many people were enthusiastic about HISA's passage. USADA and its CEO Travis Tygart are the gold standard when it comes to anti-doping and they get results. While it's true that HISA covers other areas and issues, none seem that important at the moment. This was always about bringing in USADA and letting them accomplish what the sport is incapable of doing on its own.
>
> Now what?[21]

Now what, indeed. How the suspension of negotiations would play out in the coming months was anybody's guess. It was a high-stakes game of chicken, and neither party seemed willing to blink. It was clear, though, that the Horseracing Integrity and Safety Authority needed a deal with USADA more than USADA needed a deal with the authority, especially when negotiating the details of an unfunded mandate. HISA eventually reached an agreement with a different enforcement organization, Drug Free Sport International.[22]

Meanwhile, the legislative process moved forward. On January 5, 2022, proposed rules for the safety portion of HISA were printed in the *Federal Register* for public comment.[23] They were ultimately approved and went into effect on July 1, 2022. By that date, the scheduled start date for the antidoping provisions of HISA, proposed medication rules had not yet been submitted to the FTC for approval. They were finally submitted in the fall of 2022. Implementation was delayed until at least January 1, 2023.

19

Genetics, the Wealth Gap, and the Myth of the Level Playing Field

It is almost impossible to review research, interviews, and media reports on doping in horse racing without coming across the phrase "level playing field" and the urgent need to find or create one. The phrase has become a popular sound bite that conveys the general idea of fairness in horse racing without actually saying so and without any specifics. If crafting a level playing field is the goal of a medication program, the search is a futile one, notwithstanding the Horseracing Integrity and Safety Act of 2020.

There is not, and cannot be, a truly level playing field in horse racing. Nor should there be. With actual parity, which the idea of a level playing field implies, every race would simply become a game of chance. Handicapping skills would be useless, and serious bettors would abandon horse racing in droves, favoring sports where picking a winner requires more than a roll of the dice or a Magic Eight Ball.[1]

The playing field is always tilted in favor of one or more horses, for a variety of reasons, not the least of which is money. The wealthier an owner is, the more likely he or she is to invest in the best bloodlines, the savviest trainers, and the winningest riders. Less fashionably bred horses can be excellent runners, of course, and long shots like Rich Strike can win the Kentucky Derby, but the odds definitely favor the rich. In fact, every aspect of the Thoroughbred industry is designed specifically to create a distinctly unlevel field of competition. The goal of breeders has always been to produce a faster horse—the long-standing idea behind the maxim of breeding the best to the best to get the best. Owners select trainers based on their ability to saddle winners at whatever level an owner can afford to compete, and the top jockeys vie for the best mounts on the basis of winning more races than other riders.

The trick to success in racing is not to level the playing field but rather to fashion a playing field that disadvantages the other horses in a race. The tools are breeding nicks (particular stallion and mare combinations), trainer choices, and jockey decisions that mesh so that the "best" horse—whatever that means—wins more often than not. The fundamental problem with the use of performance-enhancing drugs is not that they create an unlevel playing field, although they do that. Instead, PEDs skew the playing field in a wildly unpredictable way, and information about their use is kept secret from bettors and fans alike. But that secrecy is not the biggest problem. In horse racing—and in human athletics—the most unfair competition is, and always has been, between PED users and the regulators and chemists who are trying to catch them.

Thoroughbreds, like human athletes, are inherently different from one another, and these differences make horse racing attractive for bettors, who want to outsmart the system, and for ordinary fans, who may want nothing more than to see an exciting race. Differences in genetics, training, riders, nutrition, track surfaces, and veterinary care—the age-old debate about nature versus nurture—make for good sport.

In *The Sports Gene,* David Epstein writes that elite sports provide "a splendid stage for the fantastic menagerie that is human biological diversity."[2] Award-winning author Malcolm Gladwell elaborated on this concept in the *New Yorker:* "What we are watching when we watch elite sports, then, is a contest among wildly disparate groups of people, who approach the starting line with an uneven set of genetic endowments and natural advantage. . . .The menagerie is what makes sports fascinating. But it has also burdened high-level competition with a contradiction. We want sports to be fair and we take elaborate measures that no one competitor has an advantage over any other. But how can a fantastic menagerie ever be a contest among equals?"[3] Epstein and Gladwell are writing about human athletics, but substitute "racing" for "sports" and "horses" for "people," and the impossibility of a level playing field for horse racing is evident.

Gladwell then shifts gears in the direction of laser surgery to improve a baseball player's eyesight and Tommy John surgery to repair a pitcher's damaged throwing arm as examples of accepted ways to turn an athlete into "an improved version of his natural self." He points out the hypocrisy when drugs enter the picture: "When it comes to drugs Major League Baseball—like most sports [including horse racing]—draws the line. An athlete cannot use a drug to become an improved version of his natural self, even if the drug is used in doses that are not harmful and is something that—like testosterone—is no more than a copy of a naturally occurring hormone, available by prescription to anyone, virtually anywhere in the world." Gladwell concludes with "a vision of sports in which the object of competition is to use science, intelligence, and sheer will to conquer natural differences. [Tyler] Hamilton and [Lance] Armstrong [professional bicycle racers who doped and were caught] may simply be athletes who regard this kind of achievement as worthier than the gold medals of a man with the dumb luck to be born with a random genetic mutation."[4]

As more sophisticated drugs and other methods become available to Thoroughbred owners, breeders, and trainers—erythropoietin (EPO), gene doping and manipulation, and a constant stream of difficult-to-detect designer steroids and other PEDs, for example—will regulators and drug testers be able to keep pace? If not, will we reach a point where every horse competing is an "improved version of his natural self"? Will dumb genetic luck even be a factor moving forward?

Lance Armstrong argued that making PEDs available to all competitors is one way to achieve a level playing field. Perhaps racing secretaries should card "doping optional" races and identify horses with "PED-improved" natural selves. That's not likely to happen, but what about considering PEDs to be just another training and racing aid? That was James R. Keene's initial thought when the Jockey Club first considered regulating PEDs in the late 1890s. He relented only when he was informed that PEDs can harm horses.

What about blood doping not with EPO, which artificially increases the production of red blood cells and has been implicated in the deaths of professional cyclists, but with an autotransfusion of a horse's own blood before a race? What about genetic manipulation? Once the subject of science fiction, gene-editing technology is available and getting better all the time. The prospects are both fascinating and frightening.

Jennifer Doudna is a world-famous biochemist who helped develop the CRISPR gene-editing tool. She is also the subject of Walter Isaacson's best-selling biography *The Code Breaker*. There is a significant difference between gene editing to treat genetic diseases and using the technique for athletic enhancement. As she explains:

> The role of sports, at least since the first Olympics in 776 BC, is to celebrate two things: natural talent combined with disciplined effort. Enhancements would shift that balance, making human effort less of a component for victory. Therefore, the achievement becomes a little less praiseworthy and inspiring. There is a whiff of cheating if an athlete succeeds by obtaining some physical advantages through medical engineering.
>
> But there's a problem with this fairness argument. Most successful athletes have *always* been people who happen to have better athletic genes than the rest of us. Personal effort is a component, but it helps to be born with the genes for good muscles, blood, coordination, and other innate advantages.[5]

Doudna's concerns also apply to genetic manipulation for improved performance in Thoroughbreds. Is it fair to create ability beyond that possessed by a horse naturally? This might not be a pressing concern today, but it will be.

Unfortunately, I lack the "sprinter" gene, which should be obvious to anyone who knows me and has been confirmed by genetic testing. Ancestry.com's commercial genetic test, which provided the bad news, looks at a marker in the *ACTN3* gene, which plays an important role in athletic performance.[6] Doudna explains the connection: "Almost every champion runner has what is known as the R allele of the *ACTN3* gene. It produces a protein that builds fast-twitch fibers, and it is also associated with improving strength and recovery from muscle injury. Someday it may be possible to edit this variation of the *ACTN3* gene into the DNA of your kids. Would that be unfair? Is it unfair that some kids are born with it naturally? Why is one more unfair than the other?"[7]

The practical impact of my genetic profile is that if I were foolish enough to enter a sprint race, the playing field could never be tilted in my favor. But what if it were possible to tweak the sprinter gene to make me more competitive? What if it were possible to tweak the genetics of a Thoroughbred to make the horse more competitive? At what point does gene manipulation become doping? The answers are complicated. Solving these issues will require more than simply reciting a mantra about level playing fields.

Conclusion

The Racing Imperative

In 1999 the *New York Times* introduced "The Ethicist," a weekly advice column aimed at thorny ethical questions about charity ("What Do I Owe an Impoverished Villager?"), family problems ("May I Disinherit My Right-Wing Daughters?"), the workplace ("Should We Fire Our Unvaccinated Babysitter?"), personal relationships ("Is It OK to Drop Him Because of His Medical Condition?"), and other dilemmas. On September 5, 2014, a reader from Dallas, Texas—perhaps a Cowboys fan—broke new ground with a question about the ethics of supporting the National Football League (NFL): "I've recently begun to question my support for the N.F.L. I suspect that the recent discoveries about concussions and the prevalence of early-onset dementia among players are just the tip of the iceberg. Is it unethical to support a league that seems to know it is detrimental to the health of its participants? And if so, what should my response be? Don't go to games? Don't buy merchandise? Don't watch on television? Start actively opposing the N.F.L.? Write letters?"[1]

It was a timely question. Football was struggling to weather a significant controversy over the likelihood of players suffering traumatic brain injuries from repeated concussions and whether the NFL had been actively suppressing evidence of the risk. A best-selling book and a PBS documentary had brought public attention to the issue the year before, and professional football was still reeling from the accusations.[2]

Chuck Klosterman, the columnist for "The Ethicist" from 2012 to 2015, replied to the Dallas reader: "If an entire enterprise is corrupt, culpability is shared among participants." This would apparently include sports fans. "But that's not the dilemma troubling you," Klosterman continued. "What you are concerned about involves one disquieting aspect of one specific sport. You want to know if it's ethically acceptable to watch a game that is dangerous to the athletes who participate. And the answer to that query is yes." Klosterman added that although the reader was supporting and "financially subsidizing" a profession with "elective physical risks," players should have been aware of the danger by 2014. The risks of football, he noted, are "the risks associated with the work taken on by free people."[3]

Klosterman seems to suggest that it is ethically acceptable to enjoy and support an inherently dangerous sport as long as the participants know the risks and engage voluntarily. I don't have a problem with that logic. It's the basis of a long-standing legal principle known as "assumption of the risk." But Thoroughbreds are not "free people," and horses cannot choose to assume the risks associated with racing. And even if they could, the use of performance-enhancing drugs is not an inherent risk of harm if the game is honest. Instead, horses have to rely on the people who care for them and the regulators who police the sport to protect them from dopers. In some cases, that trust has been misplaced.

At the time, fans of Thoroughbred racing might have posed the same questions asked by the Dallas football fan, substituting "Thoroughbreds" for "athletes," "racing" for the "NFL" and "doping and breakdowns" for "concussions." Is it ethical to support horse racing when there are major doping scandals every few years, minor medication infractions much more often, and catastrophic breakdowns at a slowly diminishing but still alarming rate?

This becomes a much more perplexing ethical question because the horses—arguably among the major stakeholders in the sport—

have no say in how racing is conducted. In that context, even when all reasonable safety precautions have been taken, doping, breakdowns, and other accidents still occur. Consider, for example, the fatal injury suffered by Mongolian Groom during the running of the 2019 Breeders' Cup Classic.[4] Veterinarian Larry Bramlage, who compiled a comprehensive report on the horse's breakdown, concluded that the injury was likely the result of a preexisting condition—bilateral lameness—that was difficult to diagnose despite heightened prerace scrutiny.[5] In other words, it was an accident, with no shared fault.

Is it ethical to characterize breakdowns as an unfortunate but unavoidable cost of doing business in horse racing? That is a personal decision for every participant. I continue to watch horse racing and write about it, albeit with a palpable sense of dread at the start of every race. For me, horse racing is too big to fail but too vulnerable to embrace the status quo. Some animal welfare and animal rights organizations advocate for horses at the tracks, with objectives ranging from working within the system to enforce existing rules or change the rules to eliminating horse racing entirely. Success on these fronts has been spotty at best, disingenuous at worst.

Doping, in contrast, should never be considered an inherent cost of doing business in horse racing. State racing commissions should be actively concerned about doping and the welfare of their equine athletes, and many of them are. However, a fractured regulatory scheme in the United States makes even well-intentioned efforts difficult. The Horseracing Integrity and Safety Act (HISA), which was due to take effect on July 1, 2022 (safety provisions), and January 1, 2023 (medication provisions), was hailed as a major step toward uniform regulation. That was the rationale for selling HISA to Congress and the racing community in the first place, and it might eventually be the outcome, but significant problems developed, and the law created a rift among leading racing organizations. Most groups promoted HISA as a long-overdue solution to serious problems in the sport, but others filed lawsuits claiming that HISA is unconstitutional.[6] In addition, negotiations between the Horseracing Integrity and Safety Authority and the US Anti-Doping Agency (specifically named in HISA as the entity tasked with drafting and enforcing new rules) broke down. A substitute organization was eventually found: Drug Free Sport International.

Maintaining the public's—especially the betting public's—confidence that racing is fair and humane is vital. Otherwise, Thoroughbred racing may become nothing more than a scandal-prone, second-rate sport propped up by casinos, state subsidies, and a handful of important events. The Triple Crown races, the traveling Breeders' Cup weekends, and boutique meetings at a handful of historic tracks have significant staying power, but a much larger segment of the sport does not. Today, horse racing faces existential challenges. Consider boxing (once popular, but now, not so much) or greyhound racing (on the verge of extinction) as clues to Thoroughbred racing's possible future.

Trust in the integrity of racing, acceptance by the public, and the sport's credibility have always been cornerstones of Thoroughbred racing. The significance of those qualities came to the forefront during a February 2022 hearing involving the New York Racing Association (NYRA) and famed trainer Bob Baffert.

Days after Baffert trainee Medina Spirit finished first in the 2021 Kentucky Derby, the colt tested positive for the prohibited corticosteroid betamethasone. The positive result was confirmed when a second sample was tested.[7] However, subsequent testing performed at the request of Baffert and Medina Spirit's owners raised questions about the source of the drug in the colt's system. Nevertheless, Medina Spirit was eventually disqualified, second-place finisher Mandaloun was moved up to first place, the purse was redistributed, and Baffert was suspended for ninety days and fined $7,500. The Kentucky Horse Racing Commission affirmed the disqualification and the penalties and then refused to grant Baffert the customary stay.[8] Litigation continued, and the Kentucky Court of Appeals denied the motions of Baffert and Zedan Racing Stables Inc. for

Medina Spirit's memorial, located at Old Friends in Georgetown, Kentucky. Several weeks after crossing the finish line first in the 2021 Kentucky Derby (which was moved to the fall because of the COVID-19 pandemic), Medina Spirit collapsed during a workout and died. (Author's collection)

emergency relief.[9] That decision cleared the way for Baffert's ninety-day suspension to begin on Monday, April 4, 2022. He returned to racing at most tracks on July 3, 2022.

Well before the disqualification of Medina Spirit and Baffert's suspension became official, both Churchill Downs and NYRA took independent action against the well-known trainer. Churchill Downs suspended Baffert for two years and decreed that horses he trained could not earn Kentucky Derby qualifying points in prep races.[10] NYRA also suspended Baffert.[11] However, a federal court in New York ruled that the trainer's due process rights had been violated when he was suspended without a hearing.[12] The five-day due process hearing was held on January 24–28, 2022. Meanwhile, Baffert continued to train in New York under a permanent injunction prohibiting NYRA from enforcing the suspension.

According to a letter NYRA sent to Baffert regarding the decision to suspend him, public opinion was one of the rationales for the action: "In light of the above [a summary of Baffert's other recent drug violations], and other related information, NYRA has determined that the best interests of thoroughbred racing compel the temporary suspension of your entering horses in racing and occupying stall space at our racetracks. To do otherwise would compromise NYRA's investment in its operations as well as the public's perception of racing generally."[13] In a June 2021 press release, Churchill Downs voiced similar concerns about the impact of Baffert's spotty medication record on "public confidence in thoroughbred racing."[14]

On the second day of the Baffert-NYRA suspension hearing—January 25, 2022—the importance of the public's acceptance to horse racing's future and whether a trainer's doping issues can affect that acceptance came up, albeit under a new name: social license to operate (SLO). The concept of a social license that allows an entity to conduct operations is not new. Only in the last quarter century, however, has the term SLO emerged, initially in the context of resource-related endeavors such as mining, oil exploration and development, forest management, pulp and paper mills, and farming.[15] More recently, the concept of an SLO has been applied to racing and other horse sports.[16] Whether horse racing has an SLO, whether it needs one, and whether Baffert's reputation could damage it were at issue during the hearing. Testifying for NYRA was Camie Heleski, holder of a PhD from Michigan State University and a senior lecturer in the Department of Animal and Food Sciences at the University of Kentucky's College of Agriculture, Food, and Environment. Heleski is also a researcher in the relatively new area of applying SLO principles to racing and other horse sports.[17]

But what is a social license to operate? It is not what it sounds like. It is not legal permission to conduct business. In fact, unlike a traditional government-issued business license, a social license to operate is not a legal document at all. "Social License to Operate (SLO) is the public or 'social' acceptance, which grants permission or a 'license' [for a business] to undertake its activity; i.e., to 'operate.' . . . Today, SLO is acknowledged as the public's approval (or consent) of the activities of an institution."[18] One definition of SLO has three parts:

- Social legitimacy (how well the activity fits into the established norms of the community)
- Credibility (created by the activity's transparency and the ability to do what it says it will do)
- Trust (cooperation with the community to develop shared experiences)[19]

Put another way, "social licence can never be self-awarded, it requires that an activity enjoys sufficient trust and legitimacy and has the consent of those affected."[20]

Asked whether the unfavorable publicity in the mainstream media surrounding Baffert's violations could have a negative impact on Thoroughbred racing's SLO, Heleski suggested that it might. "Many people will talk about the issues of drugs and medications, and they have a big concern," Heleski was quoted as testifying. "They don't necessarily go into the nuance of levels. Most of the time, they feel like if there was a drug or medication noted, it's bad. They put it all under the umbrella of doping. If someone is so well known in a certain sport or industry that even the casual racing fan can identify them, they're more likely to make an impact when some news takes place."[21] Baffert may be one of the most recognizable figures in horse racing, and if ongoing accusations of wrongdoing against anyone in the game could harm racing's SLO, it would be Baffert. He was even the subject of a scathing—and hilarious—skit on *Saturday Night Live* in 2021.[22] By then, despite the two dozen individuals identified by federal indictments in 2020 (see chapter 16), Baffert was the face of racehorse doping in the public's eye.

Baffert's attorneys questioned whether it was reasonable to hold the trainer responsible for the public's apparent inability to recognize the difference between the use of various therapeutic medications and doping. Attorney W. Craig Robertson also asked whether the concept of an SLO is even valid, considering that it is not an actual license issued by a governing body.[23]

It seemed likely that the legal wrangling in both the NYRA and the Churchill Downs cases would drag on for months, and it did. On April 27, 2022, hearing officer O. Peter Sherwood issued a fifty-plus-page report recommending that Baffert receive a two-year suspension from NYRA.[24] In an effort at damage control, Baffert had announced a month earlier that four of his best Kentucky Derby candidates would be moved to other trainers. Messier, Doppelganger, and McLaren Vale would be transferred to West Coast trainer Tim Yakteen (Baffert's former assistant), and Blackadder would be shipped from California to Kentucky and train with Rodolphe Brisset. By the time Baffert's suspension in Kentucky started on April 4, 2022, all his horses had been transferred to other trainers.

Horse racing's SLO has been threatened in the past, with varying degrees of success. Tracks opened and closed with regularity from the 1890s through the first decades of the twentieth century, driven by a volatile mixture of animus toward gambling, political infighting, widespread corruption in the sport, competition between racing organizations, doping, and unfettered expansion.[25] The suspension of racing in New York from 1910 to 1912, the accompanying plunge in the sales price for bloodstock, and a wholesale exodus of stables to Europe led to a common belief that racing had shut down across the country. That was not true. Racing continued at a number of tracks in states other than New York and New Jersey, but a nationwide recovery was slow.[26]

Whether the March 2020 federal indictments of more than two dozen trainers, veterinarians, illicit drug manufacturers, and drug distributors will be a tipping point remains to be seen. What is clear, though, is that the investigation and the damning evidence of a widespread doping culture will make it easier for the public to abandon horse racing entirely and for bettors to move their dollars to legal wagering on other sports.

Perhaps the best and most straightforward approach to doping was suggested by veterinarian Joseph C. O'Dea in *The Racing Imperative,* an important but often overlooked book published in 1998. "The regulation of racing has been, and will continue to be an evolving process, but its purpose remains unchanged," O'Dea wrote:

> From racing's earliest days the integrity of each contest has been paramount. We must never forget it. When the integrity of each contest is achieved, all of the participants and all of the peripheral entities related to the race are well served and benefit therefrom.
>
> The need to ensure that each race is a true test of horses is what we call "the racing imperative." It is achieved by eliminating or adjusting so far as is humanly possible every extrinsic factor which bears adversely on the required validity of the racing contest.[27]

The Racing Imperative deals almost exclusively with performance-enhancing drugs, and it seems clear that doping was on O'Dea's mind.

It is time to pay attention to Thoroughbred racing's doping culture, if it is not already too late. If there is a wholesale defection of bettors and fans from horse racing—whether because of federal indictments, the Medina Spirit–Bob Baffert debacle, the latest doping scandal, or the next one after that—no one can claim they did not see it coming.

Acknowledgments

Writing a book is a peculiar task that is accomplished alone, but only with the help of many. Occasionally, it requires a very patient editor and a corps of doctors, nurses, and specialists to chart a course through a particularly challenging year.

During the first months of 2020, while I was putting together a schedule of necessary research trips to archives, libraries, and museums, the first cases of COVID-19 in the United States were being diagnosed. Seemingly unrelated to research for this book, the connection between the two soon became apparent. Within a few weeks, travel was problematic. All branches of the National Archives and most libraries and museums closed their doors. I contacted archivists and librarians, but they could not predict when things would return to normal.

The COVID-related shutdowns generated the first of several requests I made for deadline extensions from the University Press of Kentucky. Special thanks to Ashley Runyon, director; Patrick O'Dowd, my editor; and the staff for shepherding the book—and me—through the publishing process. As the manuscript was taking longer and longer to finish and my apologies to Patrick became more frequent, he always responded, "No worries. These things take as long as they take." The press always is a joy to work with, but Ashley and Patrick went beyond the call of duty. Special thanks to copyeditor Linda Lotz. The book is better for her efforts.

There was a bright side to the delays, however, as they allowed me extra time to add information that made the book as up to date as possible. This included the potentially disastrous breakdown of negotiations between the Horseracing Integrity and Safety Authority and the US Anti-Doping Association and the hiring of a replacement organization, Drug Free Sport International; the federal indictments that shook racing to its core in 2020; and the legal wrangling between Bob Baffert and Churchill Downs over the disqualification of 2021 Kentucky Derby winner Medina Spirit and the trainer's suspension.

The Keeneland Library was on lockdown for parts of the pandemic, but the staff worked diligently to provide remote research assistance and, once restrictions loosened a bit, limited research appointments. Thanks to director Becky Ryder, research services librarian Kelly Coffman, and archivist Dan Prater. This book would have been impossible without their help and the extraordinary resources at the library.

Special thanks to Roda Ferraro, who served as head librarian at Keeneland before moving on to a post as head of education and outreach at the National Museum of Racing and Hall of Fame in Saratoga. Roda provided a wealth of information for several award-winning articles on performance-enhancing drugs that appeared in *Blood-Horse* magazine. Her help with this book was invaluable.

Although their facilities were closed to visitors, a number of other librarians and archivists went out of their way to fulfill my research requests: Emily Goodrich at the Special Collections section of the Penn State University Library searched through Harry J. Anslinger's personal papers and provided copies of several important documents, including after-action reports from the field written by Federal Bureau of Narcotics agents. These documents from Anslinger's correspondence files were useful supplements to records I had previously reviewed in the FBN chief's "Horse Racing" file at the library. Michael Maloney, an archivist at the New York State Archives, tracked down the appellate record of Tom Smith's hearings and litigation during his unsuccessful fight to avoid suspension of his trainer's license and provided a copy of the huge file. Glenn Longacres, archivist at the Chicago division of the National Archives, located a batch of federal district court records for individuals arrested during Aslinger's raid on the Arlington Park backstretch in 1933. Those files included indictments and dispositions of numerous criminal cases that were unavailable anywhere else. Michelle Guzman, at the National Sporting Library and Museum in Virginia, managed to locate magazine articles despite the erroneous citations I provided—not an easy task. Thanks to Emily, Michael, Glenn, Michelle, and their staffs for their help during the pandemic.

Marshall Trimble, the official state historian of Arizona, expanded my understanding of drugs, doping, and horse racing in the Old West. Thanks to Marshall for providing a unique and seldom heard perspective.

Bernard Unti is senior policy adviser and special assistant to the president and CEO of the Humane Society of the United States. He works on a wide range of strategic, policy, program, and communications priorities, yet he took time from his remarkably busy schedule to copy relevant pages from *Angel in Top Hat,* an early biography of ASPCA founder Henry Bergh. Thanks, Bernie.

Blood-Horse magazine, *Paulick Report,* and *Thoroughbred Daily News* were constant sources of timely and reliable information about horse racing's war on doping. I found reporting from Frank Angst at *Blood-Horse,* Natalie Voss at the *Paulick Report,* and Bill Finley and T. D. Thornton at *TDN* particularly insightful. Splendid work, everyone, at these publications!

Thanks, also, to a world-class power lifter who explained how steroids work for training and competing.

And, as always, profound thanks to my wife, Roberta. Her expertise as an epidemiologist kept us both safe through the pandemic, and her support as she ran interference for me during a yearlong procession of doctors, surgeries, tests, scans, ER visits, and enough blood work to satisfy a vampire kept me relatively sane and occasionally productive. This book would still be a dozen file boxes and a bookcase of research without her. Love you, Sweetie!

Appendix 1

Selected Timeline: Modern Era of Doping

The use of performance-enhancing drugs (PEDs) in human athletics has often been mirrored by their use in horse racing, and vice versa. There is, however, an important difference: human athletes use PEDs by choice, while horses have no say in the matter. What follows is a comparative timeline of important events related to the use and regulation of PEDs in human athletics and Thoroughbred racing.

Human Athletics	Date	Thoroughbred Racing
	1866	The American Society for the Prevention of Cruelty to Animals is founded in New York by Henry Bergh. Organizations supporting animal welfare and animal rights would become important players in horse racing more than a century later.

Competitors in grueling six-day, round-the-clock bicycle races resort to a variety of PEDs just to finish, including cocaine, morphine, strychnine, and nitroglycerine.	Pre-1890	Horses are "helped" with drenches—prerace doses of whiskey, brandy, and a hodgepodge of drugs and chemicals—to little practical effect.
	1890	"Doc" Ring develops the "injection," utilizing cocaine, narcotics, and other ingredients. Arguably, this is the beginning of the modern era of doping in horse racing.
	1894	The Jockey Club is incorporated in New York.
	1897	The Jockey Club approves Rule 162, the first attempt to regulate PEDs. Without a reliable chemical test for PEDs, however, enforcement is impossible.
	1903	The death of the horse Dr. Riddle from an apparent drug overdose following a race at Morris Park attracts short-lived nationwide attention. Both the British and French Jockey Clubs ban doping, with little practical effect in the absence of reliable testing.

	1904	
The first recorded use of drugs in the modern Olympics occurs when marathon runner Thomas Hicks reportedly receives doses of strychnine and brandy during the late stages of the race.		
	1910	Polish pharmacist Alfons Bukowski develops a rudimentary analytical test for alkaloids (plant-based drugs, including heroin, morphine, and caffeine) in a horse's saliva, ushering in the modern era of drug testing in horse racing.
The Harrison Narcotics Tax Act is passed to regulate and tax the manufacture, importation, and use of narcotics, cocaine, and other coca products.	1914	
	1919	Sir Barton wins the Kentucky Derby, Preakness, and Belmont amid rumors of doping by trainer H. G. Bedwell.
Amphetamine becomes one of the first stimulants created in a laboratory.	1920	

The International Amateur Athletic Federation (IAAF) bans doping, a meaningless threat to athletes without a reliable chemical test for PEDs.	1928	
Harry Anslinger is named to head the new Federal Bureau of Narcotics (FBN), with a mandate to enforce the Harrison Act.	1930	
	1932	FBN agents begin undercover investigations into the possession of illegal drugs at more than a dozen East Coast and midwestern racetracks.
	1933	FBN agents raid the backstretch at Arlington Park as part of a months-long undercover investigation into Harrison Act violations. A flurry of arrests and federal indictments and a few convictions follow.

	1934	Joseph E. Widener introduces the saliva test at Hialeah during the Florida track's winter meeting. The first serious applications of and legal challenges to the absolute insurer rule, holding trainers responsible for their horses' condition, occur.
Testosterone is synthesized by a team of Austrian, Swiss, and German chemists; development of other anabolic steroids follows.	1935	
Widespread amphetamine use during World War II introduces the drug to the public. Anecdotal evidence suggests that Nazi researchers test anabolic steroids on prisoners, soldiers, and perhaps Adolf Hitler.	1941–1945	

	1945	Seabiscuit trainer Tom Smith is suspended for one year for using the prohibited stimulant ephedrine. A few months after the suspension ends, Smith trains 1947 Kentucky Derby winner Jet Pilot.
	1947	Trainers using contaminated hypodermic needles to inject horses with testosterone are suspected of spreading equine infectious anemia (swamp fever) at Rockingham Park. Dozens of Thoroughbreds are destroyed. Among the hardest hit trainers is H. G. Bedwell.
Allegedly doped with testosterone, Soviet weight lifters begin dominating the sport.	1954	
FBI chief J. Edgar Hoover finally acknowledges the existence of the Mafia and its connection with drug smuggling.	1957	
"Our Drug Happy Athletes" is published in *Sports Illustrated*.	1960	

A successful East German doping program is developed.	1960s–1970s	
	1968	Dancer's Image finishes first in the Kentucky Derby but tests positive for a prohibited medication (see 1973).
	1969	Three-part exposé of doping in sports appears in *Sports Illustrated*. Drug testing in horse racing is praised as a model for other sports.
	1972	Congressional hearings investigate supposed links between organized crime and race fixing, but no action is taken.
	1973	After five years of administrative hearings and litigation, Dancer's Image is disqualified. The gold Kentucky Derby trophy is delivered to Calumet Farm, owner of second-place Forward Pass.
International Olympic Committee bans anabolic steroids.	1975	Most states have no similar prohibition on the use of anabolic steroids in horses, including Kentucky, Maryland, and New York (hosts of the Triple Crown races).

	1981	Corrupt Horseracing Practices Act is introduced in Congress but dies in committee after multiple hearings.
Blood doping is prohibited, although no reliable test exists.	1985	
IAAF introduces an ambitious plan for year-round out-of-competition drug testing, to little immediate effect.	1988	
Canadian sprinter Ben Johnson defeats rival Carl Lewis and sets world record for 100 meters at Seoul Olympics. Johnson is later disqualified for steroid use in the "dirtiest race in history" because of other runners' links to doping.	1988	
	1988	Enzyme-linked immunosorbent assay (ELISA) test for prohibited medications, developed by Dr. Thomas Tobin and other researchers at the University of Kentucky, is introduced in horse racing.

Erythropoietin (EPO), a PED to increase the concentration of red blood cells, is developed.	1989	
Anabolic Steroids Control Act becomes law, criminalizing possession of these drugs without a valid prescription from a medical doctor or veterinarian.	1990	Anabolic steroids remain legal for racing in most states, including Kentucky, Maryland, and New York.
Festina professional cycling team is caught up in a sweep for prohibited drugs prior to the Tour de France; nearly half the original field of 189 riders drops out during the three-week race.	1998	
World Anti-Doping Agency (WADA) is established.	1999	
US Anti-Doping Agency (USADA) is formed.	2000	
Test for EPO introduced at 2000 Olympics.	2000	

Federal investigation into Bay Area Laboratory Co-operative (BALCO) begins; prominent athletes are implicated in designer steroid scheme.	2003	
First World Anti-Doping Code is introduced.	2003	
Floyd Landis wins the Tour de France; later tests positive for excessive amounts of testosterone.	2006	
Olympic gold medal winner Marion Jones admits using steroids prior to the 2000 Olympics; loses three gold medals and two bronze medals.	2007	
Mitchell Report on anabolic steroid use in Major League Baseball is released, implicating dozens of players.	2007	

	2008	Congressional hearings held on "Breeding, Drugs, and Breakdowns: The State of Thoroughbred Racing and the Welfare of the Thoroughbred Racehorse." No action is taken.
	2008	After receiving monthly injections of anabolic steroids, Big Brown wins the Kentucky Derby and Preakness Stakes and then finishes last in the Belmont Stakes. Although steroids were permitted for training in all three Triple Crown states, most racing jurisdictions rush to ban them in the aftermath of the controversial "Steroid Derby."
	2011	Rick Dutrow, trainer of Big Brown, is fined $30,000 and suspended for ten years by the New York State Racing and Wagering Board for "repeated violations and disrespect of the rules of racing." The board cites violations at fifteen tracks in nine states.

	2011	Interstate Horseracing Improvement Act is introduced in Senate; hearings are held on "Medication and Performance-Enhancing Drugs in Horseracing." The bill dies in committee.
	2011	Interstate Horseracing Improvement Act is introduced in House of Representatives; hearings are held on "A Review of Efforts to Protect Jockeys and Horses in Horseracing." The bill dies in committee.
USADA opens investigation into seven-time Tour de France winner Lance Armstrong, who is later stripped of his victories. Cycling's international governing body does not advance the second-place finishers, citing the sport's doping culture; the races are left without official winners. The Armstrong case emphasizes the successful use of nonanalytical evidence in doping cases.	2012	

	2013	Horseracing Integrity and Safety Act is introduced in House of Representatives by Joseph R. Pitts; dies in committee
	2015	Horseracing Integrity and Safety Act is introduced in House of Representatives by Pitts; dies in committee.
	2015	Bipartisan Thoroughbred Horseracing Integrity Act is introduced in House of Representatives by Andy Barr and Paul Tonko; dies in committee.
WADA reports a deeply rooted culture of cheating in Russian athletics.	2015	
	2017	Horseracing Integrity Act is introduced in House by Barr and Tonko, identifying USADA as regulatory agency; dies in committee after hearings.
	2019	Racehorse Doping Ban Act is introduced in Senate; dies in committee.
	2019	Horseracing Integrity Act is introduced in Senate; no action taken.

	2019	Horseracing Integrity Act is introduced in House by Barr and Tonko, identifying USADA as independent regulatory body with Federal Trade Commission providing oversight; hearings are held.
	2020	More than two dozen Thoroughbred trainers, veterinarians, drug manufacturers, and distributors are indicted for federal drug offenses in March.
	2020	House of Representatives passes Horseracing Integrity Act of 2019.
	2020	Horseracing Integrity and Safety Act (HISA) is introduced in Senate, recommended by committee, and passed without debate. Amended version is passed by House of Representatives and signed into law by President Trump on December 27.
	2021	Medina Spirit finishes first in the Kentucky Derby. Traces of the prohibited corticosteroid betamethasone are detected in a postrace drug test.

	2021	Negotiations between Horseracing Integrity and Safety Authority and USADA break down and are later abandoned.
	2022	After months of litigation and administrative hearings, Medina Spirit is disqualified by Kentucky Horse Racing Commission; trainer Bob Baffert is suspended.
	2022	HISA is scheduled to take effect on July 1, 2022; medication protocols are delayed until 2023.
	2022	First federal trials held for individuals indicted in 2020. Veterinarian Seth Fishman and drug distributor Lisa Giannelli are convicted of drug misbranding and adulteration. By year's end, all defendants in the original federal indictments were either convicted or had pleaded guilty.
	2022	Horseracing Integrity and Safety Authority partners with Drug Free Sport International to replace USADA as regulatory authority. Litigation delays implementation of HISA medication regulations until 2023.

Appendix 2

Federal Doping Investigations, 1932–1934

For fourteen months, from December 1932 through January 1934, agents from the Federal Bureau of Narcotics were involved in clandestine investigations at more than a dozen racetracks in the Midwest and along the East Coast. The agents sent regular reports of suspected doping incidents to the FBN, which compiled a list of 348 individual cases involving 254 horses. Entries in boldface indicate incidents included in chapter 6.

Horse	Owner	Track	Date
Action	N. E. Stanton	Pimlico	5-13-33
Adelaide A.	Jack Howard	Hialeah	2-17-33
Advising Anna	Mrs. Jack Howard	Arlington Park	7-20-33 7-27-33
Aldershot	J. A. Alder	Jefferson Park	1-5-33
Allegretto	H. Steel	Jefferson Park	12-20-32
American Smile	Bud Fisher	Hialeah	3-7-33
At Top	Shandon Farm	Jefferson Park	1-10-33
Axentea	J. B. Belk	Pimlico	5-13-33
Axtel	Deveraux Bros.	Coney Island	8-24-33

Balderdash	P. H. Krick	Jefferson Park	1-10-35
Barashkova	Mrs. R. T. Flippen	Jefferson Park	12-14-33
Bea M.	J. D. Weil	Lincoln Fields	6-12-33
Below Cost	C. S. Bancroft	Tropical Park	3-25-33
		Bowie	5-19-33
		Lincoln Fields	6-20-33
		Arlington Park	6-27-33
Benish Way	G. C. Brenton	Pimlico	5-16-33
Beton	C. C. Davison	Detroit Fair Grounds	10-3-33
Bide A Wee	A. Gaignard	Havre de Grace	4-25-33
		Pimlico	5-15-33
	Walter E. Coburn	Empire City	10-19-33
Big Bean	H. P. Headley	Arlington Park	7-12-33 7-18-33
Big Doug	N. Gunare	Jefferson Park	1-3-33
Billies Orphan	F. C. McAter	Coney Island	9-1-33
Black Comet	E. Haughton	Lincoln Fields	6-23-33
		Coney Island	8-23-33 8-25-33
	L. Thompson	Jefferson Park	12-20-33 12-26-33
Black Stockings	J. C. Ellis	Tropical Park	3-31-33
Blackstrap	C. S. Bancroft	Pimlico	5-4-33
		Arlington Park	7-11-33 7-25-33

Black Watch	Mrs. W. E. Martin	Tropical Park	3-29-33
Blessed Event	E. R. Bradley	Havre de Grace	4-24-33
Blighter	Mrs. A. Hiller	Detroit Fair Grounds	10-7-33
Bob Weidel	J. Holub	Washington Park	6-5-33
Bonnet	C. Gray	Jefferson Park	12-24-33 12-26-33
Border Patrol	Laffoon & Yeiser	Lincoln Fields	6-13-33
Bosky	R. T. Flippen	Jefferson Park	12-14-32
Bright Chestnut	Smith & Williams	Jefferson Park	12-20-32
Broad Axe	F. J. Uhlein	Jefferson Park	11-29-32 12-15-32
Broadway Lights	T. McCarthy	Hialeah	3-2-33
Brooksie	Mrs. E. McCuan	Washington Park	6-8-33
Brown Wisdom	W. C. Reichert	Hialeah	2-15-33
Burning Up	Mrs. E. Denemark	Lincoln Fields	6-23-33
		Arlington Park	7-15-33 7-22-33
Burnside	A. L. Wynston	Jefferson Park	12-23-32 12-22-33
		Laurel	10-30-33
		Pimlico	11-2-33 11-8-33
Buzzy Boo	J. W. Johnston	Jefferson Park	12-30-33

Cabouse	H. P. Headley	Lincoln Fields	6-13-33
Cains	Mrs. J. H. Pink	Washington Park	6-5-33
Calgary Kay	Mrs. B. E. Chapman	Tropical Park	3-28-33
Capitalist	G. T. Preece	Hialeah	2-24-33
Captain Ed	C. S. Bancroft	Arlington Park	7-14-33
Chance Flight	J. Beuer	Bowie	11-25-33
Charlie O.	R. M. Eastman Est.	Hialeah	2-25-33 3-11-33
Chianti	Mrs. M. F. Keller	Jefferson Park	12-23-32
Chokoloskee	D. Shaw	Hialeah	2-28-33
Claremont	G. E. Phillips	Detroit Fair Grounds	10-7-33
Come Seven	**A. Gaignard Jr.**	**Jefferson Park**	**12-26-33**
Confidential	**J. Somersby**	**Jefferson Park**	**12-19-32**
Contraband	M. Goldblatt	Jefferson Park	12-25-33
Country Tom	Mrs. H. H. Hensel	Jefferson Park	12-15-32
Crash	Mrs. C. McCuan	Washington Park	5-30-33
Cresta Run	C. V. Whitney	Coney Island	8-26-33
Cross Roads	Mrs. B. E. Chapman	Bowie	11-16-33
Curacao	Greentree Stable	Hialeah	3-4-33
Darkest Hour	G. S. C. Mifler	Jefferson Park	12-21-33 12-28-33

Dark Roma	W. B. Kilmer & B. Creech	Arlington Park	6-27-33
Decanter	C. W. Bowne Jr.	Lincoln Fields	6-21-33
Deemster	St. Louis Stable	Detroit Fair Grounds	10-5-33
Desert Call	Laffoon & Yeiser	Lincoln Fields	6-17-33 6-20-33
Dessner	J. J. Robinson	Jefferson Park	12-18-33 12-20-33 12-27-33
Dodgson	Everglade Stable	Hialeah	2-18-33
Dontara	Mrs. E. Trueman	Havre de Grace	4-25-33
Don Vern	A. J. Halliwell	Detroit Fair Grounds	10-5-33
Dr. Parrish	Mrs. A. M. Creech	Arlington Park	6-30-33 7-1-33
Drury	E. J. O'Connell	Jefferson Park	12-22-32
Ebony Lady	Mrs. Jack Howard	Hialeah	2-27-33 3-8-33
Ed Reese	R. Scoville	Jefferson Park	12-12-32 1-4-33
Enactment	W. R. Coe	Havre de Grace	4-21-33
Energetic Boy	Godfrey Preece	Hialeah	2-16-33
Entrap	A. J. Halliwell	Detroit Fair Grounds	10-3-33
Essare	Mrs. F. Preece	Arlington Park	7-3-33
Eva B.	J. J. Robinson	Jefferson Park	12-26-32
Fair Dutchess	Lou Johnson	Coney Island	8-23-33

Fancy Feathers	Greentree Stable	Jefferson Park	12-22-33
Field Goal	Laffoon & Yerser	Lincoln Fields	6-17-33
	E. Haughton	**Coney Island**	**8-22-33**
Fighting Bob	Mrs. A. M. Creech	Arlington Park	7-13-33
Finnic	Mrs. R. L. Rogers	Jefferson Park	12-12-32 1-14-33
Fire Neck	Coldstream Stud	Hialeah	3-6-33
Flaming Mamie	J. B. Belk	Pimlico	5-6-33
Flowerly Lady	W. F. Knebelkamp	Coney Island	6-7-33
Flying Don	J. J. Robinson	Jefferson Park	12-20-32 1-10-33
Foolhardy	W. A. Mikel	Jefferson Park	1-10-33
	J. D. Mikel	Arlington Park	7-7-33
Fort Dearborn	E. W. Ogle	Hialeah	2-21-33
Galland Sir	N. W. Church	Arlington Park	7-22-33
Gilbert Elston	M. Goldblatt	Jefferson Park	12-28-33
Glen Artney	C. Studer	Jefferson Park	1-12-33
Glidelia	J. J. Robinson	Havre de Grace	4-27-33
Golden Storm	N. B. Stewart	Pimlico	5-4-33
Gold Sweeper	G. E. Pillips	Tropical Park	3-17-33
Goofus	H. Teller Archibald	Bowie	11-21-33
Greenwald	J. D. Neil	Detroit Fair Grounds	10-3-33
Grimace	M. E. Johnston	Jefferson Park	1-3-33
Gunfire	P. H. Newman	Arlington Park	7-13-33

Hamilton	Mrs. A. M. Creech	Washington Park	6-1-33
Happy Sue	P. A. Shaw	Pimlico	11-11-33
Happy Warrior	C. S. Mitchell	Jefferson Park	12-5-32 12-23-32 1-12-33
Harold, Jr.	Mrs. R. T. Flipper	Jefferson Park	1-14-33
Herowin	W. S. Kilmer	Havre de Grace	4-21-33
Home Shore	A. B. Catalano	Havre de Grace	4-18-33
Hot Shot	C. E. Davison	Detroit Fair Grounds	10-7-33
Huraway	A. J. Halliwell	Detroit Fair Grounds	10-7-33
Hyklas	E. Matthews	Jefferson Park	12-14-32
Idle Along	**A. Gaignard**	**Jefferson Park**	**12-28-33**
Ilchester	Mrs. E. Trueman	Bowie	11-21-33
Ima Count	N. W. Church	Detroit Fair Grounds	10-7-33
Impish	Beau Brummel Stables	Detroit Fair Grounds	10-2-33 10-7-33
Islam	Jack Howard	Arlington Park	7-5-33 7-12-33
		Lincoln Fields	6-19-33
Jack Alexander	C. E. Davison	Jefferson Park	12-13-32
Jeff O'Neill	J. Levey	Beulah Park	9-29-33
Jim Macaw	J. L. Butler	Hialeah	2-23-33 3-3-33

Joe Patsie	P. J. Comiskey	Jefferson Park	1-2-34
John Mill	J. D. Mikel	Arlington Park	7-27-33
	R. T. Watts	Washington Park	10-10-33
Kai Finn	Camp Bell Stables	Jefferson Park	12-18-33
Keep Out	Wm. Ziegler	Pimlico	5-6-33
Kieva	Mrs. M. Weiner	Detroit Fair Grounds	10-7-33
Kievex	W. Graham	Detroit Fair Grounds	10-7-33
Kitty Williams	Mrs. E. D'Aguin	Jefferson Park	1-12-33
Knights Gal	Audley Farm	Detroit Fair Grounds	10-7-33
Kybo	H. S. Jones	Jefferson Park	12-20-32 1-2-33
Ladino	A. Gaignard	Laurel	10-26-33 10-30-33
Lady Legend	Beaucastle Farm	Havre de Grace	4-20-33
Lady Sweet	J. V. Pons	Jefferson Park	12-13-32 12-23-32
	Owner not listed	Hialeah	2-15-33
Lady Tobacco	J. J. Robinson	Jefferson Park	12-30-33 1-2-34
Laknite	E. J. Valli	Jefferson Park	1-3-34
Lamp Black	J. D. Mikel	Lincoln Fields	6-16-33
		Arlington Park	6-29-33 7-26-33
La Salle	**Shandon Farm**	**Jefferson Park**	**1-10-33**

Last Second	J. Kederis	Jefferson Park	12-20-32
Liqueur	Hall Price Headley	Hialeah	3-6-33
Little Lad	J. J. Robinson	Jefferson Park	12-16-33
Lofty Heights	Mrs. R. L. Rogers	Jefferson Park	12-16-32
Longus	J. D. Mikel	Arlington Park	7-10-33 7-26-33
Louie Dear	Jack Howard	Arlington Park	7-5-33 7-14-33 7-19-33 7-28-33
Lucky Jack	Mrs. J. Grossman	Washington Park	5-29-33
Luck Piece	Mrs. R. T. Flippen	Jefferson Park	12-21-32
Madame Snot	J. B. Belk	Pimlico	5-3-33
Madelon	Easkay Stable	Detroit Fair Grounds	10-7-33
	Riverview Stable	Jefferson Park	12-14-33 12-19-33
Marmion	Goldstream Stud	Arlington Park	7-4-33
Matthew	Mrs. B. Hernandez	Jefferson Park	12-11-32
Merrily On	Mrs. J. Grossman	Washington Park	6-3-33
		Detroit Fair Grounds	10-7-33
		Latonia	10-28-33 10-31-33

Mexico	McKinley Bryant	Empire City	10-19-33
Mike Hall	R. M. Eastman Est.	Hialeah	2-25-33
Miss Tulsa	Jack Howard	Arlington Park	7-17-33 7-22-33
Modern Maiden	J. A. Herrmann	Lincoln Fields	6-15-33
Modern Times	L. H. Miner	Havre de Grace	4-22-33
Monkey Shine	Camp-ball Stable	Jefferson Park	12-16-33
More Anon	J. C. Milam	Hialeah	2-24-33
Morning Fair	W. F. Knebelkamp	Coney Island	9-2-33
Morsun	Lone Star Stable	Detroit Fair Grounds	10-7-33
Mr. Sponge	C. Leroy King	Detroit Fair Grounds	10-7-33
		Arlington Park	7-1-33 7-4-33
Mr. Swift	P. A. Markey	Pimlico	5-15-33
My Dan	A. J. Bordes	Jefferson Park	12-23-32 12-27-32
My Dandy	W. C. Reichert	Hialeah	2-25-33 3-9-33
My Joanne	**W. C. Reichert**	**Jefferson Park**	**1-12-33**
My Kind	Le Mar Stock Farm	Lincoln Fields	6-17-33
Mynheer	J. Berry	Jefferson Park	12-18-33 12-24-33 12-28-33 12-31-33

Nell Kuhlman	W. F. Lutz	Jefferson Park	12-6-32
Night Patrol	E. O. Ferguson	Havre de Grace	4-15-33
Noah's Pride	J. F. Connors	Tropical Park	3-29-33
North Shadow	A. Van den Ende	Washington Park	5-26-33
Nurses' Boy	Mrs. G. Rotterman	Jefferson Park	1-5-33
Oaten	W. C. Reichert	Arlington Park	7-11-33
Ocean Flight	Flick, Litachgi & Bottle Stable	Coney Island	8-25-33
Oderic	A. L. Trough	Jefferson Park	1-6-33
Okapi	**Brookmeade Stable**	**Bowie**	11-25-33 **11-30-33**
Oriole Bird	Southland Stable	Arlington Park	7-7-33
Pantaloons	M. Goldblatt	Jefferson Park	12-23-33
Parahead	J. T. Taylor	Arlington Park	7-8-33
Pari-Mutual	C. Leroy King	Detroit Fair Grounds	10-7-33
Peace Lady	C. W. Vaskoetter	Hialeah	2-22-33
Petabit	Colgate Stables	Jefferson Park	12-23-32 12-27-33
Phantasime	Mrs. F. F. Fitzgerald	Jefferson Park	1-13-33
Pharahead	J. T. Taylor	Arlington Park	7-4-33 7-20-33 7-24-33

Phicky Play	N. W. Church	Arlington Park	7-22-33
Piecemeal	G. R. Allen	Lincoln Fields	6-22-33
Polar Brush	Mrs. A. J. Abel	Pimlico	5-5-33
	S. Mason	Bowie	11-30-33
Polisher	W. F. Phelan	Tropical Park	3-29-33
Polyp	A. J. Halliwell	Detroit Fair Grounds	10-7-33
Pompeius	G. H. Boshwick	Havre de Grace	4-22-33
Porgie	E. K. Bryson	Jefferson Park	12-22-32
Portcodine	Mrs. A. M. Creech	Washington Park	6-10-33
		Arlington Park	6-27-33 7-11-33
Port O'Play	S. Gorbet	Tropical Park	3-27-33
Pretty Peg	J. J. Robinson	Havre de Grace	4-18-33
Princess Peri	Mrs. A. Luzada	Jefferson Park	1-3-33
Princess Pyre	K. N. Gilpin	Jefferson Park	1-15-33
Prize Day	J. Jones	Empire City	10-19-33
Prose & Poetry	Mrs. A. McCreech & B. Parke	Washington Park	6-7-33
Race Street	Mrs. H. Veach	Jefferson Park	1-13-33
Ratscallion	J. L. McKnight	Laurel	10-27-33
Red Casino	Miss B. E. Folsom	Lincoln Fields	6-24-33
Ricciardo	J. L. Cleveland	Jefferson Park	1-4-33
Riff Raff	J. B. Theall	Washington Park	6-2-33
	Lone Star Stable	Jefferson Park	12-16-32 1-5-33

Riskulus	N. W. Church	Detroit Fair Grounds	10-7-33
Roanoke Lad	Thos. Piatt	Coney Island	9-29-33
Royal Blunder	Audley Farm	Detroit Fair Grounds	10-7-33
Ruane	C. H. Hughes	Havre de Grace	4-24-33
Rubridge	H. C. Rummage	Tropical Park	3-31-33
Sambo Brown	Harned Bros.	Lincoln Fields	6-20-33
Sand Boot	J. Rakickas	Arlington Park	7-26-33
Sandwrack	Lone Star Stable	Detroit Fair Grounds	10-7-33
Scimitar	J. D. Mikel	Arlington Park	7-10-33
Screen Idol	W. C. Weaut	Tropical Park	4-1-33
Semester	M. Simmons	Tropical Park	3-28-33
Shasta Charmer	Percy & Weston	Jefferson Park	1-10-33
Shasta Mint	R. Dollaway	Jefferson Park	12-23-33
Shiva	Mrs. E. Pollard	Hialeah	3-3-33
Sister Mary	C. E. Davison	Jefferson Park	1-5-33
Skirl	M. Goldblatt	Jefferson Park	12-23-33
Skunner	Lone Star Stable	Detroit Fair Grounds	10-7-33
Sky Haven	E. Haughton	Lincoln Fields	6-16-33 6-21-33
		Arlington Park	6-28-33
Smear	C. V. Whitney	Jefferson Park	12-24-32
Snaplock	A. A. Baroni	Arlington Park	7-14-33
Social Climber	N. Wahl	Jefferson Park	12-14-33

Solid American	G. E. Phillips	Detroit Fair Grounds	10-7-33
Sporting Pearl	C. Morris	Arlington Park	6-28-33
Spud	Jack Howard	Hialeah	2-28-33
St. Brideaux	Greentree Stable	Hialeah	3-4-33
Street Singer	Mrs. A. M. Creech	Arlington Park	7-5-33 7-7-33 7-18-33
Sun Apollo	W. S. Kilmer	Havre de Grace	4-18-33
Sun Teatime	Mrs. N. G. Fisher	Tropical Park	3-17-33
Tadcaster	W. Humphy	Jefferson Park	12-17-32
Tamerlane	C. E. Lenshen	Lincoln Fields	6-23-33
Technique	H. P. Headley	Arlington Park	7-17-33
Tela	Howard Oats	Hialeah	2-22-33
	Mrs. R. T. Flippen	Lincoln Fields	6-13-33
		Pimlico	11-2-33 11-11-33
		Jefferson Park	12-25-33
Terry Girl	R. W. Hoffman	Lincoln Fields	6-21-33
Texas Knight	W. B. Mitchell	Detroit Fair Grounds	10-7-33
The Nile	C. Studer	Jefferson Park	1-17-33
Thistle Play	Beau Brummel Stable	Detroit Fair Grounds	10-2-33 10-7-33
Threat	Mrs. A. M. Creech	Arlington Park	6-30-33 7-5-33 7-13-33 7-24-33 7-27-33

Tight Rope	J. Levy	Beulah Park	9-25-33 9-28-33
Timorous	Mrs. A. M. Creech	Arlington Park	7-28-33
Town Limit	M. Goldblatt	Jefferson Park	12-22-33 12-26-33 12-29-33
Transbird	Mrs. E. Denemark	Arlington Park	7-15-33 7-24-33
Tremendous	Mrs. L. F. Carman	Tropical Park	3-30-33
Try It	R. McIlvain	Hialeah	3-10-33
Twisted Threads	G. E. Phillips	Tropical Park	3-18-33
		Arlington Park	7-27-33
Uncle Henry	T. C. Worden	Arlington Park	7-3-33
Uncommon Gold	C. Morris	Arlington Park	7-18-33
Unencumbered	P. A. Markey	Bowie	5-19-33
Verda	B. Workman	Washington Park	6-8-33 6-10-33
Vishnu	H. T. Archibald	Pimlico	5-6-33
War Tide	A. Gaignard	Havre de Grace Laurel	4-29-33 10-28-33
War Time	A. Gaignard	Pimlico	5-15-33
Watchgirl	Boose & Davis	Jefferson Park	12-29-32 1-4-33

Watch Part	Mrs. E. Denemark	Washington Park	6-9-33
Water Port	Mrs. E. Denemark	Washington Park	6-3-33
Winifred Ana	Mrs. A. T. Langivir	Jefferson Park	11-26-32
Wise Anne	Mrs. W. C. Weant	Hialeah	3-6-33
Wise Ways	R. M. Eastman Est.	Hialeah	3-11-33
Ytfin	A. A. Baroni	Arlington Park	7-10-33
Zahn	Harned Bros.	Coney Island	9-1-33
Zorana	W. N. Adriens	Hialeah	3-1-33

Source: Harry J. Anslinger Papers, box 8, file 6, "Drugs in Horse Racing (1921–1952)," HCLA 1875, Special Collections Library, Pennsylvania State University.

Appendix 3

Doping Formulary

During the backstretch raids conducted by the Federal Bureau of Narcotics from late 1932 through early 1934, Harry Anslinger's agents collected doping recipes. Interestingly, many of the ingredients were suspected components of "Doc" Ring's "injection" nearly half a century earlier. The most popular substance found among the formulae gathered by the FBN agents was strychnine or strychnine sulfate ("strick"), reportedly the drug of choice of Sir Barton's trainer H. G. Bedwell. The most common drugs listed in the recipes are:

- Strychnine—26 times
- Heroin—16 times
- Cocaine—15 times
- Morphine—5 times
- Coca leaves—2 times

These drugs would fall out of favor with the introduction of analytical testing.

The following recipes were copied verbatim (where legible) from notes archived with Anslinger's papers.[1] These recipes are presented only to provide an accurate and necessary context for the development of PEDs from 1890 through the present. Readers are warned that the use of PEDs is prohibited in every racing jurisdiction and that possession of many of the listed components is a violation of federal law with serious legal consequences. Neither the author nor the publisher assumes any liability for harm suffered from the misuse of this information.

Selected Legend

Agua Dist. = distilled water
dr. or dp. = drops
F.E. or Fld. Ext. = fluid extract
gr. = grain (obsolete measure equivalent to 0.0648 gram)
Sig. = instructions that should be included on the medication label
Sol. = solution
Spts. = spirits
Sulf. = sulfate
Tr. = tincture
= dosage illegible

Recipes

Caffeine Citrate	1200 gr.
Morphine Sulf.	###
Strychnine Sulf.	12 gr.
Atropine Sulf.	12 gr.
Agua. Dist.	20 oz.

Alcohol sufficient to make 4 pt.

Caffeine Citrate	315 gr.
Morphine Sulfate	7 gr.
Strychnine Sulphate	3 gr.
Atropine Sulphate	3 gr.
Agua. Dist.	4 oz.
Alcohol	1 pt.

As directed.

Cocaine Hydrochloride   gr. 4
Sol. Adrenalin Chloride   dp. 10
Sol. Soda Chloride phys.   oz. 1
Sig. Doctors use.

Caffeine Citrate   gr. 315
Morphine Sulphate   gr. 7½
Strychnine Sulphate   gr. 3
Atropine Sulphate   gr. 3
Agua Dist.   oz. 8
Alcohol   pt. 1
M
Sig. Use as directed.

Cocaine   gr. 14
Tr. Digitalis   1 dp.
Tr. Strophanthus   1 dp.
F.E. Kola Nut   2 oz.
M. in solution
Sig. give as one dose ½ hour before physic.

Caff[eine] Citrate   gr. 20
Strychnine Sulph.   gr. ½
Nitroglyc[erine]   dr. 1
Arom[atic] Spts. Am[monia]   oz. 5
Heroin   gr. 12
Apple Jack   oz. 30

Stimulant
Caff[eine] Citrate   dr. 12
Arom[atic] Amm[onia]   oz. 2
Kola sufficient to make one ounce at a dose

Hop

Caffeine Cit[rate]	dr. 12
Strych[nine] Sulph.	gr. 12
Spts. Nitroglycerine	oz. 1
Spts. Ammon[ia] Ar[omati]c	oz. 5
Heroin	gr. 12
Apple Jack or Brandy	oz. 30

Strych[nine] Sulph.	gr. ½
F.E. Digitalis	dp. 15
F.E. Strophanthus	dp. 10
Spts. Nitroglycerine	dp. 10
F.E. Kola Nut	oz. 2

Heroin	gr. 2
Nitroglycerine	dp. 10
Tr. Strophanthus	dp. 5
Strychnine	gr. 4
Caffeine	gr. 4
Kola Nut	oz. 2
50 minutes.	

Cocaine	gr. 8
Strychnine	gr. ½
Heroin	gr. ¼
Sol. Nitroglycerine	dp. 12
F.E. Kola Nut	oz. 2

Heroin	gr. 1
Cocaine	gr. 14
Tr. Strophanthus	dr. 1½
Tr. Digitalis	dr. 1½
F.E. Kola Nut	oz. 2

Cocaine	gr. 4 or 6
Alcohol	oz. 1
Syrup	oz. 3

2 oz. to be given 1 hr. 15 min. before post time.
2 oz. to be given 45 min. before post time.
Veraseptol

Kola Nut	oz. 2
Digitalis	dp. 2
Strychnine	gr. ¼
Nitroglycerine	dp. 2
Heroin	gr. 1½

Give one half 50 minutes before post time.
Give one half 20 minutes before post time.

Mike's Hop

Heroin	gr. 1
Cocaine	gr. 14
Tr. Digitalis	dr. 1
Tr. Strophanthus	dr. 1

Fld. Ext. Kola Nut sufficient to make oz. 2

Hop

Strychnine	gr. ½
Tr. Strophanthus	dp. 10
Tr. Nitroglycerine	dp. 10

Fld. Ext. Kola Nut sufficient to make oz. 2

Cocaine	gr. 8
Strychnine	gr. ¼
Heroine	gr. ¼
Sol. Nitroglycerine	dp. 12

Fld. Ext. Kola Nut sufficient to make oz. 2

Cocaine   gr. 24
Aqua Rosa   oz. 1
Inject ½ the bottle ¼ hr. before going to paddock.

Caffeine Citrate   oz. 3
Spts. Ammonia Aromatic   oz. 2
Glycerine   oz. 3
Spts. Nitroglycerine   oz. 1½

Caffeine Citrate   oz. 1
Tr. Digitalis   oz. 2
Strychnine   oz. 4
Alcohol
Water sufficient to make qt. 1

Caffeine   gr. 240
Strychnine   gr 4
Spts. Nitroglycerine   dr. 3½
Digitalis   oz. 1
Aromatic Spirits   oz. 8
Alcohol sufficient to make qt. 1

Strychnine Sulphate   gr. 5
Morphine Sulphate   dr. ½
Quinine Sulphate   dr. 2
Caffeine Citrate   oz. ½
Ammonia Aromatic Spirits   oz. 2
Glycerine   oz. 2
Wyeth's mixture of Elixir of   oz. 16
    Heroin and Terpin Hydrate
Alcohol sufficient to make oz. 32

Nitro Glycerine   30 drops
Caffeine   66 grains
2 oz. Brandy or Cut Pure Grain Alcohol

Apple Brandy   15 oz.
Glycerine   1½ oz.
Strick (Strychnine)   3 gr.
Caffeine   1 oz.—437 gr.
Aromatic Spirits Ammonia   ½ oz.
Dose 1 oz. 2 hrs. before post time, 1 oz. 1 hr. before.

(1½ grain) Tincture Strephintus [*sic*]   40 drops
Nitro Glycerine   5 drops
Strychnine Sulphate   ¼ grain
Fluid Ext. Kola Nut   2 oz.
50 minutes before post time.

2 grains Heroin
10 drops Nitro Glycerine
5 [drops] Tinct. Strophanthus
4 gr. Strick
4 [gr] Caffeine
2 oz. Kola Nut
50 min.

4 gr. Cocaine
1/8 gr. Heroin
4 drops Nitro Glycerine
2 [drops] Carbolic Acid
3 cc distilled water

Heroin   gr. 1
Cocaine   gr. 14
Tincture of Digitalis   dr. 1

| Tincture of Strophanthus | dr. 1 |
| Fluid Extract of Kola nut | oz. 2 |

Strong dose.

Strychnine	gr. ¼
Tincture of Strophanthus	dp. 10
Tincture of Nitroglycerine	dp. 10
Fluid Extract of Kola nut	oz. 2

Short dose.

Cocaine	gr. 4 or 5
Alcohol	oz. 1
Syrup	oz. 3

2 oz to be given 1 hr. 15 min. before post time.
2 oz to be given 45 min. before post time.
Veraseptol

Kola nut	oz. 2
Extract Ginger	oz. ½
Cocaine	gr. 5
Heroin	gr. 1 ½
Strychnine	gr. ¼

Hot days 50 min. before post time.
Cold days 1 hr. before post time.
Green Stripe Scotch delicious.

Kola nut	oz. 2
Digitalis	dp. 2
Strychnine	gr. ¼
Nitro Glycerine	dp. 2
Heroin	gr. 1½

Give one half 50 min. before post time.
Give one half 20 min. before post time.

Strychnine	gr. ¼
Heroin	gr. 3
Nitro Glycerine	gr. 1/8
Strophanthus	dr. 1
Digitalis	dp. 4
Coca Leaves	dr. 4
Kola nut	oz. 2

Cocaine	gr. 24
Aqua Rosa	oz. 1

Sig. Inject ½ the bottle ½ hour before going to paddock.

Apple Brandy	oz. 15
Glycerine	oz. 1½
Strychnine	gr. 3
Caffeine	oz. 1
Arom[atic] Spts. Ammonia	oz. ½

1 oz. 2 hrs. before post time.
1 oz. 1 hr. before post time.

F.E. Gentian	oz. 1
F.E. Nux Vomica	oz. 1
Water sufficient to make	qt. 1

"Cooper" Tonic, 2 oz. twice a day.

Nitroglycerine	dp. 30
Caffeine	gr. 66
Brandy or cut alcohol	oz. 2

16 times this amount equal 1 qt.

Cocaine	gr. 4
Heroin	gr. 1/8
Nitroglycerine	dp. 4
Carbolic Acid	dp. 2
Distilled water	cc 3

Tr. Strophanthus	### 40
Nitroglycerine	### 5
Strychnine Sulph.	gr. ½
Fl. Ext. Kola Nut	oz. 2

50 minutes before post time.

1 quart

Apple Brandy	oz. 30
Arom[atic] Spts. Ammonia	oz. 1
Glycerine	oz. 3
Spts. Nitro	oz. ½
Heroin	gr. 15
Strychnine	gr. 4
Caffeine	oz. 2

1 qt.—2 hrs.—1 hr. 2 oz. bottle one to two hrs. a head of time. [This confusing schedule is shorthand for instructions about how long before a race to administer the mixture.]

Sweet Syrups	oz. 2
Cocaine	gr. 4
Strychnine	gr. ½

Give as soon as leaves barn.

F.E. Kola Nut	oz. 2
Strychnine Sulphate	gr. ¼
Sol. Nitroglycerine	dp. 15 or 20

At one dose 40 minutes before race.

Strychnine	gr. ###
Heroin	gr. 3
Nitroglycerine	gr. 1/8
Strophanthus	dp.1
Digitalis	dp. 4
Coca Leaves	dr. 4
Kola Nut	oz. 2

Morphine	gr. 1
Chloralhydrate	dr. 1
Aspirin	dr. 1

To be administered before race.

Strychnine Sulphate	gr. 1
Caffeine Citrate	gr. 47
Spirits of Nitroglycerine	oz. 1/8
Tr. Nux Vomica	oz. ¼
Spts. Ammonia Aromatic	oz. 1
Tr. Strophanthus	oz. ¼
Tr. Belladonna	oz. ¼
Tr. Digitalis	oz. ½
Tr. Hyoscyamus	dr. ¼
F.E. Ginger	oz. ¼
F.E. Kola Nut sufficient to make	oz. 8

Caffeine	oz. 1
Spts. Nitroglycerine	dr. 1½
Spts. Ammonia Aromatic	oz. ½
Glycerine	oz. 1½
Alcohol	oz. 14

Appendix 4

Smith v. Cole

After exhausting his administrative appeals before the Joint Board, trainer Tom Smith sought judicial relief in New York state courts. The decision that follows confirms the Joint Board's decision to revoke Smith's training license. The rationale applied here—that is, that there was substantial evidence to support the Joint Board's action—is the same used by the Kentucky Court of Appeals a quarter century later in supporting the Kentucky State Racing Commission's ruling in the Dancer's Image case.

In the Matter of TOM SMITH, Petitioner,
v.
ASHLEY T. COLE et al., as Members of the Racing Commission of the State of New York, et al., Respondents.
Supreme Court of New York, First Department.
May 17, 1946
 PROCEEDING under article 78 of the Civil Practice Act (transferred to the Appellate Division of the Supreme Court in the first judicial department by an order of the Supreme Court at Special Term, entered in New York County) to review a determination of respondent Jockey Club in revoking petitioner's license as a trainer of race horses for the year 1945, and the action of respondent Joint Board in affirming said revocation.
 COUNSEL

John T. Cahill of counsel (Mathias F. Correa with him on the brief; Cahill, Gordon, Zachry & Reindel, attorneys), for petitioner.

Orrin G. Judd of counsel (John P. Powers, Samuel A. Hirshowitz and Howard F. Danihy with him on the brief; Nathaniel L. Goldstein, Attorney-General) for Joint Board and Racing Commission, respondents.

Martin A. Schenck of counsel (Harold C. McCollom, and Kenneth W. Greenawalt with him on the brief; Davies, Auerbach, Cornell & Hardy, attorneys), for the Jockey Club, respondent.

Per Curiam.

The law relating to the issuance and revocation of licenses of participants and employees at race meetings is found in the Unconsolidated Laws of New York. (L. 1926, ch. 440, § 9-b, as added by L. 1934, ch. 310, and later amd.) This statute provides that for the purpose of maintaining a proper control over race meetings, the Jockey Club shall license owners, trainers and jockeys at running races, and the National Steeplechase Association shall license owners, trainers and jockeys at steeplechases and hunts. Each license, unless revoked by the issuing body "for cause," shall remain in force for the period of one year from April of the year in which the same is issued. Upon the application of a person whose license has been refused or revoked, such person shall be entitled to a hearing before a joint session of the State Racing Commission and two stewards of the Jockey Club or of the National Steeplechase Association.

"For cause," as used in this statute, means that a revocation must be for an occurrence which it is reasonably consistent with sound public policy to find offensive. The determination must not be arbitrary or capricious.

The Joint Board has decided in the present case that there was cause for the revocation of the license of petitioner, Tom Smith. Its decision involved the consideration of factual matters. In reviewing a determination of an administrative agency based on factual findings the courts are confined to a consideration of the question as to whether there was substantial evidence to support the findings made.

After the petitioner, a trainer of race horses, had been issued a license for the year 1945, that license was revoked on November 10, 1945. Petitioner demanded a hearing which was had before a statutory joint board consisting of members of the Racing Commission of the State of New York and certain stewards of the Jockey Club who reviewed the determination of the Jockey Club and affirmed the revocation. The petitioner now seeks to have this court review, in turn, the determination of the statutory Joint Board.

Implicit in the opinion rendered by the board is the finding that the revocation was imposed because the board determined that the trainer had violated the rules of racing in permitting the application of improper medication that would affect the racing condition of a horse under his care. Concededly, a 2.6% solution of ephedrine was sprayed into the nasal passages of a horse trained by petitioner shortly before the running of a race in which the horse was entered to participate. While the trainer was not present when the medicine was applied, there was evidence from which his responsibility for the treatment could be found to have been established.

There was substantial evidence before the administrative body that ephedrine had certain qualities as a stimulant, and that it also might affect the racing condition of a horse by increasing its respiratory capacity. Expert opinion evidence, contradictory in view, was received from both sides to the controversy concerning the possibility of the dosage administered in this case acting as a stimulant, particularly in view of the method of its application. Under the controlling authorities we may not consider the weight of the evidence relating to this question. Nor may we choose to believe one set of experts rather than the other. If we could, it might well be that we should arrive at a different conclusion from that arrived at by the board as to whether the evidence established any actual stimulation of the horse in question.

We find that a fair hearing was afforded the petitioner and that there was some substantial evidence to support the finding made. Accordingly, the determination cannot be said to be arbitrary or capricious, and we may not set it aside.

The petition for review seeks merely to annul the revocation of petitioner's license by the Jockey Club, and the affirmation thereof by the Joint Board, and to direct the restoration of the license. It does not seek review of the determination of the stewards of the Jockey Club denying the petitioner admission to and all privileges of race tracks under jurisdiction of said Jockey Club. Accordingly, we confirm the revocation of the license only, with $50 costs and disbursements to the respondents.

MARTIN, P. J., DORE, COHN, CALLAHAN and PECK, JJ., concur.

Determination revoking petitioner's license unanimously confirmed, with $50 costs and disbursements to the respondents. Settle order on notice.

Appendix 5

Kentucky State Racing Commission v. Fuller

KENTUCKY STATE RACING COMMISSION et al., etc., Appellants, v. Peter FULLER, Appellee.

Court of Appeals of Kentucky.

April 28, 1972.

Rehearing Denied June 30, 1972.

John B. Breckinridge, Atty. Gen., George F. Rabe, Asst. Atty. Gen., Squire N. Williams, Jr., Frankfort, Rufus Lisle, Harbison, Kessinger, Lisle & Bush, Lexington, for appellants.

Arthur W. Grafton, Wyatt, Grafton & Sloss, Stuart E. Lampe, Edward S. Bonnie, Brown, Eldred & Bonnie, Louisville, for appellee.

CATINNA, Commissioner.

This appeal from the Franklin Circuit Court was filed in this court on March 8, 1971. Filed with the record were five volumes, 1162 pages, of the proceedings before the Stewards and fourteen volumes, 2860 pages, of the proceedings before the Kentucky State Racing Commission. Appellants' brief was filed on July 30, 1971; appellee filed his brief on September 20, 1971. Appellants filed a reply brief on December 9, 1971, and appellee filed a responsive brief on January 13, 1972.

On Saturday, May 4, 1968, the thoroughbred, Dancer's Image, owned by Peter Fuller, crossed the finish line first in the Seventh Race at Churchill Downs, the Kentucky Derby, followed by Forward

Pass, Francie's Hat, T.V. Commercial, and Kentucky Sherry, in that order.

Thoroughbred racing in Kentucky is under the supervision of the Kentucky State Racing Commission and conducted under rules adopted by the Commission. Accordingly, a urine specimen was taken from Dancer's Image under the supervision of the state veterinarian, L. M. Roach, and delivered to the mobile laboratory of Louisville Testing Laboratory, Inc., at Churchill Downs.

The Louisville Testing Laboratory, Inc., owned by Kenneth W. Smith, was the official chemist for the Commission and, by contract, did chemical tests of samples from thoroughbred races. The purpose of these tests was to determine if there was present in the sample forbidden medication including phenylbutazone or one of its derivatives.

On May 6, 1968, the official chemist of the Kentucky State Racing Commission reported to the Stewards that the urine tests of Dancer's Image indicated the presence of a medication known as phenylbutazone or one of its derivatives.

The rules of racing of the Kentucky State Racing Commission required that responsible parties be notified and a hearing conducted with appropriate penalties for violators of the rules, including a redistribution of the purse. The Stewards held a hearing on May 13, 14, and 15, 1968, at which time all affected parties were present in person or by counsel. At the conclusion of the hearing, May 15, 1968, the Stewards found that phenylbutazone or one of its derivatives was present in the urine of Dancer's Image on May 4, 1968, in violation of the rules of racing and directed that the purse be distributed as follows:

1st money Forward Pass
2nd money Francie's Hat
3rd money T.V. Commercial
4th money Kentucky Sherry

The betting on the race and the payment of parimutuel tickets were not affected.

Peter Fuller, owner of Dancer's Image, appealed this ruling to the Kentucky State Racing Commission. The Commission conducted an extensive hearing over a period of fourteen days, commencing November 18, 1968, and concluding December 7, 1968. The Commission issued its findings of fact, conclusions of law, and order on January 6, 1969, which sustained the Stewards' order of May 15, 1968.

The order of the Kentucky State Racing Commission was appealed to the Franklin Circuit Court. While this appeal was pending, counsel for Peter Fuller introduced additional evidence in support of an alleged denial of due process of law by the Commission. On December 11, 1970, the Franklin Circuit Court issued a "Memo Opinion" which made certain findings of fact and rulings of law. On December 31, 1970, the judgment was entered. This judgment adopted the "Memo Opinion" of December 11, 1970, and directed that the order of the Kentucky State Racing Commission of January 6, 1969, be set aside for lack of substantial evidence to support it and that distribution of the purse in the Seventh Race at Churchill Downs on May 4, 1968, be made in accordance with the order of finish.

The Kentucky State Racing Commission appeals. The sole issue raised by the appellants is whether the January 6, 1969, order of the Commission was supported by substantial evidence.

The appellee filed a motion to dismiss the appeal, which was passed by this court to the merits of the case.

The motion to dismiss the appeal is overruled, and the judgment of the Franklin Circuit Court is reversed.

The Kentucky State Racing Commission is an independent agency of state government. KRS 230.220. The Commission, charged with the duty of maintaining integrity and honesty in racing, was directed to promulgate rules and regulations "for effectively preventing the use of improper devices, the administration of drugs or stimulants or other improper acts for the purpose of affecting the speed or health of horses in races in which they are to participate."

KRS 230.240. The Commission was vested with all powers necessary and proper to carry out fully and effectively those duties imposed upon it by the statutes. KRS 230.260.

All persons aggrieved by an order of the Commission are granted an appeal to the Franklin Circuit Court in the manner provided by KRS 243.560 to 243.590, being the same sections of the statute governing appeals from orders of the Alcoholic Beverage Control Board. KRS 230.330. Upon the appeal no additional evidence shall be introduced except as to the fraud or misconduct of some party engaged in the administration of the act and affecting the order appealed from. The court shall otherwise hear the case upon the record as attested by the Commission. Upon the appeal the review of the court is limited to determining whether or not (a) the Commission acted without or in excess of its powers; (b) the order appealed from was procured by fraud; (c) if questions of fact are in issue, whether or not any substantial evidence supports the order appealed from. KRS 243.570.

Any party "aggrieved" by a judgment of the Franklin Circuit Court is granted an appeal to the Court of Appeals in accordance with the Rules of Civil Procedure. KRS 243.590.

Rules adopted by the Kentucky State Racing Commission regulating the subject matter of this appeal are as follows:

14.04 Should the chemical analysis of saliva, urine or other sample taken from a horse indicate the presence of a forbidden narcotic, stimulant, depressant, local anaesthetic, or a medication which is a derivative of phenylbutazone, it shall be considered prima-facie evidence that such has been administered to the horse. * * *.

14.05 When such positive report is received from the State Chemist by the Stewards the persons held responsible shall be notified, and a thorough investigation shall be conducted by or on behalf of the Stewards. * * *.

14.06 The trainer shall be responsible for the condition of the horses he enters. Should the chemical analysis of any sample indicate the presence of any forbidden narcotic, stimulant, depressant, local anaesthetic, or a medication which is a derivative of phenylbutazone, the trainer of the horse, together with the assistant trainer, stable foreman, groom, or any other person shown to have had care and attendance of the horse shall be subject to the penalties prescribed in section XXIII, and such horse shall not participate in the purse distribution.

Appellee's motion to dismiss the appeal is grounded upon the contention that the appellants are not "aggrieved parties" within the purview of the statute and thus have no legal right to maintain this appeal. Appellee contends that as the Commission is an administrative agency it can have no partisan interest in its decisions and therefore is not aggrieved by an adverse court decision; and that the Commission, in exercising its quasi-judicial function, could not have a legal interest in maintaining its determination. Thus, an adverse decision by the court deprives it of no right or privilege.

The Kentucky State Racing Commission is more than an administrative agency having the quasi-judicial function of finding the facts and applying the law to the facts. The Commission was created for the purpose of maintaining integrity and honesty in racing; the promulgation and enforcement of rules and regulations effectively preventing the use of improper devices, the administration of drugs or stimulants, or other improper acts for the purpose of affecting the speed or health of horses; and the promotion of interest in the breeding of and improvement of the breed of thoroughbred horses. The Commission is vested with extensive authority over all persons on racing premises for the purpose of maintaining honesty and integrity and orderly conduct of thoroughbred racing. On the basis of the statutes heretofore referred to, the Commission is charged with the duty of protecting substantial public interest and is therefore a representative of this interest in all proceedings.

The expression "person aggrieved" or "party aggrieved" has no technical meaning. What it means depends on the circumstances involved. It has been defined as meaning adversely affected in respect of legal rights, or suffering from an infringement or denial of legal rights. "One may be aggrieved within the meaning of the various statutes authorizing appeals when he is affected only in a representative capacity." In re Halifax Paper Company, Inc., 259 N.C. 589, 131 S.E.2d 441 (1963).

In Minnesota Water Resources Board v. County of Traverse et al., 287 Minn. 130, 177 N.W.2d 44 (1970), the Water Resources Board appealed from an adverse judgment of the district court. Appellee filed a motion to dismiss the appeal, claiming that the Water Resources Board was not an aggrieved party under either the Watershed Act or the Administrative Procedures Act. The Watershed Act provided in part: "Any party aggrieved by a final order or judgment * * * may appeal therefrom to the supreme court * * * ." Minn.St. § 112.82, subd. 1. The Administrative Procedures Act provided in part: "An aggrieved party may secure a review of any final order or judgment * * * by appeal to the supreme court." Minn.St. § 15.0426.

On the question of the Water Resources Board's being an aggrieved party, the court said:

" * * * Whether it is an aggrieved party under either the Administrative Procedures Act or the Watershed Act depends, as we see it, on whether it is essentially an administrative agency of the state empowered to initiate proceedings within the sphere of its jurisdiction and to establish and implement policy on behalf of the state, or whether its functions are limited to resolving disputes between conflicting interests of other agencies, subdivisions of government, and individuals."

Following a discussion of the rule in other jurisdictions, the court said:

"A review of these and other authorities leads us to the conclusion that the right of appeal depends largely on whether express provision is made in the particular statute involved. As we have previously indicated, where the language is broad as in §112.82, subd. 1, relating to any 'party aggrieved,' the test seems to be whether the agency is created to represent the interests of the public or whether it is to act only in deciding controversies between other entities of government or individual members of the public."

In Workmen's Compensation Board of Kentucky v. Abbott, 212 Ky. 123, 278 S.W. 533 (1925), this court, in holding that the Workmen's Compensation Board had the right to appeal from an adverse ruling of the circuit court, said:

> Before taking up the questions argued on the merits of the case, we will first briefly consider a question of practice raised by an amicus curiae brief filed in the case by permission of this court. It is that the Board has no right or authority to prosecute an appeal in this class of cases from the circuit court to this one. Involved in that question is the further one as to the extent of the Board's interest in the matters involved, i.e., whether under the act it is only a mere nominal party to the proceedings on appeal either to the circuit or to this court; or whether it has, as the representative of the public, a substantial interest beyond that of a mere nominal party and which question will be hereinafter answered to the effect that it is more than a mere nominal party. Notwithstanding that fact, however, it, perhaps, would have been competent for the Legislature to deny it the right of appeal to this court and to have conferred it alone on the employer and the employee; but the fact that the Board is more than a nominal party and represents some substantial interests of the public in the due and proper administration of the act (as hereinafter shown) is persuasive that the Legislature did not intend to withhold

from it the right of appeal so that it might protect that interest in this court to which an appeal may be taken; and, therefore, such right should not be denied, unless the act does so in clear and explicit terms. The provisions for an appeal to the circuit court are contained in section 52 of the act, now section 4935 of our Statutes, and, of course, the Board could scarcely be an appellant to the circuit court, since the appeal is from its award, which, however, is untrue with reference to the judgment of the circuit court on review of the award. Therefore, we do not attribute any particular significance to the word "party" in that section with reference to who may appeal from the award of the Board to the circuit court. Section 53 of the act, now section 4936 of our Statutes, makes provisions for an appeal to this court from the judgment of the circuit court, and it is therein provided that the scope of this court's review "shall include all matters herein made the subject of review by the circuit court and also errors of law arising in the circuit court," etc. It is then further provided that—

"The procedure as to appeal to the Court of Appeals shall be the same as in civil actions, so far as the same may be applicable to and not in conflict with the provisions of this act, except as follows."

There is then prescribed what evidence shall be brought to this court and the method by which it may be done, as well as the duty of "the appellant" in the premises, after which certain provisions are made as to the duties of the circuit clerk upon direction of "the parties" with reference to the transmission of the record to this court, as well as what it should contain. The section, supra, providing for an appeal to the circuit court, says, inter alia, "The Board and each party shall have the right to appear in such review proceedings," and the right to appear carries with it the further one to be heard, which latter right is not usually accorded to a mere nominal party. We therefore hold that it was the purpose of the act to give the Board, which must be summoned on appeal to the circuit court, the right to be heard in that court, and the section providing for an appeal to this court, as we have seen, vests it with the right to review the same matters that were reviewed by the circuit court, and it would seem naturally to follow that if the Board had the right to be heard in the review by the circuit court, it would likewise have the same right in this court. We therefore hold that it is competent for the Board to appeal to this court from any judgment rendered by the circuit court in all cases where the amount involved is appealable to this court.

See also Boyd & Usher Transport v. Southern Tank Lines, Inc., Ky., 320 S.W.2d 120 (1959).

We conclude that the Kentucky State Racing Commission is a "party aggrieved" within the purview of KRS 243.590 and can, therefore, maintain this appeal. The motion to dismiss this appeal is overruled.

The real issue before this court is whether there was substantial evidence on the record as a whole to support the findings of the Kentucky State Racing Commission.

The rules of the Commission prohibiting the use of phenylbutazone require that the presence of this medication be determined by chemical analysis. Rules 14.04–14.06. The Commission is authorized by statute to contract with a laboratory for the making of chemical tests of saliva and urine. KRS 230.240. On May 4, 1968, Louisville Testing Laboratory, Inc., was, by contract, making the tests required by the Commission. Kenneth W. Smith was the president and chief chemist of the laboratory. Smith is a graduate of the University of Louisville with Bachelor's and Master's degrees in chemistry. He had performed chemical tests for the Commission for more than twenty-eight years during which time he had tested approximately 50,000 urine samples. Smith had two assistants, Maurice K. Cusick and

James W. Chinn. Cusick had a degree in chemistry and eighteen years of experience in racetrack chemistry. He was laboratory supervisor. Chinn was a laboratory technician and had been with Smith since 1960.

Five chemical tests of the urine sample are required in order to indicate the presence of phenylbutazone. Smith performed each of these tests on a urine sample designated as 3956U, or for laboratory purposes 9, and was unaware of the fact that the sample was from Dancer's Image until long after the results of the tests had been reported to the Stewards. The tests used had been recommended by the Association of Official Racing Chemists as those necessary for reporting the presence of phenylbutazone. The tests performed by Smith were as follows:

1. Vitali's color test;
2. Spectrophotometric curve in base solution of pH 11 to 13, and spectrophotometric curve at pH2;
3. Typical crystal test with copper chloride ethlenediamine;
4. Typical crystal test with palladous chloride ethlenediamine;
5. Mandelin's color test.

There is an abundance of expert testimony in the record to the effect that better practice would require a chemist to make additional tests before a positive finding would be acceptable. However, all witnesses agreed that a positive result on the five tests given by Smith would be sufficient to support a positive finding of phenylbutazone.

We do not attempt to detail the procedures followed in the making of these tests, but rather concern ourselves with the results obtained.

Smith testified that he did the Vitali's color test on a part of the sample with a positive result, being a color change to black or bluish black, thereby indicating the presence of phenylbutazone.

Cusick and Chinn testified that they had each observed the Vitali's test and its positive indication of phenylbutazone. Of the results Cusick said, "It was the strongest one I have ever seen." Chinn said, "The Vitali's test that we made on Saturday night was the strongest Vitali's that I have ever seen."

Appellee Peter Fuller attacked the positive Vitali's test by contending that there were other chemicals that would produce a positive reaction and also that a black-and-white picture made by Smith of his test completely refuted the positive results claimed. Dr. Gerald Umbreit testified that a great number of chemicals would produce a positive Vitali's test. Yet, he admitted to the Commission that very few of them would ordinarily be found in the urine of a horse. All witnesses agreed that phenylbutazone produces a positive Vitali's test. John L. McDonald, Director of the Illinois Bureau of Racetrack Police Laboratory, when questioned about the black-and-white picture of Smith's Vitali's test, testified that the picture confirmed neither the presence nor absence of phenylbutazone.

Smith testified in regard to the results of the spectrophotometric curves as follows:

Q   Mr. Smith, is there any question in your mind about the DK-2 curve which is Exhibit Number 6, center of Exhibit Number 6 in the Stewards Hearing being a phenylbutazone curve?
A   None whatsoever.
Q   Base and acid?
A   Both curves to me were characteristic of phenylbutazone at the time I made them. * * * .
Q   Has there ever been any doubt in your mind that these curves were produced by phenylbutazone?
A   None whatsoever.

Cusick, the laboratory supervisor, testified that there was no doubt in his mind that both curves were phenylbutazone curves.

Witness Lewis E. Harris, a highly qualified racing chemist, after examining the Smith spectrophotometric curve, testified as follows:

Q   Does the fact that there was an acid curve produced in this case, is that acid curve consistent with phenylbutazone?

A   Yes.

Q   Does the fact that there is no minimum on the curve, alkaline curve produced by Mr. Smith, does that detract from your opinion that the testing he did was sufficient to indicate the presence of phenylbutazone?

A   No.

George Jaggard, another racing chemist, after an examination of the Smith curve, testified:

Q   Mr. Jaggard, do you have an opinion as to whether or not that the alkaline curve on that page was produced by phenylbutazone?

A   Yes, I do.

Q   And what is that opinion?

A   I think it was produced by phenylbutazone.

The accuracy of the tests with the resultant curves was seriously questioned, the question being predicated in part on the fact that one curve did not have a minimum reading, thereby indicating that a rather serious mistake had been made in the procedural and mechanical aspects of the test.

Appellee's expert, Dr. Hans H. Jaffe, a spectroscopist, examined the curves that resulted from Smith's test. He detailed the mechanics and theory of the spectrophotometric curve and the numerous defects and errors detected by him in his examination of the Smith curves. However, Jaffe, after considering these defects and errors, testified:

A   * * * The acid curve does resemble that of phenylbutazone. * * * .

Q   * * * can you state individually if these (curves) have any meaning as far as the identification of phenylbutazone?

A   I cannot, of course, say that these curves demonstrate that there was no phenylbutazone. This is a determination that is pretty hard to make. But as far as I can see, they do not demonstrate the presence of phenylbutazone in these specimens.

This witness further testified that he could not say that the curve was not caused by phenylbutazone. The witness James L. McDonald, after studying the curves that resulted from the Smith test, testified that they did not affirm or disaffirm the presence of phenylbutazone. Of the crystal tests Smith said:

Q Was there any question in your mind about the results of these crystal tests?
A No sir, none whatsoever.
Q Have you concluded from those crystal tests that they were what?
A I concluded from the series of tests that the sample contained phenylbutazone and the characteristic crystals were concluded to be from phenylbutazone with this particular agent.

While the crystal tests were in progress Smith made several pictures of the crystal formations with a Polaroid camera. These pictures were filed in the record at the time Smith testified. Characteristic crystals produced by the tests were not readily, if at all, identifiable in the pictures. Appellee seeks to discredit Smith and the positive showing of these tests because the pictures did not depict the crystals and, consequently, Smith could not have observed the formation of these characteristic crystals.

George Jaggard, a racing chemist with more than fifty years of experience, testified that these crystal tests required at least fifteen minutes to complete, while a picture of the process would represent only one thousandth of the whole and, therefore, was not very representative of what you see. Appellee's witness, Dr. Gerald Umbreit, also testified that crystals were constantly changing during the test, and that a picture would show only one phase of the test. Dr. Umbreit also testified that even with the help of a professional photographer he had encountered serious difficulties in getting acceptable pictures. In one instance he had made fifteen to twenty attempts before he was satisfied with the picture. Appellee's witness, John L. McDonald, after examining the Smith pictures, testified that they neither affirmed nor disaffirmed the presence of phenylbutazone.

Smith had the following to say in regard to the Mandelin's color test:

A   * * * These color tests were conducted along with a known. And the known gave the same results as the sample did.

Q   By the known, you mean that you take a substance that you know to be or to contain phenylbutazone, and run the tests along with this in the unknown substance, is that right?

A   That's correct.

Q   And then you compare them as you run your tests?

A   (Affirmative nod.)

Q   Is that right?

A   That's correct.

Q   And then, this test was positive?

A   For Mandelin's reagent color.

Q   Can you describe how positive?

A   Unquestionably.

Q   Was that the degree of certainty in all the tests you conducted?

A   Yes sir.

Q   Having observed the Mandelin's test, was there any doubt in any of your minds as to whether the Mandelin's test gave a positive reaction?

A   None whatsoever.

Smith made no photographs of this test; whether it was made and the results obtained depend solely upon oral testimony. The appellee would have this court believe that where no demonstrative evidence is introduced oral testimony alone cannot be considered substantial evidence, and further that the court can no longer rely on what is termed "the honor system" and give any weight to oral testimony where it is not supported by demonstrative evidence.

Cusick and Chinn both testified that they observed the Mandelin's tests performed by Smith and that the tests were positive. Upon cross-examination the evidence was highly contradictory concerning the date, time, and place where each of these witnesses observed the Mandelin's tests. However, no evidence was introduced that might have indicated that either of them did not see a positive Mandelin's test.

On the question of whether the tests performed by Smith were sufficient to indicate the presence of phenylbutazone, Smith testified:

Q   Mr. Smith, do you have an opinion as to whether or not the series of tests which you ran are sufficient to establish the presence of phenylbutazone?

A   Yes sir. In my report I stated that phenylbutazone was present and from all the tests that I made and as many times as I made them, there was no question in my mind whatsoever it was there.

Q   Let's try once more, Mr. Smith. Do the results you obtained in running all of these tests, which were observed with you by two of your employees, indicate to you whether or not phenylbutazone was present?

A   They do. There was no question in my mind but what phenylbutazone was present.

Appellee's expert, Dr. Gerald Umbreit, was asked by Commission member Bell if using the tools and tests employed by Smith he could conclude that there was an indication of phenylbutazone. In answer to this question, he said, "With those tools, I could reach a private conclusion that it might be. But I would not reach a public conclusion that it is."

This witness also testified that in all of the tests that he had run with different compounds he did not find one that produced a positive in all the tests that Smith had run, with the exception of phenylbutazone.

Witness McDonald testified that he would not report an indicated presence of phenylbutazone even if he should get a positive on all of the Smith tests. His reasoning was that there were other compounds which could produce a positive in some of the tests used; yet, he was unable to name a single compound that would have the same reaction as phenylbutazone on these five tests.

The Kentucky State Racing Commission heard all the testimony in the record now under consideration. The direct examination of the witnesses was generally long and detailed, with the cross-examination being prolonged, repetitious, and argumentative, which facts are amply substantiated by the size of the record. There are numerous contradictions and even contradictions of contradictions throughout this entire record.

The Commission, as the trier of the facts, saw each witness and was in a superior position to evaluate the situation as well as the conduct and demeanor of each witness as he testified; to consider the credibility of the witness; and to determine the weight as between conflicting statements of witnesses or even a single witness.

In cases where an administrative agency acts in its capacity as a trier of the facts, we have held that the findings of the agency are conclusive if supported by substantial evidence.

We will consider first the rule; second, the definition of substantial evidence; and finally, the province of the agency in its evaluation of the evidence heard and considered.

Commonwealth v. Mudd, Ky., 255 S.W.2d 989 (1953). The act establishing the Board of Claims limited judicial review of its orders of a determination of whether "the finding of fact supports the award or judgment." In discussing the authority of the courts of review, we said:

"The Board of Claims was created to provide a method for the processing of claims against the Commonwealth with a minimum of formality and delay, and, as we construe the Act, the Legislature did not intend that the courts would retry a case on conflicting facts after it has been heard by the Board. It was held in Shrader v. Commonwealth, 309 Ky. 553, 218 S.W.2d 406, and reaffirmed in Morrison v. Department of Highways, Ky., 252 S.W.2d 426, that findings of fact by the Board of Claims are conclusive if supported by substantial evidence." In Taylor v. Coblin, Ky., 461 S.W.2d 78, we said:

"If there is any substantial evidence to support the action of the administrative agency, it cannot be found to be arbitrary and will be sustained."

See also Board of Education of Ashland School District v. Chattin, Ky., 376 S.W.2d 693 (1964), and H. Smith Coal Company v. Marshall, Ky., 243 S.W.2d 40 (1951).

Substantial evidence is defined in Chesapeake and Ohio Railway Company v. United States, 298 F.Supp. 734 (D.C.1968), as follows:

" * * * Substantial evidence is such relevant evidence as a reasonable mind might accept as adequate to support a conclusion; it is something less than the weight of the evidence, and the possibility of drawing two inconsistent conclusions from the evidence does not prevent an administrative agency's finding from being supported by substantial evidence." (Citations omitted.)

In O'Nan v. Ecklar Moore Express, Inc., Ky., 339 S.W.2d 466 (1960), this court said:

" * * * We have defined 'substantial' evidence as being evidence of substance and relevant consequence, having the fitness to induce conviction in the minds of reasonable men."

The test of substantiality of evidence is whether when taken alone or in the light of all the evidence it has sufficient probative value to induce conviction in the minds of reasonable men. Blankenship v. Lloyd Blankenship Coal Company, Inc., Ky., 463 S.W.2d 62 (1970).

The Kentucky State Racing Commission, as trier of the facts is afforded great latitude in its evaluation of the evidence heard and the credibility of witnesses appearing before the Commission.

The authority of the Bureau of Land Management, Department of Interior, was questioned in Noren v. Beck, 199 F.Supp. 708 (D.C.1961). The Court, in limiting the scope of its review of a ruling of the department, said:

> In the development of the doctrine and rule of administrative finality, courts have uniformly held that it is the exclusive province and function of administrative agencies to draw legitimate inferences of fact and make findings and conclusions of fact, to appraise conflicting testimony or other evidence, to judge the credibility of witnesses and the evidence adduced by the parties, and to determine the weight of the evidence (see cases cited in Schaffer v. United States, 139 F.Supp. 444 (S.D.1956)). See also In the Matter of Adolfe Cartellone, 148 F.Supp. 676 (N.D.Ohio) 1957.
>
> It therefore follows that the review by this court in this case is to determine from the record whether the exercise of discretion of the agency in rejecting plaintiffs' applications was arbitrary, capricious, discriminatory, unlawful, illegal, or a denial of their rights. The scope of judicial review in this respect does not provide for a trial de novo.

In Wheatley v. Shields, 292 F.Supp. 608 (D.C.1968), the findings of a Coast Guard Hearing Examiner were contested. The Court, in upholding the examiner, said:

> Accordingly, after a thorough consideration of the entire record of the administrative hearing, the decision and order of the Examiner, and the Decision of the Commandant, it is the opinion of this Court that "substantial evidence" exists upon which a reasonable mind could properly arrive at the conclusion reached below. Regardless of the fact that this Court might have reached a contrary result if it were hearing this case de novo, it is required on the basis of its

posture as a reviewing body to affirm the administrative determination. For it must be borne in mind that it is the exclusive province of the administrative trier of fact to pass upon the credibility of witnesses, and the weight of the evidence. (Citations omitted.)

The basic rule in Kentucky was expressed in Irvin v. Madden, 281 Ky. 7, 134 S.W.2d 942 (1939), as follows:

" * * * Under a doctrine too well recognized to require citation of authority, the credibility of witnesses and the weight to be given their evidence are matters exclusively within the province of a jury. A jury may accept the evidence of one set of witnesses to the exclusion of that of another or the evidence of one witness as against the evidence of a number of witnesses and may also judge and determine the weight as between the conflicting statements of a single witness."

Wilson v. Haughton, Ky., 266 S.W.2d 115 (1954), involved the question of evidence required to prove a contract. In that opinion it is stated:

> * * * appellant insists that the verdict was flagrantly against the weight of the evidence and states that appellee's testimony was vague, uncertain and unconvincing and such testimony, when contradicted by the clear and convincing testimony of appellant, his wife and daughter, does not carry that quality of proof and fitness to induce conviction necessary to sustain the verdict.
>
> We do not take the view that appellee's testimony is unconvincing. The fact that testimony is denied does not constitute proof of its lack of plausibility. Louisville & N.R. Co. v. Thomas, 298 Ky. 494, 183 S.W.2d 19. Neither is superiority of numbers conclusive in evaluating the testimony of witnesses. Hale v. James E. Hannah Realty Corp., Ky., 249 S.W.2d 733. Here, the jury accepted the testimony of appellee and his witness and fixed the damage for the

breach of contract at an amount they believed to be equivalent to his loss. We are of opinion that the verdict should not be disturbed.

H. Smith Coal Company v. Marshall, Ky., 243 S.W.2d 40 (1951), is a workmen's compensation case where the cause of death of an employee was in issue. Dr. Howze testified that death was due to an acute coronary occlusion. Dr. Weiss testified that death was caused by carbon monoxide poison. The Board ruled that the employee's death was due to a coronary occlusion. In sustaining the Board, this court said:

"As competent substantial evidence supported the Board's finding that Mr. Marshall's death was due to a coronary occlusion rather than from carbon monoxide poisoning, the circuit court could not weigh the evidence for itself but was bound by the finding of the Board and was without authority to disturb it."

In Chesapeake & Ohio Railway Company v. United States, 298 F.Supp. 734 (D.C.1969), the rule is stated as follows:

"In determining whether the findings of the Commission challenged by plaintiffs are arbitrary or capricious or unsupported by substantial evidence, the Court is not free to substitute its judgment for that of the Commission as to the weight of the evidence or the inferences to be drawn from the evidence."

This court, after having considered the entire record and the law of the case as set out herein, finds and now holds that there was an abundance of substantial evidence supporting the findings and rulings of the Kentucky State Racing Commission.

The Franklin Circuit Court ruled that there had been no denial of due process of law or arbitrary action on the part of the Kentucky State Racing Commission. This court, upon its consideration of the record, finds nothing to indicate that this particular ruling of the Franklin Circuit Court was erroneous.

The judgment is reversed with directions to set it aside and enter one sustaining the order of the Kentucky State Racing Commission.

All concur.

Appendix 6

Dutrow v. New York State Racing and Wagering Board

In 2011 Rick Dutrow, trainer of Kentucky Derby and Preakness Stakes winner Big Brown, was fined $30,000 and suspended for ten years by the New York State Racing and Wagering Board for "repeated violations and disrespect of the rules of racing." The next year, the Appellate Division of the New York State Supreme Court concluded that the "revocation of petitioner's license for a period of at least 10 years and the imposition of a fine was not so disproportionate to his proven, recurrent misconduct as to shock one's sense of fairness." The text of the decision follows.

2012 N.Y. Slip Op. 05699
In the Matter of Richard E. DUTROW, Petitioner,
v.
NEW YORK STATE RACING AND WAGERING BOARD, Respondent.
Supreme Court, Appellate Division, Third Department, New York.
July 19, 2012.
Hinkley, Allen & Snyder, LLP, Albany (Michael L. Koenig of counsel), for petitioner.
Eric T. Schneiderman, Attorney General, Albany (Kathleen M. Arnold of counsel), for respondent.

Before: MERCURE, J.P., ROSE, LAHTINEN, STEIN and McCARTHY, JJ.

MERCURE, J.P.

Proceeding pursuant to CPLR article 78 (transferred to this Court by order of the Supreme Court, entered in Schenectady County) to review a determination of respondent which, among other things, revoked petitioner's license to participate in pari-mutuel racing for a period of 10 years.

Respondent prohibits licensed horse trainers, such as petitioner, from possessing hypodermic needles at race tracks (*see* 9 NYCRR 4012.1[a]) and, during a November 2010 search, investigators found three syringes in petitioner's desk at the Aqueduct Racetrack. Although the administration of the drug butorphanol to horses within 96 hours of racing is also prohibited (*see* 9 NYCRR 4043.2[g]), Fastus Cactus, a horse that was trained by petitioner, tested positive for the drug after racing at Aqueduct. Petitioner was found, by the state racing steward, to have violated both rules and his license was suspended for a total of 90 days, prompting his administrative appeal to respondent.

By order to show cause, respondent then sought to suspend or revoke petitioner's license and exclude him from New York race-tracks due to the foregoing violations, the presence of the drug xylazine in the unlabeled syringes (*see* 9 NYCRR 4012.1[c]), and the inadvisability of his continued involvement in horse racing given his history of rule violations and improper conduct (*see* Racing, Pari-Mutuel Wagering and Breeding Law §220[2]; 9 NYCRR 4002.9[a]; 4003.46). A Hearing Officer sustained the charges in their entirety and recommended that petitioner permanently lose his license and be fined a total of $50,000. Respondent adopted the Hearing Officer's findings of fact and conclusions of law, although it permitted petitioner to reapply for a new license after 10 years. Petitioner thereafter commenced this CPLR article 78 proceeding, and Supreme Court transferred the matter to this Court and stayed respondent's determination.

Initially, we reject petitioner's claim that he was deprived of a fair hearing by the refusal of respondent's chair, John Sabini, to recuse himself. Sabini was an unpaid officer for the Association of Racing Commissioners International, an organization devoted to maintaining a multijurisdictional database of licensed horse racing professionals' disciplinary histories. Sabini had no prior official involvement with, and made no appearance in, petitioner's case stemming from that role (*cf. Matter of Beer Garden v. New York State Liq. Auth.*, 79 N.Y.2d 266, 278–279, 582 N.Y.S.2d 65, 590 N.E.2d 1193 [1992]), but the association's president informed Sabini that a United States Senator's office had inquired about the case; the president also publicly urged respondent to assess petitioner's "suitability to continue his participation in racing." Petitioner's bare allegation that those communications led to bias is insufficient absent "a factual demonstration to support the allegation . . . and proof that the outcome flowed from it" (*Matter of Warder v. Board of Regents of Univ. of State of N.Y.*, 53 N.Y.2d 186, 197, 440 N.Y.S.2d 875, 423 N.E.2d 352 [1981], *cert. denied* 454 U.S. 1125, 102 S.Ct. 974, 71 L.Ed.2d 112 [1981]; *see* [97 A.D.3d 1036] *Matter of Yoonessi v. State Bd. for Professional Med. Conduct*, 2 A.D.3d 1070, 1071, 769 N.Y.S.2d 326 [2003], *lv. denied* 3 N.Y.3d 607, 785 N.Y.S.2d 24, 818 N.E.2d 666 [2004]). Sabini was not bound to follow any suggestions made by the association or its president, and the record is devoid of evidence that he took any action based upon the communications or otherwise "gave the impression that [he] had prejudged the facts" (*Matter of Beer Garden v. New York State Liq. Auth.*, 79 N.Y.2d at 278, 582 N.Y.S.2d 65, 590 N.E.2d 1193; *see Matter of Kole v. New York State Educ. Dept.*, 291 A.D.2d 683, 686, 738 N.Y.S.2d 420 [2002]; *cf. Matter of 1616 Second Ave. Rest. v. New York State Liq. Auth.*, 75 N.Y.2d 158, 161–162, 551 N.Y.S.2d 461, 550 N.E.2d 910 [1990]). Inasmuch as petitioner thus failed "to rebut the presumption of honesty and integrity accorded to administrative bodies" (*Matter of Kole v. New York State Educ. Dept.*, 291 A.D.2d at 686, 738 N.Y.S.2d 420), it cannot be said that he was denied a fair hearing.

Turning to the charges themselves, substantial evidence—in the form of the positive test, the horse's veterinary records, and the testimony of veterinarian and pharmacologist George Maylin—supports respondent's determination that Fastus Cactus received a dose of butorphanol less than 96 hours before racing (*see Matter of Dutrow v. New York State Racing & Wagering Bd.*, 18 A.D.3d 947, 947, 795 N.Y.S.2d 106 [2005]). A rebuttable presumption of petitioner's responsibility thus arose, which he attempted to rebut with expert testimony that the sample had not been tested to eliminate the possibility of cross contamination (*see Matter of Mosher v. New York State Racing & Wagering Bd.*, 74 N.Y.2d 688, 690, 543 N.Y.S.2d 374, 541 N.E.2d 403 [1989]; *see* 9 NYCRR 4043.4). Respondent credited Maylin's testimony that Fastus Cactus had been administered butorphanol and, in our view, properly rejected the speculative testimony of petitioner's expert regarding possible alternative explanations for the positive test as insufficient to rebut the presumption (*see Matter of Pletcher v. New York State Racing & Wagering Bd.*, 35 A.D.3d 920, 922, 826 N.Y.S.2d 468 [2006], *lv. denied* 9 N.Y.3d 802, 840 N.Y.S.2d 567, 872 N.E.2d 253 [2007]; *Matter of Zito v. New York State Racing & Wagering Bd.*, 300 A.D.2d 805, 806–807, 752 N.Y.S.2d 109 [2002], *lv. denied* 100 N.Y.2d 502, 760 N.Y.S.2d 765, 790 N.E.2d 1194 [2003]).

As for the remaining charges, unlabeled syringes containing xylazine were recovered from petitioner's desk at Aqueduct, and the chain of custody of those syringes was appropriately established through the testimony of the individuals who handled them (*see Matter of Spano v. New York State Racing & Wagering Bd.*, 72 A.D.3d 404, 405, 899 N.Y.S.2d 19 [2010], *lv. denied* 16 N.Y.3d 709, 2011 WL 1237390 [2011]; *Matter of Case v. New York State Racing & Wagering Bd.*, 61 A.D.3d 1313, 1314, 877 N.Y.S.2d 526 [2009], *lv. denied* 13 N.Y.3d 705, 2009 WL 2924116 [2009]). Further, while respondent previously renewed petitioner's license despite his prior disciplinary history, it properly relied upon that history in tandem with the instant violations to determine that petitioner engaged in conduct that was improper and inconsistent with the public interest and best interests of racing (*see* 9 NYCRR 4002.9, 4003.46).

Finally, we conclude that the revocation of petitioner's license for a period of at least 10 years and the imposition of a fine was not so disproportionate to his proven, recurrent misconduct as to shock one's sense of fairness (*see Matter of Fusco v. New York State Racing & Wagering Bd.,* 88 A.D.3d 1240, 1243, 931 N.Y.S.2d 439 [2011], *lv. denied* 18 N.Y.3d 809, 2012 WL 996693 [2012]). Petitioner's assertion that aspects of the regulatory scheme are unconstitutionally vague is unpreserved for our review (*see Matter of McCollum v. Fischer,* 61 A.D.3d 1194, 1194, 876 N.Y.S.2d 766 [2009], *lv. denied* 13 N.Y.3d 703, 2009 WL 2779303 [2009]), and his remaining argument has been considered and found to lack merit.

ADJUDGED that the determination is confirmed, without costs, and petition dismissed. ROSE, LAHTINEN, STEIN and McCARTHY, JJ., concur.

Notes

Introduction

1. The word "dope" as a reference to opium may have originated in China in the early 1600s, when Portuguese and Dutch sailors began to mix small balls of raw opium with tobacco to smoke—a mixture called "doop." John H. Halpern and David Blistein, *Opium: How an Ancient Flower Shaped and Poisoned Our World* (New York: Hachette Books, 2019). The phrase "Dutch courage" sometimes appears in early accounts of stimulants being given to racehorses, lending credence to a Dutch-Portuguese origin of the word "dope." The *Oxford English Dictionary* includes these relevant definitions of "dope" as a noun—"A drug etc. administered to a racehorse or greyhound to interfere with its performance or to an athlete as a stimulant"—and as a verb—"Administer stimulating or stupefying drugs to (a horse, a person)." The *OED* dates the origins of these definitions between 1870 and 1899. As used throughout this book, "dope" refers generally to performance-enhancing drugs used in Thoroughbred racing and human athletics, whether legal or illegal, prohibited or allowed by regulators. (In a different and more innocuous context, "dope" refers to information about the horses running in a race contained in form sheets and other compilations of past performances.)

2. A three-year research study into the performance-enhancing qualities of Lasix (trade name of the drug furosemide) is required by the Horseracing Integrity and Safety Act of 2020, which may finally put to rest the question of whether it is a PED. Lasix, which is used to treat exercise-induced pulmonary hemorrhage in horses (commonly called "bleeding"), also gained a reputation as a "masking" drug behind which PEDs could hide. According to veterinarian Rick Arthur, who, along with Dr. George Maylin, researched Lasix in the mid-1980s, diuretics like Lasix do not mask other drugs but can reduce their concentration in a horse's urine, making it more difficult to

detect a PED. See Bill Finley, "Horse Racing, Robinson Cano and Can Lasix Really Mask Other Drugs?" *Thoroughbred Daily News,* May 17, 2018, https://www.thoroughbreddailynews.com/horse-racing-robinson-cano-and-can-lasix-really-mask-other-drugs.

3. As of this writing, my award-winning *Dancer's Image: The Forgotten Story of the 1968 Kentucky Derby* (Charleston, SC: History Press, 2011) is the only book about that controversial race.

4. Yogi Berra, *The Yogi Book: I Really Didn't Say All the Things I Said* (New York: Workman Publishing, 2010), 45. The famed Yankee catcher said he came up with the phrase "after Mickey Mantle and Roger Maris hit back-to-back home runs for the umpteenth time."

5. *Murphy v. National Collegiate Athletic Association,* 138 S.Ct. 1461 (2018).

6. L. John Wertheim, "Follow the Money," *Sports Illustrated,* September 2021, 26.

7. John W. Jeffries, *Wartime America: The World War II Homefront,* 2nd ed. (New York: Rowman and Littlefield, 2018), 148.

8. See https://mostpopularsports.net/in-america.

9. Bennett Liebman, "Reasons for the Decline of Horse Racing," *New York Times,* June 6, 2010, https://therail.blogs.nytimes.com/2010/06/06/reasons-for-the-decline-of-horse-racing/.

10. Claudio Gatti, "Looking Upstream in Doping Cases," *New York Times,* January 16, 2013, B11, https://www.com/2013/01/16/sports/cycling/critics-take-a-look-upstream-in-doping-scandals.html?searchResultPosition=1.

11. The video interview can be viewed at https://www.youtube.com/watch?v=CCXtrpUo49U. For more information about the prisoner dilemma, see Steven Kuhn, "Prisoner's Dilemma," in *The Stanford Encyclopedia of Philosophy* (Winter 2019), ed. Edward N. Zalta, https://plato.stanford.edu/archives/win2019/entries/prisoner-dilemma/.

12. Andrew M. Homan, *Iron Mac: The Legend of Roughhouse Cyclist Reggie McNamara* (Lincoln: University of Nebraska Press, 2016), 111–15.

13. Dr. Grigory Rodchenkov, *The Rodchenkov Affair: How I Brought Down Putin's Secret Doping Empire* (London: WH Allen, 2020); Werner W. Franke and Bridgitte Berendonk, "Hormonal Doping and Androgenization of Athletes: A Secret Program of the German Democratic Government," *Clinical Chemistry* 43, no. 7 (1997): 1262–79.

14. See David R. Mottram and Neil Chester, eds., *Drugs in Sport,* 7th ed. (New York: Routledge, 2018); Paul Dimeo, *A History of Drug Use in Sport, 1876–1976: Beyond Good and Evil* (New York: Routledge, 2007); Mike

McNamee and William J. Morgan, eds., *Routledge Handbook of the Philosophy of Sport* (New York: Routledge, 2017).

15. See John Gleaves, "Enhancing the Odds: Horse Racing, Gambling, and the First Anti-Doping Movement," *Sport in History* 32, no. 1 (March 2012): 26–52; Steven Riess, "The Cyclical History of Horse Racing: The USA's Oldest and (Sometimes) Most Popular Spectator Sport," *International Journal of the History of Sport* 31 (2014): 29–54.

1. The Death of Dr. Riddle

1. Racing in England, Iroquois also won the Newmarket Two-Year-Old plate, the Two-Year-Old Stakes, the Chesterfield Stakes, and the Levat Stakes as a juvenile; the Prince of Wales's Stakes, the St. James's Palace Stakes, the St. Leger Stakes, and the Newmarket Derby at age three; and the Stockbridge Cup as a five-year-old. See American Classic Pedigrees, http://www.americanclassicpedigrees.com/iroquois.html. For more information on the next American-bred to win the Epsom Derby in 1954, see James C. Nicholson, *Never Say Die: A Kentucky Colt, the Epsom Derby, and the Rise of the Modern Thoroughbred Industry* (Lexington: University Press of Kentucky, 2013).

2. William H. P. Robertson, *The History of Thoroughbred Racing in America* (Englewood Cliffs, NJ: Prentice-Hall, 1964), 93.

3. W. C. Vreeland, "Dope to Stimulate Speed First Used on Horses at Guttenberg," *Brooklyn (NY) Daily Eagle,* January 21, 1932, 23.

4. "Gossip of Racing Men," *New York Times,* December 26, 1892, 2.

5. Paul Gallico, "Quick, Watson, the Needle," *New York Daily News,* April 8, 1934, 69.

6. *Buffalo (NY) Morning Express and Illustrated Buffalo Express,* May 16, 1903, 3.

7. *Buffalo (NY) Commercial,* May 16, 1903, 4.

8. *Brooklyn (NY) Times-Union,* May 16, 1903, 8.

9. *Detroit Free Press,* May 16, 1903, 11.

10. *Chicago Tribune,* May 16, 1903, 7.

11. *Pittsburg Press,* May 16, 1903, 12.

12. "Doping the Racehorses," *Cincinnati Enquirer,* June 6, 1903, 12.

13. "Doping of Dr. Riddle Was Apparent to All," *Brooklyn (NY) Times-Union,* May 16, 1903, 8.

14. "New Record Made at Morris Park," *Standard Union* (Brooklyn, NY), May 16, 1903, 5.

15. "Doping of Dr. Riddle Was Apparent to All," 8. The paddock judge was later identified as a man named Hall. "S.P.C.A. Agent at Morris Park," *Inter Ocean* (Chicago), May 26, 1903, 14.

16. "Doping of Dr. Riddle Was Apparent to All," 8.

17. For a comprehensive discussion of the often contentious relationship between the New York tracks and bookmakers around the turn of the century, see Steven A. Riess, *The Sport of Kings and the Kings of Crime* (Syracuse, NY: Syracuse University Press, 2011), 253–57.

18. "A Strange Rule about Bets," *New York Times*, May 20, 1893, 9.

19. "'Doped' Racehorse Dies," *Chicago Tribune*, May 16, 1903, 7.

20. *Daily Racing Form*, May 16, 1903, 1, https://drf.uky.edu/catalog /1900s/drf1903051601/drf1903051601_.

21. The description of Dr. Riddle's last race is based on several contemporaneous sources, including "'Doped' Race Horse Died," *New York Times*, May 16, 1903, 7; "A Scandal of the Turf," *Pittsburg Press*, May 16, 1903, 12; "Horse Killed by Overdose of Drugs," *San Francisco Chronicle*," May 16, 1903, 5; and "New Record Made at Morris Park," *Standard Union* (Brooklyn, NY), May 16, 1903, 5.

22. "Died from Being Doped," *Cincinnati Enquirer*, May 16, 1903, 3.

23. John Boden, "How 'Doc' Ring 'Doped' the Horses," *Buffalo (NY) Sunday Morning News*, April 30, 1911, 37.

24. "Horse Racing Gossip: Trainer Howell Ruled off for Doping Dr. Riddle," *Washington, DC, Evening Star*, May 23, 1903, 10.

25. "Trainer Wm. Howell Ruled off the Turf," *Washington (DC) Times*, May 23, 1903, 8.

26. "Doping of Dr. Riddle Was Apparent to All," 8.

27. "S.P.C.A. Agent at Morris Park," 14.

28. Ernest Freeberg, "The Horse Flu Epidemic that Brought 19th-Century America to a Stop," https://www.smithsonianmag.com/history /how-horse-flu-epidemic-brought-19th-century-america-stop-180976453/.

29. Zulma Steele, *Angel in Top Hat* (New York: Harper and Brothers, 1942), 87. This lack of interest in horse racing is reflected in a recent biography: Ernest Freeberg, *A Traitor to His Species: Henry Bergh and the Birth of the Animal Rights Movement* (New York: Basic Books, 2020).

30. For an account of the incident, see Steele, *Angel in Top Hat*, 89–90. For newspaper accounts, see "Racing at Jerome Park," *New York Tribune*, October 10, 1884, 8; "No Decision in the Jerome Park Case," *New York Tribune*, October 15, 1884, 2; "Gotham Gossip," *New Orleans Times-Picayune*, October 23, 1884, 3.

31. Riess, *Sport of Kings*, 257–59.

32. Bob McGarry, "'Ringing' Racehorses to the Tune of $6,000,000," *New York Daily News,* December 3, 1932, 24.

33. David Ashworth, *Ringers & Rascals: The True Story of Racing's Greatest Con Artists* (Lexington, KY: Eclipse Press, 2004), 85.

2. "Doc" Ring and the Modern Era of Doping

1. "Of Winter Racing," *Lewiston (ME) Evening Journal,* February 26, 1892, 6.

2. Audax Minor [G. F. T. Ryall], "The Race Track: Sticky Wicket," *New Yorker,* December 14, 1957, 86. Ryall made an error regarding the site of Guttenberg. The track was located in the New Jersey Palisades, directly across from 100th Street on the New York side of the Hudson River.

3. For more about Guttenberg's role in pioneering winter racing, see T. D. Thornton, "Outlaw Tracks Gave Rise to Winter Racing," *Daily Racing Form,* February 20, 2014, www.drf.com/news/outlaw-tracks-gave-rise-winter-racing.

4. "No Game at Guttenberg," *New York Times,* January 21, 1892, 5.

5. Steven A. Riess, *The Sport of Kings and the Kings of Crime* (Syracuse, NY: Syracuse University Press, 2011), 105–6.

6. "Of Winter Racing," 6.

7. Turn-of-the-century racetracks in the metropolitan area included Empire City, Jerome Park, and Morris Park in the Bronx; Gravesend, Brighton Beach, and Sheepshead Bay in Brooklyn; Aqueduct, Belmont Park, and Jamaica in Queens; and Guttenberg, Clifton, Elizabeth, and Linden in New Jersey. Riess, *Sport of Kings,* 22.

8. "The Outlaws of the Turf," *New York Times,* December 28, 1891, 2.

9. Riess, *Sport of Kings,* 122–35.

10. "The 'Big Four' Must Go to Jail," *New York Times,* May 14, 1895, 9.

11. "Gossip of Racing Men," *New York Times,* December 26, 1892, 2.

12. Guttenberg, along with competitors at Clifton, Linden, and Elizabeth, were so-called outlaw or proprietary tracks because they were not associated with any turf organization that set standards and enforced rules of conduct. Guttenberg "exemplified the worst" that horse racing had to offer. Riess, *Sport of Kings,* 107.

13. "Races at Clifton," *St. Louis Globe-Democrat,* December 23, 1890, 9.

14. For a discussion of westward expansion and the impact of the 1890 census, see Frederick J. Turner, "The Significance of the Frontier in American History," American Historical Association, https://www.historians.org

/about-aha-and-membership/aha-history-and-archives/historical-archives
/the-significance-of-the-frontier-in-american-history.

15. Erik Larson, *The Devil in the White City: Murder, Magic and Madness at the Fair that Changed America* (New York: Crown, 2003).

16. For a discussion of the vanishing frontier, see Richard A. Serrano, *American Endurance: Buffalo Bill, the Great Cowboy Race of 1893, and the Vanishing Wild West* (Washington, DC: Smithsonian Books, 2016).

17. "Testimony of Bennett Liebman to the Ad Hoc Committee on the Future of Racing," Albany (NY) Law School, January 24, 2005, 3, https://www.albanylaw.edu/media/user/glc/barretttestimony.pdf.

18. Marshall Trimble, email messages to the author, December 17–18, 2020.

19. Marshall Trimble, "Drugs on the Frontier," *True West Magazine,* June 27, 2017, https://truewestmagazine.com/drugs-on-the-frontier/.

20. Tom Clavin, *Dodge City: Wyatt Earp, Bat Masterson, and the Wickedest Town in the American West* (New York: St. Martin's Press, 2017), 402–3.

21. Alysha Strongman, "Mrs. Winslow's Soothing Syrup: The Baby Killer," Museum of Health Care blog, July 28, 2017, https://museumofhealthcare.wordpress.com/2017/07/28/mrs-winslows-soothing-syrup-the-baby-killer/.

22. Trimble, "Drugs on the Frontier."

23. Edward Marshall, "Uncle Sam Is the Worst Drug Fiend in the World," *New York Times,* March 12, 1911, 64.

24. John H. Halpern and David Blistein, *Opium: How an Ancient Flower Shaped and Poisoned Our World* (New York: Hachette Books, 2019), 199–215.

25. Dan Baum, "Legalize It All: How to Win the War on Drugs," *Harper's,* April 2016, https://harpers.org/archive/2016/04/legalize-it-all/.

3. The Injection

1. Walt Whitman, *Leaves of Grass: The Death-Bed Edition* (Overland Park, KS: Digireads, 2017), 93 (verse 51).

2. Very little has been written about Doc Ring's background, and much of what appeared in the press was based on rumor and speculation. Of the half dozen newspaper articles, only one was written contemporaneously. Unless otherwise noted, this chapter is based on the following sources: John Boden, "How 'Doc' Ring 'Doped' the Horses," *Buffalo (NY) Sunday Morning News,* April 30, 1911, 3; "Doping Race Horses: Practice Originated at

the Old Guttenberg Track," *Oshkosh (WI) Daily Northwestern,* September 25, 1903, 10; "'Dope' an American Term," *New York Times,* April 7, 1901, 19; "How Horses Are Doped," *Los Angeles Times,* January 5, 1896, 23; "Slow Horses Made Fast: The Rejuvenating Device of a Broken Down Sport," *New York Times,* September 25, 1892, 17; "How to Makes Horses Win: Hypodermic Injections Administered to Soft-Hearted Animals Successfully," *Louisville (KY) Courier-Journal,* April 18, 1890, 7. Although the farthest removed from Ring's time at Guttenberg, Boden's article (the only one with a byline) is likely the most reliable. Boden served as secretary of the New York State Racing Association, a post that would have put him behind the scenes and in a position to know the details of Ring's story.

3. "History of Veterinary Medicine," *Iowa State University Veterinarian* 2, no. 1 (1939): article 1, https://lib.dr.iastate.edu/cgi/viewcontent.cgi?article=1037&context=iowastate_veterinarian.

4. "The City: Race at Dexter Park," *Chicago Tribune,* October 2, 1867, 4.

5. See "Local New St. Louis Trotting Park," *Daily Missouri Republican,* October 18, 1867, 1, for a reference to "P. B. Ring's Magoozler." The horse previously raced for John Watson (trainer) and Samuel Keys (driver) from Pittsburgh. "Pittsburg Races: Oakland Park Race Course," *Pittsburg Weekly Gazette,* October 20, 1866, 1. With regard to Ring's name, newspaper references to Magoozler and T. B. King and T. B. Ring complicate matters; however, P. B. Ring appears to be the most reliable.

6. "Slow Horses Made Fast," 17.

7. "The Big Race," *New York Evening World,* June 18, 1889, 1.

8. "Taviston Had an Easy Victory," *New York Evening World,* October 31, 1889, 1.

9. "At Elizabeth," *New York Evening World,* December 4, 1889, 1.

10. "How to Make Horses Win," 7.

11. *New York Tribune,* August 4, 1889, 2.

12. "Another Record Broken," *Chicago Tribune,* August 28, 1889, 3.

13. See "A Strange Rule about Bets," *New York Times,* May 20, 1893, 9.

14. "How to Make Horses Win," 7.

15. Boden, "How 'Doc' Ring 'Doped' the Horses," 3.

16. "Slow Horses Made Fast," 17.

17. "'Dope' an American Term," 19.

18. W. S. Vosburgh, *Racing in America, 1866–1922* (New York: Scribner Press, 1922; private printing for the Jockey Club), 133.

19. "Trainer Dyer Tells How Tom Sawyer Upsets a Good Thing," *Portage (WI) Daily Democrat,* December 14, 1900, 4.

20. Boden, "How 'Doc' Ring 'Doped' the Horses," 3.

21. "Guttenberg Races," *St. Louis Globe-Democrat,* April 4, 1890.

22. "How to Make Horses Win," 7.

23. Boden, "How 'Doc' Ring 'Doped' the Horses," 3.

24. See https://www.healthline.com/nutrition/gentian-root#what-it-is.

25. See https://www.smithsonianmag.com/science-nature/how-advertising-shaped-first-opioid-epidemic-180968444/.

26. Boden, "How 'Doc' Ring 'Doped' the Horses," 3.

27. Advertisement in *Breeder and Sportsman,* October 22, 1898, 271.

28. *Obsolete American Securities and Corporations,* vol. 2 (New York: R. M. Smythe, 1911), 948.

29. Thomas Tobin, *Drugs and the Performance Horse* (Springfield, IL: Charles C. Thomas, 1981), 185.

30. Tobin, 85–98. For a discussion of the Dancer's Image case, see chapters 13 and 14.

31. For a report on the disqualification of Maximum Security, see Dan Wolken, "Country House Wins Kentucky Derby after Maximum Security Is Disqualified," *USA Today,* May 4, 2019, https://www.usatoday.com/story/sports/horseracing/2019/05/04/kentucky-derby-country-house-wins-maximum-security-disqualified/1101698001/.

32. See "Full Release on Monday's Indictments in Horse Racing," *Blood-Horse,* March 9, 2020, https://www.usatoday.com/story/sports/horseracing/2019/05/04/kentucky-derby-country-house-wins-maximum-security-disqualified/1101698001/.

33. Kent Hollingsworth, *The Great Ones* (Lexington, KY: Blood-Horse, 1970), 265–67.

34. *Thoroughbred Champions: Top 100 Racehorses of the 20th Century* (Lexington, KY: Blood-Horse Publications, 1999), 108–9. The selections, including a controversial decision to rank Man o' War first, ahead of second-place Secretariat, were made by a panel of racing officials and journalists: Howard Battle, Lennie Hale, Jay Hovdey, William R. Nack, Pete Pedersen, Jennie Rees, and Tommy Trotter.

35. For Sysonby's complete record, see *Champions: The Lives, Times, and Past Performances of America's Greatest Thoroughbreds,* rev. ed. (New York: Daily Racing Form, 2005), 38.

36. Alden Hatch and Foxhall Keene, *Full Tilt: The Sporting Memories of Foxhall Keene* (New York: Derrydale Press, 1938), 42–43.

37. For more about Chubb's work at the Museum of Natural History, see A. Katherine Berger, "Mounting Horse Skeletons to Exemplify Different Gaits and Actions," *Natural History Magazine,* https://images.library.amnh.org/digital/index.php/items/show/24889.

38. John H. Lewy, "Rancocas Filly Is Needled While on the Way from Barn to Paddock for Third Race," *Brooklyn (NY) Times-Union,* August 14, 1931, 14.

39. "Stewards of Saratoga Meeting Bar Famous Stable Entries When Ladana Is Found to Be Poisoned," *Brooklyn (NY) Citizen,* August 16, 1931, 11.

40. "Sinclair Sells Entire Stable," *Bridgewater (NJ) Courier-News,* September 4, 1931, 20.

41. Steve Cady, "A Fixer Describes Drugging Hundreds of Race Horses," *New York Times,* June 14, 1972, 55.

42. Steve Cady, "Turf Charges Held Unfounded," *New York Times,* June 16, 1972, 28.

43. "Slow Horses Made Fast," 17.

44. For an example of race charts from Gravesend, see *New York World,* June 12, 1896, 8.

45. Paul Dimeo, *A History of Drug Use in Sport, 1876–1976: Beyond Good and Evil* (New York: Routledge, 2007), 7.

46. Boden, "How 'Doc' Ring 'Doped' the Horses," 3.

47. "How to Make Horses Win," 7.

48. "Doping Race Horses," 10.

49. Gendarme's race record in 1890 was pieced together from reports in several newspapers and may be incomplete.

50. *New York Times,* May 28, 1885, 4.

4. Rule 162

1. Statistical information was gathered from several sources, including Jockey Club, "Trends in US Racing," http://www.jockeyclub.com/default.asp?section=FB&area=12; "$1 in 1905 Is Worth $22.19 in 2005," https://www.in2013dollars.com/us/inflation/1905?endYear=2005&amount=1; "Millions Distributed in Racing Last Year," *New York Times,* March 4, 1906, 11.

2. William H. P. Robertson, *The History of Thoroughbred Racing in America* (Englewood Cliffs, NJ: Prentice-Hall, 1964), 174.

3. "The Peril of the Turf," *New York Tribune,"* April 25, 1886, 4.

4. For a comprehensive discussion of efforts to organize the Board of Control and later the Jockey Club, see Steven A. Riess, *The Sport of Kings and the Kings of Crime* (Syracuse, NY: Syracuse University Press, 2011), chap. 6.

5. Robertson, *History of Thoroughbred Racing,* 175.

6. Riess, *Sport of Kings*, 151.

7. "A Strange Rule about Betting; It Seems to Open the Door for Fraud in Racing," *New York Times*, May 20, 1893, 9.

8. "Race-Horse Owners Aroused: To Organize a Club for Their Own Protection," *New York Times*, December 29, 1893, 6.

9. See Robertson, *History of Thoroughbred Racing*, 174–76; Riess, *Sport of Kings*, 163–64; "The History of the Jockey Club," http://www.jockeyclub.com/default.asp?section=About&area=0.

10. Riess, *Sport of Kings*, 162.

11. As cited in *Jockey Club v. United States*, 157 F. Supp. 419, 420–27 (Fed. Cl. 1956). The issue was whether the Jockey Club was exempt from paying federal income tax because of its status as a business league. The court ruled that the Jockey Club did not qualify for tax exemption.

12. "The Jockey Club Blocked," *New York Times*, January 23, 1894, 7.

13. Robertson, *History of Thoroughbred Racing*, 175.

14. *Jule Fink v. Ashley T. Cole*, 97 N.E.2d 873 (NY 1951).

15. "Jockey Club Meeting: Important Amendments to the Racing Rules Adopted," *Brooklyn (NY) Standard Union*, February 12, 1897, 8.

16. "Changes in the Rules," *Brooklyn (NY) Times-Union*, December 12, 1902, 8.

17. W. C. Vreeland, "Turf Authorities Are Awake to the Menace of Old Jockey Tricks," *Brooklyn (NY) Daily Eagle*, August 6, 1933, 32.

18. "Paddock's Case Is Put over to Aug 6," *Boston Globe*, July 28, 1928, 8.

19. "Rubien Is Displaced; Post Goes to Maccabe," *New York Times*, August 8, 1928, 21.

20. "Sports for Women Kept in Olympics," *New York Times*, August 8, 1928, 21.

21. "Horse Racing Gossip: Trainer Howell Ruled off for Doping Dr. Riddle," *Washington (DC) Evening Star*, May 23, 1903, 10; "Trainer Censured," *Elmira (NY) Star-Gazette*, May 25, 1903, 3.

22. "Brown Ruled off the Saratoga Track," *Washington (DC) Times*, August 8, 1903, 4; "Ruled off the Turf for 'Doping' Horse," *New York Evening World*, August 8, 1903, 4; "Will Continue to Bet," *Buffalo (NY) Courier*, December 24, 1903, 10.

23. "Ruled off for Life," *Lexington (KY) Leader*, October 31, 1906, 7; "Horse Ruled off with His Owner," *Meriden (CT) Daily Journal*, October 30, 1906, 8.

24. "Turf Officials Show Activity," *Chicago Tribune*, September 15, 1902, 6.

25. "Fizer Is Ruled off for Life: New Orleans Stewards Charge Horseman with 'Doping' to Accelerate Speed," *Chicago Tribune*, March 11, 1903, 6.

26. "Ruled off for Life," 4.

27. "Reformed Racing Medication Rules," http://www.jockeyclub.com /pdfs/reformed_rules.pdf.

28. Chris McGrath, *Mr. Darley's Arabian: A History of Racing in 25 Horses* (New York: Pegasus Books, 2017), 237. McGrath was quoting trainer George Lambton, *Men and Horses I Have Known* (London: Thornton Butterworth, 1924), 255.

29. Lambton, *Men and Horses I Have Known*, 253.

30. "Royal Hunt Cup," June 17, 2020, https://www.racingbetter.co.uk /royal_ascot/royal_hunt_cup.html.

31. Lambton, *Men and Horses I Have Known*, 252.

32. Lambton, 253.

33. Lambton, 256.

34. "2 Horse Trainers Ruled off in Doping Exposé," *Tampa (FL) Times*, October 31, 1930, 19.

35. Thomas B. Cromwell, "'Dope' in England and America," *Blood-Horse*, October 11, 1930, 1179. Over the years, *Blood-Horse* has been one of the most frequent and vocal critics of doping. As noted later in this book (chapter 7), a March 1929 editorial by Cromwell triggered a Federal Bureau of Narcotics investigation into illegal drugs at American racetracks.

36. "Chapman Gets Damages," *Blood-Horse*, December 12, 1931, 721.

5. The Drug Czar Goes Racing

1. For more information, see "18th Amendment to the U.S. Constitution: Primary Documents in American History," *Library of Congress Research Guides*, https://guides.loc.gov/18th-amendment#:~:text=Introduction-,18th% 20Amendment%20to%20the%20U.S.%20Constitution%3A%20Primary %20Documents%20in%20American,or%20transportation%20of%20 intoxicating%20liquors%22.

2. "Utah Decides to Vote after 9 P.M. Our Time," *New York Times*, December 5, 1933, 1; Christopher Klein, "The Night Prohibition Ended," *History Stories*, December 5, 2013, updated December 10, 2018, https://www.history .com/news/the-night-prohibition-ended#:~:text=In%20February%20 1933%2C%20Congress%20easily,earlier%20now%20approved%20its%20 repeal.

3. For the official report of the Utah vote, see https://images.archives
.utah.gov/digital/collection/6300/id/22/rec/3.

4. "Prohibition Repeal Is Ratified at 5:32 P.M.," *New York Times,* December 6, 1933, 1; "Repeal Cuts Price of Drinks in Half," *New York Times,*
December 5, 1933; "Large Order for Bottle Caps," *New York Times,* December 5, 1933, 41.

5. Klein, "Night Prohibition Ended."

6. Joseph Lynn Lyon, "Word of Wisdom," in *The Encyclopedia of Mormonism* (New York: Macmillan, 1992), 1584–85, https://eom.byu.edu
/index.php/Word_of_Wisdom.

7. Allen Kent Powell, "Prohibition," in *Utah History Encyclopedia,*
https://www.uen.org/utah_history_encyclopedia/p/PROHIBITION
.shtml.

8. Dave Roos, "How Prohibition Put the 'Organized' in Organized
Crime," *History Stories,* January 14, 2019, updated March 9, 2021, https://
www.history.com/news/prohibition-organized-crime-al-capone.

9. David Pietrusza, *Rothstein: The Life, Times, and Murder of the Criminal
Genius Who Fixed the 1919 World Series* (New York: Basic Books, 2011).

10. Brien Bouyea, "How Arnold Rothstein, One of the Prohibition Era's
Most Infamous Gangsters, Fixed the 1921 Travers Stakes (Or Did He?),"
Saratoga Living, July 28, 2018, https://saratogaliving.com/how-arnold-
rothstein-one-of-the-prohibition-eras-most-infamous-gangsters-fixed-the-
1921-travers-stakes-or-did-he/.

11. Thom Loverro, "The Gangster, the Gamble and the Horse that Paid Off,"
Washington (DC) Times, October 17, 2017, https://www.washingtontimes
.com/news/2017/oct/17/loverro-gangster-gamble-and-horse-paid/.

12. Pietrusza, *Rothstein,* 316–29.

13. Landis was inducted into the Baseball Hall of Fame in 1944. See
https://baseballhall.org/hall-of-famers/landis-kenesaw.

14. The Horseracing Integrity and Safety Act of 2020 (HISA) created an
independent body to establish and enforce national regulations related to
medication and safety issues, with oversight through the Federal Trade
Commission. The new law was scheduled to take effect on July 1, 2022, but
its constitutionality is being challenged in court. Frank Angst, "Suit Aims to
Halt Horseracing Integrity and Safety Act," *Blood-Horse,* March 16, 2021,
https://www.bloodhorse.com/horse-racing/articles/246665/suit-aims-to-
halt-horseracing-integrity-and-safety-act.

15. G. F. T. Ryall, "A New Year of Racing," *Polo,* January 1934, 13.

16. Harry J. Anslinger Papers, box 8, file 6, Drugs and Horse Racing
(1921–52), HCLA 1875, Special Collections Library, Pennsylvania State

University (hereafter cited as Anslinger Papers). The Drugs and Horse Racing file contains approximately two hundred unnumbered pages, including handwritten notes from Anslinger on a variety of subjects and statistical information collected by his associates in the Federal Bureau of Narcotics.

17. Walter H. Donovan to Treasury Secretary Henry Morgenthau, Anslinger Papers, box 3, file 6, Correspondence (1934).

18. "Statement of H. J. Anslinger, Commissioner," in *Hearing before the Subcommittee of House Committee on Appropriations, Seventy-Third Congress* (Washington, DC: US Government Printing Office, 1934), 179.

19. Harrison Narcotics Tax Act, Pub. L. 82-223, 38 Stat. 785–90 (1914). For more about the Harrison Act and predecessor legislation, see John H. Halpern and David Blistein, *Opium: How an Ancient Flower Shaped and Poisoned Our World* (New York: Hachette Books, 2019), chap. 25.

20. "Asks Government Help," *Louisville (KY) Courier-Journal,* October 11, 1933, 13. Judge Murphy ran horse racing in Chicago, Detroit, New Orleans, Arlington Downs, and Tanforan, and he offered to cooperate with the official veterinarian and set up laboratories for drug testing. He said there was no cooperation between racetracks and the Federal Bureau of Narcotics because its agents "were snoopers who made a play for the galleries and publicity."

21. "Statement of Anslinger," 186–87.

22. Russell Oakes, "New 'Dope' Plan," *Baltimore Evening Sun,* October 9, 1935, 31.

23. "Waging War on the Cruel Horse Dopers," *Dayton (OH) Daily News,* November 12, 1933, 54.

24. "$1,000,000 Dope Seizure Is Bared," *Baltimore Sun,* October 17, 1930, 2.

25. John C. McWilliams, "Unsung Partner against Crime: Harry J. Anslinger and the Federal Bureau of Narcotics, 1930–1962," *Pennsylvania Magazine of History and Biography* 113, no. 2 (April 1989): 207–36.

26. Nick Dedina, "Billie Holiday's Searing 'Strange Fruit' Still Has the Power to Startle," in *Independent Lens in Beyond the Films,* February 19, 2020, https://www.pbs.org/independentlens/blog/billie-holidays-searing-strange-fruit-still-has-the-power-to-startle/.

27. Josh Sanburn, "Strange Fruit," *Time,* October 21, 2011, https://entertainment.time.com/2011/10/24/the-all-time-100-songs/slide/strange-fruit-billie-holiday/.

28. Anslinger served under Republican Herbert Hoover (who appointed him to head the Federal Bureau of Narcotics), Democrats Franklin D. Roosevelt and Harry S. Truman, Republican Dwight D. Eisenhower, and Democrat John F. Kennedy.

29. McWilliams, "Unsung Partner against Crime," 235.

30. Albin Krebs," Harry J. Anslinger Dies at 83; Hard-Hitting Foe of Narcotics," *New York Times,* November 18, 1975, 40.

31. For more comprehensive assessments of Harry Anslinger and the Federal Bureau of Narcotics, both pro and con, see John C. McWilliams, *The Protectors: Harry J. Anslinger and the Federal Bureau of Narcotics, 1930–1962* (Newark: University of Delaware Press, 1990); Johann Hari, *Chasing the Scream: The First and Last Days of the War on Drugs* (New York: Bloomsbury, 2015); Alexandra Chasin, *Assassin of Youth: A Kaleidoscopic History of Harry J. Anslinger's War on Drugs* (Chicago: University of Chicago Press, 2016); Halpern and Blistein, *Opium,* chap. 26.

32. "Statement of Anslinger," 188–93.

33. "Federal Ban Is Being Planned on Shipment of 'Doped' Horses," *St. Louis Post-Dispatch,* March 29, 1936, 22.

34. The use of performance-enhancing drugs in horse racing generally mirrors PED use in human athletics. For a timeline of PED use by human athletes, see David R. Mottram and Neil Chester, eds., *Drugs in Sport,* 6th ed. (New York: Routledge, 2015), 21–37.

35. "Statement of Anslinger," 179.

36. "No Narcotics," *Blood-Horse,* December 5, 1931, 683.

37. "Firm Stand against Use of Narcotics," *Daily Racing Form,* November 30, 1933.

38. Anslinger Papers.

39. Anslinger Papers.

6. Reports from the Field

1. W. C. Vreeland, "Florida Secret Narcotics Agents Place Three Horsemen under Arrest," *Brooklyn (NY) Daily Eagle,* January 21, 1932, 23.

2. Harry J. Anslinger Papers, box 3, files 7 and 8, Correspondence (1932–33), HCLA 1875, Special Collections Library, Pennsylvania State University. Most field reports from the investigation are included in Federal Bureau of Narcotics files archived at the National Archives in College Park, Maryland. However, because this archive closed during the first months of the pandemic in 2020 and remained closed throughout much of 2021, those records were not reviewed.

3. *Daily Racing Form,* January 13, 1933, #78553. The second race at Jefferson Park was six furlongs for $1,500 claimers. My Joanne was second choice in the betting.

4. Richard Sowers, *The Kentucky Derby, Preakness and Belmont Stakes: A Comprehensive History* (Jefferson, NC: McFarland, 2014), 119–21; "Mrs. Isabel Dodge Sloane Dead; Owner of the Brookmeade Stable," *New York Times*, March 11, 1962, 86.

7. *The United States v. Parke*

1. "Harry Anslinger Retains Federal Narcotics Post," *Altoona (PA) Tribune*, March 20, 1933, 1; "Dope Addicts Hit," *Paterson (NJ) News*, February 16, 1933; 8; "New Drug More Effective in Relieving Pain than Heroin Being Developed," *Longview (TX) News-Journal*, January 22, 1933, 8.

2. H. E. C. Bryant, "See Patronage Appointments at Early Date," *Charlotte (NC) News*, July 9, 1933, 22.

3. For reference, 1 gram = 15.43236 grains. Oyler's estimate of the amount of drugs seized was equivalent to 26 to 32 grams of drugs. https://calculator-converter.com/grams-to-grains.htm. "National Horse-Doping Ring Charged in Arrest of Seven," *Washington (DC) Evening Star*, July 30, 1933.

4. Frank G. Menke, "U.S. Investigation Reveals Startling Horse 'Dope' Ring" and subsequent articles in the series, *San Francisco Examiner*, October 11–24, 1933; Frank G. Menke, "Hopping Horses," *Esquire*, April 1936, 57.

5. Memo to Anslinger, October 18, 1933, Harry J. Anslinger Papers, box 3, file 7, Correspondence (1933), HCLA 1875, Special Collections Library, Pennsylvania State University.

6. Anslinger to Hearst, November 23, 1933, Anslinger Papers, box 3, file 7, Correspondence (1933).

7. "The Hearst Blast," *Blood-Horse*, October 28, 1933, 405.

8. Thomas B. Cromwell, "Dope," *Blood-Horse*, October 21, 1933, 367.

9. John C. McWilliams, *The Protectors: Harry J. Anslinger and the Federal Bureau of Narcotics, 1930–1962* (Newark: University of Delaware Press, 1990), 87–88. Attention to doping and illegal drugs on the backstretch would be a very small part of the drug czar's legacy. McWilliams devoted only two pages to the campaign, and other biographers generally followed suit. See Alexandra Chasin, *Assassin of Youth: A Kaleidoscopic History of Harry J. Anslinger's War on Drugs* (Chicago: University of Chicago Press, 2016); Johann Hari, *Chasing the Scream: The First and Last Days of the War on Drugs* (New York: Bloomsbury, 2015).

10. "7 Men Held in Race Horse 'Doping' Plot," *Tampa Tribune*, July 30, 1933, 1; "U.S. Nabs 7 in Doping of 200 Race Horses," *San Francisco*

Examiner, July 30, 1933, 1; "Seize Seven in Inquiry on Race Horse Doping at Arlington," *Chicago Tribune,* July 30, 1933, 21; "National Horse-Doping Ring Charged in Arrest of Seven," *Washington (DC) Evening Star,* July 30, 1933, 1.

11. "Asks Government Help," *Louisville (KY) Courier-Journal,* October 11, 1933, 13.

12. Thoroughbred Racing Hall of Fame, https://www.racingmuseum .org/hall-of-fame/jockey/ivan-h-parke.

13. An indictment initiates a criminal prosecution and is issued by a grand jury that determines, based on evidence presented by a prosecutor, that there is probable cause to believe that a crime has been committed and that the defendant committed that crime. An indictment provides a defendant notice of the charges and is not a finding of guilt. Indictment by a grand jury is required for felony charges. See https://www.justice.gov/usao /justice-101/charging.

14. Federal District Court for the Northern District of Illinois, case number 27518, Federal Court file, National Archives, Chicago.

15. Anslinger Papers, box 8, file 6, Drugs and Horse Racing (1921–52).

16. *Patterson, et al. v. United States,* 82 F.2d 937 (Sixth Circuit, 1936).

17. "Appeal Decision in Detroit Race Dope Conviction," *Windsor (ON) Star,* July 12, 1935, 26.

18. Anslinger Papers, box 8, file 6, Drugs and Horse Racing (1921–52).

19. "After the Horse Hoppers," *Blood-Horse,* August 5, 1933, 108.

20. Federal District Court for the Northern District of Illinois, case number 27523, Federal Court file, National Archives, Chicago.

21. *Patterson,* 82 F.2d 937.

22. Ernest Knaebel, reporter, "Cases Adjudged in the Supreme Court at October Term 1935," in *United States Reports,* vol. 298 (Washington, DC: US Government Printing Office, 1936), 657.

23. "Dope: Arrests at Detroit," *Blood-Horse,* October 14, 1933, 355.

24. Federal District Court for the Northern District of Illinois, case number 27514, Federal Court file, National Archives, Chicago.

25. "Dope: Bonds Are Executed," *Blood-Horse,* September 2, 1933, 202.

26. Federal District Court for the Northern District of Illinois, case number 27515, Federal Court file, National Archives, Chicago.

27. "Dope: Three to Prison," *Blood-Horse,* August 26, 1933, 177.

28. Frank G. Menke, "Drugging of Horses to Be Thing of Past," *Minneapolis Star Tribune,* November 5, 1933, 26.

29. *Blood-Horse* magazine reported the arrest of a Maryland veterinarian for writing prescriptions for stimulants and a dozen arrests at Latonia.

"Maryland Vet Arrested," *Blood-Horse,* August 26, 1933, 177; "Dope: Arrests at Latonia," *Blood-Horse,* November 18, 1933, 178.

30. McWilliams, *Protectors,* 87–88.

31. "Federal Ban Is Being Planned on Shipment of 'Doped' Horses," *St. Louis Post-Dispatch,* March 29, 1936, 22.

32. "Dope: Action in Maryland," *Blood-Horse,* August 26, 1933, 177; "Dope: California Action," *Blood-Horse,* September 2, 1933, 202; "Dope: The First Ruling Off," *Blood-Horse,* December 6, 1933, 580.

33. "Formal Opinions: Note," *New York Attorney General Reports and Opinions,* 1934, 247–48.

34. John H. Halpern and David Blistein, *Opium: How an Ancient Flower Shaped and Poisoned Our World* (New York: Hachette Books, 2019), 208–9.

8. The Spit Box, Trainer Responsibility, and the Modern Era of Drug Testing

For readers unfamiliar with the term "spit box," it refers to a secure location on the backstretch of a racetrack where drug testing samples are taken. It originated because the first drug tests developed for racehorses used saliva.

1. Carlos Baker, *Ernest Hemingway: A Life Story* (New York: Charles Scribner's Sons, 1969), 51.

2. Given Hemingway's affinity for horse racing, it is surprising that he published little of note about the sport. The lone exception was "My Old Man," a short story included in the anthology *The Best Short Stories of 1923.*

3. Ernest Hemingway, *A Moveable Feast* (New York: Scribner, 1964), 42–43, 51–52, 82–83, 179.

4. Hemingway, 83. The author's self-imposed exile from horse racing was not permanent. The restored edition of *A Moveable Feast* includes a back-cover photograph of a much older Hemingway reading about past performances at Auteuil.

5. Nancy Milford, "'A Million Little Pieces' Is Part of a Long Debate that Dates to the Origins of Writing," *Washington Post,* February 5, 2006, https://www.washingtonpost.com/archive/entertainment/books/2006/02/05/all-the-shouting-about-a-million-little-pieces-is-part-of-a-long-debate-that-dates-to-the-origins-of-writing/b1f6085a-2620–42de-9010–64b0f0e15db1/; Hemingway, preface to *Moveable Feast,* vii.

6. Cheats and scoundrels have been plying their trade for as long as horse racing has existed. The use of sophisticated chemical stimulants and the equally sophisticated tests and laboratory equipment to detect them are

more recent developments. Thomas Tobin, an equine veterinarian with a PhD in pharmacology, has been investigating performance-enhancing drugs in horse racing at the University of Kentucky since the mid-1970s. For an entertaining history of PEDs in horses and humans, see Tobin's *Drugs and the Performance Horse* (Springfield, IL: Charles C. Thomas, 1981), 21–39.

7. PBS, "Drug Wars: A Social History of America's Most Popular Drugs," https://www.pbs.org/wgbh/pages/frontline/shows/drugs/buyers/socialhistory.html.

8. For a thorough discussion of opium's history from the ancient Assyrians and Egyptians to the present day, see John H. Halpern and David Blistein, *Opium: How an Ancient Flower Shaped and Poisoned Our World* (New York: Hachette Books, 2019); for the development of heroin and competing claims about the invention of the hypodermic, see Halpern and Blistein, 164–74.

9. United Nations Office on Drugs and Crime, "History of Heroin," January 1, 1953, https://www.unodc.org/unodc/en/data-and-analysis/bulletin/bulletin_1953-01-01_2_page004.html.

10. PBS, "Drug Wars."

11. See, for example, Sir Arthur Conan Doyle, *The Sign of Four* and *A Scandal in Bohemia*, in *Sherlock Holmes: The Complete Novels and Stories*, vol. 1 (New York: Bantam Dell, 1986), 123–24, 239.

12. Peter Burnaugh, "Thoroughbreds and Blackguards: Inside the Sordid World of Horse Racing," *Atlantic*, July 1925, https://www.theatlantic.com/magazine/archive/1925/07/thoroughbreds-and-blackguards/304908/. Earl Sande and John Maiben were among the leading riders of the era. Two years after this article appeared, while covering opening day at the old Empire City Racing Association track in New York, Burnaugh fell ill and was rushed to a nearby hospital. He died a few days later at age thirty-five.

13. Jennifer S. Kelly, *Sir Barton and the Making of the Triple Crown* (Lexington: University Press of Kentucky, 2019), 17, 104.

14. Andrzej Pokrywka, Damian Gorczyca, Anna Jarek, and Dorota Kwiatowska, "In Memory of Alfons Bukowski on the Centenary of Anti-Doping Research," *Drug Testing Analysis* 2 (2010): 538–41.

15. Pokrywka et al., 539.

16. The Florida State Racing Commission voted to adopt the saliva test at all tracks statewide and determined that the "rules shall be strengthened otherwise to prevent the use of drugs as stimulants." "Florida: Saliva Test," *Blood-Horse*, October 21, 1933, 376. After a study of the new Florida rule, the Ohio Racing Commission voted to adopt the saliva test for all racing

where there was betting. "Saliva Test Will Be Used," *Massillon (OH) Evening Independent,* December 21, 1933, 2.

17. "May Reform Sport of Kings: Exposé of Use of Narcotics at Arlington in 'Doping' Race Horses Bids to Rid Game of Sordid Practices that Have Invaded It," *Dayton (OH) Herald,* August 4, 1933, 33.

18. Rena Baer, "Drug Testing of Horses Begins," in *Horse Racing's Top 100 Moments* (Lexington, KY: Blood-Horse Publications, 2006), 122–23; Bryan Field, "Hialeah to Adopt 'Dope Box' System," *New York Times,* October 14, 1933, 1.

19. "Eradicating Use of Drugs: J. E. Widener Speaks to National Association of Racing Commissioners at Louisville," *Daily Racing Form,* May 7, 1934, 29, https://drf.uky.edu/catalog/1930s/drf1934050701/drf1934050701_29.

20. Harry J. Anslinger Papers, Special Collections Library, Pennsylvania State University.

21. W. C. Vreeland, "No Evidence of Doping at Tropical Park," *Brooklyn (NY) Daily Eagle,* January 11, 1934, 20.

22. Today, "horsemen" is archaic, politically incorrect, sexist, and discriminatory. But in 1934 the term was accurate. Mary Hirsch, daughter of Hall of Fame trainer Max Hirsch, applied for a trainer's license from the Jockey Club in 1933, but her application was tabled. She persisted, and in 1934 Hirsch was licensed in Illinois and Michigan. The Jockey Club eventually relented, and by 1935 Hirsch was the first female trainer to be licensed across the country. In her first full year as a trainer, Hirsch's horses won ten races and earned $10,365.

23. Baer, "Drug Testing of Horses Begins," 122–23.

24. W. C. Vreeland, "Nat Ray Exonerated by Hialeah Stewards on Doping Charge," *Brooklyn (NY) Daily Eagle,* February 7, 1934, 21.

25. "Soon Over 3–1 Favorite Today in Miami Derby," *Nashville (TN) Banner,* March 17, 1934, 10; "Horsemen Strike at Hialeah but Florida Derby Is on Today," *Fort Worth (TX) Star-Telegram,* March 17, 1934.

26. Bob Heleringer, "An Abbreviated History of Absolute Insurer Rule," *Blood-Horse,* August 30, 2017, https://www.bloodhorse.com/horse-racing/articles/223352/an-abbreviated-history-of-absolute-insurer-rule. For a more thorough discussion, see Robert Heleringer, *Equine Regulatory Law* (Louisville, KY: Robert L. Heleringer, 2012), chap. 7.

27. "Time Clock Winner of Florida Derby," *New York Daily News,* March 19, 1934, 94. The instigators of the strike were identified as Laurence Jones, field representative for the Thoroughbred Horse Owners and Trainers Association and spokesperson for the horsemen, along with trainers R. C. Watts, J. Shevlin, and C. Caferelli.

28. "Horsemen Strike at Hialeah Park: But Florida Derby Is Scheduled to Be Run Today," *Reading (PA) Times,* March 17, 1934, 16.

29. "Seventh Annual Report of the Florida State Racing Commission for Fiscal Year Ending June 30, 1938," issued July 1, 1938, and sent to Governor Fred P. Cone.

9. "Those Bastards"

The chapter title, "Those Bastards," comes from Tom Smith's terse response when a reporter asked how he felt about the stewards of the Jockey Club who had revoked his trainer's license for a medication violation in 1945. "Sport: Lady's Day in Louisville," *Time,* May 6, 1946, http://content .time.com/time/magazine/article/0,9171,1,887019,00.html.

The narrative is based on the appellate record in *Smith v. Cole,* 270 A.D. 675 (1946), 62 N.Y.S.2d 226 (1946). The record, which runs more than nine hundred pages, is archived at the New York State Library in Albany. Unless otherwise noted, quoted material is taken directly from that record. In cites to *Smith v. Cole,* page numbers refer to the sequentially numbered pages in that record, not to page numbers of individual documents therein.

1. Red Smith, "A Day of Beauty: Jet Pilot Wins Kentucky Derby," in *American Pastimes: The Very Best of Red Smith,* ed. Daniel Okrent (New York: Literary Classics of the United States, 2013), 141–43.

2. Tommy Devine, "Thoroughbreds Are Valued at Half a Million," *Reno (NV) State Journal,* May 3, 1946, 10.

3. For a thorough review of the Triple Crown races, see Richard Sowers, *The Kentucky Derby, Preakness and Belmont Stakes: A Comprehensive History* (Jefferson, NC: McFarland, 2014).

4. "Sport: Lady's Day in Louisville."

5. David Grening, "War Horses: The 1940s," in *Champions: The Lives, Times, and Past Performances of America's Greatest Thoroughbreds,* rev. ed. (New York: Daily Racing Form Press, 2005), 71–119.

6. Statistical information is from *The American Racing Manual,* 666, 672. The Jockey Club took over publication of the manual in 2021. A pdf version of the nearly two thousand–page volume is available free of charge at http://www.jockeyclub.com/factbook/ARM/2021_arm.pdf.

7. Grening, "War Horses," 82, 86, 112.

8. The record suggests that the caller was one of the stewards, Marshall Cassidy. *Smith v. Cole,* 26.

9. *Smith v. Cole,* 109.

10. *Smith v. Cole,* 816–17.

11. *Smith v. Cole,* 109–10.

12. Testimony from the stewards' hearing can be found in *Smith v. Cole:* Tom Smith, 20–30; Pevler, 30–34; Choate, 34–36; Shelley, 36–40; Turner, 40–43; Lacey Smith, 43–45.

13. *Smith v. Cole,* 65.

14. *Smith v. Cole,* 32; emphasis in original.

15. *Smith v. Cole,* 33.

16. For more about stakeouts of the Maine Chance barns, see *Smith v. Cole,* 104–7.

17. Testimony and exhibits from the Jockey Club stewards' hearing can be found in *Smith v. Cole:* Dr. Cattlett, 52, 66–72; Dr. Gilman, 53–54; Dr. Corwin, 55–56; MacAllister, 56; Dr. Davis, 58; La Boyne, 59–60; excerpt from *New and Non-Official Remedies,* 60–63; state chemist reports, 64–65; Tom Smith, 73–90; Ernest Pevler, 90–104; discussion, 104–7.

18. See Uniform Classification Guidelines for Foreign Substances and Recommended Penalties and Model Rules, September 2020, https://www.arci.com/wp-content/uploads/2020/09/Uniform-Classification-Guidelines-Version-14.3.pdf.

19. "Tom Smith and His Atomizer," *Blood-Horse,* November 17, 1945, 1007.

20. J. A. Estes, "Commentary on Burning Words," *Blood-Horse,* December 1, 1945.

21. *Smith v. Cole,* 749–50.

10. The Joint Board and the Courts

The narrative in this chapter is based on the appellate record in *Smith v. Cole,* 270 A.D. 675 (1946), 62 N.Y.S.2d 226 (1946). The record, which runs more than nine hundred pages, is archived at the New York State Library in Albany. Unless otherwise noted, quoted material is taken directly from that record. In cites to *Smith v. Cole,* page numbers refer to the sequentially numbered pages in that record, not to page numbers of individual documents therein.

1. "Tom Smith and His Atomizer," *Blood-Horse,* November 17, 1945, 1007.

2. "Tom Smith and His Atomizer," 1008.

3. "Tom Smith and His Atomizer," 1008–9.

4. "Sport: Flit-Gun Hop," *Time,* November 19, 1945, http://content.time.com/time/subscriber/article/0,33009,886671,00.html.

5. Testimony and exhibits from the Joint Board hearing can be found in *Smith v. Cole:* Marshall Cassidy, 190–200; Stella Sachs, 191; Dr. Thomas Corwin, 208–11; Dr. Manual Gilman, 212–21, 543–688; Frank G. Lorentzen, 223–28; James F. La Boyne, 237–42; Charles E. Morgan, 244–46; Dr. James C. Cattlett, 246–62; Dr. Hubert S. Howe, 390–437, 693–709; Bernard L. Oser, 500; Dr. Harry Gold, 276–89, 439–49; 723–38; Dr. Robert S. MacKellar, 292–95, 739; Dr. David E. Buckingham, 297–307; Ernest Pevler, 307–43; Tom Smith, 344–85; racing commission exhibits, 749–55; stewards' exhibits, 758–806; petitioner (Tom Smith) exhibits, 809–43.

6. Although the Smith hearings attracted most of the press attention, the absolute insurer rule was on trial in Maryland. See chapter 11.

7. Alex Bower, "The Smith Hearing in New York," *Blood-Horse,* December 22, 1945, 1360–67.

8. Bower, 1360.

9. *Smith v. Cole,* 64.

10. *Smith v. Cole,* 65.

11. *Smith v. Cole,* 816.

12. *Smith v. Cole,* 248.

13. "The Defense Rests," *Blood-Horse,* December 29, 1945, 1486.

14. Grantland Rice, "Coast Sportsman Defends Smith in N.Y. Drug Case," *Baltimore Sun,* December 4, 1945, 18.

15. For the full text of the ruling, see "The Tom Smith Ruling Stands," *Blood-Horse,* February 23, 1946, 521–28.

16. "Tom Smith Scores a Point," *Blood-Horse,* April 13, 1946, 940.

17. Whether a reviewing court has the authority to question the decision of an administrative agency would come up again, and ultimately be resolved, following the disqualification of Dancer's Image in the 1968 Kentucky Derby. See Milton C. Toby, *Dancer's Image: The Forgotten Story of the 1968 Kentucky Derby* (Charleston, SC: History Press, 2011).

18. *Smith v. Cole,* 270. See appendix 4 for the full ruling.

19. "Tom Smith Withdraws Appeal," *Blood-Horse,* September 21, 1946, 684.

20. "Trainer Smith Restored to Good Standing," *Syracuse (NY) Post-Standard,* April 2, 1947, 17.

11. The Not-so-Absolute Insurer Rule?

1. "Horse Drugger Ruled Off: Jockey Club Officials Act in Case of Trainer Howell for 'Doping' of Dr. Riddle," *New York Times,* May 22, 1903, 7.

2. See https://www.racingmuseum.org/hall-of-fame/trainer/tom-smith.

3. Amendment XIV, section 1 of the US Constitution reads: "No State shall . . . deprive any person of life, liberty, or property, without due process of law; nor deny to any person within its jurisdiction the equal protection of the laws."

4. Robert L. Heleringer, *Equine Regulatory Law* (Louisville, KY: Robert L. Heleringer, 2012), 236–37. Heleringer has written extensively about the absolute insurer rule; see also "An Abbreviated History of Absolute Insurer Rule," *Blood-Horse*, August 30, 2017, https://www.bloodhorse.com/horse-racing/articles/223352/an-abbreviated-history-of-absolute-insurer-rule; "Will the Absolute Insurer Rule Save Racing . . . Again?" *Paulick Report*, May 17, 2021, https://www.paulickreport.com/news/ray-s-paddock/heleringer-will-the-absolute-insurer-rule-save-racing-again/.

5. See *Barry v. Barchi*, 443 U.S. 55 (1979), in which the US Supreme Court noted, "it is clear that Barchi [the defendant, a Thoroughbred trainer whose license was suspended] had a property interest in his license sufficient to invoke the protection of the Due Process Clause."

6. "Maryland Faces Crisis in Racing: Suspensions and Countersuits over Doping Cases Threatens Game," *Wichita (KS) Eagle*, December 24, 1945, 3.

7. For more about this saliva testing kerfuffle, see "N.Y. Chemist Disagrees: Says He Found More than 4 Dope Cases in Eight Years," *Baltimore Sun*, December 1, 1945, 11; "New Row in 'Dope' Case," *San Francisco Examiner*, December 1, 1945, 14; "Race Bodies in Open Break," *Passaic (NJ) Herald-News*, December 1, 1945, 15; "Break Threatens over Pimlico 'Fake' Saliva Tests," *Windsor (ON) Star*, December 1, 1945, 27.

8. "Pimlico Trainer Suspended on Dope Charge," *Baltimore Evening Sun*, December 10, 1945, 28.

9. Dan Parker, "The Truth about Doping of Horses at Race Tracks," *Pittsburg Sun-Telegraph*, December 16, 1945, 29.

10. John F. Chandler, "Horse Doping Probe Opens in Maryland," *Owensboro (KY) Messenger*, December 11, 1945, 8.

11. "Horse Trainers Accused of Dope Tactics in Race," *Twin Falls (ID) Times-News*, December 12, 1945, 10.

12. "Race Hearings to Continue: Section of Commission Rule Held Unconstitutional," *Baltimore Sun*, February 21, 1946, 30.

13. "The Racing Commission Has Another Bad Day in Court," *Baltimore Sun*, March 2, 1946, 8.

14. *Mahoney et al. v. Byers*, 187 Md. 81, 48 A.2d 600 (Md. 1946).

15. "Powerless to Act in Horse Dopings, Mahoney Says," *Baltimore Evening Sun*, August 2, 1946.

16. "Two Men Fined in Racing Case," *Baltimore Sun,* September 24, 1946, 18.

17. "3 Reinstated by Race Body," *Baltimore Sun,* March 12, 1946, 15.

18. "Plan Backed by Anslinger: Narcotics Chief Endorses on-the-Spot Saliva Tests," *Baltimore Sun,* March 6, 1946, 16.

19. Harry J. Anslinger Papers, box 8, file 6, Drugs and Horse Racing (1921–52), HCLA 1875, Special Collections Library, Pennsylvania State University.

20. William Boniface, "Compromise Ends Laurel Turf Threat," *Baltimore Sun,* October 1, 1946, 28.

21. J. E. Wild, "State's Horse Guards Parade at First 'Protected' Race Meeting," *Baltimore Sun,* October 3, 1946, 22.

22. Thomas Tobin, *Drugs and the Performance Horse* (Springfield, IL: Charles C. Thomas, 1981), 29. For a lengthy and dense scientific study of the Straub reaction, see https://www.ncbi.nlm.nih.gov/pmc/articles /PMC3922199/.

23. *A Report by the TRPB,* December 3, 1946, 13, 22.

24. "Mice Are Item in Racing Cost," *Baltimore Sun,* December 16, 1946, 19.

25. An in-depth review of the absolute insurer rule is beyond the scope of this book. For more information, see Heleringer, *Equine Regulatory Law,* 236–380; Bennet Liebman, "The Trainer Responsibility Rule in Horse Racing," *Virginia Sports and Entertainment Law Journal* 7, no. 1 (Fall 2007): 1–40.

26. *Kentucky Horse Racing Commission v. H. Graham Motion and George Strawbridge Jr.,* 592 S.W.3d 739 (Ky.App. 2019).

27. Frank Angst, "Small Fine Wraps up Motion's Important Regulatory Case," *Blood-Horse,* March 26, 2020, https://www.bloodhorse.com/horse-racing/articles/239310/small-fine-wraps-up-motions-important-regulatory-case.

28. Natalie Voss, "Kentucky Approves Changes Allowing Trainers to Push Back on Absolute Insurer Rule," *Paulick Report,* September 25, 2018, https://www.paulickreport.com/news/the-biz/kentucky-commission-approves-rule-changes-allowing-trainers-to-push-back-on-absolute-insurer-rule/.

29. 810 KAR 8:025: Drug, medication, and substance withdrawal guidelines, section (3)(k)(i).

30. Jason Frakes, "Bob Baffert Acknowledges Using Ointment on Medina Spirit that Includes Betamethasone," *Louisville (KY) Courier-Journal,* May 11, 2021, https://www.courier-journal.com/story/sports/horses/horse-racing /2021/05/11/bob-baffert-says-ointment-used-medina-spirit-includes-betamethasone/5019077001/.

31. Des Bieler, "Kentucky Derby winner Medina Spirit disqualified," *Washington Post,* February 22, 2022, https://www.washingtonpost.com /sports/2022/02/21/medina-spirit-disqualified/.

32. Liebman, "Trainer Responsibility Rule," 38–39.

12. The Thoroughbred Racing Protective Bureau and the Defection of Dr. Kater

1. Anthony Summers, *Official and Confidential: The Secret Life of J. Edgar Hoover* (New York: G. P. Putnam's Sons, 1993), 234.

2. Scott Van Wynsberghe, "Mobster's Ball," *Toronto National Post,* November 14, 2007, 21.

3. Curt Gentry, *J. Edgar Hoover: The Man and the Secrets* (New York: W. W. Norton, 1991), 452–55.

4. Jim McCulley, *25 Years After: A Quarter Century Report on the TRPB; Its Vital Role in the Ecology of Thoroughbred Racing* (New York: Thorough-bred Racing Associations, [1971]), 7–8. For more about the history of the TRPB, see https://www.trpb.com/history.html.

5. Incorporated as a private investigative agency whose principal mission was to address issues of integrity and security in the Thoroughbred horse racing industry, the TRPB remains a wholly owned subsidiary of the Thoroughbred Racing Associations. https://www.trpb.com/history .html.

6. Oscar Otis, "Spencer Drayton Was Racing Fan while Serving with FBI," *Daily Racing Form,* December 2, 1971.

7. Don Grisham, "Drayton Keeps Zest for Racing," *Daily Racing Form,* March 2, 1982.

8. "Editor's Note," in *A Report by the TRPB,* December 3, 1946, 8.

9. "Ex-NY State Turf Vet Held in Doping Case," *New York Daily News,* October 22, 1946, 45.

10. "Collared from Bottom to Top," in *Report by the TRPB,* 23.

11. "Drayton Calls Racing 'Cleanest of Sports,'" *New York Sunday Graphic,* June 13, 1955.

12. *The First 10 Years* (Thoroughbred Racing Associations, 1956).

13. "The Case of the Sugar Pill," in *First 10 Years,* 31–32.

14. Doug McCoy, "Dr. Harthill, Mr. Hyde?" *Thoroughbred Racing Action* 4, no. 22 (August 1990): 25.

15. "Harthill Arrested on Drug Charges," *Louisville (KY) Courier-Journal,* March 6, 1955, 30; "Charge State Health Official, Two Others in Horse Doping," *Shreveport (LA) Times,* March 6, 1955, 1.

16. For more about the trial, see "New Trial Slated on Bribery Charge," *Alexandria (LA) Town Talk*, February 28, 1946, 7; "N.O. Bribery Trial Ended in Mistrial," *Shreveport (LA) Times*, February 28, 1946, 4; "Call Witness in Horse-Dope Orleans Case," *Alexandria (LA) Town Talk*, March 27, 1946, 9; "Bribery Trial Nearing Close," *Shreveport (LA) Journal*, March 29, 1946, 3; "Two Acquitted on Charges of Horse Doping," *Shreveport (LA) Journal*, March 30, 1946, 3.

17. See Milton C. Toby, *Dancer's Image: The Forgotten Story of the 1968 Kentucky Derby* (Charleston, SC: History Press, 2011), 36–37.

18. Dr. John McA. Kater, "Horse Doping, Still a Blot on Racing: An Expert Shows How New Drugs Defy Detection, Making a Farce out of the Tests Used at Tracks," *Life*, January 31, 1955, 93–104.

19. Kater, 93.

20. Dorothy Ours, *Man o' War: A Legend Like Lightning* (New York: St. Martin's Press, 2006), 163.

21. Kater, "Horse Doping," 93, 97, 102.

22. "Notes of How to Dope Horses," *Blood-Horse*, February 5, 1955, 387.

23. "Raps Racing for Failure to Answer Dope Charges," *Troy (NY) Times Record*, April 27, 1955, 28.

24. "No More Lip: TRPB Set for 2020 Digital Tattoo Mandate," *Paulick Report*, September 20, 2019, https://www.paulickreport.com/news/the-biz/no-more-lip-trpb-set-for-2020-digital-tattoo-mandate/#:~:text=The%20TRPB%20provides%20authentication%20of,microchipped%20prior%20to%20being%20registered. Two years earlier, the Jockey Club began requiring any Thoroughbred foaled in 2017 or later to be microchipped prior to registration.

25. See https://www.trpb.com/mission.html.

26. Natalie Voss, "Horse Racing's FBI: A Look Back at the Old Days of the Thoroughbred Racing Protective Bureau," *Paulick Report*, June 8, 2020, https://www.paulickreport.com/news/ray-s-paddock/horse-racings-fbi-a-look-back-at-the-old-days-of-the-thoroughbred-racing-protective-bureau/.

13. The Derby and the Doctor

1. Information about Dr. Harthill's checkered history was gleaned from a variety of sources, including reports in *Blood-Horse* magazine, the *Louisville (KY) Courier-Journal*, and the *Daily Racing Form*. Among the more comprehensive sources of information are Jim Bolus, "The Alex Harthill Story," *Louisville (KY) Courier-Journal*, September 1, 1972; Doug McCoy,

"Dr. Harthill, Mr. Hyde?" *Thoroughbred Racing Action* 4, no. 22 (August 1990): 24–26, 46; and Ryan Goldberg, "Secret to Success: A Derby Win and Racing's Doping Addiction," *ProPublica,* May 2, 2014, https://www.propublica.org/article/secret-to-success.

2. Bolus, "Alex Harthill Story," A21.

3. Gregory Gordon, "Harthill: Greatest Vet or Racetrack Rogue?" *New Orleans Times Picayune,* April 23, 1981.

4. "Voltaren: How It Works and How to Get It," https://www.medicalnewstoday.com/articles/voltaren-otc.

5. Quoted in Goldberg, "Secret to Success."

6. Bill Christine, *Bill Hartack: The Bittersweet Life of a Hall of Fame Jockey* (Jefferson, NC: McFarland, 2016), 122.

7. Jim Squires, "The Doc's Legacy at the Derby," *New York Times* blog, April 30, 2009, https://archive.nytimes.com/therail.blogs.nytimes.com/2009/04/30/the-docs-legacy-at-the-derby/?searchResultPosition=2.

8. McCoy, "Dr. Harthill," 46.

9. From the transcript of an unidentified educational program.

10. "DEA Lawsuit Says Horse Vet Failed to Keep Proper Records," *Louisville (KY) Courier-Journal,* January 20, 1996, 8.

11. Barry Irwin, "Derby Doc," *Blood-Horse,* July 19, 2005.

14. Permissive Medication and the "E" in PED

1. Information about the phone calls to Jones came from a recorded interview of Peter Fuller by journalist Jim Bolus, archived at the Kentucky Derby Museum in Louisville, Kentucky. For a comprehensive report on the 1968 Kentucky Derby, see Milton C. Toby, *Dancer's Image: The Forgotten Story of the 1968 Kentucky Derby* (Charleston, SC: History Press, 2011).

2. "Vet Hits Handling of Dancer's Image: Strikes Back on Scandal over Derby," *Chicago Tribune,* August 18, 1968, Sports section, 1.

3. For a comprehensive discussion of Bute and other NSAIDs, see Thomas Tobin, *Drugs and the Performance Horse* (Springfield, IL: Chares C. Thomas, 1981), 85–110.

4. Tom Easterling, "Dancer's Image Loses Derby Purse," *Daily Racing Form,* May 8, 1968.

5. Ephedrine is a stimulant, closely related to methamphetamine. See David R. Mottram and Neil Chester, eds., *Drugs in Sport,* 7th ed. (New York: Routledge, 2018), 246.

6. David Condon, "That Derby Medication No Bad Word," *Chicago Tribune,* May 8, 1968, 65.

7. Thomas Rivera, "Dancer Drug Not Dope, but a Pain-Killer," *Chicago Tribune,* May 8, 1968, 65. Also see Joe Caldwell, "Will It Be a Household Word Now?" *Lexington (KY) Leader,* May 7, 1968, 1.

8. Thomas H. Hunt, Scott R. Jedlicka, and Matthew T. Bowers, "Drugs, the Law, and the Downfall of Dancer's Image at the 1968 Kentucky Derby: A Case Study on Human Conceptions of Domesticated Animals," *International Journal of the History of Sport* 31, no. 8 (2014): 902–13.

9. Transcript of Proceedings before the Kentucky State Racing Commission, Re: Appeal of Peter Fuller, vol. 1, 95–96. See appendix 5.

10. Toby, *Dancer's Image,* 107–8.

11. Steven Crist, "Lasix: Opposing Sides Consult the Evidence," *New York Times,* May 8, 1990, 103. For the results of the study, see Corinne Raphel Sweeney, Lawrence R. Soma, Abby D. Maxxon, Joseph E. Thompson, Susan J. Holcomb, and Pamela A. Spencer, "Effects of Furosemide on the Racing Times of Thoroughbreds," *American Journal of Veterinary Research* 51, no. 5 (May 1990). For an excellent but somewhat dated source of information about Lasix, see Bill Heller, *Run, Baby, Run: What Every Owner, Breeder, & Handicapper Should Know about Lasix in Racehorses* (Neenah, WI: Russell Meerdink, 2002). Also see Joseph C. O'Dea, *The Racing Imperative* (Geneseo, NY: Castlerea Press, 1998).

12. Victor Ryan, "Lasix-Free Stakes Racing Comes to Fruition in 2021," *Horse Racing Nation,* December 31, 2020, https://www.horseracingnation.com/news/Lasix_free_stakes_racing_comes_to_fruition_in_2021_123.

13. Ryan.

14. "HISA Finds Partner to Build Enforcement Agency," *Blood-Horse,* May 3, 2022, https://www.bloodhorse.com/horse-racing/articles/258532/hisa-finds-partner-to-build-enforcement-agency.

15. Frank Angst, "Breeders' Cup Presents Lasix-Free World's Championships," *Blood-Horse,* December 2021, 20.

15. The Steroid Derby

Anabolic androgenic steroids come in many forms. Unless a particular drug is named (e.g., Winstrol), the term "steroids" here and elsewhere in this book refers to the general class of drugs. For a concise summary of steroid regulation in the United States, see Bradley S. Friedman, "Oats, Water, Hay, and Everything Else: The Regulation of Anabolic Steroids in Thoroughbred Horse Racing" (Lewis and Cark Law School, 2009), https://www.animallaw.info/article/oats-water-hay-and-everything-else-regulation-anabolic-steroids-thoroughbred-horse-racing.

1. See https://www.rxlist.com/winstrol-drug.htm.

2. Richard Moore, *The Dirtiest Race in History: Ben Johnson, Carl Lewis, and the Olympic 100m Final* (London: Wisden, 2012), 246.

3. Joe Drape, "Big Brown Will Run Belmont Stakes without Steroids, His Trainer Says," *New York Times,* June 5, 2008, D1.

4. Personal interview with an anonymous source.

5. Richard Sowers, *The Kentucky Derby, Preakness and Belmont Stakes: A Comprehensive History* (Jefferson, NC: McFarland, 2014), 338–42.

6. Sowers, 341.

7. "Big Brown's Stud Fee Set at $65,000," https://www.bloodhorse.com/horse-racing/articles/151419/big-browns-stud-fee-set-at-65-000.

8. See http://www.dutchessviewsfarm.com/bigbrown.html.

9. Statement of Alexander M. Waldrop, CEO, National Thoroughbred Racing Association, in *Hearing before the Subcommittee on Commerce, Trade, and Consumer Protection of the Committee on Energy and Commerce, House of Representatives* (Washington, DC: US Government Printing Office, 2008), 168–69.

10. "Trainer Blames Barn Mistake for Suspension," *Columbia Daily Tribune,* June 28, 2008, https://www.columbiatribune.com/story/sports/2008/06/28/trainer-blames-barn-mistake-for/21533280007/.

11. A. J. Perez, "House Testimony Heartens Barbaro Owners," *USA Today,* June 20, 2008.

12. Ron Mitchell, "KY Stewards Suspend Trainer Dutrow," *Blood-Horse,* June 25, 2008, https://www.bloodhorse.com/horse-racing/articles/153403/ky-stewards-suspend-trainer-dutrow.

13. Although clenbuterol is not an anabolic steroid, the drug has some of the muscle-building characteristics of steroids. In 1993 the International Olympic Committee changed the name of a class of prohibited drugs from "anabolic steroids" to "anabolic agents" to allow the inclusion of clenbuterol. See David R. Mottram and Neil Chester, eds., *Drugs in Sport,* 7th ed. (New York: Routledge, 2018), 25.

14. Joe Drape, "Detrow Faces Steroid Ban," *New York Times,* June 25, 2008, https://www.nytimes.com/2008/06/25/sports/othersports/25racing.html.

15. "Trainer Dutrow Suspended for Doping," *Philadelphia Inquirer,* July 8, 2009, https://www.inquirer.com/philly/hp/sports/20090708_Trainer_Dutrow_suspended_for_doping.html.

16. "What Is the History of Anabolic Steroid Use?" in *Steroids and Other Appearance and Performance Enhancing Drugs (APEDs),* Research Report, National Institute on Drug Abuse, February 2018, https://www.drugabuse

.gov/publications/research-reports/steroids-other-appearance-performance-enhancing-drugs-apeds/what-history-anabolic-steroid-use.

17. Bill Finley, "In Horse Racing, Test of Beefed-up Champions," *New York Times,* June 2, 2008, D1.

18. Mottram and Chester, *Drugs in Sport,* 24.

19. For the complete Mitchell report, see http://mlb.mlb.com/mlb /news/mitchell/index.jsp.

20. Don Clippinger, "Pennsylvania Testing Reduces Positives," *Thoroughbred Times,* July 19, 2008, http://grayson-jockeyclub.org/newsimages /penn_testing.pdf.

16. Indictments and Wiretaps

1. For more information about the indictments, see Department of Justice, US Attorney's Office, Southern District of New York, press release, March 9, 2020 (hereafter, DOJ press release), https://www.justice.gov/usao-sdny/pr/manhattan-us-attorney-charges-27-defendants-racehorse-doping-rings. To read the original indictments, available through the online service PACER (Public Access to Court Electronic Records), see https:// ecf.nysd.uscourts.gov/doc1/127126533694; https://ecf.nysd.uscourts.gov /doc1/127126537502; https://ecf.nysd.uscourts.gov/doc1/127126537260; https://ecf.nysd.uscourts.gov/doc1/127126536581.

2. DOJ press release, March 9, 2020.

3. Statistical information is from Equibase, accessed October 19, 2021, https://www.equibase.com/stats/View.cfm?tf=year&tb=trainer.

4. "No Final Decision Yet on Maximum Security's Saudi Cup," *Blood-Horse,* August 10, 2020, https://www.bloodhorse.com/horse-racing/articles /242772/no-final-decision-yet-on-maximum-securitys-saudi-cup.

5. Bob Ehalt, "West Would Support Saudi Cup DQ of Maximum Security," *Blood-Horse,* December 10, 2022, https://www.bloodhorse.com/horse-racing/articles/265351/west-would-support-saudi-cup-dq-of-maximum-security.

6. Eric Mitchell, "Maximum Security Retired to Ashford Stud," *Blood-Horse,* November 10, 2020, https://www.bloodhorse.com/horse-racing /articles/244668/maximum-security-retired-to-ashford-stud.

7. DOJ press release, March 9, 2020 (note 1).

8. DOJ press release, March 9, 2020 (note 1).

9. To read the superseding indictments (available through PACER), see https://ecf.nysd.uscourts.gov/doc1/127127929792; https://ecf.nysd.uscourts .gov/doc1/127127928216; https://ecf.nysd.uscourts.gov/doc1/127128690722.

10. "Sealed Indictment," 16 (available through PACER), https://ecf.nysd.uscourts.gov/doc1/127126533694.

11. See https://www.justice.gov/archives/jm/criminal-resource-manual-923-18-usc-371-conspiracy-defraud-us (general conspiracy statute); https://www.law.cornell.edu/uscode/text/18/1512 (obstruction); https://www.law.cornell.edu/uscode/text/18/545 (smuggling).

12. Letter to District Court Judge Mary Kay Vyskocil, March 12, 2020 (available through PACER), https://ecf.nysd.uscourts.gov/doc1/127126562908.

13. Letter to District Court Judge J. Paul Octken, April 3, 2020 (available through PACER), https://ecf.nysd.uscourts.gov/doc1/127126678516.

14. Letter to District Court Judge P. Kevin Castel, April 18, 2020 (available through PACER), https://ecf.nysd.uscourts.gov/doc1/127126678516.

15. For the motion to suppress (available through PACER), see https://ecf.nysd.uscourts.gov/doc1/127129557919. For the omnibus brief, see https://ecf.nysd.uscourts.gov/doc1/127129739284.

16. "Thoroughbred Trainer Jorge Navarro and Head of New York Veterinary Clinic Plead Guilty in Federal Doping Case," Department of Justice press release, August 11, 1021, https://www.justice.gov/usao-sdny/pr/thoroughbred-trainer-jorge-navarro-and-head-new-york-veterinary-clinic-plead-guilty.

17. "Prolific Thoroughbred Trainer Sentenced to Five Years in Federal Doping Case," Department of Justice press release, December 17, 2021, https://www.justice.gov/usao-sdny/pr/prolific-thoroughbred-trainer-sentenced-five-years-federal-doping-case.

18. Judgment in Criminal Case no. 1:20-cr-00160-MKV, document 608, filed December 17, 2021 (available through PACER), https://ecf.nysd.uscourts.gov/doc1/127130371985.

17. The Balkanization of Thoroughbred Racing in America

For information about access to full transcripts of the congressional hearings referenced in this chapter and elsewhere in this book, see https://ask.loc.gov/law/faq/300694.

1. Robert L. Heleringer, *Equine Regulatory Law*, 1st ed. (Louisville, KY: Robert L. Heleringer, 2012), 45–75. For more information about the Percy-Gray Act, see Steven A. Riess, *The Sport of Kings and the Kings of Crime: Horse Racing, Politics, and Organized Crime in New York 1865–1913* (Syracuse, NY: Syracuse University Press, 2011), 221–27.

2. *Grainger v. Douglas Park Jockey Club*, 148 F. 513 (6th Cir. 1906). See also Heleringer, *Equine Regulatory Law*, 76–77.

3. *Fink v. Cole*, 97 N.E.2d 873 (N.Y. 1951).

4. T. D. Thornton, "Federal Judge Dismisses HBPA Constitutionality Suit vs. HISA," *Thoroughbred Daily News*, March 31, 2022, https://www.thoroughbreddailynews.com/federal-judge-dismisses-hbpa-constitutionality-suit-vs-hisa/; Dick Downey, "Challenge to HISA Fails in Kentucky-Based Federal Court," *Blood-Horse*, June 22, 2022, https://www.bloodhorse.com/horse-racing/articles/259275/challenge-to-hisa-fails-in-kentucky-based-federal-court.

5. Garry Valk, "Letter from the Publisher," *Sports Illustrated*, June 23, 1969; Bil Gilbert, "Problems in a Turned-on World," *Sports Illustrated*, June 23, 1969, 64; Bil Gilbert, "Something Extra on the Ball," *Sports Illustrated*, June 30, 1969, 32; Bil Gilbert, "High Time to Make Some Rules," *Sports Illustrated*, July 7, 1969, 30.

6. George Walsh, "Our Drug-Happy Athletes," *Sports Illustrated*, November 21, 1960, 64.

7. Gilbert failed to recognize the sentimental attachment many owners, trainers, jockeys, grooms, fans, and even bettors have with horses. For more about the dichotomy between horses as personal property and horses as competitors in their own right, see chapter 14.

8. Gilbert, "High Time to Make Some Rules," 30–32.

9. *A Report by the Select Committee on Crime, Together with Additional and Separate Views* (Washington, DC: US Government Printing Office, 1973), v.

10. "Statement of Bobby Byrne, Horseracing Specialist and Fixer of Races," in *Hearings before the Select Committee on Crime, House of Representatives* (Washington, DC: US Government Printing Office, 1973), vol. 3, 1104.

11. "Statement of Byrne," 1120.

12. "Statement of Byrne," 1089, 1091, 1120.

13. Steve Cady, "Horse Racing Inquiry Seen Paving Way for Federal Control of All Sports," *New York Times*, May 28, 1978, S9.

14. "Statement of Joseph (The Baron) Barboza, Syndicate Crime Enforcer; Presently in Protective Custody, U.S. Government," in *Hearings before the Select Committee on Crime*, vol. 2, 737, 752; "Statement of Frank Sinatra, Entertainer, Hollywood, Calif., Accompanied by Milton A. Rudin, Counsel," in *Hearings before the Select Committee on Crime*, vol. 4, 1411.

15. Quoted in Steve Cady, "Turf Charges Held Unfounded," *New York Times*, June 16, 1972, 28.

16. Bill Surface, "Racing's Biggest Scandal," *Sports Illustrated*, November 6, 1978, 26.

17. *Report by the Select Committee on Crime*, v.

18. 15 U.S. Code §3001 et seq.

19. "Pari-Mutuel Handle," in *The Jockey Club Fact Book*, 2022, https://www.jockeyclub.com/efaukt.asp?section=FB&area=8.

20. For more about the Department of Justice's challenge to the constitutionality of the Interstate Horseracing Act, see M. Shannon Bishop, "And They're Off: The Legality of Interstate Pari-Mutuel Wagering and Its Impact of the Thoroughbred Horse Industry," *Kentucky Law Journal* 88 (2001): 711.

21. Congressional findings and policy for the Interstate Horseracing Act (15 U.S. Code §3001) were as follows:

a) The Congress finds that—
  1) the States should have the primary responsibility for determining what forms of gambling may legally take place within their borders;
  2) the Federal Government should prevent interference by one State with the gambling policies of another, and should act to protect identifiable national interests; and
  3) in the limited area of interstate off-track wagering on horseraces, there is a need for Federal action to ensure States will continue to cooperate with one another in the acceptance of legal interstate wagers.

b) It is the policy of the Congress in this Chapter to regulate interstate commerce with respect to wagering on horseracing, in order to further the horseracing and legal off-track betting industries in the United States.

22. The commerce clause (Article I, section 8, clause 3) gives Congress the exclusive authority to "regulate Commerce with foreign Nations, among the several States, and with the Indian tribes."

23. "Testimony of the American Horse Protection Association Inc.," in *Hearings before the Subcommittee on Criminal Justice of the Committee on the Judiciary, House of Representatives* (Washington, DC: US Government Printing Office, 1983), 63.

24. Andrew Beyer, "Drug Lasix Ruining Racing in Maryland," *Miami News,* January 27, 1977, 36; Andrew Beyer, "Untangling the Maze of Sublimaze," *Newsday* (Nassau ed.), December 15, 1978, 136. Bettors today are probably more familiar with Beyer as the developer of a widely recognized method to calculate speed; a horse's "Beyer number" is an important tool for handicappers and for advertising purposes.

25. Beyer, "Drug Lasix Ruining Racing," 36.

26. Beyer, "Untangling the Maze of Sublimaze," 136.

27. Quoted in William Boniface, "Jockeys' Guild Voices Opposition to Doping," *Baltimore Evening Sun,* March 19, 1979, 31.

28. "Testimony of American Horse Protection Association," 63.

29. "Prepared Statement of Congressman Bruce F. Vento," in *Hearings before the Subcommittee on Criminal Justice,* vol 1. (1982), 5.

30. "Opening Statement of Senator Charles McC. Mathias Jr.," in *Hearings before the Subcommittee on Criminal Law of the Committee on the Judiciary, United States Senate* (Washington, DC: US Government Printing Office, 1983), 1–2.

31. "Opening Statement of Hon. Jan Schakowsky, a Representative in Congress from the State of Illinois," in *Hearings before the Subcommittee on Commerce, Trade, and Consumer Protection of the Committee on Energy and Commerce, House of Representatives* (Washington, DC: US Government Printing Office, 2008), 2.

18. Legislating Integrity?

For information about access to full transcripts of congressional hearings referenced in this chapter and elsewhere in this book, see https://ask.loc .gov/law/faq/300694. To stay current with developments regarding HISA and USADA, see www.hisaus.org. and www.usada.org.

1. Statement of Ogden Mills Phipps Jr., 2007 Annual Round Table Conference on Matters Pertaining to Racing, https://www.jockeyclub.com /default.asp.section=RT&year=2007+area=14.

2. "Opening Statement of Hon. Joseph R. Pitts, a Representative in Congress from the Commonwealth of Pennsylvania," in *Hearing before the Subcommittee on Health of the Committee on Energy and Commerce, House of Representatives* (Washington, DC: US Government Printing Office, 2013), 2.

3. "Opening Statement of Hon. Tom Udall, U.S. Senator from New Mexico," in *Hearing before the Committee on Commerce, Science, and Transportation, United States Senate* (Washington, DC: US Government Printing Office, 2013), 2.

4. See https://www.congress.gov/bill/112th-congress/house-bill/1733?q= %7B%22search%22%3A%5B%22hr+1733+interstate+horseracing+ improvement+act+2011%22%2C%22hr%22%2C%221733%22%2C% 22interstate%22%2C%22horseracing%22%2C%22improvement%22%2 C%22act%22%2C%222011%22%5D%7D&r=2&s=1.

5. See https://www.congress.gov/bill/113th-congress/house-bill/2012?q= %7B%22search%22%3A%5B%222013+horseracing+integrity+act%22%

2C%222013%22%2C%22horseracing%22%2C%22integrity%22%2C%22act%22%5D%7D&s=3&r=3.

6. "Statement of Travis T. Tygart," in *Hearing before the Subcommittee on Commerce, Manufacturing, and Trade of the Committee on Energy and Commerce, House of Representatives* (Washington, DC: US Government Printing Office, 2015), 47 (testimony), 49 (prepared statement), 158 (answers to submitted questions).

7. See https://www.congress.gov/bill/114th-congress/house-bill/3084?q=%7B%22search%22%3A%5B%22horse+racing+integrity+act+of+2015%22%2C%22horse%22%2C%22racing%22%2C%22integrity%22%2C%22act%22%2C%22of%22%2C%222015%22%5D%7D&s=2&r=5.

8. See https://www.congress.gov/bill/115th-congress/house-bill/2651?q=%7B%22search%22%3A%5B%22Horseracing+integrity+act+of+2017%22%2C%22Horseracing%22%2C%22integrity%22%2C%22act%22%2C%22of%22%2C%222017%22%5D%7D&s=1&r=2.

9. Quoted in Frank Angst, "House Subcommittee Weighs Equine Drug Testing," *Blood-Horse,* June 22, 2018, https://www.bloodhorse.com/horse-racing/articles/228173/house-subcommittee-weighs-equine-drug-testing-bill.

10. "A Daily Double for the Reform Our Sport so Desperately Needs," emailed press release from Water, Hay, Oats Alliance, September 9, 2020.

11. Ray Paulick, "Horseracing Integrity and Safety Act Signed into Law," *Paulick Report,* December 27, 2020, https://www.paulickreport.com/news/the-biz/horseracing-integrity-and-safety-act-signed-into-law/.

12. See https://www.congress.gov/bill/116th-congress/house-bill/1754?q=%7B%22search%22%3A%5B%22horseracing+integrity+and+safety+act+of+2020%22%2C%22horseracing%22%2C%22integrity%22%2C%22and%22%2C%22safety%22%2C%22act%22%2C%22of%22%2C%222020%22%5D%7D&s=3&r=1.

13. For stakeholder comments, see Bill Finley, "Horseracing Integrity and Safety Act Passes in Congress," *Thoroughbred Daily News,* December 22, 2020.

14. See Civil Action no. 5:21-CV-00071-H. See also *Carter v. Carter Coal Co.*, 56 S.Ct. 855, 873 (1936), in which the court describes the delegation of regulatory authority to a private entity as "legislative delegation in its most obnoxious form."

15. See Civil Action no. 5:21-CV-00104, Joseph M. Hood, presiding judge.

16. T. D. Thornton, "Feds: HBPA 'Jumped the Gun' in HISA Lawsuit," *Thoroughbred Daily News,* May 4, 2021.

17. Statement from Travis T. Tygart, November 23, 2021, https://www.usada.org/announcement/equine-protocols-definitions/.

18. Jim Mulvihill, "Spotlight on HISA as Global Symposium on Racing Opens," *Blood-Horse,* December 7, 2021, https://www.bloodhorse.com/horse-racing/articles/255438/spotlight-on-hisa-as-global-symposium-on-racing-opens.

19. "Statement from USADA CEO Travis T. Tygart on Equine Anti-Doping and Medication Control Programs," December 23, 2021, https://www.usada.org/statement/equine-negotiations/.

20. Daniel Ross, "USADA Unable to Reach Deal with HISA," *Thoroughbred Daily News,* December 23, 2021, https://www.thoroughbreddailynews.com/usada-unable-to-reach-deal-with-hisa-authority/.

21. Bill Finley, "The Week in Review: USADA-HISA Must Settle Their Differences," *Thoroughbred Daily News,* December 26, 2021, https://www.thoroughbreddailynews.com/the-week-in-review-usada-hisa-must-settle-their-differences/.

22. "HISA Tabs Drug Free Sport International as Enforcement Agency Partner," *Thoroughbred Daily News,* https://www.thoroughbreddailynews.com/hisa-tabs-drug-free-sport-international-as-enforcement-agency-partner/.

23. See https://www.federalregister.gov/documents/2022/01/05/2021-28513/hisa-racetrack-safety.

19. Genetics, the Wealth Gap, and the Myth of the Level Playing Field

1. When I asked the Magic Eight Ball "Could this scenario ever happen?" the response was "Very likely." Readers can take that prognostication for what it's worth.

2. David Epstein, *The Sports Gene: Inside the Science of Extraordinary Athletic Performance* (New York: Portfolio/Penguin, 2014).

3. Malcolm Gladwell, "Man and Superman: In Athletic Competitions, What Qualifies as a Sporting Chance?" *New Yorker,* September 2, 2013, https://www.newyorker.com/contributors/malcolm-gladwell.

4. Gladwell.

5. Walter Isaacson, *The Code Breaker: Jennifer Doudna, Gene Editing, and the Future of the Human Race* (New York: Simon and Schuster, 2021), 349.

6. For more information about the sprinter gene in horses, see "How the 'Speed Gene' Works in Thoroughbred Horses," *Science Daily,* November 6, 2018, https://www.sciencedaily.com/releases/2018/11/181106111616.

htm; Mary F. Rooney, Emmaline W. Hill, Vincent P. Kelly, and Richard K. Porter, "The 'Speed Gene' Effect of Myostatin Arises in Thoroughbred Horses Due to a Promoter Proximal SINE Insertion," *PLOS One*, October 31, 2018, https://journals.plos.org/plosone/article/comments?id=10.1371/journal.pone.0205664.

7. Isaacson, *Code Breaker*, 349.

Conclusion

1. Chuck Klosterman, "Is It Wrong to Watch Football?" *New York Times*, September 5, 2014, https://www.nytimes.com/2014/09/07/magazine/is-it-wrong-to-watch-football.html.

2. Mark Fainaru-Wada and Steve Fainaru, *League of Denial: The NFL, Concussions, and the Battle for Truth* (New York: Crown Archetype, 2013); PBS, *League of Denial: The NFL's Concussion Crisis*, https://www.pbs.org/video/frontline-league-denial-nfls-concussion-crisis/.

3. Klosterman, "Is It Wrong to Watch Football?" It's worth noting that the decision to hire Klosterman, a well-regarded author and rock music critic but not an academic, was a controversial one. Wrote one columnist: "How did they pick the Bearded One? It's as if someone dared them to find an ethicist less qualified than his predecessor Ariel Kaminer." Lindsay Beyerstein, "Chuck Klosterman Is the Ethicist?" *In These Times*, June 8, 2012, https://inthesetimes.com/article/chuck-klosterman-is-the-ethicist.

4. Claire Crosby, "Breeders Cup Releases Report on Mongolian Groom," *Blood-Horse*, January 15, 2020, https://www.bloodhorse.com/horse-racing/articles/237936/breeders-cup-releases-report-on-mongolian-groom.

5. The full report is available at https://www.breederscup.com/sites/default/files/MongolianGroomEvaluation.pdf.

6. One of those lawsuits was dismissed on March 31, 2022. A second was dismissed several weeks later. Appeals are likely. A third lawsuit was filed days before the safety portion of HISA went into effect on July 1, 2022. That action is pending as of this writing.

7. For those unfamiliar with drug testing protocols in Kentucky, samples are divided into two parts: A and B. If the test of sample A is negative, there is no subsequent testing. If sample A is positive for a prohibited substance, the horse's owner or trainer can request a test of sample B. If sample B is negative, no further action is taken. If the test of sample B confirms the positive result, it is considered a violation. See 810 KAR 8:010, §§12–14.

8. The Medina Spirit–Bob Baffert–Kentucky Derby debacle was widely reported at the time. See, for example, Des Bieler, "Kentucky Derby Winner Medina Spirit Disqualified: Trainer Bob Baffert Suspended for 90 Days," *Washington Post,* February 21, 2022, https://www.washingtonpost.com /sports/2022/02/21/medina-spirit-disqualified; Frank Angst and Byron King, "Medina Spirit Disqualified from 2021 Derby Win," *Blood-Horse,* February 21, 2022, https://www.bloodhorse.com/horse-racing/articles /256644/medina-spirit-disqualified-from-2021-kentucky-derby-win; Natalie Voss, "Kentucky Commission Votes Not to Give Baffert a Stay," *Paulick Report,* March 4, 2022, https://paulickreport.com/news/the-biz /kentucky-commission-votes-not-to-give-baffert-a-stay/.

9. *Bob Baffert and Zedan Racing Stables, Inc., v. Kentucky Horse Racing Commission,* Case no. 2022-CA-0317, Kentucky Court of Appeals, April 1, 2022.

10. Baffert challenged that suspension in US District Court for the Western District of Kentucky. See *Bob Baffert and Bob Baffert Racing Stables, Inc. v. Churchill Downs, Inc., William C. Carstanjen, and R. Alex Rankin,* Case no. 3.22-cv-123. The case was pending as of March 2022.

11. Pat McKenna, "NYRA Suspends Bob Baffert," *NYRA Headlines,* May 17, 2021, https://www.nyra.com/belmont/news/nyra-suspends-bob-baffert.

12. *Bob Baffert v. The New York Racing Association, Inc.,* Memorandum and Order, 21-CV-3329, filed January 22, 2022.

13. The letter is included as an exhibit in *Baffert v. New York Racing Association.*

14. "Churchill Downs Incorporated Suspends Bob Baffert for Two Years," Churchill Downs press release, June 2, 2021, https://www .kentuckyderby.com/uploads/wysiwyg/assets/uploads/20210602_Baffert_ Suspension.pdf.

15. For a comprehensive discussion of SLOs, see Joel Gehman, Lianne M. Lefsrud, and Stuart Fast, "Social License to Operate: Legitimacy by Another Name?" *Canadian Public Administration* 60 (2017): 293–317, https://doi.org/10.1111/capa.12218.

16. Elizabeth Duncan, Raewyn Graham, and Phil McManus, "No One Has Even Seen . . . Smelt . . . or Sensed a Social Licence: Animal Geographies and Social Licence to Operate," *Geoforum,* October 2018, https://doi.org/10.1016/j.geoforum.2018.08.020.

17. Camie Heleski, C. J. Stowe, Julie Fiedler, Michael L. Peterson, Colleen Brady, Carissa Wickens, and James N. MacLeod, "Thoroughbred Racehorse Welfare through the Lens of 'Social License to Operate'—With

an Emphasis on a U.S. Perspective," *Sustainability* 12, no. 5 (2020), https:// doi.org/10.3390/su12051706.

18. Heleski et al., 1.

19. "What Is the Social License?" https://socialicense.com/definition. html.

20. John Morrison, "Business and Society: Defining the 'Social Licence,'" *Guardian,* September 29, 2014, https://www.theguardian.com/sustain-able-business/2014/sep/29/social-licence-operate-shell-bp-business-leaders.

21. Natalie Voss, "Baffert/NYRA Hearing, Day 2: Social License to Operate, Ethics of Therapeutic Drugs Debated," *Paulick Report,* January 25, 2022, https://paulickreport.com/news/the-biz/baffert-nyra-hearing-day-2-social-license-to-operate-ethics-of-therapeutic-drugs-debated/.

22. Mary Ramsey, "Fake Bob Baffert Sits Down with Saturday Night Live's Michael Che to Talk Medina Spirit," *Louisville (KY) Courier-Journal,* May 16, 2021, https://www.courier-journal.com/story/sports/horses /kentucky-derby/2021/05/16/saturday-night-live-weekend-update-takes-bob-baffert-medina-spirit/5120965001/.

23. Voss, "Baffert/NYRA Hearing."

24. For a summary of the hearing officer's report, see Bob Ehalt, "Hear-ing Officer Recommends 2-Year NYRA Ban for Baffert," *Blood-Horse,* April 27, 2022, https://www.bloodhorse.com/horse-racing/articles/258359 /hearing-officer-recommends-2-year-nyra-ban-for-baffert. To read the com-plete report, see http://i.bloodhorse.com/pdfs/HearingReport_BobBaffert .pdf.

25. For a discussion of the perils facing horse racing more than a century ago and the sport's recovery, see William H. P. Robertson, *The History of Thoroughbred Racing in America* (Englewood Cliffs, NJ: Prentice-Hall, 1964), 194–201.

26. Robertson, 196–97.

27. Joseph C. O'Dea, *The Racing Imperative* (Geneseo, NY: Castlerea Press, 1998), 14.

Appendix 3

1. Harry J. Anslinger Papers, box 8, file 6, Drugs in Horse Racing (1921–1952), HCLA 1875, Special Collections Library, Pennsylvania State University.

Selected Bibliography

Books, Articles, and Dissertations

Ashworth, David. *Ringers & Rascals: The True Story of Racing's Greatest Con Artists*. Lexington, KY: Eclipse Press, 2004.

Bowen, Edward L. *Legacies of the Turf: A Century of Great Thoroughbred Breeders*. 2 vols. Lexington, KY: Eclipse Press, 2003, 2004.

Brooks, Graham, Azeem Aleem, and Mark Button. *Fraud, Corruption and Sport*. New York: Palgrave Macmillan, 2013.

Chasin, Alexandra. *Assassin of Youth: A Kaleidoscopic History of Harry J. Anslinger's War on Drugs*. Chicago: University of Chicago Press, 2016.

Clarke, E. G. C. "A Brief History of Dope Detection in Horse." *British Journal of Sports Medicine* (October 1976): 100–102.

Clavin, Tom. *Dodge City: Wyatt Earp, Bat Masterson, and the Wickedest Town in the American West*. New York: St. Martin's Press, 2017.

Dasgupta, Lovely. *The World Anti-Doping Code: Fit for Purpose?* New York: Routledge, 2019.

de Boer, Douwe. "Sports Doping: Closing Pandora's Box." *Analytical Scientist* (March–April 2022): 14–25. https://theanalyticalscientist.com/fileadmin/tas/pdf-versions/issues/0422_TAS_Issue.pdf.

Dimeo, Paul. *A History of Drug Use in Sport, 1876–1976: Beyond Good and Evil*. New York: Routledge, 2007.

Doudna, Jennifer A., and Samuel H. Sternberg. *A Crack in Creation: Gene Editing and the Unthinkable Power to Control Evolution*. New York: First Mariner Books, 2017.

Duncan, Elizabeth, Raewyn Graham, and Phil McManus. "No One Has Even Seen . . . Smelt . . . or Sensed a Social Licence: Animal Geographies and Social Licence to Operate." *Geoforum*, October 2018. https://doi.org/10.1016/j.geoforum.2018.08.020.

Edwardes-Evans, Luke, Serge Laget, and Andy McGrath. *The Official History of the Tour de France*. London: Welbeck, 2021.

Epstein, David. *The Sports Gene: Inside the Science of Extraordinary Athletic Performance*. New York: Portfolio/Penguin, 2014.

Freeberg, Ernest. *A Traitor to His Species: Henry Bergh and the Birth of the Animal Rights Movement*. New York: Basic Books, 2020.

Gehman, Joel, Lianne M. Lefsrud, and Stuart Fast. "Social License to Operate: Legitimacy by Another Name?" *Canada Public Administration* 60 (2017): 293–317. https://doi.org/10.1111/capa.12218.

Gentry, Curt. *J. Edgar Hoover: The Man and the Secrets*. New York: W. W. Norton, 1991.

Gleaves, John. "Enhancing the Odds: Horse Racing, Gambling and the First Anti-Doping Movement in Sport, 1889–1911." *Sport in History* 32, no. 1 (March 2012): 26–52.

Gleaves, John. "From Science to Sport: A Cross Disciplinary Examination of the Justification for Doping Bans." PhD diss., Pennsylvania State University, 2011. https://www.smithsonianmag.com/science-nature/how-advertising-shaped-first-opioid-epidemic-180968444/.

Gleaves, John, and Thomas M. Hunt, eds. *A Global History of Doping in Sport: Drugs, Policy, and Politics*. New York: Routledge, 2015.

Green, Brigadier H. J. L. "Dope: The Enemy of the Racehorse." *British Journal of Sports Medicine* (October 1976): 103–5.

Halpern, John H., and David Blistein. *Opium: How an Ancient Flower Shaped and Poisoned Our World*. New York: Hachette Books, 2019.

Hamilton, Tyler, and Daniel Coyle. *The Secret Race: Inside the Hidden World of the Tour de France*. New York: Bantam Books, 2013.

Hari, Johann. *Chasing the Scream: The First and Last Days of the War on Drugs*. New York: Bloomsbury, 2015.

Hass, Ulrich, and Deborah Healey. *Doping in Sport and the Law*. Oxford: Hart, 2019.

Hatch, Alden, and Foxhall Keene. *Full Tilt: The Sporting Memories of Foxhall Keene*. New York: Derrydale Press, 1938.

Heleski, Camie, C. J. Stowe, Julie Fiedler, Michael L. Peterson, Colleen Brady, Carissa Wickens, and James N. MacLeod. "Thoroughbred Racehorse Welfare through the Lens of 'Social License to Operate'— With an Emphasis on a U.S. Perspective." *Sustainability* 12, no. 5 (2020): 1706. https://doi.org/10.3390/su12051706.

Heller, Bill. *Run, Baby, Run: What Every Owner, Breeder, & Handicapper Should Know about Lasix in Racehorses*. Neenah, WI: Russell Meerdink, 2002.

Hoberman, John. *Mortal Engines: The Science of Performance and the Dehumanization of Sport*. New York: Free Press, 1992.

Hoberman, John. *Testosterone Dreams: Rejuvenation, Aphrodisia, Doping.* Berkeley: University of California Press, 2005.

Hollingsworth, Kent. *The Great Ones.* Lexington, KY: Blood-Horse Publications, 1970.

Homan, Andrew M. *Iron Mac: The Legend of Roughhouse Cyclist Reggie McNamara.* Lincoln: University of Nebraska Press, 2016.

Horse Racing's Top 100 Moments. Lexington, KY: Blood-Horse Publications, 2006.

Hunt, Thomas H., Scott R. Jedlicka, and Matthew T. Bowers. "Drugs, the Law, and the Downfall of Dancer's Image at the 1968 Kentucky Derby: A Case Study on Human Conceptions of Domesticated Animals." *International Journal of the History of Sport* 31, no. 8 (2014): 902–13.

Isaacson, Walter. *The Code Breaker: Jennifer Doudna, Gene Editing, and the Future of the Human Race.* New York: Simon and Schuster, 2021.

Jeffries, John W. *Wartime America: The World War II Homefront.* 2nd ed. New York: Rowman and Littlefield, 2018.

Johnson, Mark. *Spitting in the Soup: Inside the Dirty Game of Doping in Sports.* Boulder, CO: Velopress, 2016.

Lambton, George. *Men and Horses I Have Known.* London: Thornton Butterworth, 1924.

Larson, Erik. *The Devil in the White City: Murder, Magic, and Madness at the Fair that Changed America.* New York: Crown, 2003.

McDermott, Vanessa. *The War on Drugs in Sport: Moral Panics and Organizational Legitimacy.* New York: Routledge, 2016.

McGrath, Chris. *Mr. Darley's Arabian: A History of Racing in 25 Horses.* New York: Pegasus Books, 2017.

McGraw, Eliza. *Here Comes Exterminator.* New York: Thomas Dunne Books, 2016.

McNamee, Mike, and William J. Morgan, eds. *Routledge Handbook of the Philosophy of Sport.* New York: Routledge, 2015.

McWilliams, John C. *The Protectors: Harry J. Anslinger and the Federal Bureau of Narcotics, 1930–1962.* Newark: University of Delaware Press, 1990.

McWilliams, John C. "Unsung Partner against Crime: Harry J. Anslinger and the Federal Bureau of Narcotics, 1930–1962." *Pennsylvania Magazine of History and Biography* 113, no. 2 (April 1989): 207–36.

Moore, Richard. *The Dirtiest Race in History: Ben Johnson, Carl Lewis, and the 1988 Olympic 100m Final.* London: Wisden, 2012.

Mottram, David R., and Neil Chester, eds. *Drugs in Sport.* 7th ed. New York: Routledge, 2018.

Nicholson, James C. *1968: A Pivotal Moment in American Sports*. Knoxville: University of Tennessee Press, 2019.

Nicholson, James C. *Racing for America: The Horse Race of the Century and the Redemption of a Sport*. Lexington: University Press of Kentucky, 2021.

O'Dea, Joseph C. *The Racing Imperative*. Geneseo, NY: Castlerea Press, 1998.

Okrent, Daniel, ed. *American Pastimes: The Very Best of Red Smith*. New York: Literary Classics of the United States, 2013.

Pietrusza, David. *Rothstein: The Life, Times, and Murder of the Criminal Genius Who Fixed the 1919 World Series*. New York: Basic Books, 2011.

Poundstone, William. *Prisoner's Dilemma: John Von Neumann, Game Theory, and the Puzzle of the Bomb*. New York: Anchor Books, 1992.

Riess, Steven. "The Cyclical History of Horse Racing: The USA's Oldest and (Sometimes) Most Popular Spectator Sport." *International Journal of the History of Sport* 31 (2014): 29–54.

Riess, Steven A. *The Sport of Kings and the Kings of Crime: Horse Racing, Politics, and Organized Crime in New York 1865–1913*. Syracuse, NY: Syracuse University Press, 2011.

Robertson, William H. P. *The History of Thoroughbred Racing in America*. Englewood Cliffs, NJ: Prentice-Hall, 1964.

Rodchenkov, Dr. Grigory. *The Rodchenkov Affair: How I Brought Down Putin's Secret Doping Empire*. London: WH Allen, 2020.

Rooney, Mary F., Emmeline W. Hill, Vincent P. Kelly, and Richard K. Porter. "The 'Speed Gene' Effect of *Myostatin* Arises in Thoroughbred Horses Due to a Promoter Proximal SINE Insertion." *PLOS One* 13, no. 10 (October 2018): 312. https://dooi.org/10.1371/jpotma;pone.0205664.

Serrano, Richard A. *American Endurance: Buffalo Bill, the Great Cowboy Race of 1893, and the Vanishing Wild West*. Washington, DC: Smithsonian Books, 2016.

Sides, Hampton. *Blood and Thunder: An Epic of the American West*. New York: Doubleday, 2006.

Sowers, Richard. *The Kentucky Derby, Preakness and Belmont Stakes: A Comprehensive History*. Jefferson, NC: McFarland, 2014.

Steele, Zulma. *Angel in Top Hat*. New York: Harper and Brothers, 1942.

Summers, Anthony. *Official and Confidential: The Secret Life of J. Edgar Hoover*. New York: G. P. Putnam's Sons, 1993.

Tobin, Thomas. *Drugs and the Performance Horse*. Springfield, IL: Charles C. Thomas, 1981.

Tobin, Thomas, Kimberly Brewer, and Kent H. Stirling. *World Rules for Equine Drug Testing & Therapeutic Medication Regulation: 2012 Policy of the National Horsemen's Benevolent and Protective Association, Inc.* Nicholasville, KY: Wind Publications, 2012.

Toby, Milton C. *Dancer's Image: The Forgotten Story of the 1968 Kentucky Derby.* Charleston, SC: History Press, 2011.

Vamplew, Wray, "Playing with the Rules: Influences on the Development of Regulation in Sport." *International Journal of the History of Sport* 24, no. 7 (2007): 843–71.

Vamplew, Wray. *The Turf: A Social and Economic History of Horse Racing.* 2nd ed. Brighton, UK: Edward Everett Root, 2016.

Wall, Maryjean. *How Kentucky Became Southern: A Take of Outlaws, Horse Thieves, Gamblers, and Breeders.* Lexington: University Press of Kentucky, 2010.

Weinreb, Michael. "The Complicated Legacy of Harry Anslinger." *Penn-Stater,* January–February 2018, 32–41.

World Anti-Doping Code 2021. Montreal: World Anti-Doping Agency, 2021.

Transcripts of Congressional Hearings and Other Federal Legislative Material

H.R. 1733. Interstate Horseracing Improvement Act of 2011. House Subcommittee on Health of the Committee on Energy and Commerce, 2013. 1 vol.

H.R. 2012. Horseracing Integrity and Safety Act of 2013. Hearing before the House Subcommittee on Commerce, Manufacturing, and Trade of the Committee on Energy and Commerce Committee. 1 vol.

H.R. 2331. Corrupt Horseracing Practices Act of 1981. House Subcommittee on Criminal Justice, 1982 (1 vol.), 1983 (2 vols.).

H.R. 2641. Horseracing Integrity and Safety Act of 2015.

H.R. 2651. Horseracing Integrity Act of 2017. Hearing before the House Subcommittee on Digital Commerce and Consumer Protection of the Committee on Energy and Commerce, 2018. 1 vol.

H.R. 3084. Horseracing Integrity Act of 2015.

Organized Criminal Influence in Sports (Racing). House Select Committee on Crime, Committee Hearings, 1972. 4 vols.

Organized Criminal Influence in Sports (Racing). House Select Committee on Crime, Committee Report, 1973. 1 vol.

S. 886. Interstate Improvement Act of 2011. Senate Committee on Commerce, Science, and Transportation. 1 vol.

S. 1043. Corrupt Horseracing Practices Act of 1981. Senate Subcommittee on Criminal Law. 1 vol.

S. 1488. Racehorse Doping Ban Act of 2019. Senate Committee on Commerce, 2018. 1 vol.

S. 1820. Horseracing Integrity Act of 2019. "Legislation to Promote the Health and Safety of Racehorses," House Subcommittee on Consumer Protection of the Energy and Commerce Committee, 2020. 1 vol.

S. 4547. Horseracing Integrity and Safety Act of 2020.

Transcripts of State Racing Commission Hearings

Appellate file, *Tom Smith v. Cole.* Includes transcripts of hearings before the stewards and the Joint Board and litigation files from the judicial review of Smith's suspension. 900+ pages.

RE: Appeal of Peter Fuller. Hearing before the Kentucky State Racing Commission (1968 Kentucky Derby). 15 vols.

Index

Page numbers in italics refer to illustrations.

Rule 146(d), 156, 157
Rule 162, 18, 56–58
Rule 216(f), 125, 136, 139, 143
Russia, sports doping in, 6
Ryall, G. F. T. (Audax Minor), 24, 70
Ryan, Victor, 194

saliva tests, 64, 98–99, 109, 136, 143, 176; absolute insurer rule and, 152; Anslinger's campaign and, 70, 80, 110; Bukowski's development of, 112–13; "dope boxes" and, 113; ephedrine and, 130, 131; first adoption at Hialeah (1934), 80, 113, 114, *115,* 150; mobile laboratories and, 158–59; state racing commissions and, 106; Straub reaction and, 159–60
Salix (furosemide), 43
Salling, Oscar, 17
Salter, Leslie E., 99
Salute the Count (horse), 200–201
Sams, Dr. Richard, 162
San Diego Handicap, 210
San Francisco Examiner, 93–94
Santa Anita Derby, 122
Saratoga racetrack (upstate New York), 45, 50, 69
Scaffidi, James, 169
Schakowsky, Rep. Jan, 249
Scheeler, Charles, 264
Schenk, Martin A., 140, 141, 146
Schofield, Major, 116
Scorpio (horse), 13
Seabiscuit (horse), 3, 42, 123, 132, *132,* 133, 135
Seattle Slew (horse), 244
Secretariat (horse), 244

Select Committee on Crime, House of Representatives, 45
selling races, 11
Sertürner, Frederick, 110
Servis, Jason, 207, 208–9, 210, 213, 216, 219–33
SGF-1000 (customized PED), 211, 220–22, 223, 224, 228–29
Shandon Farm, 83
Sharp, Matthew, 20
Sheepshead Bay, 45, 51, 53
Sheetz, Harold O., 169
Shelley, James, 126, 127, 135
Sherwood, O. Peter, 280
Shilstone, Cecil M., 172, 173
Sinclair, Harry F., 45
Sir Barton (horse), 112, 174
Sixth Circuit Court of Appeals, 97–98, 101, 103, 105, 237
Sky Haven (horse), 85
sleeping pills, 187
SLO (social license to operate), 278–80
Sloan, A. B., 160
Sloane, Isabel Dodge, 90
Smasher (horse), 172, 173
Smith, J. W. "Jimmy," 122, 124
Smith, Lacey, 126, 129
Smith, Morton, 99, 101, 102–3
Smith, "Silent" Tom, 121, 152, 161, 191; Jockey Club hearing and, 131–37; Joint Board hearing and, 140–50; license revocation, 122, 123, 136, 149–50, 185; Seabiscuit trained by, 3, 42, 123, *132;* stewards' hearing and, 126–29, 138
Smith, Walter Wellesley "Red," 121
"snow men," 23–24

Horses in History

Series Editor: James C. Nicholson

For thousands of years, humans have utilized horses for transportation, recreation, war, agriculture, and sport. Arguably, no animal has had a greater influence on human history. Horses in History explores this special human-equine relationship, encompassing a broad range of topics, from ancient Chinese polo to modern Thoroughbred racing. From biographies of influential equestrians to studies of horses in literature, television, and film, this series profiles racehorses, warhorses, sport horses, and plow horses in novel and compelling ways.